CAVENDISH

Q&A

SERIES

CIVIL LIBERTIES AND HUMAN RIGHTS

THIRD EDITION

Helen Fenwick
Professor of Law, University of Durham

Howard Davis
Reader in Law, Bournemouth University

Cavendish
Publishing
Limited

London • Sydney • Portland, Oregon

Third edition first published in Great Britain 2004 by
Cavendish Publishing Limited, The Glass House,
Wharton Street, London WC1X 9PX, United Kingdom
Telephone: + 44 (0)20 7278 8000   Facsimile: + 44 (0)20 7278 8080
Email: info@cavendishpublishing.com
Website: www.cavendishpublishing.com

Published in the United States by Cavendish Publishing
c/o International Specialized Book Services,
5824 NE Hassalo Street, Portland,
Oregon 97213-3644, USA

Published in Australia by Cavendish Publishing (Australia) Pty Ltd
45 Beach Street, Coogee, NSW 2034, Australia
Telephone: + 61 (2)9664 0909   Facsimile: + 61 (2)9664 5420
Email: info@cavendishpublishing.com.au
Website: www.cavendishpublishing.com.au

© Fenwick, H and Davis, H	2004
Fenwick, H and Davis, H	
First edition	1994
Second edition	2001
Third edition	2004

British Library Cataloguing in Publication Data
Fenwick, Helen
Civil liberties and human rights 2004–2005 – 3rd ed (Q&A series)
1 Civil rights – England – examinations, questions, etc
2 Civil rights – Wales – examinations, questions, etc
I Title II Davis, Howard
342.4'2'085

Library of Congress Cataloguing in Publication Data
Data available

ISBN 1-85941-770-1

1 3 5 7 9 10 8 6 4 2

PREFACE

These are exciting and confusing times in which to study civil liberties or, as it is becoming more commonly known, domestic human rights. Since the first edition of this book, there has been a rapid acceleration of development of this field of law, which has become almost all-pervasive. There are many new statutes and cases which have been incorporated into the questions in this edition, most notably the Human Rights Act 1998, which has finally incorporated the European Convention on Human Rights and Fundamental Freedoms into domestic law. The Act has now been fully in force for three years. This is an extremely significant change and so it is affecting every civil liberties and human rights course across the country; the new law and the early cases taking the Human Rights Act into account form the focus of many of the questions in this edition. Students will be expected to have a thorough knowledge of the 1998 Act, its implications and the relevant cases, including ECHR cases decided at Strasbourg, as they relate to each and every area of their course, and so these topics have been addressed in depth. The speed of change in this field and the sheer volume of new human rights-related statutes requires some selectivity in the topics chosen for discussion here, but the core areas of any human rights/civil liberties course are examined. New questions have also been included on topics of current and likely future interest, such as privacy, freedom of information, immigration and asylum provisions and discrimination law.

This book is intended for students studying civil liberties who feel that they have acquired a body of knowledge, but don't feel confident about using it effectively in exams. This book sets out to demonstrate how to apply the knowledge to the question and how to structure the answer. Students often find the technique of answering problem questions particularly hard to grasp, so this book contains a large number of answers to such questions. Such technique is rarely taught in law schools and the student who comes from studying science or Maths 'A' level may find it particularly tricky. Equally, a student who has studied English literature may find it difficult to adapt to the impersonal, logical, concise style which problem answers demand. It is hoped that this book will be particularly useful at exam time, but may also prove useful throughout the year.

The book provides examples of the kind of questions which are usually asked in end of year examinations, along with suggested solutions. Each chapter deals with one of the main topics covered in civil liberties courses and contains typical questions on that area. The aim is not to include questions covering every aspect of a course, but to pick out the areas which tend to be examined because they are particularly contentious or topical. Many courses contain a certain amount of material which tends not to be examined, although it is important as background.

Some areas tend to be examined only by essays, some mainly, although not invariably, by problems and some by both. The questions chosen reflect this mix and the introductions at the beginning of each chapter discuss the type of question usually asked. It is important not to choose a topic and then assume that it will appear on the exam paper in essay form unless it is in an area where a problem question is never set. If an area might appear as an essay or a problem, revision should be geared to either possibility; a very thorough knowledge of the area should be acquired, but also an awareness of critical opinion in relation to it.

The answers in this book are about the length of an essay that a good student would be expected to write in an exam; some are slightly longer. There are a number of reasons for this: some students can write long answers – about 1,800 words – under exam conditions; some students can't, but nevertheless can write two very good and lengthy essays and two reasonable, but shorter ones. Such students tend to do very well, although it must be emphasised that it is always better to aim to spread the time evenly between the four essays. Therefore, some answers indicate what might be done if very thorough coverage of a topic was undertaken. Also, since some courses are assessed partly by coursework, the longer essays give an indication as to what might be expected from a coursework essay.

Each essay also provides notes exploring some areas of the answer in more depth, which should be of value to the student who wants to do more than cover the main points. Some answers provide a number of notes; it would not be expected that any one student would have time to make all the points they contain, but they demonstrate that it is possible to choose to explore, say, two interesting areas in more depth in an answer once the main points have been covered. It can't be emphasised enough that the main points have to be covered before interesting, but less obvious issues can be explored.

Civil liberties' exam papers normally include one question on each of the main areas. For example, a typical paper might include problem questions on public order, police powers, and contempt of court, and essay questions on the Human Rights Act, freedom of expression, 'open' government, privacy of information, and prisoners' rights. Therefore, the questions have to be fairly wide ranging in order to cover a reasonable amount of ground on each topic. Some answers in this book therefore have to cover some of the same material especially where it is particularly central to the topic in question.

The law is stated as at 30 September 2003.

Helen Fenwick, University of Durham
Howard Davis, Bournemouth University

CONTENTS

TABLE OF CASES

TABLE OF LEGISLATION

Statutory Instruments

Directives

CHAPTER 1

FREEDOM OF EXPRESSION

Introduction

This area is obviously a key element in a civil liberties course and therefore it may arise in two or possibly more questions on the exam paper. Examiners tend to set general essays in this area; the emphasis is usually on the degree to which a balance is struck between freedom of expression and a variety of other interests. However, problem questions are sometimes set, particularly in the area of contempt of court.

There is a large amount of overlap between this area and that of freedom of information, since freedom of information may broadly be viewed as one aspect of freedom of expression. The case of *Shayler* (2002), considered in Chapter 2, could readily be viewed as relating to both freedoms. Therefore, what may be termed 'freedom of information issues' may well be treated as aspects of freedom of expression. However, the overlap is not complete: in some circumstances, information may be sought where there is no speaker willing to disclose it and, therefore, such instances tend to fall only within the area of freedom of information. The current interest in further media regulation to protect privacy may well be reflected in civil liberties examinations; as such, you may well be called upon to consider the conflict between freedom of expression and privacy. In this book, that issue is covered in the chapter on privacy but, of course, the freedom of expression dimension is taken into account.

It is now essential in your answers to take the European Convention on Human Rights (ECHR) into account, especially Art 10, which provides a guarantee of freedom of expression. The Convention was received into UK law when the Human Rights Act (HRA) 1998 came fully into force in October 2000. Until that time, Art 10 and other Convention Articles relevant in this area were not directly applicable in UK courts, but the judiciary referred to the Convention more and more in resolving ambiguity in statutes in the run up to the inception of the HRA. The HRA has now been in force for three years and there are certain early significant decisions in the field of freedom of expression (such as *ProLife Alliance v BBC* (2003); *AG v Punch* (2003)). Section 3 will require that: 'So far as it is possible to do so, primary and subordinate legislation must be read and given effect in a way which is compatible with the Convention rights ...' Section 3(2)(b) reads: 'this section does not affect the validity, continuing operation or enforcement of any incompatible primary legislation.' This goes beyond the *current* obligation to resolve ambiguity in statutes.

All statutes affecting freedom of expression and media freedom therefore have to be interpreted so as to be in harmony with the Convention if that is at all possible. Under s 6 of the HRA, Convention guarantees are binding only against public authorities. These are defined as bodies which have a partly public function. The definition is therefore quite wide, but means that private bodies, including most of the media (apart from the 'public bodies', such as the BBC, the Independent Television Commission (now replaced by Ofcom) and the Press Complaints Commission) can violate Convention rights unless a part of the common law, which will also be interpreted in conformity with the Convention, bears on the matter.

Thus, exam questions will reflect this extremely significant development and will require an awareness of the Art 10 jurisprudence and of the impact of the HRA on freedom of expression.

Checklist

You should be familiar with the following areas:

- Art 10 of the ECHR, other relevant rights such as Art 6, Art 10 jurisprudence and the HRA 1998;

- common law free speech jurisprudence pre-HRA (see, for example, *Reynolds v Times Newspapers* (1999); *Derbyshire CC v Times Newspapers* (1993); *R v Secretary of State for the Home Department ex p Simms* (1999));

- early decisions taking account of the HRA and Art 10 such as *ProLife Alliance v BBC* (2003); *AG v Punch* (2003);

- key aspects of the Contempt of Court Act 1981 and common law contempt;

- the doctrine of breach of confidence;

- key aspects of the Broadcasting Acts 1990 and 1996, and the Communications Act 2003 ('taste and decency', impartiality provisions);

- the Obscene Publications Act 1959 as amended; common law indecency: *Gibson* (1990);

- the Cinemas Act 1985; the Video Recordings Act 1984, as amended;

- blasphemy; the Religious Offences Bill 2003.

Question 1

Critically evaluate the current regime governing the regulation and censorship of films and videos in relation to the demands of Art 10 of the European Convention on Human Rights as received into domestic law under the Human Rights Act.

Answer plan

This is a reasonably straightforward essay question. Bear in mind the implications flowing from the fact that the ECHR has been afforded further effect in domestic law under the HRA 1998: you need to consider the key provisions of the HRA as they relate to the regulation and censorship of films and videos; you also need to examine the relevant Strasbourg jurisprudence. The mere fact that Art 10 of the ECHR has been received into domestic law under the HRA does not necessarily mean that change is needed.

Essentially, the following areas should be considered:

- Article 10 of the Convention and the HRA 1998;
- relevant Strasbourg jurisprudence under Art 10;
- classification and censorship of cinema films;
- the statutory regime relating to videos;
- conclusions regarding compatibility of the statutory provisions and Art 10 of the Convention.

Answer

At the present time it is arguably necessary for public authorities and the courts to take a stronger stance than previously in favour of freedom of expression due to the impact of the HRA 1998 which incorporates the Convention, including the guarantee of freedom of expression under Art 10, into domestic law. The legislation governing censorship of films and videos (the Video Recordings Act 1984 as amended and the Cinemas Act 1985) must be read by the courts in a manner which gives effect, so far as is possible, to the Convention rights (s 3 of the HRA); if this is not possible, a declaration of incompatibility may be issued (s 4), and remedial action may be taken as a result (s 10). Further, the HRA gives special regard to the importance of freedom of expression in s 12. Public authorities are bound by the Convention rights under s 6 unless s 6(2) applies. The term 'public authorities' is likely to include media bodies such as the British Board of Film Classification (BBFC) and the Video Appeals Committee (VAC). Assuming that they are public authorities, these bodies must ensure that Art 10 is not infringed in their decision making. Ultimately, decisions of media regulators or of other media bodies that are also public authorities can be challenged in the courts, which should seek to ensure that Art 10 is being complied with. In such decisions, the courts could, if necessary, use s 3 of the HRA to modify overly restrictive statutory provisions. Alternatively, the court could decide that as a public authority, it could itself find that Art 10 has been infringed by a restrictive decision of, for example, the BBFC (as the Court of Appeal – but not the House of Lords – did in the context of broadcasting in the *ProLife Alliance* case (2003)). Thus, it is submitted that restrictions on freedom of expression in this context may undergo fresh scrutiny, with a possible change in the balance against restraints on the showing of explicit material.

The regulation of films does not necessarily in itself infringe Art 10. Article 10(1) specifically provides that the Article 'shall not prevent States from requiring the licensing of broadcasting, television or cinema enterprises'. It is significant that this provision arises in the *first* paragraph of Art 10, thereby providing a limitation of the primary right that on its face is not subject to the test of para 2. However, a very restrictive approach to this sentence has been adopted. It has been found to mean that a licensing system is allowed for on grounds not restricted to those enumerated in para 2; the State may determine who is to have a licence to broadcast. But in general, other decisions of the regulatory bodies are not covered by the last sentence of para 1 and must be considered within para 2 (*Groppera Radio AG v Switzerland* (1990)). Thus, content requirements must be considered under para 2. Certain forms of expression which may be said to be of no value may fall outside the scope of Art 10(1) and it is arguable that, for example, material gratuitously offensive to religious sensibilities (*Otto-Preminger Institut v Austria* (1994)) or depictions of genitals in pornographic magazines intended merely for entertainment (*Groppera Radio AG v Switzerland* (1990)) may fall outside its scope. On the other hand, 'hardcore' pornography has been found by the Commission to fall within Art 10(1) (*Hoare v UK* (1997)).

Clearly political speech receives a much more robust degree of protection than other types of expression. Thus, the 'political' speech cases of *Sunday Times v UK* (1979), *Jersild v Denmark* (1994), *Lingens v Austria* (1986) and *Thorgeirson v Iceland* (1992) all resulted in findings that Art 10 had been violated and all were marked by an intensive review of the restriction in question in which the margin of appreciation was narrowed almost to vanishing point. By contrast, in cases involving artistic speech, an exactly opposite pattern emerges: applicants have tended to be unsuccessful and a deferential approach to the judgments of the national authorities as to its obscene or blasphemous nature has been adopted (*Müller v Switzerland* (1991); *Handyside v UK* (1976); *Otto-Preminger Institut v Austria* (1994); *Gay News v UK* (1982)). In *Otto-Preminger Institut v Austria* (1994), the Court found that a State may restrict expressions which may offend a particular population, although, otherwise, freedom of expression includes freedom to disseminate unpopular, shocking and disturbing information and ideas. Although there is no universal concept of morality (*Handyside* (1976)), the European Court of Human Rights (ECtHR) does give high value to public interest arguments in favour of publication, as demonstrated in recent cases. Under Art 10(2), an interference with the guarantee of freedom of expression under Art 10 can be justified if it is prescribed by law, has a legitimate aim and is necessary in a democratic society. Strasbourg affords a very high value to freedom of expression and, in particular, as indicated, views the scope for interference with political expression as very limited. Even in respect of artistic expression, which appears to have a lower place in the hierarchy of expression, no decisions defending restrictions on the freedom of expression of adults can be found, except in respect of hardcore pornography, or where a risk to children is also present, or in the context of offending religious sensibilities. Thus, there are grounds for suggesting that restraints on the showing of explicit material in films and videos could undergo further relaxation by reference to Art 10.

Currently, in the UK, censorship of films operates in practice on two levels: first, the BBFC, a self-censoring body set up by the film industry itself in 1912, may insist on cuts before issuing a certificate allowing a film to be screened or may refuse to issue a certificate at all. Films are classified by age: 'U' films are open to anybody as, in effect, are 'PG' (parental guidance) classified films. After that are '12', '15' and '18' certificate films. 'R18' films (restricted viewing) may be viewed only on segregated premises. An 'R18' certificate means that the BBFC considers that the film would survive an Obscene Publications Act prosecution; it will refuse a certificate if a film is thought to fall within the Act. In coming to its decision, the BBFC will take the 'public good' defence under s 4(1A) of the 1959 Act, as amended, into account. This defence is the more restricted defence under s 3 of the Theatres Act 1968; s 4(1A) provides that a film or soundtrack can be justified as being for the public good 'on the ground that it is in the interests of drama, opera, ballet or any other art or of literature or learning'. Therefore, the BBFC may grant a certificate on the grounds of artistic merit to a film that contains some obscene matter. Clearly, most film distributors have no interest in achieving only a restricted publication for a film and are, therefore, prepared to make cuts to achieve a wider circulation. Thus, the system of control may be driven largely by commercial motives: a distributor may make quite stringent cuts in order to ensure that, for example, a film receives a '15' certificate and so reaches a wider audience.

The second level of censorship is operated by local authorities under the Cinemas Act 1985, which continues the old power arising under the Cinematograph Act 1909. The local authority will usually follow the Board's advice; authorities are reluctant to devote resources to viewing films and will tend to rely on the BBFC's judgment. However, authorities may, on occasion, choose not to grant a licence to a film regardless of its decision. Films which have been licensed but which nevertheless have been banned in some areas include *A Clockwork Orange, The Life of Brian, The Last Temptation of Christ* and *Crash*. There is no requirement of consistency between authorities and thus discrepancies have arisen between different local authority areas. It is notable that the cinema is the only art form subject to moral judgment on a local level and it may be asked why it should be so singled out. This dual system of censorship was criticised by the Williams Committee in 1979 partly on the ground of the anomalies caused by having two overlapping levels and partly due to the inconsistency between local authorities. In particular, it criticised a system which allowed adult films to be censored both in general and on a local level beyond the requirements of the Obscene Publications Act 1959.

The Video Recordings Act (VRA) 1984 was introduced after a campaign about the dangers posed by video 'nasties' to children. Under the VRA 1984, the BBFC was established as the authority charged with classifying videos for viewing in the home. Videos are classified and therefore censored in almost the same way as films, and under s 9 of the 1984 Act, it is an offence to supply a video without a classification certificate, unless it is exempt on grounds of its concern with education, sport, music or religion. Under s 2(2), the exemption will not apply if the video portrays human sexual activity or gross violence or is designed to stimulate or encourage this. Section 4 of the VRA 1984 requires that the BBFC should have 'special regard to the likelihood of video works being viewed in the home'. Thus, makers of videos may find that videos are censored beyond the requirements of the Obscene Publications Act. The 1984 Act places the BBFC in the position of official censors and, in that role, their work has often been criticised as over-strict and arbitrary.

The regime in respect of videos was made potentially more restrictive in 1994. Fears that children might be more likely to commit violence after watching violent videos led the government to include a number of provisions in the Criminal Justice and Public Order Bill 1994 which was then before the Commons. Under s 90 of the Criminal Justice and Public Order Act (CJPOA) 1994, inserting s 4A into the VRA 1984, the BBFC must have 'special regard' to harm which may be caused to 'potential viewers or through their behaviour to society' by the manner in which the film deals with criminal behaviour, illegal drugs, violent behaviour or incidents, horrific incidents or behaviour, or human sexual activity. These criteria are non-exhaustive. The BBFC can consider any other relevant factor. The kind of harm envisaged to a child or to society is not specified and nor is the degree of seriousness envisaged. Once the Board has taken the above factors 'into account', s 4A does not prescribe the Board's response.

Section 89 of the CJPOA 1994 also amended s 2(2) in respect of the scope of exemptions. It is no longer necessary to show that the video is designed to stimulate or encourage the activity mentioned above, but only that it is likely to do so. Further, the exemptions will not apply if a video 'depicts techniques likely to be useful in the commission of offences' or 'criminal activity likely to any significant extent to stimulate or encourage the commission of offences'.

There is a right of appeal from the decisions of the BBFC to the VAC, under s 4, which operates as a tribunal. In 2000, the BBFC and the VAC came into conflict in respect of a number of explicit videos which depicted actual, rather than simulated, sexual scenes. The BBFC considered that no certificate should be issued, but, on appeal, the VAC disagreed. The BBFC sought review of the decision of the VAC (*Video Appeals Committee of the BBFC ex p BBFC* (2000)), but was unsuccessful on the basis that the VAC had taken all the relevant factors into account, including any risk to children. The judgment appeared to be based on the legal view that the access of adults to explicit material should not be prevented on the basis that it might be harmful to children if it happened to come into their hands. It was thought that since the videos were to be sold in adult sex shops, the risk that they would come into the hands of children was very slight.

The stance of the BBFC is obviously influenced by the composition of the Board, but its effect on film and video makers has been criticised as militating against creativity. It has been suggested by Robertson that a cosy relationship has developed that is insufficiently challenging – the acceptable boundaries are not fully explored in the name of artistic integrity and creative freedom. The age-based classification system encourages commercial judgments rather than artistic considerations to dominate; the most pressing consideration is to find the widest audience, which may mean instituting cuts in order to obtain a '15' certificate. These factors lead to a heavier censorship of films in the UK than in Europe or the US.

It seems possible that the inception of the HRA could have some impact on this situation. For example, a film maker whose film was refused a classification without certain cuts could seek to challenge the decision of the BBFC or, in the case of a video, that of the VAC, upholding the BBFC's decision. The VAC and BBFC are, assuming that they are public authorities, bound by the Convention rights under s 6 of the HRA. Therefore, they should ensure that their decisions do not breach Art 10 or any other relevant Article.

The 1984 Act, as amended, must be interpreted compatibly with the Convention rights under s 3 of the HRA. Given that a number of its terms are very open-ended, there is room for a range of interpretations. The VAC is a body set up under statute with a public function in the sense of hearing appeals regarding the classification of material to be promulgated to the public; it is also subject to judicial review. It is therefore almost certainly a public authority under s 6 of the HRA. The BBFC has a public function which is also statutory in respect of providing classification certificates for videos. Its function in relation to films is not statutory, but can clearly be termed public. Had it not undertaken the classification of films, the government would have been likely to set up a statutory body (see *Poplar Housing v Donoghue* (2001) on this point). It is suggested that it is probably a functional public authority. Therefore, there are grounds for taking the view that private bodies or persons could bring an action against either body under s 7(1)(a) of the HRA, relying on Art 10. In such an action, the court would have to give effect to s 12 of the HRA.

The stance taken by Strasbourg in relation to films likely to offend religious sensibilities was indicated in the leading decision, *Otto-Preminger* (1994). The film in question was not likely to be viewed by children, but was found to be offensive to religious sensibilities. The seizure and forfeiture of the film was not found to breach Art 10. Further guidance derives from the decision of the Court of Human Rights in *Wingrove v UK* (1996). This judgment concerned a decision of the BBFC, upheld by the VAC, to refuse a certificate to the short, explicit film *Visions of Ecstasy*. The Court found that the decision to refuse a certificate was within the national authorities' margin of appreciation. However, the film, which was to be promulgated as a short video, was viewed as offensive to religious sensibilities and as quite likely to come to the attention of children, since it could be viewed in the home. No breach of Art 10 was found.

In the case of a sexually explicit or violent film, the problem would be, as indicated above, that the Strasbourg jurisprudence appears to support quite far-reaching restrictions. However, where the risk of children viewing the film is very slight due to the use of age restrictions relating to films to be shown in the cinema, *and* the question of offending religious sensibilities does not arise, it is suggested that the jurisprudence can be viewed as supporting the availability of even very explicit films. This contention derives from the principles underlying the jurisprudence, which, as indicated above, relate to the familiar free speech justifications, including that of self-fulfilment.

It is concluded that where the question of offence to religious sensibilities does not arise, and bearing in mind the expectation that the domestic courts will not adopt the margin of appreciation doctrine, it would be consonant with the general Strasbourg freedom of expression jurisprudence to leave little scope under Art 10(2) for interferences with the freedom of expression of film makers in respect of films targeted at adults. Following this argument, it would be expected that they would be afforded an '18' certificate and, possibly, appropriate warnings would have to be posted at cinemas so that an unwitting viewer would not be offended. Different considerations would apply to videos, owing to the possibility that they might be viewed by children, although this argument should be considered carefully in terms of its impact on adults. The question of the harm that might be caused should also be considered, bearing in mind the lack of evidence mentioned above regarding a connection between behaviour seen on film and actual behaviour. The mere invocation of the possibility that children might view a video should not be enough. Guidance on this matter might usefully be sought from other jurisdictions, since it is not a matter that Strasbourg has inquired into in any depth. The question of the validity of taking the stance adopted in *Wingrove* and *Otto-Preminger* is considered in the next section.

The Strasbourg cases discussed above appear to show that freedom of expression may in future be given greater guarantees in UK courts. It does appear, to an extent, that the domestic means of protecting freedom of speech pre-HRA were weak; its protection depended partly on the discretion of the government and prosecuting authorities, rather than the law. Therefore, it is arguable that the HRA may provide greater protection. Domestic judges could find that some sections of the statutes considered here are unsustainable now that freedom of speech has been given primacy. The chances that they will do so may not be high, especially as in relation to the protection of morality, the Strasbourg jurisprudence leaves open room for a number of interpretations domestically. It is arguable, as indicated, that the provisions considered are compatible with Art 10 and strike a balance which is broadly consistent with its demands, but the HRA may inculcate a greater awareness of freedom of expression jurisprudence among judges and even among media bodies themselves.

Question 2

In what ways does Art 10 of the European Convention on Human Rights, as given effect by the Court of Human Rights, require States to strike an effective balance between those forms of political speech that should be permitted in a democratic society and those which can legitimately be restricted?

Answer plan

This question requires a critical approach to the case law of the Court of Human Rights on Art 10 and also a sense of how the principles developed by the Court may be significant for aspects of the law in the UK. It also requires an understanding of a number of issues in relation to which political expression can legitimately be curtailed and of the general approach the Court of Human Rights has adopted to such issues. There is no definitive list and any answer is bound to be selective.

The essential matters to be discussed are:

- the structure of Art 10 of the European Convention on Human Rights (ECHR);
- its general impact under the HRA 1998;
- the main principles governing the approach of the Court of Human Rights to political speech;
- examples of Art 10 jurisprudence which impact upon circumstances in which political speech is restricted.

Answer

The common law recognises freedom of expression and media freedom as fundamental values capable of influencing the way the law develops and the way judicial discretion, such as in respect of remedies, is exercised. Since the coming into effect of the HRA 1998, Art 10 of the ECHR ('freedom of expression'), which is a scheduled Convention right, now provides an additional and significant basis for ensuring that speech, particularly political speech, receives proper protection under the law. UK courts' understanding of Art 10 will now influence the way Acts of Parliament are interpreted and it will be a standard against which the legality of the actions of public authorities (as defined by s 6 of the HRA) will be measured. Even where neither Act of Parliament nor the actions of public authorities are in issue, Art 10 may also influence the way private law develops as the courts give effect to being, themselves, public authorities who are required to act compatibly with the scheduled Convention rights.

As with Arts 8, 9 and 11, Art 10 has two paragraphs. Article 10(1) identifies a general right to freedom of expression and it specifically mentions that this includes the freedom to hold opinions and to receive and impart information and ideas without interference from a public authority. Article 10(2) identifies the exclusive circumstances under which the freedom in Art 10(1) can be restricted. It also notes that the exercise of freedom of expression carries with it duties and responsibilities.

In resolving freedom of expression issues, the courts must firstly decide whether the issue is within the terms of Art 10(1). Freedom of expression has been broadly interpreted by the Strasbourg Court to include matters that go beyond simple speech. Acts of political protest, for example, are likely to be covered by the term, as in *Steel v UK* (1999), and so the law on public order will need to be formulated, as far as possible, to take the right to freedom of expression into account. It should be noted that both commercial speech, such as advertising, and artistic expression are included in the reach of Art 10(1). Both these forms of expression are capable of having political significance, and since, as we shall see, political speech receives the highest degree of protection under Art 10, the question may well arise whether political aspects outweigh any commercial or artistic aspects in any particular case. In one matter of political significance, Art 10 appears to be of little relevance. This is in respect of freedom of information and access to personal information. Although Art 10(1) includes the right to 'receive' information, this is understood as preventing State interferences with people's receipt of information which others are prepared to give, and does not impose a correlating duty on State agents to impart information (see *Gaskin v UK* (1989)). The point was illustrated in domestic law in *R (Persey) v SSEFRA* (2002) involving a challenge to the government's refusal to hold a public inquiry into the foot and mouth outbreak.

Article 10(2) lays down the exclusive circumstances under which expression, including political speech, can be made subject to any 'formalities, conditions, restrictions or penalties'. Of course, the terms of Art 10(2) have to be interpreted by judges and nothing in Art 10 indicates what, if any, priority is to be given to expression amongst the other rights and freedoms the Convention aims to secure.

First, any restrictions, etc, on freedom of expression must be 'prescribed by law': the restriction must have a basis in law and its application be reasonably foreseeable. Unlike in the context of privacy under Art 8, this provision has not caused significant problems for English law regarding freedom of expression. Even vague, common law offences, such as outraging public decency, seem to pass the test, as in *S and G v UK* (1991) where the prosecution of those responsible for an art exhibition which included the display of freeze-dried foetuses was found not to violate Art 10.

Secondly, restrictions on freedom of expression can only be imposed if they are intended to serve one or more of the purposes listed in Art 10(2). Most of the major areas of English law where freedom of expression is limited can be brought within these purposes. They include, for example, restrictions aimed at protecting national security (including official secrets legislation) or at preventing the disclosure of confidential material (including breach of confidence injunctions) or at maintaining the authority and impartiality of the judiciary (such as convictions for contempt of court). Protecting the 'rights of others' is a purpose that could play a wide-ranging, justifying role.

The most important requirement of Art 10(2) is, thirdly, that any restriction of freedom of expression must be 'necessary in a democratic society', and this means that any particular restriction must be a proportionate means of meeting a pressing social need. It is in this context that the judgments of the courts can be controversial, particularly in a political context. The job of the court, giving effect to Art 10, is to ensure a fair balance between the rights of individuals to freedom of expression and the public interest, such as it is, in restricting or suppressing speech.

Various guidelines can be discerned. The Court of Human Rights has been clear that political speech is to be given the highest priority, more than artistic or commercial speech, in the sense that any public interest purporting to justify restriction must be particularly strong and persuasive (the leading case is *Lingens v Austria* (1986)). Freedom of political speech is a requirement of a democratic society, which is the form of society under which the protection of human rights is most likely to be secured. In this context, political speech is broadly defined to include information about, and discussion of, matters of general public concern in society and is not confined to matters of State politics or the concerns of political parties. Free expression in a democracy also requires that the protection of the law should extend to unpopular expression that others, perhaps the majority or those in social, economic or political power, may find offensive, shocking or disturbing. In this context, the Court of Human Rights has also sought to defend media freedom. Reporting and comment may be vigorous and hostile to those affected. Furthermore, the Court upholds the general principle that journalists should be able to report allegations and should not be subject to criminal penalty merely because they are unable to prove the truth of what they report. This is a matter of great importance for effective investigative journalism (*Thorgeirson v Iceland* (1992)).

The effectiveness of Art 10, as interpreted by the Court of Human Rights, in the context of political speech is hard to measure. Any judgment will, of course, depend upon the point of view adopted for evaluation. ECHR cases are highly dependent on their individual facts and circumstances. Nevertheless, the Court's approach to some difficult questions about political speech can be considered. Its position tends to be complex. It does not take an absolutist position in favour of freedom of expression, but will strike down disproportionate or over-rigid restrictions on speech even if they are aimed at a legitimate, democratic purpose.

For example, it can be argued that the needs of a democratic society justify significant restrictions on political advertising both by political parties and other organisations and companies. The point is to try and prevent those who have the most wealth from being able to set and dominate the political agenda. The Court of Human Rights accepts the general legitimacy of this purpose but may find that general bans have disproportionate impacts in individual cases, particularly where a ban does not, in fact, serve the purpose. In *Vgt Verein Gegen Tierfabriken v Switzerland* (2002), the Court found that a ban on a TV advertisement by an animal welfare organisation violated Art 10. Following that case, the UK ministers introducing the Communications Bill into Parliament in 2002–03, were unable to certify, under s 19 of the HRA, that the ban on political advertising in the Bill was compatible with Art 10 (see ss 319 and 321 of the new Communications Act 2003).

A major issue about political speech relates to the question of the degree to which a tolerant society should permit intolerant speech. The inclusion of offensive and unpopular expression within the sphere which is protected by Art 10 means that the banning of, for example, racist speech is likely to require convincing justification. Protecting the rights of others, perhaps preventing disorder and crime, are legitimate purposes for restricting speech, but bans must also be proportionate. In *Jersild v Denmark* (1994), for instance, the banning of a programme, whose intention was anti-racist, but in which racists were allowed to speak for themselves, was held to be disproportionate. Of course, under Art 17, racist organisations will not be able to assert any Convention rights which they can then use to violate the rights of others.

Article 10 permits speech and expression to be restricted 'for the protection of morals'. In *Handyside v UK* (1979–80), the Court of Human Rights allowed a wide margin of appreciation to the States in this context. The problem is that matters impinging on moral questions can also be of political importance and a wide margin of appreciation may not allow sufficient protection to be given to this political dimension. This may be important in the UK where, for example, broadcasting organisations are required by law not to broadcast matter which offends against good taste and decency. The point was illustrated in *R (ProLife Alliance) v BBC* (2003), where the House of Lords upheld the right of the BBC to ban a party political broadcast (which was anti-abortion and contained graphic, disturbing images of aborted foetuses) on the grounds that it offended good taste. The Court of Appeal, whose judgment was overturned, had seen the matter as one of illegal censorship.

The question of political violence and the advocacy of causes associated with violence is a pressing one in the climate of the 'war against terrorism'. States are permitted to restrain political speech if it is an incitement to violence but, at the same time, need to recognise that, in a democratic society, the population is entitled to be informed and for difficult issues to be discussed. In *United Communist Party of Turkey v Turkey* (1998), for example, the Court upheld the linked rights of freedom of expression and freedom of association in respect of advocacy and campaigning for major constitutional change taking place against a background of political violence, albeit not violence that could be attributed to the applicants. The border between advocacy and incitement is, of course, hard to identify. In *Baskaya and Okçuoglu v Turkey* (2001), where the conviction of a university professor and journalist for publishing a book on the Kurdish problem was held to violate Art 10, the Court nevertheless seemed to accept that, in the context of political violence, a greater margin of appreciation, even on the suppression of political speech, was acceptable. The way the border between legitimate advocacy in a context of violence and incitement to violence is drawn by the courts as they review the activities of State authorities is clearly a matter of importance and relevant in the UK today as regards some of the offences in the Terrorism Act 2000 which relate to the activities of members of proscribed organisations.

In conclusion, we can see that the Strasbourg Court does not take an absolutist approach, as is taken by some judges of the US Supreme Court, on free speech issues. Nevertheless, given the importance of political speech in the Convention scheme, restrictions on political speech can only be justified if it is clear that the purpose served and the need for any particular restriction are very compelling. Justifications for restricting political speech must, above all, be demonstrated to meet a social need of the most pressing kind. In some areas where restrictions are compatible with Art 10, there is little controversy in principle, though, of course, there may be great disagreement in respect of the proportionality of any particular restriction. Restrictions on matters mentioned such as incitements to violence or racist politics are widely accepted in principle. As the issues about elections and political advertising show, however, there remain areas of reasonable disagreement about political speech where the Convention position may be at odds with alternative views about how best to promote fair democratic procedures in terms of which human rights can flourish. Under the HRA, of course, through the device of the declaration of incompatibility, the choice of the UK Parliament on such matters, the way it sets the balance, can prevail.

Question 3

'The Obscene Publications Act 1959 strikes a balance between freedom of expression and the interest in maintaining proper standards of taste and decency, which can be viewed as in accordance with the demands of Art 10 of the European Convention on Human Rights.' Discuss.

Answer plan

This is a reasonably straightforward essay question. It is important to consider the statute only and not the common law in this area. Obviously, the question could be 'attacked', in the sense that you might argue that no balance at all should be struck between, for example, freedom of expression on the one hand and maintaining proper standards of taste and decency: freedom of expression should entirely outweigh the other value, since it is too broad and vague to justify restrictions. You could argue that allowing freedom of expression to outweigh that other value entirely would be in accordance with Art 10. You need to remember that the European Convention on Human Rights (ECHR) has been afforded further effect in domestic law under the HRA 1998; it cannot merely be considered as an instrument administered at Strasbourg or afforded some effect domestically as a means of resolving statutory ambiguity as in the pre-HRA era.

Essentially, the following areas should be considered:

- Art 10 of the Convention and the HRA;
- relevant Strasbourg jurisprudence;
- subsequent restraints under the Obscene Publications Act 1959;
- the forfeiture regime under the 1959 Act;
- conclusions regarding compatibility of the statutory provisions and Art 10 of the Convention.

Answer

At the present time, it is arguably necessary for public authorities and the courts to take a stronger stance than previously in favour of freedom of expression, due to the impact of the HRA 1998, which incorporates the Convention, including the guarantee of freedom of expression under Art 10 of the Convention, into domestic law. The Obscene Publications Act 1959, as amended, must be read by the courts in a manner which gives effect, so far as is possible, to the Convention rights (s 3 of the HRA); if this is not possible, a declaration of incompatibility may be issued (s 4), and remedial action may be taken as a result (s 10). Further, the HRA gives special regard to the importance of freedom of expression in s 12. Public authorities are bound by the Convention rights under s 6 unless s 6(2) applies. The term covers all the bodies including courts who are involved in prosecutions, seizures and forfeitures under the 1959 Act. All these bodies must ensure that Art 10 is not infringed in their decision making. The courts could, if necessary, use s 3 of the HRA to modify overly restrictive statutory provisions, or the court could decide that, as a public authority, it could itself apply the Act in such a way as to avoid infringing Art 10. On the face of it, it is possible that restrictions on freedom of expression created by the 1959 Act may undergo fresh scrutiny, with a possible change in the direction of allowing the publication of explicit material which could not currently be published.

However, the impact of the HRA in this context depends on the requirements of Art 10. Certain forms of expression which may be said to be of no value may fall outside the scope of Art 10(1) and it is arguable that, for example, material gratuitously offensive to religious sensibilities (*Otto-Preminger Institut v Austria* (1994)) or depictions of genitals in pornographic magazines intended merely for entertainment (*Groppera Radio AG v Switzerland* (1990)) may fall outside its scope. On the other hand, 'hardcore' pornography has been found by the Commission to fall within Art 10(1) (*Hoare v UK* (1997); *Scherer v Switzerland* (1993)).

Assuming that most explicit material falls within Art 10(1), how high a level of protection does it receive? Clearly, political speech receives a much more robust degree of protection than other types of expression. Thus, the 'political' speech cases of *Sunday Times v UK* (1979), *Jersild v Denmark* (1994), *Lingens v Austria* (1986) and *Thorgeirson v Iceland* (1992) all resulted in findings that Art 10 had been violated and all were marked by an intensive review of the restriction in question in which the margin of appreciation was narrowed almost to vanishing point. By contrast, in cases involving artistic speech, an exactly opposite pattern emerges: applicants have tended to be unsuccessful and a deferential approach to the judgments of the national authorities as to its obscene or blasphemous nature has been adopted (*Müller v Switzerland* (1991); *Handyside v UK* (1976); *Otto-Preminger Institut v Austria* (1994); *Gay News v UK* (1982)). In *Otto-Preminger Institut v Austria* (1994), the Court found that a State may restrict expressions which may offend a particular population, although, otherwise, freedom of expression includes freedom to disseminate unpopular, shocking and disturbing information and ideas. The film in question was not likely to be viewed by children, but was found to be offensive to religious sensibilities. The seizure and forfeiture of the film was not found to breach Art 10. Further guidance derives from the decision of the Court of Human Rights in *Wingrove v UK* (1996). This judgment concerned a decision of the BBFC, upheld by the VAC, to refuse a certificate to the short, explicit film *Visions of Ecstasy*. The Court found that the decision to refuse a certificate was within the national authority's margin of appreciation. However, the film, which was to be promulgated as a short video, was viewed as offensive to religious sensibilities and as quite likely to come to the attention of children since it could be viewed in the home. No breach of Art 10 was found.

Although there is no universal concept of morality (*Handyside* (1976)), the ECHR does give high value to public interest arguments in favour of publication, as demonstrated in recent cases. Under Art 10(2), an interference with the guarantee of freedom of expression under Art 10 can be justified if it is prescribed by law, has a legitimate aim and is necessary in a democratic society. Strasbourg affords a very high value to freedom of expression and, in particular, as indicated, views the scope for interference with political expression as very limited. However, even in respect of artistic expression, which appears to have a lower place in the hierarchy of expression, there are no decisions defending restrictions on the freedom of expression of adults, except in respect of hardcore pornography where the distributor cannot ultimately control access to the material (*Hoare v UK* (1997)), or where a risk to children is also present, or in the context of offending religious sensibilities. This stance is in accordance with the principles underlying the jurisprudence, which relate to the familiar free speech justifications, including that of self-fulfilment.

It is concluded that where the question of offence to religious sensibilities does not arise, and bearing in mind the expectation that the domestic courts will not adopt the margin of appreciation doctrine, it would be consonant with the general Strasbourg freedom of expression jurisprudence to leave little scope under Art 10(2) for interferences with the freedom of expression of publishers of explicit material targeted at adults. The case of *Scherer v Switzerland* (1993) supports the contention that restraints on the material that can be offered to a willing adult audience should be minimal. Different considerations would apply to material aimed at children or teenagers and the possibility that children might access the material would be relevant.

The Obscene Publications Act covers all media under s 1(2), once the Broadcasting Act 1990 brought radio and television within its ambit. The Act makes a specific attempt at creating a balance between protecting morality on the one hand and safeguarding freedom of speech on the other. The provisions aimed at achieving this balance are s 1(1) and s 4. Section 1(1) prohibits publication of material which tends to deprave and corrupt its likely audience. The meaning of this test has caused the courts some difficulty: the House of Lords held in *Knuller v DPP* (1973) that it did not connote something which might lead to social evil in the sense that the material in question would be likely to cause a person to act in an anti-social fashion. The House of Lords found that such a test would be too narrow and would fail to catch a great deal of material.

It is balanced by the 'public good' defence contained in s 4. This defence requires a jury to ask first whether an article is obscene and, if so, to consider whether its merits outweigh its obscenity. This test was included as a means of giving protection to freedom of expression in relation to publications of artistic merit. However, it has been criticised by Robertson as requiring a jury to embark on the very difficult task of weighing an intrinsic quality against a predicted change for the worse in the minds of the group of persons likely to encounter the article. Further, the defence can be avoided by bringing a charge of indecency at common law; as *Gibson* (1990) demonstrated, the merits of an obscene object may, paradoxically, prevent its suppression, while the merits of less offensive objects will not.

However, the application of these tests at the present time, as seen in the trial for obscenity of the book *Inside Linda Lovelace* in 1976, suggests that no book of any conceivable literary merit will be prosecuted for obscenity.[1] Other publications, however, are a different matter: under s 3 of the Act, magazines and other material such as videos can be seized in forfeiture proceedings, which may mean that the full safeguards provided by the Act can be bypassed: full consideration may not be given to the possible literary merits of such material. It seems, therefore, that the protection afforded by the Act to freedom of speech depends more on the willingness of the prosecuting authorities to refrain from bringing prosecutions or on the tolerance of magistrates, rather than on the law itself.[2]

Clearly, any prosecutions under the Act or forfeiture actions constitute interferences with the Art 10 guarantee of freedom of expression under the HRA, although subject to justification. In relation to any particular decision, the public authorities involved are bound by s 6 of the HRA to ensure that the tests under Art 10 are satisfied, while the provisions of the 1959 Act must be interpreted consistently with Art 10 under s 3 of the HRA. Section 12 of the HRA does not apply to criminal proceedings. Forfeiture proceedings have the hallmarks of criminal proceedings in certain respects, although a conviction is not obtained, and therefore they may be outside the ambit of s 12.

Given the wide margin of appreciation afforded to the domestic authorities in the relevant decisions, little guidance as to the requirements of Art 10 in this context is available, especially where the material is directed at a willing adult audience. The domestic judiciary are, therefore, theoretically free to take a different stance. The decisions considered above at Strasbourg on the 1959 Act (*Handyside, Hoare*) indicate that the statutory regime relating to publication of an obscene article under s 2 is broadly in harmony with Art 10 of the European Convention. Nevertheless, a specific decision might not meet the proportionality requirements if scrutinised more intensively than at Strasbourg.

The UK forfeiture regime has not itself been tested at Strasbourg. The HRA requirements may be especially pertinent in relation to forfeiture: the magistrates conducting the proceedings are, of course, bound by Art 10 and therefore would be expected to approach the task with greater rigour. In particular, it is arguably necessary to examine each item, even where a large-scale seizure has occurred, rather than considering a sample of items only (see *Snaresbrook Crown Court ex p Commissioner of the Metropolis* (1984)). However, since, in practice, a vast amount of material is condemned as obscene in legal actions for forfeiture, the practical difficulties facing magistrates make it possible, especially initially, that the impact of the HRA will be more theoretical than real. It seems probable that, in practice, magistrates will not examine each item and will give only cursory attention, if any, to considering the application of the somewhat elusive Strasbourg case law. However, if on occasion publishers seek to contest s 3 orders before a jury, the proportionality of the measures adopted may receive more attention. Moreover, it is arguable that Art 6 of the Convention might be breached by the procedure since it could be said to lack impartiality, given that the same magistrate may sign the seizure order and determine forfeiture.

The Strasbourg cases discussed appear to show that freedom of expression may in future be given greater guarantees in UK courts, since the margin of appreciation doctrine – so influential in this particular area – is inapplicable. Therefore, it is arguable that the HRA may provide an impetus towards liberality. The chance that this will occur may not be high, especially as in relation to the protection of morality, the Strasbourg jurisprudence leaves open room for a number of interpretations domestically. It is arguable that the provisions of the 1959 Act and their application in practice are compatible with Art 10 and strike a balance which is broadly consistent with its demands (following *Handyside*), but the HRA may inculcate a greater awareness of freedom of expression jurisprudence among judges and magistrates in this context.

Notes

1   This is an important point which could be pursued further – the test is known as 'the contemporary standards' test – it derives from *Calder and Boyers* (1969). Because juries will apply this test, the concept of obscenity is, at least theoretically, able to keep up to date.

2   Proposals for reform could be mentioned. The Williams Committee recommended in 1979 that the printed word should not be subject to any restraint and that other material should be restrained on the basis of two specific tests: first, material which might shock should be available only through restricted outlets; and secondly, material should not be prohibited unless it could be shown to cause specific harm. Clearly, these proposals would give greater weight to freedom of speech than the protection of morals, in that they would allow greater differentiation between the kind of harm which might be caused by the various media. These proposals have not been implemented and, therefore, the uncertain 'deprave and corrupt' test remains as an arguably unacceptable restraint on artistic freedom.

Question 4

Do you consider that the Contempt of Court Act 1981 has succeeded in creating a balance between freedom of speech and the administration of justice that is in accordance with Art 10 of the European Convention on Human Rights as scheduled in the Human Rights Act 1998?

Answer plan

A reasonably straightforward essay question if you are familiar with the reforms in this area undertaken after the *Sunday Times* decision by means of the Contempt of Court Act 1981. The following matters should be discussed:

- the need to show a substantial risk of serious prejudice under s 2(2) of the Contempt of Court Act 1981;
- the concept of 'active' proceedings under s 2(3) of and Sched 1 to the 1981 Act;
- discussions in good faith under s 5;
- the survival of common law contempt and its relationship with the 1981 Act;
- intention to prejudice the administration of justice;
- the concept of imminence in common law contempt;
- the possibility of establishing a 'trial by newspaper';
- contempt of court and the Strasbourg jurisprudence.

Answer

The Contempt of Court Act 1981 brought about various reforms which were intended to give greater weight to freedom of speech in order to bring about harmonisation between UK contempt law and Art 10 of the ECHR. In particular, it created a stricter test for risk of prejudice, which gave less weight to the administration of justice, it created a shorter *sub judice* period and it allowed discussions in good faith of public affairs to escape liability.

The basic Convention requirement is to strike a proper relationship between freedom of expression in Art 10, and the right to a fair trial in Art 6. Article 10 permits restrictions on freedom of expression aimed at maintaining the 'integrity and impartiality of the judiciary'. The leading Strasbourg case is *Worm v Austria* (1998) in which a journalist had been convicted for contempt for publishing an article implying the guilt of a politician who, at the time of publication, was on trial. The Court held that the conviction was not a violation of Art 10 and upheld the view that it was legitimate to restrain the media in order to maintain the function of the courts as the forum for deciding legal disputes and criminal trials, and to ensure that everyone, including prominent persons, has their right to a fair trial protected. Articles and programmes prejudging particular issues before the courts can be restricted, as can those that seriously undermine the general integrity of the courts. At the same time, the Court of Human Rights, as in earlier cases such as *Sunday Times v UK* (1979), stressed that the needs of a free press in a democratic society included permitting vigorous debate on matters of public interest and these could include both the judiciary and court system and also matters forming the context of cases before the courts. In *AG v Guardian Newspapers Ltd* (1999), which involved press comment prejudicial to a defendant on trial for stealing body parts, the Divisional Court said that the Contempt of Court Act 1981 can be applied in a manner that is compatible with these Convention principles.

The new test for risk of prejudice arises under s 2(2) and requires that a substantial risk of serious prejudice must be shown. According to the Court of Appeal in *AG v News Group Newspapers* (1987), both limbs of this test must be satisfied; showing a slight risk of serious prejudice or a substantial risk of slight prejudice would not be sufficient. In *AG v English* (1983), Lord Diplock interpreted 'substantial risk' as excluding a 'risk which is only remote', which implies that fairly slight risks are sufficient. Later cases, however, have created a test which, it is submitted, requires there to be a fairly or reasonably substantial risk. It is therefore suggested that it has moved the balance somewhat away from the administration of justice towards freedom of speech.

Under s 4(2) of the 1981 Act, a judge may make an order postponing contemporaneous reporting of any public legal proceedings if such an order 'appears necessary for avoiding a substantial risk of prejudice to the administration of justice in those proceedings'. This is quite a wide provision, more extensive than at common law, which on its face provides little protection for media freedom.[1] Generally, such orders are likely to be compatible with Art 10 (see, for example, *Hodgson and Others v UK* (1998)). Any particular ban, of course, must be proportionate. In *Telegraph Group plc v Sherwood* (2001), the Court of Appeal laid down the proper approach, compatible with Convention rights, to the issue. There had been a controversial shooting by police and the issue was whether reporting the trial of one officer for murder would prejudice the later trial of the senior officers who planned the operation. Building on earlier cases, it was held that a court had, first, to be satisfied that reporting would create a 'not insubstantial' risk to the proceedings in issue (here, the later trials) and, secondly, it had to be satisfied that reporting restrictions would prevent that risk materialising. If so, however, an order does not follow necessarily; the existence of an overriding public interest in allowing reporting needs to be considered. At that third stage, value judgments about the relationship between free speech and fair trials could be made. This approach expressly permits a value-laden balancing of different public interests. Whether it gives Art 6 its proper significance can be doubted. Reporting, even of a matter which involved serious public interests, which clearly denied a person a fair trial, is likely to be hard to justify in Convention terms.

The test for the *sub judice* period which arises under s 2(3) is more clearly defined than the test at common law and, therefore, proceedings are 'active' (or *sub judice*) for shorter periods. Thus, the test is intended to have a liberalising effect and, since it produces greater certainty about the time from which the contempt jurisdiction runs, it is easier to show consistency with the pervasive 'legality' principle in human rights law.

Even where a publication is published in the active period and satisfies s 2(2), it may still escape liability if the prosecution cannot show that it does not amount to 'a discussion in good faith of public affairs or other matters of general public interest', or that, 'the risk of impediment or prejudice to particular legal proceedings is not merely incidental to the discussion' (s 5). In other words, media discussions of various issues are less stifled under the Act than they were previously under the common law.

AG v English (1983) is the leading case on s 5 and is generally considered to provide a good example of the kind of case for which s 5 was framed. After the trial had begun of a consultant who was charged with the murder of a Down's syndrome baby, an article was published in the *Daily Mail*, which made no direct reference to him, but was written in support of a pro-life candidate, Mrs Carr, who was standing in a by-election. Mrs Carr had no arms; the article referred to this fact and continued: '... today the chances of such a baby surviving are very small; someone would surely recommend letting her die of starvation. Are babies who are not up to scratch to be destroyed before or after birth?'

Lord Diplock adopted a two-stage approach in determining the s 5 issue. First, could the article be called a 'discussion'? Lord Diplock considered that the term 'discussion' could not be confined merely to abstract discussions, as the Divisional Court had suggested, but could include consideration of examples drawn from real life and could include accusations about actual practices going on in society. The article was about Mrs Carr's election and also the general topic of mercy killing. The main point of her candidature was that killing of sub-standard babies did happen and should be stopped; if the article had not asserted that babies were allowed to die, she would have been depicted as tilting at imaginary windmills. Thus, the term 'discussion' could include implied accusations.

Secondly, was the risk of prejudice to Dr Arthur's trial merely an incidental consequence of expounding the main theme of the article? Lord Diplock held that the issue was not whether the article could have been written without including the offending words, as the Divisional Court had proposed, but rather the principal meaning of the article as derived from its words. The main theme of the article was Mrs Carr's election policy; Dr Arthur was not mentioned – unlike the article in the *Sunday Times* case, which was concerned entirely with the actions of Distillers. Clearly, Dr Arthur's trial could be prejudiced by the article, but that prejudice could properly be described as incidental to its main theme. Thus, s 5 applied; the article did not therefore fall within the strict liability rule. This ruling was generally seen as giving a liberal interpretation to s 5. Had the narrower interpretation of the Divisional Court prevailed, it would have meant that all debate in the media on the topic of mercy killing would have been prevented for almost a year – the period of active proceedings against Dr Arthur.

Section 5 does not give the media *carte blanche* to discuss issues arising from or relating to any particular case during the 'active' period. For example, an article which is focused predominantly on the alleged bad character of the defendant and does not raise a major independent matter of public interest is likely to fall outside the scope of s 5 (*AG v Guardian Newspapers Ltd* (1999)). The ruling in *AG v English* gave an emphasis to freedom of speech. Indeed, it may go beyond what Art 10 requires since it permits the publication of an article which creates a substantial risk of serious prejudice to a trial. Section 5 does not, in its own terms, limit what can be published by the fair trial requirement in Art 6, and s 3 of the HRA 1998 may require this to be interpreted into the section.

Due largely to the operation of s 5, the strict liability rule seems to have created a fairer balance than was the case at common law between freedom of speech and protection for the administration of justice. However, the uncertainty as to the application of s 5 where the article focuses on the case itself means that s 5 will allow some legitimate debate in the press to be stifled and, therefore, it might be argued that further relaxation is needed, such as a general public interest defence. What remains unclear is the role of Art 6: is the right to a fair trial simply an important matter to be weighed against the importance of the free speech interests, or is it a 'trump' right in the sense that it justifies restraints on media comment, no matter how important the public interests involved, at that point when fair trial rights are seriously affected? Article 10 may authorise simplifying the s 5 test, but not relaxing it too far.

It may be argued, then, that the tests under the 1981 Act, especially the s 5 test, have tended to afford recognition to the free speech principle, but the possibility of escaping from the 'balance' created by the Act by using the common law has been preserved by s 6(c). Common law contempt presents such an alternative in all instances in which proceedings are not active, assuming, of course, that the *mens rea* requirement can be satisfied, and it has proved to be of great significance in this context, due to the readiness with which it is sometimes accepted that the common law tests have been fulfilled. Even more controversially, common law contempt may be an alternative in instances where proceedings are active, but liability under the Act cannot be established; again, the provisions of s 5 could be undermined.

In the *Hislop* case (1991), it appeared that a finding of intention to prejudice the administration of justice necessary to found liability for contempt at common law would probably preclude a finding of good faith under s 5. In the majority of cases, a finding of good faith under s 5 would preclude a finding of intention to prejudice proceedings. A situation is imaginable in which a newspaper recognised a strong risk that proceedings would be prejudiced, and did not desire such prejudice but felt that publication was justified by an overriding need to bring iniquity to public attention (as may have been the case in *AG v Newspaper Publishing plc* (1990)). Section 5 might cover such a situation, thereby preventing liability under statute. However, liability could still arise at common law if the necessary intention can be proved. This would allow a newspaper to be punished for contempt where proceedings were active and where publication of material covered by an injunction fell within s 5. Thus, in this sense, common law contempt clearly has the ability to undermine the statutory protection for freedom of speech. Also, it may be noted that the upholding of an interlocutory injunction by the House of Lords in *AG v Punch* (2003) indicates that there is little inclination on the part of the senior judiciary to narrow down the common law tests in favour of freedom of expression in the post-HRA era.

Similarly, common law contempt in respect of 'active' proceedings is possible in other circumstances. Section 2(2) might not be satisfied on the basis that, although some risk of prejudice arose, it could not be termed serious enough. In such an instance, there appears to be no reason why the common law could not be used instead, on the basis that the test of showing 'a real risk of prejudice' is less difficult to satisfy. If so, it would be possible to circumvent the more stringent s 2(2) requirement. Of course, it would be necessary to prove an intention to prejudice the administration of justice. Thus, due to the possible difference between the test under s 2(2) and the equivalent common law test of 'real risk of prejudice', the safeguards for media freedom in s 5 could be avoided even when there was a good faith

problem would be, as indicated above, that the Strasbourg jurisprudence appears to support quite far-reaching restrictions. There is always the possibility that a broadcast might be viewed by children, although this argument should be considered carefully, in terms of its impact on adults.

The broadcasting regime should be considered in the light of the HRA and the relevant Strasbourg jurisprudence. The predecessor of the Communications Act 2003 was the Broadcasting Act 1990. As part of the 'deregulation' of television, the Act set up the Independent Television Commission (ITC) to replace the Independent Broadcasting Authority (IBA) as a public body charged with licensing and regulating non-BBC television services. Under s 6(1)(a), the ITC had to attempt to ensure that every licensed television service ensured that nothing was included in its programmes 'which offends against good taste and decency'. The ITC published an updated Programme Code dealing with those matters in 2001. The Code attempts to strike a balance between preserving good taste and decency on the one hand and avoiding too great a restraint on freedom of speech on the other. It therefore allows sexual scenes, so long as they are presented with tact and discretion. As far as films are concerned, it follows the guidelines laid down by the BBFC: '18' rated films may be shown, but only after 'the watershed', which varies according to the channel. Furthermore, the BBFC standards are to be regarded as minimum ones; the mere fact that a film has an '18' certificate is not to be taken as implying that it would be proper to broadcast it. The role of the ITC in this respect was, to an extent, duplicated by the Broadcasting Standards Council, set up in 1988 to monitor the standards being maintained in programmes.

The Broadcasting Act 1996 replaced the Council with the Broadcasting Standards Commission (BSC), an independent body to which appointments are made by the Home Secretary (now itself subsumed in Ofcom under the 2003 Act). The BSC was placed under a duty to create and implement a Code of Guidance for broadcasters which dealt with matters of decency, with particular attention to the depiction of sex and violence (s 108). The BSC was also under a duty to deal with complaints about indecency, sex or violence in broadcasts, and it may have held a hearing to enable it to reach a decision (ss 110 and 116). The BBC has similar duties under its Royal Charter and Licence Agreement. The flouting of viewer expectations and in particular the fact that people tune in and tune out of programmes is thought to provide a rationale for such regulation – it is not thought to be sufficient merely to provide warnings and to show explicit films or other material late at night – that is the main reason advanced for providing a different and stricter regime for broadcasting as opposed to videos. The BSC made this point by referring in its Code on Standards (to be policed in future by Ofcom, the new all-inclusive regulator) to an implied contract between viewer and broadcaster about the terms of admission to the home (para 2 of the Code).

This regulation, affecting broadcasting in the interests of preventing offence to viewers, clearly curbs the freedom of expression of broadcasters, although it is viewed as indicated as a part of a 'contract' for the privilege of coming directly into the home, which should be adhered to by responsible broadcasters. The inception of the HRA might have been expected to call this regime into question since freedom of expression as protected under Art 10 can only be curbed where it is necessary in a democratic society and proportionate to the aim of protecting morality or the rights of others.

The Communications Act 2003 largely creates a new regime governing *inter alia* restrictions on the basis of causing offence to viewers. The new regime is, in essentials, based on the old one, but more detailed statutory guidance is afforded to broadcasters. Overly restrictive decisions of public sector broadcasters and of Ofcom under the taste and decency provisions of s 319 (the term taste and decency is not used – the reference is to offensive material) could be challenged under the HRA for the first time, not merely on the grounds that a decision was irrational but on the ground of infringing freedom of expression. As indicated above, the Convention jurisprudence – interpreting Art 10 – notoriously does not uphold freedom of expression very strongly where matters of taste and decency in respect of non-political speech are concerned – broadly, artistic speech – but the jurisprudence defends political expression very strongly. Therefore, where the regulatory regime upholding standards of taste and decency appeared to come into conflict with the standards maintained by Art 10 – most likely in the realm of political broadcasting – it appeared possible that broadcasters' and regulators' decisions as to the balance to be struck in this instance between freedom of expression and the responsibilities of broadcasters in relation to allowing for the intrusion of offensive material into the home might be determined by the courts.

The challenge in question arose in the *ProLife Alliance* case (2003) which has just been to the House of Lords. The ProLife Alliance is a registered political party which opposes abortion. At the 2001 general election, the applicant put up enough parliamentary candidates to qualify for a party election broadcast (PEB). The applicant submitted a video showing *inter alia* an abortion being carried out. The broadcasters refused to broadcast the video on the grounds that it offended against good taste and decency and would cause widespread offence. The applicant applied for permission to seek judicial review and appealed against the refusal of permission. The applicant did not challenge s 6(1) of the Broadcasting Act 1990 (the predecessor of s 319 of the 2003 Act) imposing the taste and decency standards itself, as inconsistent with Art 10 under the HRA. The applicant argued rather that the broadcasters had not properly applied those standards – on the basis that they had failed to attach sufficient significance to the electoral context – in which freedom of expression would be even more crucial. The Court of Appeal found that under the HRA, it had itself to decide whether the censorship (as it put it) in question was justified. The court found that considerations of taste and decency could not prevail over freedom of speech by a political party at election time except wholly exceptionally, and this instance did not require an exception to be made. Very little deference to the broadcasters' expertise and experience was accorded by the court.

The BBC appealed to the House of Lords, which considered that the Court of Appeal decision amounted to a finding that the taste and decency standards should not be applied to PEBs. However, Parliament had decided that such broadcasts should not be exempt: despite the importance of free speech at such times, and that decision of Parliament as encapsulated in the Broadcasting Acts 1990 and 1996 (in respect of the BSC) and now in the 2003 Act had not itself been challenged, although it could have been. Thus, once it was accepted that those standards should be applied to PEBs, the question was whether the broadcasters had applied them wrongly; that did not appear to be the case on the facts, bearing in mind the clear findings of expert broadcasters, and in giving weight to their views, the Lords made it clear that greater deference should be accorded to the broadcasters on the basis that, due to their audience research, they were likely to be in touch with audience expectations.

So, the appeal of the BBC was allowed. The outcome means that broadcasters' freedom within that particular statutory framework – which in essence is now encapsulated in the 2003 Act – was reaffirmed. The HRA did not operate as a mechanism enabling the courts to claim significantly greater powers of interference in broadcasters' decisions as to their responsibilities in respect of standards – even in respect of political speech. The same stance is now likely to be taken in respect of the new statutory framework if a similar case arises. It is clear that outside the context of political speech, a serious challenge under the HRA to the restrictions on broadcasting offensive material under the 2003 Act is highly unlikely to succeed. However, if a challenge similar to that in the *ProLife Alliance* case was brought, there would be a chance of success if the claim was based on the new statutory framework itself – specifically on s 319 – as being incompatible with the demands of Art 10. The courts might accept that difficulties in reconciling the two required a declaration of the incompatibility under s 4 of the HRA or quite a radical modification of the provisions under s 3 of the HRA. Such a modification could include minimising the demands of the standards set where political broadcasting – not necessarily only in relation to PEBs or party political broadcasts – is concerned.

Restraints on, and regulation of, television programmes may be based on political grounds, not only on those of taste and decency. An impartiality clause was introduced by s 6 of the Broadcasting Act 1990, requiring the ITC to set up a Code to require that politically sensitive programmes must be balanced to ensure impartiality. Such programmes can be balanced by means of a series of programmes; it is not necessary that any one programme should be followed by one specific balancing programme. However, the requirement may have meant that some politically controversial programmes are not made, since the expense and difficulty of setting up balancing programmes may have proved to have a deterrent effect. The ITC Code makes it clear that a company cannot use the argument that a programme which might be said to have an anti-government bias may be balanced by programmes broadcast by other companies; the company has to achieve impartiality in its own programming. In interpreting this Code, the companies may again act cautiously and may interpret what is meant by 'bias' broadly. Thus, although this provision may seek to balance a need for impartiality against the need to protect freedom of expression, it may not achieve that balance in practice. The Communications Act 2003 continues the restrictions in relation to impartiality in s 319(2)(c) and s 320. Section 320(4) makes it clear that programmes can continue to be balanced by means of a series of programmes.

It may be noted that the 2003 Act was *not* declared compatible with the Convention rights under s 19 of the HRA. The lack of a declaration was due to the view taken that s 321(2), which continues the ban on political advertising, was incompatible with Art 10, based on the decision of the European Court of Human Rights (ECtHR) in *VGT v Switzerland* (2002). However, it can be assumed that the rest of the Act was viewed by Parliament as compatible with Art 10. Therefore, it should be treated in the same way as any other Act of Parliament.

Journalists, film makers and groups such as Amnesty, whose advertising has been rejected, could challenge media regulators, including, in future, Ofcom (which has replaced the BSC) directly by invoking s 7(1)(a) of the HRA. They could alternatively bring judicial review proceedings and then rely on s 7(1)(b) in those proceedings. They could also challenge media bodies such as the BBC which are also public authorities. They could challenge the application of the Communications Act 2003 – as occurred in the *ProLife Alliance* case – or the statutory restrictions based on impartiality and relating to political advertising themselves. Decisions as to licensing, political advertising and adjudications regarding impartiality could be subjected thereby to a more intensive scrutiny. Assuming that the independent television companies are not public authorities under s 6 of the HRA, which is almost certainly the case, they could also bring such proceedings as 'victims' under the HRA. For example, an independent broadcaster could seek a preliminary ruling from Ofcom as to whether a particular programme might infringe the political advertising ban and/or the impartiality requirements, if broadcast, or Ofcom might find, post-broadcast, that those restrictions had been infringed. Such findings could then be challenged as indicated and s 3 of the HRA could be relied upon to seek modification of the provisions, relying on Art 10. The use of the HRA would mean that the provisions themselves and decisions made under them would be tested more directly against Convention standards than they have been by means of judicial review. Section 12 of the HRA would be applicable. The application of the various Codes of Practice could also be challenged in such proceedings. Provisions of such Codes could be struck down by the courts unless primary legislation prevented the removal of the incompatibility. Given that the detailed provisions are commonly contained in the Codes, this is a significant possibility. Although the *ProLife Alliance* case did not afford much encouragement to those wishing to challenge the decisions of broadcasters or Ofcom in relation to the taste and decency provisions, a different stance might be taken in respect of political broadcasting that did not infringe those requirements. Such a stance could be based partly on the Strasbourg political speech jurisprudence discussed above and partly on the established common law stance in favour of such speech (see, for example, *Reynolds v Times Newspapers* (1999); *Derbyshire CC v Times Newspapers* (1993); *R v Secretary of State for the Home Department ex p Simms* (1999)). If compatibility could not be achieved – as is unlikely in respect of the ban on political advertising under s 321 of the 2003 Act – a declaration of that incompatibility could be made.

In conclusion, it can be said, as indicated above, that the Convention standards applied to broadcasting under the HRA are themselves quite flexible in respect of the 'protection of morals' – they very clearly leave room for the adoption of a range of approaches. The stance under Art 10 considered above at Strasbourg and in the *ProLife Alliance* case might well support quite far-reaching restrictions on broadcasting owing to the possibility that children might be affected, since it comes into the home. But the Strasbourg standard as regards political expression is much stricter. The use of the Convention jurisprudence considered above on both political and, if afforded a creative interpretation, artistic expression might enable pressure to be brought to bear, tending to promote the representation of a wider range of views, including views of minority groups, in broadcasting. In various broadcasting contexts, domestic judges could theoretically find that ss 319, 320, 321 and other relevant provisions under the 2003 Act fail to give freedom of speech the primacy it is given under Art 10. The chances that they will do so are probably not high, especially as, in relation to the protection of morality, the Strasbourg jurisprudence leaves open room for a number of interpretations, domestically. It is arguable that the provisions considered are compatible with Art 10 and strike a balance which is broadly consistent with its demands, but at the least the HRA may inculcate a greater awareness of freedom of expression jurisprudence among judges and even among media bodies and media regulators themselves.

Question 6

There are currently proposals before Parliament to abolish blasphemy law. Evaluate the case for such abolition in the Human Rights Act era.

Answer plan

A reasonably straightforward essay question if you are familiar with this particular area. You need to consider whether reform should mean complete abolition – as is proposed – or whether the function of blasphemy law (if you think it has a legitimate one) can be taken over by changes to another area of law, or whether blasphemy law instead requires extension to cover all religions. Bear in mind the need to create a balance between freedom of expression on the one hand and protection for religious sensibilities on the other under the HRA. Would the current proposals create such a balance? Essentially, the following matters should be considered:

- ambit of blasphemy law (the *Lemon* rulings);
- The Law Commission's 1985 Report;
- *Chief Metropolitan Magistrates' Court ex p Choudhury* (1991);
- Arts 9 and 10 of the ECHR under the HRA and their implications for domestic law in this context;
- incitement to racial hatred under the Public Order Act 1986 – the proposal for the addition of incitement to religious hatred under the Religious Offences Bill 2003;
- conclusions as to the desirability of abolition and the introduction of the offence of incitement to religious hatred.

Answer

The Religious Offences Bill 2003 will abolish the offence of blasphemy if it becomes law. This essay will argue that abolition is readily defensible due to the current width of the offence and its discriminatory nature. By the middle of the 19th century and, in particular, after the case of *Ramsay and Foote* (1883), it became clear that the basis of blasphemy had narrowed: it required a scurrilous attack on Christianity, rather than merely reasoned and sober arguments against it. It was thought by 1950 that the offence no longer existed, but it was resurrected in *Lemon* (1979). *Gay News* published a poem 'The love that dares to speak its name', by a Professor of English Literature, James Kirkup. It expressed religious sentiment in describing a homosexual's conversion to Christianity and, in developing its theme, it metaphorically attributed homosexual acts to Jesus. A private prosecution was brought against *Gay News* and the editor and publishing company were convicted of the offence of blasphemous libel. This decision led to an arguably unacceptable broadening of the offence.

The Court of Appeal held that the intention or motive of the defendants was irrelevant, since blasphemy was a crime of strict liability and the Lords confirmed that mere intention to publish the material constituted the *mens rea* of the offence. Moreover, it could be committed by a Christian, as there was no need to show that the material had mounted a fundamental attack on Christianity (as had been thought). There was no defence of publication in the public interest; serious literature could therefore be caught. The work in question need not be considered as a whole. All that needed to be shown was that the material in question, which was published with the defendants' knowledge, had crossed the borderline between moderate criticism on the one hand and immoderate treatment of objects sacred to Christians on the other. There was no need to show indecent or offensive treatment of such objects, nor was it necessary to show that resentment would be likely to be aroused. Neither was the past requirement to show that a breach of the peace might be occasioned by publication of the material necessary.

This decision has been much criticised, since it inhibits juxtaposition of sexuality with aspects of the Anglican religion by writers and broadcasters. In common with other parts of the common law, it allows the Obscene Publications Act 1959 to be circumvented, because it admits of no public good defence. Moreover, there are already various areas of liability arising at common law and under statute which could be used to prevent offence being caused to Christians.

Gay News applied to the European Court of Human Rights (ECtHR) on a number of grounds, including that of a breach of Art 10. This application was ruled inadmissible in a cautious judgment. It was found that the Art 10 guarantee of freedom of expression had been interfered with, but that the interference fell within the 'rights of others' exception of Art 10(2). Was the interference necessary in a democratic society? It was found that once it was accepted that the religious feelings of citizens may deserve protection if attacks reach a certain level of savagery, it seemed to follow that the domestic authorities were best placed to determine when that level was reached. The argument used in the *Handyside* case (1976) seemed to underlie the decision: a very wide margin of appreciation is required in sensitive areas linked closely to national culture. A similar stance was taken in *Otto-Preminger Institut v Austria* (1994), which concerned suppression of a film which was deemed to be an abusive attack on Catholicism. The ECtHR found that no breach of Art 10 had occurred because the rights of others exception applied. It seems, therefore, that UK blasphemy law, despite its width, is compatible with Art 10. This was implicitly recognised in *Wingrove v UK* (1997), which allowed restraint of publication of any item which would infringe criminal law.

The argument in favour of extension of the offence was put and rejected in *Chief Metropolitan Magistrates' Court ex p Choudhury* (1991), a case which arose out of the publication of Salman Rushdie's *The Satanic Verses*. The applicants applied for judicial review of the refusal of a magistrates' court to grant summonses against Salman Rushdie and his publishers for, *inter alia*, the common law offence of blasphemous libel. The Court of Appeal determined, after reviewing the relevant decisions, that the offence of blasphemy was clearly confined only to publications offensive to Christians. Extending the offence would, it was determined, create great difficulties as it would be virtually impossible to define the term 'religion' sufficiently clearly. Freedom of expression would be curtailed, as authors would have to try to avoid offending members of many different sects.

The applicants did not, however, rely only on domestic law; during argument that the offence should be extended, it was said that UK law must contain a provision to give effect to the Convention guarantee of freedom of religion under Art 9. In response, it was argued and accepted by the Court of Appeal that the Convention need not be considered, because the common law on the point is not uncertain. However, the respondents nevertheless accepted that, in this particular instance, the Convention should be considered.

It was found that the UK was not in breach of the Convention, because extending the offence of blasphemy would breach Arts 10 and 7; the exceptions of Art 10(2) could not be invoked, as nothing in the book would support a pressing social need for its suppression. Furthermore, it was uncertain that Art 9 was applicable: it would be infringed if Muslims were prevented from exercising their religion, but such restrictions were not in question. Moreover, Art 9(2) contains a number of exceptions, including that of protection for the rights of others, which would be relevant.

The applicants put forward the further argument that UK blasphemy law discriminated against Muslims and, therefore, a violation of Art 14 read in conjunction with Art 9 had occurred. This interpretation of Art 9, read alongside Art 14, had been rejected by the European Commission in the *Gay News* case (1982). In this case, it also failed on the ground that the envisaged extension of UK law to protect Islam would involve a violation of Art 10, which guarantees freedom of expression. Such an extension was not, therefore, warranted. It seems clear from this ruling and from statements made by Lord Scarman in the House of Lords in *Lemon*, which were relied upon in the *Choudhury* case, that the judiciary are not minded to extend this offence.

It is clear that some change is needed in the current law for at least two reasons. First, from a pragmatic point of view, the present situation, since it is perceived by Muslims as unfair, is a considerable source of racial tension; it both engenders feelings of anger and alienation in the Muslim community and, when these feelings are expressed through such activities as book burning and attacks on booksellers stocking *The Satanic Verses*, increased feelings of hostility towards Muslims in certain sections of the non-Muslim population. Secondly, it is indefensible that the State should single out one group of citizens and protect their religious feelings while others are without such protection. It is submitted that the only justification for continuance of the blasphemy law, which could offer it even *prima facie* support, is the argument from the right to religious freedom, which is protected under Art 9 of the Convention. The need to provide such protection is also viewed as falling within the 'rights of others' exception to Art 10 and, therefore, as arguably justifying the banning of publications that might offend religious sensibilities, as the Court of Human Rights found in *Otto-Preminger* and *Wingrove*. It is contended that the argument accepted by the Court that such publications infringe Art 9 is deeply flawed. However, the argument, as expressed by the Court of Human Rights, goes on to assume that the State is under a positive duty to facilitate the full enjoyment in practice of its citizens' right to freedom of religion, taking that term to encompass a duty to prevent attacks on religion which take a certain objected-to form. This is surely a mistaken view; rather, it is submitted, the right to religious freedom is violated if one is not free to choose, express and manifest one's religious beliefs (this is indicated in the text of Art 9): the right is not so violated simply because one is not protected from mental suffering caused by verbal attacks upon one's religion or offensive portrayals of it.

However, consideration of the Strasbourg jurisprudence suggests that the inception of the HRA does not necessarily require reform of UK blasphemy law, since such reform is not required in order to ensure harmony with Art 10 of the ECHR as interpreted at Strasbourg. This suggestion is borne out by the findings of the European Commission in the *Gay News* case and of the ECtHR in *Otto-Preminger Institut v Austria* (1994). Of course, UK courts, which do not adhere to the margin of appreciation doctrine, could take a different view of the demands of Art 10.

It seems fairly clear that the solution is not to extend this offence beyond Anglicanism and this alternative is rejected in the new Bill. It is suggested that extension would not have been justifiable for a number of reasons. The Law Commission, in their 1985 Report, concluded that an offence of wounding the feelings of adherents of any religious group would be impossible to construct, because the term 'religion' could not be defined with sufficient precision. Since extension of the law does not seem a realistic alternative due to the difficulty of defining 'religion' and the impact on freedom of expression, it would appear that abolition of blasphemy as an offence – as currently proposed in the Religious Offences Bill 2003 – would be the simplest way of remedying the current unfairness of the law in this area. However, it is arguable that abolition should be coupled with creation of a new offence of incitement to religious hatred – as also proposed in the Bill – and this is the argument this essay will now turn to.

The International Covenant on Civil and Political Rights, of which the UK is a signatory, requires contracting States to prohibit the advocacy of 'national, racial or *religious* hatred that constitutes incitement to discrimination, hostility or violence' (Art 20). In practical terms, it would be fairly straightforward to amend ss 17, 18, 19 and 23 of Pt III of the Public Order Act 1986, which prohibit incitement to racial hatred, to include religious groups. This would remedy the present situation, which permits the advocacy of hatred against Muslims, while Sikhs and Jews (as racial groups) are protected from such speech. The problem of defining religion of course still remains; however, since such incitement represents a far narrower area of liability than blasphemy, the danger that a wide interpretation of 'religion' would lead to the courts being overrun by claims from obscure groups is accordingly less great. Furthermore, prosecutions in this area can only be brought with the consent of the Director of Public Prosecutions, so the possibility of frivolous prosecutions being brought would be slight. There appears, therefore, to be an arguable case for extending the offence of incitement to racial hatred to cover religious groups.

Clause 38 of the Anti-Terrorism, Crime and Security Bill 2001 introduced this offence, so that in all the contexts mentioned, offences of stirring up religious hatred could also be committed. Clause 38 did not become law but the clause forms the main part of the 2003 Bill. If the 2003 Bill becomes law, the effect on freedom of expression will be very significant. However, the impact of the provisions can be curbed. Prosecutions for the offences of stirring up racial or religious hatred can only be brought with the consent of the Attorney General, which has so far been sparingly given in respect of race hatred. Since the Attorney General is a public authority under the HRA, he or she should give careful consideration to Art 10 before giving consent. If prosecutions are brought, the courts are in the same position. They need not, as argued above, give weight to Art 9, on the ground that protection for religious freedom does not include protection against attacks on religion. The term 'hatred' should be given full weight, while the term 'insulting' should, it is argued, be interpreted as meaning insulting to the reasonable, tolerant religious adherent rather than in relation to adherents of a particular sect (or group within a religion) which may be of an extreme nature.

The acceptability of the proposal to create such a new offence is dependent on the assumption that the prohibition of incitement to racial hatred under the Public Order Act does not already create an unacceptable infringement of freedom of speech. The ECtHR has previously stated that race-hate speech is outside the protection of Art 10 (*Glimmerveen and Haagenback v Netherlands* (1999)) or that prosecution is necessary in a democratic society. It may be argued, however, that the offences as currently conceived go beyond the mischief they are intended to prevent. There is an argument that some provision should be available to prevent racist speech due to its special propensity to lead to disorder and that such protection should be extended to religious groups, but it is suggested that one could comfortably support the addition of incitement to religious hatred to Public Order Act offences only once they had been reformed to encompass a much narrower area of liability.

Question 7

(a) Relatives of old people in the Sunnymede Old People's Home become suspicious after a number of the residents become ill. Evidence of neglect comes to light and certain of the relatives decide to sue the Home. The owners of the Home enter into negotiations with the relatives' legal representatives, with a view to settling out of court. Meanwhile, the *Daily Argus*, a national newspaper, intends to publish the following article (article (a)) on its 'Personal Lives' page:

'Caring for old people in the 90s

Joan Smith set out one day last June to visit her mother in the Sunnymede Old People's Home in Southton. It was a lovely day and she was looking forward to the visit. But when she arrived, she was appalled by the state of the Home. Some of the residents were sitting around unwashed in nightclothes, others were still in bed, although it was midday and they were able to get up. They all looked bored, listless and passive. The floors were filthy, as were the beds. For lunch, Joan's mother was offered a small bowl of soup. Joan was absolutely devastated and is now desperately trying to get her mother into another Home. But how can these conditions exist? Do we want to neglect our old people in this way? It is time the government woke up to this problem and instituted a rigorous system of inspection for these Homes. Otherwise, people like Joan's mother will continue to suffer.'

Advise the *Daily Argus* whether contempt proceedings in respect of this article would be likely to succeed.

(b) A year later, criminal charges are brought against the officer in charge of the Sunnymede Home, Mrs Sly, for assaults allegedly committed by her on a resident of the Home. At this point, the *Daily Screech*, a national tabloid newspaper with a large circulation, intends to publish the following article (article (b)):

'"Care" Workers?

How do you get a job in an Old People's Home? Does your background have to be investigated? Do you have to have good qualifications? The answer to both these questions appears to be 'no' if the case of Mrs Sly, a 'care' worker who has just been charged with assaulting an old person, is anything to go by. Mrs Sly has had four posts in Old People's Homes in the last five years. She was dismissed from the second one after a disciplinary hearing, which found that she had neglected old people in her charge. How is it that she went on to obtain two more posts? It is time that the appointment of workers to these Homes was looked into carefully; their background should be fully investigated. At present, there seems to be no control at all: this is a scandal which the *Daily Screech* is determined to root out.'

Advise the *Daily Screech* whether contempt proceedings in respect of this article would be likely to succeed.

Answer plan

Contempt of court is an area that lends itself very readily to setting problem questions. A problem question should not be attempted unless a student is very familiar with the area and, crucially, can determine when proceedings are 'active'. It is essential to take account of the HRA 1998 and relevant Convention jurisprudence in the answer, since the discussion concerns a potential interference with freedom of expression. Essentially, the following matters should be discussed:

Part (a)

- the concept of 'active' proceedings under s 2(3) of and Sched 1 to the Act;
- intention to prejudice the administration of justice under common law contempt;
- the concept of imminence in common law contempt;
- creating a 'real risk of prejudice';
- the possibility of narrowing down common law contempt by reliance on s 6 of the HRA;

Part (b)

- the concept of 'active' proceedings under s 2(3) of and Sched 1 to the Act;
- the creation of a substantial risk of serious prejudice under s 2(2) of the Contempt of Court Act 1981;
- discussions in good faith under s 5 and the effect of Art 10 under the HRA, relevance of s 3 of the HRA;
- intention to prejudice the administration of justice under common law contempt.

Answer

This question concerns the rules governing contempt of court arising under the Contempt of Court Act 1981 (hereafter 'the Act') and at common law. In advising the newspapers, it is necessary to take account of the HRA and relevant Convention jurisprudence since the discussion concerns a potential interference with freedom of expression. The two newspaper articles will be considered separately.

Liability in respect of article (a) will not arise under the Act, since the proceedings are not 'active'. This test arises under s 2(3) and the starting and ending points for civil proceedings are defined in Sched 1. The starting point for civil proceedings occurs when the case is set down for a hearing in the High Court or a date for the hearing is fixed (Sched 1, ss 12 and 13). Since the civil proceedings in question are only at the negotiating stage, this starting point has not yet arisen.

However, liability may arise at common law in respect of article (a). Section 6(c) of the Act preserves liability for contempt at common law if intention to prejudice the administration of justice can be shown. 'Prejudice (to) the administration of justice' clearly includes prejudice to particular proceedings. Once the requirement of intent is satisfied, it is easier to establish contempt at common law, rather than under the Act, as it is only necessary to show 'a real risk of prejudice' and proceedings need only be imminent, not 'active'. However, the court is a public authority under s 6 of the HRA and therefore must seek to ensure that the common law is compatible with the demands of Art 10 (see in a different context *Douglas v Hello!* (2001)), bearing in mind that the law of contempt also plays a role in protecting the guarantee of a fair trial under Art 6(1).

The test for intention to prejudice the administration of justice was established in *AG v Newspaper Publishing plc* (1990) and *AG v News Group Newspapers plc* (1988). It was recently reaffirmed in *AG v Punch* (2003). It was made clear that 'intention' connotes specific intent and therefore cannot include recklessness. The test may be summed up as follows: did the defendant either wish to prejudice proceedings or foresee that such prejudice was a virtually inevitable consequence of publishing the material in question? This test is based on the meaning of intent arising from rulings on the *mens rea* for murder from *Hancock and Shankland* (1986), *Nedrick* (1986) and *Woolin* (1999).

This is a subjective test, but a number of circumstances may allow the inference of intention to prejudice the proceedings to be made. In *AG v News Group Newspapers plc* (1988), the newspaper's support for the prosecution in its columns and in funding a private prosecution allowed the inference to be made. This case may be contrasted with *AG v Sport Newspapers Ltd and Others* (1991), in which the test for intention was more strictly interpreted. One David Evans, who had previous convictions for rape, was suspected of abducting Anna Humphries. He was on the run when the *Sport* published his convictions; the proceedings were not therefore active and so the case arose at common law. Could it be said to be foreseeable as a virtual certainty that prejudice to Evans' trial would occur as a result of the publication? It was held that there was a risk of such prejudice, of which the editor of the *Sport* was aware, but that such awareness of risk was not sufficient. Clearly, had the *mens rea* of common law contempt included recklessness, it would have been established. Similarly, article (a) may create a risk of prejudice to the future proceedings, but even if the editor of the *Argus* recognises this risk (which is unclear), it cannot be said that prejudice is virtually certain to be created, since the proceedings are such a long way off. Desire to prejudice proceedings cannot be established since the feature allowing an inference of such desire to be drawn in the *AG v News Group Newspapers plc* case – the personal involvement of *The Sun* – is not present.

Although the test for intent cannot be satisfied, as argued, the other test for common law contempt will be considered for the sake of offering complete advice to the *Argus*. At common law, the *sub judice* period began when proceedings could be said to be imminent (*Savundranayagan*). It is arguable that in the instant case the proceedings are such a long way off that they cannot be viewed as 'imminent'. However, it may not always be necessary to establish imminence. In *AG v News Group Newspapers plc,* it was held *obiter* that where it is established that the defendant intended to prejudice proceedings, it is not necessary to show that proceedings are imminent. Bingham LJ concurred with this dilution of the imminence test in *AG v Sport,* although in the same case, Hodgson J considered that proceedings must be 'pending'. He interpreted 'pending' as synonymous with 'active', an interpretation which would have greatly curtailed the scope of common law contempt.

It is questionable whether the interference with freedom of expression this broad test represents could be said to be 'prescribed by law' under Art 10(2) scheduled in the HRA, due to the lack of precision and therefore of foreseeability present in this area of the common law. Probably the most satisfactory method of ensuring that the requirements of quality are met would be – under s 6 of the HRA – to adopt the course suggested by Hodgson J. The 'active' test is laid down with reasonable precision and would, therefore, probably meet those requirements. Obviously, this would confine common law contempt to instances in which the statute could also be used. In the instant case, it is virtually certain, following this discussion, that the test of imminence cannot be met. First, if the test were to be narrowed down under s 6 of the HRA, it would become even less likely that it could be met in the instant case. Even if it were not narrowed down as suggested, it could not be met since the requirement of intent was not established and therefore the extension of the test undertaken in the *AG v News Group Newspapers plc* case would be inapplicable. The only way of meeting this test would be to argue that although the proceedings are a long way off, they can be viewed as imminent following *Savundranayagan* and that s 6 of the HRA does not require a narrowing down of this test.

Further, it is also suggested that the *actus reus* of common law contempt cannot be established since the risk of prejudice is very uncertain: the proceedings will not occur for some time and the article may therefore be forgotten by those involved in the case.[1] Moreover, no jury will be involved, since the action seems to be either in tort (for negligence) or in contract and, although a judge or witnesses might be prejudiced by this article, it is suggested that this is less likely.

In *Hislop and Pressdram* (1991), it was found that the defendants, who were one party in an action for defamation, had interfered with the administration of justice because they had brought improper pressure to bear on the other party, Sonia Sutcliffe, by publishing material in *Private Eye* intended to deter her from pursuing the action. There was a substantial risk that the articles might have succeeded in their aim; had they done so, the course of justice in Mrs Sutcliffe's action would have been seriously prejudiced, as she would have been deterred from having her claim decided in a court. However, the pressure placed on Sunnymede Old People's Home as a litigant is less immoderate than that brought to bear in the *Hislop* case; it is therefore argued that a real risk of prejudice does not arise on this argument either. Thus, on this reasoning, no liability will arise in respect of article (a), since intention has not been shown and, further, a real risk of prejudice is unlikely to arise.

Liability in respect of article (b) may arise under the Act. The first question to be determined is whether the publication in question could have an effect on any 'particular proceedings' under s 1 of the Act. The article makes reference to Mrs Sly; therefore, the strict liability rule under s 1 of the Act may apply if the following three tests are satisfied.

First, proceedings must be active under s 2(3) of and Sched 1 to the Act. Mrs Sly (hereinafter 'D') has been charged and proceedings are therefore active under Sched 1, s 4(a).

Secondly, it must be shown that the article creates a substantial risk of serious prejudice to D's trial (s 2(2) of the Act). According to the Court of Appeal in *AG v News Group Newspapers plc*, both limbs of this test must be satisfied; showing a slight risk of serious prejudice or a substantial risk of slight prejudice would not be sufficient. As regards the first limb, can it be argued that there is a substantial risk that a person involved in D's trial, such as a juror, would: (a) encounter the article; (b) remember it; and (c) be affected by it so that he or she could not put it out of his or her mind during the trial? As this is a national newspaper, it is possible that jurors and others may encounter the article; however, if the *Screech* has a very small circulation, this risk might be seen as too remote. It was found in *AG v Independent Television News Ltd* (1994) that a small circulation would clearly be one factor predisposing a court to determine that prejudice to proceedings did not occur. The principles to be applied were comprehensively reviewed by the Court of Appeal in *AG v Mirror Group Newspapers* (1997). It was emphasised that the prosecution must prove the risk beyond reasonable doubt. Relevant factors will include the prominence of the article and the novelty of its content (which will affect its impact on the reader). The length of time between publication and trial is also very significant. In *AG v News Group Newspapers plc* (1986), a gap of 10 months was held to obviate the risk of prejudice. On the other hand, in *AG v BBC* (1996), a risk was held to exist despite a gap of six months.

It is unclear what interval of time will elapse between charging Mrs Sly and the trial. This is clearly a crucial point, since, as indicated above, the longer the period, the less likely it is that a substantial risk of prejudice will be proved. If it is more than nine months, it is unlikely that the article will be held to be prejudicial. Moreover, the Court of Appeal in *AG v Mirror Group Newspapers* noted that the residual impact of a prejudicial article could be reduced by the effects of the jury's listening to evidence over a prolonged period, and the judge's directions. In this case, therefore, it could be argued that, although there is a risk that a juror might see and remember the article, it is of a relatively mild nature and might therefore be blotted out by the immediacy of the trial. The article is not couched in particularly vitriolic language, although it does convey information about Mrs Sly, which is likely to create an unfavourable impression.

The stronger argument appears to be to the effect that s 2(2) is not fulfilled. However, since this is not absolutely certain, it must next be established that s 5 does not apply. Following *AG v English* (1983), the test to be applied seems to be – looking at the actual words written (as opposed to considering what could have been omitted) – is the article written in good faith and concerned with a question of general legitimate public interest which creates an incidental risk of prejudice to a particular case? This test will cover direct references to the particular case according to *AG v Times Newspapers*. It is possible on this basis to argue that s 5 does apply on the basis that the conditions in Old People's Homes are clearly a matter of genuine public interest, the article appears to be written in good faith and seems merely to be using Mrs Sly as an example of the problem it is concerned with. It therefore bears comparison with the articles which escaped liability in the two cases mentioned. On this argument, liability cannot be established under the Act. Since s 5 was introduced as a measure to protect freedom of expression, it may be argued that it should be afforded a generous interpretation, relying if necessary on s 3 of the HRA to achieve this result, under Art 10, especially bearing in mind the emphasis placed on the media's 'watchdog' role in judgments such as *Castells v Spain* (1992) and *Thorgeirson v Iceland* (1992).

There is the alternative possibility of establishing liability at common law if intention to prejudice proceedings is present, although it should be noted that in the only case in which such liability was established when proceedings were active, the *Hislop* case, the tests under the Act and at common law were satisfied. It might be said that the Act would be undermined if liability could be established at common law in an instance where proceedings were active, but the Act did not establish liability. This argument is reinforced by the obligation under the HRA to give proper weight to the right to freedom of expression under Art 10 of the Convention. In any event, a finding that the article was written in good faith under s 5 would almost certainly preclude a finding that the editor of the paper in question intended to prejudice proceedings (a necessary ingredient of liability at common law). This would seem to be the end of the matter, but it will further be argued that, in any event, intention to prejudice proceedings cannot be shown.

Section 6(c) of the Act preserves liability for contempt at common law if intention to prejudice the administration of justice can be established. 'Prejudice (to) the administration of justice' clearly includes prejudice to particular proceedings; therefore, the instant case will fall within s 6(c) if the following three tests can be satisfied. First, an intention to prejudice the proceedings against D must be established. The test for intention established in the following cases should be considered: *AG v Newspaper Publishing plc; AG v The Observer and The Guardian Newspapers Ltd* (1989); *AG v News Group Newspapers; AG v Hislop and Pressdram; AG v Sport Newspapers Ltd.* The test is – did the defendant either wish to prejudice proceedings or foresee that such prejudice was a virtually inevitable consequence of publishing the material in question?

In the instant case, given the lack of any particular involvement that the *Screech* has in the case, it would be hard to show a desire to prejudice D's trial. It would also be difficult to establish that an objective observer would have foreseen that such prejudice would be a virtually inevitable consequence of the publication. Such an observer might consider such a result to be probable (see the argument as to the substantial risk of serious prejudice above), but that is not sufficient.

The argument above tends towards the conclusion that liability cannot be established under either the Act or at common law.

Note

1   Had it appeared that the article might well create a real risk of prejudice and had the first test for intention been satisfied, it would have been necessary to consider in more detail the question whether proceedings were 'imminent'. This test would probably be readily satisfied as *dicta* in *AG v Newspapers* and, in the *Sport* case, suggested that even 'imminence' need not be established once the *mens rea* is shown.

CHAPTER 2

OFFICIAL SECRECY AND FREEDOM OF INFORMATION

Introduction

Freedom of information and freedom of expression are very closely linked since some speech is dependent on access to information which is in turn a form of speech. Therefore, what may be termed 'freedom of information' issues could also be treated as aspects of freedom of expression. However, the overlap is not complete: in some circumstances, information may be sought where there is no speaker willing to disclose it. Such a situation would tend to be considered purely as a freedom of information issue (more accurately, as a question of access to information). This distinction receives support from the wording of Art 10 of the European Convention, which speaks of the freedom to 'receive and impart information', thus appearing to exclude from its provisions the right to demand information from the unwilling speaker. Also, the phrase 'without interference from public authorities' does not suggest that governments should come under any duty to act in order to ensure that information is received.

The most important value associated with freedom of information is the need for the citizen to understand as fully as possible the working of government, in order to render it accountable. One of the main concerns of the questions in this chapter is therefore the methods employed by governments to ensure that official information cannot fall into the hands of those who might place it in the public domain, and with methods of preventing or deterring persons from publication when such information has been obtained. This chapter also places a strong emphasis on the choices that were made as to the release of information relating to public authorities – not only to central government – in the Freedom of Information Act 2000.

Examiners tend to set general essays, rather than problem questions, in this area; the emphasis is usually on the degree to which a balance is struck between the interest of the individual in acquiring government information and the interest of the State in withholding it. The balance between what may be termed State interests, such as defence or national security, and the individual entitlement to freedom of expression and information is largely struck by the Official Secrets Act (OSA) 1989 and various common law provisions. However, the interpretation of the 1989 Act and the application of those provisions may be affected by the Convention rights as applied under the Human Rights Act (HRA) 1998. Where information held by central government or by other public authorities is not covered by the OSA 1989, the citizen may be able to obtain access to it under the Freedom of Information Act 2000, when it comes fully into force. The 2000 Act is a very significant new development that is highly likely to feature on exam papers.

Checklist

Students should be familiar with the following areas:

- the OSA 1989;
- DA Notices;
- basic scheme of the Public Records Act 1958 and data protection legislation, particularly the 1998 Act;
- basic aspects of freedom of information measures in other countries, particularly Canada and the US;
- relevant aspects of common law contempt;
- the doctrine of breach of confidence as used by the government;
- aspects of the voluntary Government Code on access to information;
- key aspects of the Freedom of Information Act 2000.

Question 8

'In recent years, there has been a significant movement towards more open government which is largely, but not wholly, attributable to decisions under the European Convention on Human Rights.' Critically evaluate this statement.

Answer plan

This is clearly a fairly narrowly focused question, since the need to consider recent developments limits its scope. It should be borne in mind that the statement makes a number of separate assertions, each of which must be evaluated. Essentially, the following issues should be considered:

- possible movement towards openness in government – the Official Secrets Act (OSA) 1989, the Security Services Act 1989, the Intelligence Services Act 1994 and the Interception of Communications Act 1985, as well as the influence of the European Convention on Human Rights (ECHR) in bringing about changes in the area of official secrecy;

- features of the Security Services Act 1989, the Intelligence Services Act 1994 and the Regulation of Investigatory Powers Act (RIPA) 2000 – ousting of the jurisdiction of the courts – secrecy as to tribunal decisions;
- use of the common law as a means of preventing disclosure of information – common law contempt – breach of confidence – response of the European Court of Human Rights (ECtHR);
- the OSA 1989 – 'harm tests' – lack of a public interest defence – the Public Interest Disclosure Act 1998;
- limitations of the Convention;
- the Freedom of Information Act 2000.

Answer

A general survey of certain recent developments might indeed suggest that a movement towards more open government has been taking place over the last 15 years. Scrutiny of interception of communications was apparently made possible under the Interception of Communications Act 1985 (now replaced by the RIPA 2000); MI5 was acknowledged to exist and placed for the first time on a statutory basis in 1989; disclosure of a range of information was decriminalised under the OSA 1989; MI6 and GCHQ were placed on a statutory basis by the Intelligence Services Act 1994, which also set up a Parliamentary Committee to oversee the work of the security and intelligence services. The voluntary Code on access to government information put in place in 1994 seemed to indicate a clear desire to move towards more open government. The Freedom of Information Act 2000 represented a further step in that direction. A closer look at some of these developments reveals, it will be argued, that they did not arise due to a sudden perception of the value of freedom of information, but were imposed on the government. However, they were not invariably imposed due to decisions of the ECtHR, although such decisions have had a significant impact in this context. It will further be argued that, in general, in any event, these changes have not had a very clear or significant liberalising impact.

The Interception of Communications Act 1985 came into being after the decision of the ECtHR in the *Malone* case (1984), which found that the tapping of Mr Malone's telephone constituted a breach of Art 8 of the Convention, which protects the right to privacy. However, the decision only required the UK government to introduce legislation to regulate the circumstances in which the power to tap could be used, rather than giving guidance as to what would be acceptable limits on the right to privacy. The limits of the Act (not applying to private telephone systems, for example –

see *Halford v UK* (1997)) and massive technological development led to its replacement by the RIPA 2000.

The limits to open government, found in the 1985 Act, are continued by the RIPA 2000, and information about authorised (let alone unauthorised) phone taps remains hard to obtain. Complaints, including allegations of human rights violations, can be made only to a tribunal set up under the Act, with no possibility of scrutiny by a court. Furthermore, tribunal decisions are not published and, although an annual report giving some information on the number of intercept warrants issued must be made available, it is first subject to censorship by the Prime Minister. Interestingly, *Secretary of State for the Home Department ex p Ruddock* (1987) established the principle that the courts were entitled to review unfair actions by government arising from failure to live up to legitimate expectations such as the promise, in issue in the case, that phone tapping would not be used for party political purposes. The judge, Taylor J, also stated that the jurisdiction of the court to look into such a complaint against a minister should not be totally ousted. That case was the last time such statements would be heard publicly in respect of telephone tapping: the 1985 Act, now ss 17 and 18 of the RIPA 2000, precluded the possibility of their repetition.

Similarly, the Security Service Act 1989 came into being largely as a response to the finding of the ECtHR that a complaint against MI5 was admissible (*Harman and Hewitt v UK* (1986)). The case was brought by two former NCCL officers, Patricia Hewitt and Harriet Harman, who were complaining of their classification as 'subversive' by MI5, which had placed them under surveillance. Part of their complaint concerned a breach of Art 13 of the ECHR on the basis that no effective remedy for complainants existed. The Security Service Act places MI5 on a statutory basis, but prevents almost all effective scrutiny of its operation. Even where a member of the public has a grievance concerning its operation, it will not be possible to use a court action as a means of scrutinising such operation. Complaints, including those involving the HRA, can only be made to the tribunal established under s 65 of the RIPA 2000. The proceedings of this tribunal are not open and its decisions are not questionable in any court of law.

This measure was not solely due to the operation of the ECtHR. Its inception was probably also influenced by the challenge to the legality of the tapping of the phones of CND members already mentioned in *Secretary of State for the Home Department ex p Ruddock*, which proved embarrassing to the government, although it failed. In any event, these statutes are unlikely to open up the workings of internal security to greater scrutiny. They suggest a perception that no breach of the Convention will occur so long as a mechanism is in place that is able to consider the claims of aggrieved citizens, however ineffective that mechanism might be.

The two statutes mentioned will work in tandem with the OSA 1989, which was not brought into being in response to pressure from Europe, but largely due to pressure from other sources. In particular, the failure of the government to secure a conviction under s 2 of the OSA 1911 in *Ponting* (1985) probably had a significant effect. It had been recognised for some time even before the *Ponting* case that s 2 was becoming discredited due to its width. Obviously, the criminal law is brought into disrepute if liability is possible in respect of extremely trivial actions. The 1911 Act had no test of substance and although obtaining a conviction should therefore have been relatively straightforward, the decisions in *Aitken* (1971) and *Ponting* suggested that the very width of the section was undermining its credibility.

It was made clear from the outset that the 1989 Act was unconcerned with freedom of information. Thus, one must be cautious in heralding the OSA 1989 as amounting to a move away from obsessive secrecy; it does not allow the release of any official documents into the public domain, although it does mean that if certain pieces of information are released, the official concerned will not face criminal sanctions. (He or she might, of course, face an action for breach of confidence as well as disciplinary proceedings.)

It is, however, fair to accept that the 1989 Act covers much less information than its predecessor, due to its introduction of a 'harm test', which takes into account the substance of the information. Clearly, such a test is to be preferred to the width of s 2 of the OSA 1911, which covered all official information, however trivial. However, there is no test for harm at all under s 1(1), which prevents members or former members of the security services disclosing anything at all about the operation of those services. All such members come under a lifelong duty to keep silent, even though their information might reveal serious abuse of power in the security services or some operational weakness. These provisions also apply to anyone who is notified that he or she is subject to the provisions of the sub-section. Equally, there is no test for harm under s 4(3) which covers information obtained by, or relating to, the issue of a warrant under the RIPA 2000 or the Intelligence Services Act 1994.[1]

The Act contains no explicit public interest defence and it follows from the nature of the harm test that one cannot be implied into it; any good flowing from disclosure of the information cannot be considered, merely any harm that might be caused. This was confirmed by the House of Lords in *R v Shayler* (2002) and was said to be compatible with Art 10 of the ECHR. Moreover, no express defence of prior publication is provided. Prior publication can be in issue, however, since the prosecution might find it hard to establish the appropriate type of harm where there had been a great deal of prior publication. Thus, although in likelihood it may be said that some features of the Act suggest a move towards some liberalisation of official secrecy law, it was clearly intended that this move should not be fully carried through. Both public interest and prior publication defences are available, although in limited circumstances, under the Public Interest Disclosure Act 1998, though the Act excludes from its protection a disclosure the making of which is a criminal offence, such as under the 1989 Act.

On the other hand, the OSA 1989 may prove more effective than the 1911 Act in deterring the press from publishing the revelations of a future Peter Wright in respect of the workings of the security service. Despite publication of the book *Spycatcher* in the US in 1987, the House of Lords decided (relying on *American Cyanamid Co v Ethicon Ltd* (1975)) to continue the temporary injunctions against the newspapers on the basis that the Attorney General still had an arguable case for permanent injunctions (*AG v Guardian Newspapers Ltd* (1987)). The injunctions continued until, in the hearing of the permanent injunctions, the House of Lords rejected the Attorney General's claim on the basis that the interest in maintaining confidentiality was outweighed by the public interest in knowing of the allegations in *Spycatcher*. Moreover, it was impossible to sustain a restriction based on confidentiality when the worldwide publication of the book meant that the information it contained was clearly in the 'public domain'.

When the ECtHR considered the case (*The Observer and The Guardian v UK* (1991); *The Sunday Times v UK* (1991)), it found that, given the extent of publication in the US, the temporary injunctions, though for a legitimate purpose, were disproportionate and a violation of Art 10. The injunctions obtained before publication in the US were not found to breach Art 10; therefore, this ruling will do nothing to discourage use of such injunctions in many instances where a disclosure of official information is threatened.

The *Spycatcher* cases (*AG v Newspaper Publishing plc* (1990) as approved by the House of Lords in *Times Newspapers and Another v AG* (1991)) had confirmed the principle that once an interlocutory injunction has been obtained restraining one organ of the media from publication of allegedly confidential material, the rest of the media may be in contempt if they publish that material, even if their intention in doing so is to bring alleged iniquity to public attention. In *AG v Punch* (2003), a magazine published articles written by an ex-security services officer in breach of an injunction restraining the officer from publishing. The magazine could only have the *mens rea* for contempt if, by publication, it intended to destroy the purpose of the injunction. The Court of Appeal's view, that the purpose of such an injunction was to prevent damaging confidential material from being published, was rejected by the House of Lords, for whom the point of the injunction was to protect the interest of the court as the effective tribunal in which the issue of confidentiality should be determined. This decision makes it easier for the State to prove that the media are in contempt if they publish in breach of a temporary injunction imposed on others.

Access to personal information, particularly where it is held as records, is governed by the Data Protection Act 1998, which lays down basic principles which are enforced by the Information Commissioner and provides various basic rights which the courts enforce. Access to non-personal government information is currently based on a 1993 government White Paper, which led to the setting up of a voluntary *Code of Practice on Access to Government Information* in 1994. This Code was revised in 1997 and 1998. It commits government departments to publishing the facts and analysis behind government decisions. It is subject to many exceptions, however, including information relating to international relations, defence, national security, law enforcement, legal proceedings and Whitehall 'internal discussions and advice'. A much more significant development is the passing of the Freedom of Information Act 2000, which will be brought fully into force by 2005. This will require public bodies to publish information and to disclose information on request. The Act is a major step forward in that, under it, access to information will now become a statutory right rather than a discretionary privilege. It will be enforced by the Information Commissioner and, ultimately, the courts. There are, however, many exceptions and the success of the Act will depend on how these exceptions are interpreted. A particularly worrying exception is that, under s 53, a government department can substitute its view for that of the Commissioner on whether the public interest does or does not require disclosure of information on a wide range of policy matters involving the department. Despite these worries, the Act is, at least, an important symbolic commitment towards far more open government and should have real practical impact on individual rights.

It may be concluded that claims under the Convention have led to some breaking down of the tradition of secrecy in government. The failings of the Security Services Act, the RIPA 2000 and the caution of the European Court judgment in the *Spycatcher* case do not, however, support the suggestion that radical change has occurred, or can occur, by this means. The ECtHR appears to have contented itself with half measures, with the result that the impact of its decisions in this area has been, and almost certainly will be, minimal. This is also true in respect of freedom of information where the ECtHR has generally denied that Art 10 provides a right to receive information which others, including the State, wish not to give. British courts adopted that view in *R (Persey) v SSEFRA* (2002) in denying a legal challenge to the government's refusal to hold a public inquiry into the foot and mouth epidemic. In respect of personal information, the Strasbourg court, on the basis of Art 8, has given a stronger push to rights to obtain personal information. The main impetus behind the Data Protection Act 1998, however, has been European Community law rather than the Convention. The

Freedom of Information Act 2000 was not introduced as a result of a decision at Strasbourg but rather as a response to a general pressure to come into line with most democracies on this matter. Thus, if greater openness in government has been achieved – a claim which, as indicated, is itself debatable – it is fair to say that Strasbourg can claim only a part of the credit for it.

Note

1   It could be argued that the harm tests under the OSA are further diluted in various ways. Under s 3(1)(b), which covers confidential information obtained abroad, the mere fact that the information is confidential 'may' be sufficient to establish the likelihood that its disclosure would cause harm. In other words, a fiction is created that harm may automatically flow from such disclosure. Under s 1(3), which applies to civil servants who disclose matters relating to security, the test for damage may be fulfilled merely by proving that the document belongs to a class of documents likely to cause harm. Thus, not only need there be no proof that disclosure of the document itself actually caused harm, but there need not even be proof that it was likely to do so.

Question 9

'The Freedom of Information Act 2000 is a grave disappointment to those who are genuinely committed to the principle of freedom of information.'
    Do you agree?

Answer plan

This is a very specific essay question which requires a detailed and critical evaluation of the 2000 Act. It should not be attempted unless the student has quite a detailed knowledge (with references to sections) of the complex Act of 2000. In a form likely to be similar to that taken here, this question is highly likely to appear on exam papers at the present time.

    Essentially, the following matters should be discussed:

- the general right of access to information under the Act;
- the exemptions under the Act; implications of the tests for exemptions;
- the use of and nature of the harm tests;
- the role of the Information Commissioner;
- the enforcement mechanisms in general;
- concluding evaluation of the Act.

Answer

'Unnecessary secrecy in government leads to arrogance in governance and defective decision making ... people expect much greater openness and accountability from government than they used to ...' (White Paper: *Your Right to Know*, Cm 3818). These words expressed the intention of the Labour government in introducing the new freedom of information legislation.

The Act of 2000 provides a general right of access to the information held by a range of bodies. The Act covers 'public authorities' and s 3 sets out the various ways in which a body can be a public authority. In Sched 1, the Act covers all government departments: the House of Commons, the House of Lords, quangos, the NHS, administrative functions of courts and tribunals, police authorities and chief officers of police, the armed forces, local authorities, local public bodies, schools and other public educational institutions, and public service broadcasters. Under s 5, private organisations may be designated as public authorities in so far as they carry out statutory functions, as may the privatised utilities and private bodies working on contracted-out functions.

Section 1(1) provides that any person making a request for information to a public authority is entitled to be informed whether it holds information of the description specified in the request and, if it holds the information, it must communicate it. Thus, the right of access to the information is accompanied by a right to know whether or not the information is held by the body in question; this is referred to in the Act as 'the duty to confirm or deny'. Once it comes fully into force in 2005, individuals will be able to gain access to information relating to them personally, such as tax and medical records. They will also have the right to obtain information on other general matters from the departments and bodies covered. For example, journalists and consumer groups might wish to obtain information concerning food safety, medical safety and pollution.

Thus, the Act begins with an apparently broad and generous statement of the rights it confers; it is also generous in its coverage.[1] However, the rights are subject to a wide range of exceptions and exemptions. In this crucial respect, it will be argued, the Act is indeed a disappointment to those who were committed to the freedom of information ideal. In particular, the Act came as a disappointment after the White Paper, which did not propose a wide range of exemptions. Under the White Paper, seven specified interests were indicated. The test for disclosure was, with one exception: will this disclosure cause substantial harm to one of these interests? The first of these interests covered national security, defence and international relations. A further five interests were: law enforcement, personal privacy, commercial confidentiality, the safety of the individual, the public and the environment, and information supplied in confidence.

Thus, the exemptions under the White Paper were relatively narrow and were subject to quite a strict harm test. They may be sharply contrasted with those that emerged under the Act. The harm-based exemptions under the Act are similar to those indicated in the White Paper: they require the public authority to show that the release of the information requested would, or would be likely to, cause prejudice to the interest specified in the exemption. However, this test for harm is of course less restrictive than that proposed under the White Paper. Further, a number of exemptions are class-based, meaning that in order to refuse the request, the authority only has to show that the information falls into the class of information covered by the exemption, not that its release would cause or be likely to cause harm or prejudice.

However, the Act provides a public interest test in relation to some, but not all, of the class exemptions, and almost all the 'harm exemptions'. The authority, having decided that the information is *prima facie* exempt (either because the information falls into the requisite class exemption, or because the relevant harm test is satisfied, as the case may be), must still then go on to consider whether it should be released under the public interest test set out in s 2. This requires the authority to release the information unless 'in all the circumstances of the case, the public interest in maintaining the exemption outweighs the public interest in disclosing the information'. It has been argued that the application of the public interest test to class exemptions in effect transformed them into 'harm'-based exemptions. However, where information falls into a class exemption, and an authority objects to disclosure even under the public interest test, it will be able not only to argue that the specific disclosure would have harmful effects, but also that the public interest would be harmed by any disclosure from within the relevant class of documents, regardless of the consequences of releasing the actual information in question. By contrast, under a prejudice test, the authority must be able first to identify that harm would be caused by releasing the *specific information* requested, and then go on to show that that specific harm outweighs the public interest in disclosure.

The discussion in this essay cannot cover all of the Freedom of Information Act class exemptions, but will consider some of the more controversial ones. Section 23(1) covers information supplied by, or which relates to, the intelligence and security services. The bodies mentioned in this exemption are not themselves covered by the Act at all. This exemption therefore applies to information which is held by *another public authority*, but which has been supplied by one of these bodies. Because it is a class exemption, it could apply to information which had no conceivable security implications, such as evidence of a massive overspend on MI5 or MI6's headquarters. Bearing in mind the complete exclusion of the security and intelligence services from the Act, the use of this class exemption unaccompanied by a harm test and not subject to the public interest test, is likely to mean that sensitive matters of great political significance remain undisclosed, even if their disclosure would ultimately benefit those services or national security. Section 32 covers information *which is only held* by virtue of being contained in a document or record served on a public authority in proceedings, or made by a court or tribunal or party in any proceedings, or contained in a document lodged with or created by a person conducting an inquiry or arbitration for the purposes of the inquiry or arbitration. The public interest test does not apply.

Certain class exemptions are subject to the public interest test. In relation to these exemptions, in practice, while the Commissioner will always have the last word on whether the information falls into the class in question, she will not always be able to enforce a finding that it should nevertheless be released on public interest grounds if the information is held by certain governmental bodies, since the ministerial veto may be used (see below). Section 30(1) provides a sweeping exemption, covering all information, whenever obtained, which relates to investigations that may lead to criminal proceedings. It represents a specific rejection of the recommendation of the Macpherson Report that there should be no class exemption for information relating to police investigations. It overlaps with the law enforcement exemption of s 31, which does include a harm test. There are certain aspects of information relating to investigations which would appear to require disclosure in order to be in accord with the principle of openness enshrined in the Act. For example, a citizen might suspect that his or her telephone had been tapped without authorisation or that he or she had been unlawfully placed under surveillance by other means. Under the Act, no satisfactory method of discovering information relating to such a possibility will exist. It is therefore unfortunate that telephone tapping and electronic surveillance were not subjected to a substantial harm or even a simple harm test.

The s 30(1) exemption extends beyond protecting the police and the Crown Prosecution Service (CPS). Other bodies will also be protected: it will cover all information obtained by safety agencies investigating accidents. It will cover routine inspections as well as specific investigations, since both can lead to criminal prosecution. Thus, anything from an inspection of a section of railway track by the Railway Inspectorate to a check upon hygiene in a restaurant by the Health and Safety Executive could be covered. It is particularly hard to understand the need for such a sweeping class exemption when s 31 specifically exempts information which could prejudice the prevention or detection of crime, or legal proceedings brought by a public authority arising from various forms of investigation. That exemption will ensure that no information is released which could damage law enforcement and crime detection.

The other major class exemption in this category, under s 35, has been just as criticised. It amounts to a very broad exemption covering virtually all information relating to the formation of government policy. This exemption is presumably intended to prevent government from having to decide policy in the public gaze – to protect the freeness and frankness of Civil Service advice and of internal debate within government – but, once again, it appears to go far beyond what would sensibly be required to achieve this aim. Section 36 contains a harm-based exemption which covers almost exactly the same ground. Since it covers all information whose release might cause damage to the working of government, and is framed in very broad terms, it appears to be unnecessary to have a sweeping class exemption covering the same ground. Moreover, this exemption is not restricted to Civil Service advice; it covers also the background information used in preparing policy, including the underlying facts and their analysis.

The Act is much more restrictive in this respect than the present, voluntary *Code of Practice on Access to Government Information.* The latter requires both facts and the analysis of facts underlying policy decisions, including scientific analysis and expert appraisal, to be made available, once decisions are announced. Material relating to policy formation can only be withheld under a harm test if disclosure would 'harm the frankness and candour of internal discussion'. The White Paper preceding the Bill proposed that there should be no class exemption for material in this area, but rather that, as under the Code, a harm test would have had to be satisfied to prevent disclosure. While information in this category is subject to a public interest test, it is important to note that, because, by definition it will generally be information held by a government department, if the Commissioner orders disclosure on public interest grounds, the ministerial veto will be available to override him or her.[2]

The enforcement review mechanism under the Act is clearly crucial, but it is also open to criticism in certain key respects. The rights granted under the Act are enforceable by the Information Commissioner. Importantly, the Commissioner has security of tenure, being dismissible only by the Crown following an address by both Houses of Parliament. An appeal lies from decisions of the Commissioner to the Information Tribunal which is made up of experienced lawyers and 'persons to represent the interests' of those seeking information and of public authorities (Sched 2, Part II).

Section 50 provides that any person can apply to the Commissioner for a decision whether a request for information made by the complainant to a public authority has been dealt with in accordance with the Act. In response, the Commissioner has the power to serve a 'decision notice' on the authority stating what it must do to satisfy the Act. She may also serve 'information notices' upon authorities, requiring the authority concerned to provide her with information about a particular application or its compliance with the Act generally. The Commissioner may ultimately force a recalcitrant authority to act by serving upon it an enforcement notice (s 52(1)) requiring it to take the steps specified in the notice. If a public authority fails to comply with a decision, enforcement or information notice, the Commissioner can notify the High Court, which can deal with the authority as if it had committed a contempt of court (s 52(2)).

However, the Commissioner's decisions are themselves subject to appeal to the Information Tribunal, and this power of appeal is exercisable upon the broadest possible grounds. The Act provides that either party may appeal to the Tribunal against a decision notice and a public authority against an enforcement or information notice (s 57(2) and (3)), either on the basis that the notice is 'not in accordance with the law', or 'to the extent that the notice involved an exercise of discretion by the Commissioner, that he ought to have exercised his discretion differently' (s 58(1)). The Tribunal is also empowered to review any finding of fact on which the notice was based. There is a further appeal from the Tribunal to the High Court, but on a 'point of law' only (s 59). In practice, this will probably be interpreted so as to allow review of the Tribunal's decisions, not just for error of law, but also on the other accepted heads of judicial review. The Convention rights under the HRA could be invoked at this point.

Enforcement can be affected by the ministerial veto, which is another highly controversial aspect of the Act. The veto can be exercised if two conditions are satisfied under s 53(1): first, the notice which the veto will operate to quash must have been served on a government department, the Welsh Assembly or 'any public authority designated for the purposes of this section by an order made by the Secretary of State'; secondly, the notice must order the release of information which is *prima facie* exempt, but which the Commissioner has decided should nevertheless be released under the public interest test in s 2. The White Paper made no provision for such a power of veto, on the basis that to do so would undermine confidence in the regime. Such a veto clearly dilutes the basic freedom of information principle that a body independent from government should enforce the rights to information.

In conclusion, it is suggested that the Act is indeed disappointing. It creates so many restrictions on the basic right of access that, depending upon its interpretation, much information of any conceivable interest could still be withheld. Whether this turns out to be the case in practice will depend primarily upon the robustness of the stance taken by the Commissioner, particularly in applying the public interest test to the class exemptions under the Act, where it will provide the only means of obtaining disclosure. However, certain restrictions, in particular that represented by the ministerial veto, will be difficult, if not impossible to overcome, however robust a stance is taken. Nevertheless, the Act does represent a turning point in British democracy since for the first time in its history, the decision to release many classes of information has been removed from government and from other public authorities and placed in the hands of an independent agency, the Information Commissioner. Most importantly, for the first time, a statutory 'right' to information, enforceable if necessary through the courts, has been established.

Notes

1   The use of statutory publication schemes under the Act could be considered briefly here as part of the discussion of the more favourable aspects of the Act.

2   The issue of exemptions could be considered further and it could be pointed out that the Act, through amendments to the Public Records Act, provides that some of the exemptions will cease to apply after a certain number of years, though these limitations are hardly generous. Examples of exemptions that will cease to apply at all after 30 years (s 63(1)) can be given, for example, s 28 (inter-UK relations), s 30(1) (information obtained during an investigation), s 32 (documents generated in litigation) and s 36 (information which could prejudice effective conduct of public affairs). Still less generously, information relating to the bestowing of honours and dignities (s 37(1)(b)) only ceases to be exempt after 60 years, while it will be necessary to wait 100 years before the expiry of the exemption for information falling within s 31. One of the absolute exemptions – information provided by the security, intelligence, etc, services (s 23(1)) – will cease to be absolute after 30 years; that is, the public interest in disclosure must be considered once 30 years has expired.

Question 10

Douglas Hurd (the then Home Secretary) called the Official Secrets Act 1989 'a great liberalising measure'. Do you agree with his view? How far might the Human Rights Act be used to 'liberalise' aspects of the Act?

Answer plan

This essay clearly demands close analysis of the provisions of the new Act; however, the context in which it must be placed should also be considered. The following matters should be discussed:

*   s 2 of the Official Secrets Act (OSA) 1911 compared with the 1989 Act;
*   categories of information covered by the OSA 1989; harm tests in different

categories – lack of a harm test in s 1(1); *R v Shayler* (2001) and the impact of the HRA;

* defences under the 1989 Act – actual and potential – 'reversed' *mens rea*;
* other measures creating liability in respect of the disclosure of official information;
* conclusion: lack of liberalising effect; failure of the HRA to bring about liberalisation.

Answer

The OSA 1989 was brought into being largely in response to the failure of the government to secure a conviction under s 2 of the OSA 1911 in *Ponting* (1985). However, it had been recognised for some time, even before the *Ponting* case, that s 2 was becoming discredited due to its width: it criminalised the unauthorised disclosure of any official information at all.

Once the decision to reform the area of official secrecy had been made, an opportunity was created for radical change which could have included freedom of information legislation along the lines of the instruments in the US and Canada. However, it was made clear from the outset that the legislation was unconcerned with freedom of information; it did not allow the release of any official documents into the public domain.[1] Thus, any claim that it is a liberalising measure must rest on other aspects of the Act. The aspects which are usually considered in this context include the introduction of tests for harm, the need to establish *mens rea*, the defences available and decriminalisation of the receiver of information. In all these respects, the Act differs from its predecessor. However, the extent to which these differences have brought about any real change, any real liberalisation, is open to question. This essay will argue that the 1989 Act was not a liberalising measure in any real sense and, further, that the HRA is unlikely to have a significant impact on it in terms of ameliorating its more illiberal aspects.

Clearly, if only to avoid bringing the criminal law into disrepute, a 'harm test' which takes into account the substance of information is to be preferred to the width of s 2 of the OSA 1911, which covered all official information, however trivial. However, will the harm tests have a liberalising effect in other respects? There is no test for harm at all under s 1(1), which is intended to prevent members or former members of the security services disclosing anything at all about the operation of those services. All such members come under a lifelong duty to keep silent, even though their information might reveal serious abuse of power in the security service or some operational weakness. These provisions also apply to anyone who is notified that he or she is subject to the provisions of the sub-section. Equally, there is no test for harm under s 4(3), which covers information obtained by or relating to the issue of a warrant under the Interception of Communications Act 1985 or the Security Services Act 1989.

The harm tests under the OSA are further diluted in various ways. Under s 3(1)(b), which covers confidential information obtained abroad, the mere fact that the information is confidential 'may' be sufficient to establish the likelihood that its disclosure would cause harm. In other words, a fiction is created that harm may automatically flow from such disclosure. Under s 1(3), which criminalises disclosure of information relating to the security services by a Crown servant as opposed to a member of MI5, it is not necessary to show that disclosure of the actual document in question would be likely to cause harm, merely that the document belongs to a class of documents disclosure of which would be likely to have that effect. Even in categories where it is necessary to show that the actual document in question would be likely to cause harm, such as s 2(1) or s 4(1), the task of doing so is made easy in two ways: first, it is not necessary to show that any damage actually occurred; and secondly, the tests for harm themselves are very wide. Under s 2(2), for example, a disclosure of information relating to defence will be damaging if it is likely to obstruct seriously the interests of the UK abroad. The tests for harm are not made any more stringent in instances where a non-Crown servant discloses information. Under s 5, if anyone discloses information which falls into one of the categories covered, the test for harm will be determined by reference to that category.

The Act contains no explicit public interest defence and it follows from the nature of the harm test that one cannot be implied into it; any good flowing from disclosure of the information cannot be considered, merely any harm that might be caused. However, s 3 of the HRA could be used creatively to seek to introduce such a defence, in effect, through the back door, by relying on Art 10. Whether or not this is possible in respect of categories of information covered by a harm test, it appears that it is not possible in respect of ss 1(1) and 4(1). In *Shayler* (2001), the conclusion of the House of Lords that ss 1(1) and 4(1) are not in breach of Art 10 was reached on the basis that Mr Shayler did have an avenue by which he could seek to make the disclosures in question. There were various persons to whom the disclosure could have been made, including those identified in s 12. Also, the House of Lords found a refusal of authorisation would be subject, the Crown accepted in the instant case, to judicial review. The refusal to grant authority would have to comply with Art 10 due to s 6 of the HRA; if it did not, the court in the judicial review proceedings would be expected to say so. The Lords therefore found that the interference with freedom of expression was in proportion to the legitimate aim pursued under Art 10(2) – that of protecting national security.

The Lords found that for the reasons given, the absence of a harm test or 'public interest' defence in ss 1(1) and 4(1) of the 1989 Act does not breach Art 10 of the Convention. The decision meant that s 3 of the HRA need not be used in relation to ss 1(1) and 4(1). It is probable that the same arguments would apply if, in respect of disclosure of information falling within other categories, the defence sought to introduce a public interest defence, relying on Art 10. The problem with the House of Lords' analysis in *Shayler* is that the avenues available to members or former members of the Security Services to make disclosures are unlikely to be used. It seems highly improbable that such a member would risk the employment detriment that might be likely to arise, especially if he then proceeded to seek judicial review of the decision. It is argued that the right to freedom of expression – one of the central rights of the Convention – is rendered illusory by ss 1(1) and 4(1) of the OSA in relation to allegedly unlawful activities of the Security Services – a matter of great significance in a democracy.

No express defence of prior publication is provided in the OSA; the only means of putting forward such an argument would arise in one of the categories in which it was necessary to prove the likelihood that harm would flow from the disclosure; the prosecution might find it hard to establish such a likelihood where there had been a great deal of prior publication. Section 6 expressly provides that information which has already been leaked abroad can still cause harm if disclosed in the UK. The test for harm will depend on the category the information falls into. If the information fell within s 1(3), the test for harm might be satisfied even where newspapers all over the world were repeating the information in question, on the basis that although no further harm could be caused by disclosure of the particular document, it nevertheless belonged to a class of documents disclosure of which was likely to cause harm. Thus, the harm tests under the Act are deceptive; the readiness with which they may be satisfied suggests that the Act is unlikely to have a liberalising impact on the publication of official information.

One of the objections to the old s 2 of the 1911 Act was the failure to include a requirement to prove *mens rea*. The new Act includes such a requirement only in two instances – in all the others, it creates a reversed *mens rea*: the defence can attempt to prove that the defendant did not know (or have reasonable cause to know) of the nature of the information or that its disclosure would be damaging. However, because the defence is tied into the harm tests, it does not operate in the same way in every category. Under ss 1(1) and 4(3), only the first part of the defence is relevant. Under s 3(1), although it appears that both parts are relevant, in fact, where the information falls within s 3(1)(b), the defence may have no opportunity to prove that there was no reasonable cause to believe that disclosure of the document would be damaging. However, under ss 5 and 6, the prosecution must prove *mens rea*, in the sense that it must be shown that the disclosure was made in the knowledge that it would be damaging. This is a step in the right direction and a clear improvement on the 1911 Act; nevertheless, the burden of proof on the prosecution would be very easy to discharge if the information fell within s 1(3) or s 3(1)(b) due to the nature of the tests for damage included in those sections.

However, where a journalist had disclosed information falling within one of the categories in which a harm test applies, a narrow interpretation of the term 'damaging' could be adopted under s 3 of the HRA, relying on Art 10, on the basis that Strasbourg has placed particular stress on the role of the press as a public watchdog. The press, it has been found, has a duty 'to impart information and ideas on matters of public interest' which the public 'has a right to receive' (*Castells v Spain* (1992)). It could be found that where the effect of the disclosure could arguably be to the public benefit in the context in question, or where the journalist had a belief that that would be the case, the burden on the prosecution to prove *mens rea* should be viewed as almost impossible to discharge.

The other clear improvement is the decriminalisation of the receiver of information. The receiver will often be a journalist; if he or she refrains from publishing the information, no liability will be incurred. Of course, this advantage might be said to be more theoretical than real, in that it was perhaps unlikely that the mere receiver would be prosecuted under the 1911 Act, even though that possibility did exist. Similarly, although the tests for harm are to be welcomed, it must be remembered that prosecution under the 1911 Act, theoretically possible in respect of extremely trivial disclosures, was not in practice undertaken; therefore, given the width of the harm tests, it could be said that very little has changed. Furthermore, the fact that journalists were included at all in the net of criminal liability under s 5 has been greatly criticised on the basis that some recognition should be given to the important role of the press in informing the public about government actions.[2]

Finally, in making a determination as to the liberalising impact of the Act, it must be borne in mind that other sanctions for the unauthorised disclosure of information exist. A very large number of statutes already invoke criminal sanctions to enforce secrecy on civil servants in the particular areas they cover.[3] For example, s 11 of the Atomic Energy Act 1946 makes it an offence to communicate to an unauthorised person information relating to an atomic energy plant. Further, s 1 of the OSA 1911 is still available to punish spies. The government also made it clear that actions for breach of confidence would be used against civil servants in instances falling outside the protected categories.

Thus, while it may be accepted that the Act at least allows argument as to a defendant's state of knowledge in making a disclosure to be led before a jury, it does not allow for argument as to the good intentions of the persons concerned, who may believe with reason that no other effective means of exposing iniquity exists. However, it is arguable that a statute aimed specifically at those best placed to know of corruption or malpractice in government should, in a democracy, contain such a defence. The fact that it does not argues strongly against the likelihood that it will have a liberalising impact. As indicated above, *Shayler* does not suggest that there is a willingness on the part of the judiciary to ameliorate the more illiberal aspects of this Act by use of s 3 of the HRA. However, where the words of the statute allow for a gateway to arguments as to the nature of the term 'damaging', it is possible that s 3 could be used, as argued above, to reinterpret the term in such a way as to allow for argument as to the intention behind a disclosure to be heard.

Notes

1 Steps towards far greater freedom of information were taken by the Public Interest Disclosure Act 1998 and the Freedom of Information Act 2000, both of which could be considered briefly here.

2 This point could be considered further: a comparison could be drawn with the constitutional role of the press recognised in the US by the Pentagon Papers case (*New York Times Co v US* (1971)). The Supreme Court determined that no restraining order on the press could be made so that the press would remain free to censure the government.

3 The overlap between the OSA, the Security Services Act 1989 and the RIPA 2000 could be considered here: see ss 1 and 4 of the OSA 1989.

Question 11

Critically evaluate recent developments in the law of confidence and their likely impact on freedom of information and government secrecy.

Answer plan

This topic might obviously appear as part of a general and wide-ranging essay or, as here, in its own right. It is concerned with the use of prior restraint under the doctrine of breach of confidence as a means of preventing publication of information and, of course, will involve consideration of the

Spycatcher case and then of the impact of the HRA 1998 in this area as indicated in *AG v Times Newspapers* (2001).

Essentially, the following matters should be considered:

- breach of confidence – balancing public interest in disclosure of information against the interest in keeping it confidential;
- the nature of the public interest defence (*Lion Laboratories v Evans and Express Newspapers* (1985));
- duty of confidence can bind third parties – use of interim injunctions (*AG v Guardian Newspapers Ltd* (1987));
- essential aspects of the judgment of the European Court of Human Rights (ECtHR) on the Art 10 issue (*The Observer and The Guardian v UK* (1991); *The Sunday Times v UK* (1991));
- the use of common law contempt in conjunction with the law of confidence;
- s 12 of the HRA and Art 10 of the European Convention on Human Rights (ECHR);
- *AG v Blake* (2000);
- *AG v Times Newspapers* (2001).

Answer

Breach of confidence is a civil remedy affording protection against the disclosure or use of information which is not generally known, and which has been entrusted in circumstances imposing an obligation not to disclose it without authorisation from the person who originally imparted it. This area of law developed as a means of protecting secret information belonging to individuals and organisations. However, it can also be used by the government to prevent disclosure of sensitive information and is, in that sense, a back-up to the other measures available to government, including the Official Secrets Act (OSA) 1989. In some respects, it may be more valuable than the criminal sanction provided by the Act. It may attract less publicity than a criminal trial, it offers the possibility of quickly obtaining an interim injunction and no jury will be involved. The possibility of obtaining an interim injunction is very valuable since, in many instances, the other party (usually a newspaper) will not pursue the case to a trial of the permanent injunctions, since the secret will probably no longer be newsworthy by that time. The government has in the past found it very useful to obtain interim injunctions to suppress information. However, with the advent of the HRA, limitations have been placed upon its use of this tool.

In the pre-HRA era, some restrictions were apparent: where the government, as opposed to a private individual, was concerned, the courts did not merely accept that it was in the public interest that the information should be kept confidential. The government had to show that the public interest in keeping it confidential, due to the harm its disclosure would cause, was not outweighed by the public interest in disclosure. Thus, in *AG v Jonathan Cape* (1976), when the Attorney General invoked the law of confidence to try to stop publication of Richard Crossman's memoirs on the ground that they concerned Cabinet discussions, the Lord Chief Justice accepted that such public secrets could be restrained, but only on the basis that the balance of the public interest came down in favour of suppression. Since the discussions had taken place 10 years previously, it was not possible to show that harm would flow from their disclosure; the public interest in publication therefore prevailed. The nature of the public interest defence – the interest in disclosure – was clarified in *Lion Laboratories v Evans and Express Newspapers* (1985). The Court of Appeal held that the defence extended beyond situations in which there had been serious wrongdoing by the plaintiff. Even where the plaintiff was blameless, publication would be excusable where it was possible to show a serious and legitimate interest in the revelation.

The leading case in this area is the House of Lords' decision in *AG v Guardian Newspapers Ltd (No 2)* (1990), which confirmed that the *Lion Laboratories Ltd v Evans* approach to the public interest defence was the correct one, and also clarified certain other aspects of this area of the law. As will be indicated below, the findings in this case should now be considered in the light of the HRA. In 1985, the Attorney General commenced proceedings in Australia in an attempt to restrain publication of *Spycatcher* by Peter Wright. The book included allegations of illegal activity engaged in by MI5. In 1986, after *The Guardian* and *The Observer* published reports of the forthcoming hearing which included some *Spycatcher* material, the Attorney General obtained temporary *ex parte* injunctions preventing them from further disclosure of such material. In 1987, the book was published in the US and many copies were brought into the UK. After that point, the House of Lords decided (relying on *American Cyanamid Co v Ethicon Ltd* (1975)) to continue the injunctions against the newspapers on the basis that the Attorney General still had an arguable case for permanent injunctions since publication of the information was an irreversible step. The House of Lords' decision, which gave little weight to freedom of expression, was eventually found to be in breach of Art 10 of the Convention; the effect of that decision will be considered below.

In the trial of the permanent injunctions (*AG v Guardian (No 2)* (1988)), the Crown argued that confidentiality should be maintained in the public interest, since unauthorised disclosure of the information was thought likely to damage the trust which members of the service have in each other and might encourage others to follow suit. On the other hand, some of the information in *Spycatcher*, if true, disclosed that members of MI5 in their operations in England had committed serious breaches of domestic law; the book also included the allegations that members of MI5 attempted to destabilise the administration of Mr Harold Wilson, and that the Director General or Deputy Director General of MI5 was a spy. The newspapers contended that the duty of confidentiality did not extend to allegations of serious iniquity of this character. It was determined that no detriment to national security had been shown that could outweigh the public interest in free speech, given the publication of *Spycatcher* that had already taken place, and therefore continuation of the injunctions was not necessary.[1] Thus, the massive publication of *Spycatcher* seems to have tipped the balance in favour of the newspapers.

In the judgment in the ECtHR on the temporary injunctions granted in the *Spycatcher* case (*The Observer and The Guardian v UK*; *The Sunday Times v UK*) it was found that the injunctions in force before publication of the book in the US had the aim of preventing publication of material which, according to evidence presented by the Attorney General, might have created a risk of detriment to MI5.[2] The injunctions did not prevent the papers pursuing a campaign for an inquiry into the operation of the security services and, though preventing publication for a long time – over a year – the material in question could not be classified as urgent news. Thus, the interference complained of was proportionate to the ends in view, but proportionality was not established in relation to the injunctions obtained after publication of the book in the US, since their aim was no longer to keep secret information secret; it was to attempt to preserve the reputation of MI5 and to deter others who might be tempted to follow Peter Wright's example.[3] Thus, a breach of Art 10 was found. It is arguable that this was a very cautious judgment. The court seems to have been readily persuaded by the Attorney General's argument that a widely framed injunction was needed in July 1986, but it is arguable that it was wider than it needed to be to prevent a risk to national security.[4]

Further developments occurred during the *Spycatcher* saga, which allowed breach of confidence a greater potential than it previously possessed to prevent dissemination of government information. While the temporary injunctions were in force, *The Independent* and two other papers published material covered by them. It was determined in the Court of Appeal (*AG v Newspaper Publishing plc* (1990)) that such publication constituted the *actus reus* of contempt. The case therefore affirmed the principle that once an interlocutory injunction has been obtained restraining one organ of the media from publication of allegedly confidential material, the rest of the media may be in contempt if they publish that material, even if their intention in doing so is to bring alleged iniquity to public attention. Such publication must be accompanied by an intention to prejudice the eventual trial of the permanent injunctions. Thus, the laws of confidence and contempt were allowed to operate together as a significant prior restraint on media freedom, and this principle was upheld by the House of Lords (*Times Newspapers and Another v AG* (1991)).

In *AG v Punch* (2003), the effect of common law contempt in this respect was re-affirmed by the House of Lords, despite the inception of the HRA. The Lords found that the purpose the court seeks to achieve by granting the interlocutory injunction is that, pending a decision by the court on the claims in the proceedings, the restrained acts shall not be done. Third parties are in contempt of court if they wilfully interfere with the administration of justice by thwarting the achievement of this purpose in those proceedings. It was found that this would be the case even if in the particular instance, the injunction was drawn in apparently over-wide terms.

It seems fairly clear that although the government eventually lost in the *Spycatcher* case, the decision did not have any liberalising impact as far as enhancing the ability of newspapers to publish information about government is concerned. The most pernicious aspect of breach of confidence – the ease with which interim injunctions may be obtained – will remain unaffected by this case, except in instances where a great deal of prior publication has occurred. Where such an injunction is obtained, it continues to affect all of the media, in the sense that they will not wish to risk criminal liability for contempt of court.

Case law since *Spycatcher* has, however, indicated that there are limits to the scope of breach of confidence and similar doctrines. In *Lord Advocate v The Scotsman Publications Ltd* (1990), a former member of MI6 published privately a book of memoirs. The Lord Advocate sought an injunction restraining any publication of extracts from the book in *The Scotsman*. The House of Lords, however, refused to grant an injunction. In the light of the Lord Advocate's concession and the fact that the book had already received some circulation (albeit limited), there was no reason to restrain publication by the press. More recently, in *AG v Blake* (2000), the courts considered the publication of the memoirs of a notorious spy. The Attorney General did not even seek to base his case on breach of confidence in this instance, since the events described took place more than 30 years previously. The House of Lords, however, while not restraining publication, ordered that all royalties otherwise payable to Blake should be forfeited to the Attorney General. This was on the basis that Blake was in breach of a contractual obligation dating from his employment by the security services not to disclose any information about his work, and this was a case where, exceptionally, an account of profits was the appropriate remedy for a breach of contract.

In the area of statutory provisions which affect the liability for breach of confidence, there has been the Public Interest Disclosure Act 1998. This aims to protect 'whistleblowers' by providing a defence of public interest and overriding the law of confidence. It renders such whistleblowers vulnerable, however, if they disclose the information to a person other than an employer or a relevant regulatory body. It remains to be seen how effective this legislation will be in restricting actions based on breach of confidence.

However, the doctrine is being affected most significantly by the HRA. Just as the OSA 1989 creates a direct interference with political speech, the doctrine of confidence as employed by the government can do so too. Therefore, the use of the doctrine in such instances will require careful scrutiny, with Art 10 in mind. Since this is a common law doctrine, s 3 will not apply, but the courts have a duty under s 6 of the HRA to develop the doctrine compatibly with Art 10. The duty of the courts in relation to the doctrine of confidence under the HRA was considered by Sedley LJ in *Douglas and Others v Hello! Ltd* (2001). He found that, following ss 2 and 6 of the Act, the courts must themselves act compatibly with the Convention rights. Thus, a court, as itself a public authority under s 6, is obliged to give effect to Art 10, among other provisions of the Convention, when considering the application of this doctrine. Section 12(4) of the HRA is also applicable where interference with the right to freedom of expression is in issue, as it inevitably will be in this context. Section 12(4) requires the court to have particular regard to the right to freedom of expression under Art 10. Thus, s 12(4) provides added weight to the argument that in the instance in which the State seeks to suppress the expression of an individual using this doctrine, the court must consider the pressing social need to do so and the requirements of proportionality very carefully, interpreting those requirements strictly. In considering Art 10, the court should, under s 12(4)(a), take into account the extent to which the material is or is about to become available to the public and the public interest in publication. These two matters are central in breach of confidence actions. They imply that the State's task in obtaining an injunction where a small amount of prior publication has taken place – or is about to – has been made harder.

Section 12(3) of the HRA provides that prior restraint on expression should not be granted except where the court considers that the claimant is 'likely' to establish at trial that publication should not be allowed. Moreover, *ex parte* injunctions cannot be granted under s 12(2) unless there are compelling reasons why the respondent should not be notified or the applicant has taken all reasonable steps to notify the respondent. All these requirements under the HRA must now be taken into account in applying the doctrine of confidence and the rule from *AG v Newspaper Publishing plc* (1990). Current developments suggest that the result is likely to be that the doctrine will undergo quite a radical change from the interpretation afforded to it in the *Spycatcher* litigation. The case of *AG v Times Newspapers* (2001) is significant. A former MI6 officer wrote a book, *The Big Breach*, about his experiences in MI6 which *The Sunday Times* intended to serialise. There had been a small amount of publication of the material in Russia. The Attorney General sought an injunction to restrain publication.

The key issue concerned the degree of prior publication required before it could be said that the material had lost its quality of confidentiality. The two parties agreed on a formula: that the material had already been published in any other newspaper, magazine or other publication whether within or outside the jurisdiction of the court. The Attorney General, however, contended that the defendants had to demonstrate that this was the case, which meant that they had to obtain clearance from the Attorney General before publishing. The newspaper invoked Art 10 and also relied on s 12(4) of the HRA. It was argued that the restriction proposed by the Attorney General would be disproportionate to the aim pursued and therefore could not be justified in a democratic society. The decision in *Bladet-Tromsø v Norway* (1999) was referred to, in which the Court said that it is incumbent on the media to impart information and ideas concerning matters of public interest. It was found that the Attorney General had failed to demonstrate why there was a public interest in restricting publication; therefore, no injunction was granted. The requirement to seek clearance should not, it was found, be imposed: the editor had to form his own judgment as to whether the material could be said to be already in the public domain. That position was, the Court found, most consonant with the requirements of Art 10 and s 12.

This decision suggests that, bearing in mind the requirements of the HRA, an injunction is unlikely to be granted where a small amount of prior publication has already taken place. It does not, however, decide the question of publication where no prior publication has taken place, but the material is of public interest (which could clearly have been said of the Wright material). Following *Bladet-Tromsø v Norway*, it is suggested that an injunction should not be granted where such material is likely, imminently, to come into the public domain, a position consistent with the demands of s 12(4), which refers to such a likelihood. Even where this cannot be said to be the case, it would be consonant with the requirements of Art 10 and s 12 to refuse to grant an injunction on the basis of the duty of newspapers to report on such material. The burden would be placed on the State to seek to establish that a countervailing pressing social need was present and that the injunction did not go further than necessary in order to serve the end in view. Thus, although breach of confidence remains a fairly important weapon in the government's armoury, it is likely to be of more limited effect in the future than seemed probable at the time of the *Spycatcher* litigation. Nevertheless,

once an injunction has been granted, it is clear, from *AG v Punch*, that it will –
indirectly – affect all of the media.

Notes

1   It was further determined that an injunction to restrain future publication of
matters connected with the operations of the security service would amount to a
comprehensive ban on publication and would undermine the operation of
determining the balance of public interest in deciding whether such publication
was to be prevented; accordingly, an injunction to prevent future publication
which had not yet been threatened was not granted.

2   It could be pointed out that the House of Lords wanted to preserve the Attorney
General's right to be granted a permanent injunction; if *Spycatcher* material had
been published before that claim could be heard, the subject matter of the action
would have been damaged or destroyed. In the court's view, these factors
established the existence of a pressing social need.

3   It could be noted further that, after publication in the US, it was not possible to
maintain the Attorney General's rights as a litigant, since the substance of his
claim had already been destroyed; had permanent injunctions been obtained
against the papers, that would not have preserved the confidentiality of the
material in question.

4   This point could be pursued further: the injunction could have required the
newspapers to refrain from publishing Wright material which had not been
previously published by others until (and if) the action to prevent publication of
the book was lost. Such wording would have taken care of any national security
interest; therefore, wording going beyond that was disproportionate to that aim.
The judgment could also have set itself against the narrow view that the
authority of the judiciary is best preserved by allowing a claim of confidentiality
set up in the face of a strong competing public interest to provide a basis for an
infringement of freedom of speech for over a year.

Question 12

Critically evaluate the means currently available to the government in
order to prevent disclosure of information. Taking some account of recent
developments, including the introduction of the Freedom of Information
Act 2000, would it be fair to say that the tradition of government secrecy is
finally breaking down?

Answer plan

This is clearly quite a general and wide-ranging essay, which requires
knowledge of a number of different areas. It is concerned both with methods
of ensuring that information cannot fall into the hands of those who might

place it in the public domain and with methods of preventing or deterring persons from publication when a leak has occurred. Both issues are aspects of freedom of expression and are touched on in Chapter 1, but the first is given greater prominence here. The question asks you, in essence, to present a critical analysis of the current scheme preventing disclosure of certain information and to consider whether the right of access to information recently introduced in the 2000 Act (not yet fully in force) will dramatically improve the public's access to information. Since the essay is so wide-ranging, you are not expected to engage in a detailed analysis of the 2000 Act.

Essentially, the following areas should be considered:

- the impact of the Official Secrets Act (OSA) 1989: 'harm tests' and the Public Interest Disclosure Act 1998;
- the relationship between the OSA, the Security Services Act 1989, the Intelligence Services Act 1994, the Interception of Communications Act 1985 and the Regulation of Investigatory Powers Act (RIPA) 2000;
- use of the common law as a means of preventing disclosure of information – common law contempt and breach of confidence;
- comparison with the DA Notice system – criticism of the system as currently operated;
- freedom of information measures in other countries;
- the operation of the Public Records Acts 1958 and 1967, as amended, and the Data Protection Act 1998, as amended;
- efficacy of the current voluntary Code and likely effect of the Freedom of Information Act 2000.

Answer

It has often been said that the UK is more obsessed with keeping government information secret than any other Western democracy. It is clearly advantageous for the party in power to control the flow of information in order to ensure that citizens are unable to scrutinise some official decisions. The justification for this climate of secrecy is that freedom of information would adversely affect 'ministerial accountability'. In other words, ministers are responsible for the actions of civil servants in their departments and must therefore be able to control the flow of information emanating from the department in question. However, this doctrine is not easy to defend in a democracy; it might be thought that ministers would be made more accountable, not less, if the workings of officials were made fully open to public scrutiny. However, s 2 of the OSA 1911 created a climate of secrecy in the civil service which greatly hampered the efforts of those who wished to obtain and publish information about the workings of government.

The OSA 1989, which decriminalised disclosure of some official information, was therefore heralded as amounting to a move away from obsessive secrecy. However, since it was in no sense a freedom of information measure, it did not allow the release of any official documents into the public domain, although it does mean that if certain information is disclosed, outside the categories it covers, the official concerned will not face criminal sanctions. (He or she might, of course, face an action for breach of confidence as well as disciplinary proceedings.)

The narrowing down of the official information covered by the Act was supposed to be achieved by introducing 'harm tests', which took into account the substance of the information. Clearly, such tests are to be preferred to the width of s 2 of the OSA 1911, which covered all official information, however trivial. However, there is no test for harm at all in the category of information covered by s 1(1) of the 1989 Act, which prevents members or former members of the security services disclosing anything at all about the operation of those services. All such members come under a lifelong duty to keep silent, even though their information might reveal serious abuse of power in the security services or some operational weakness. Equally, there is no test for harm under s 4(3) of the Act, which covers information obtained by or relating to the issue of a warrant under the Interception of Communications Act 1985 or the Security Services Act 1989. These tests are compatible with Art 10 scheduled in the HRA according to the House of Lords in *R v Shayler* (2002).

The harm tests under the Act are further diluted in various ways. Under s 3(1)(b), which covers confidential information obtained abroad, the mere fact that the information is confidential 'may' be sufficient to establish the likelihood that its disclosure would cause harm. In other words, a fiction is created that harm may automatically flow from such disclosure. The Act contains no explicit public interest defence and it follows from the nature of the harm test that one cannot be implied into it; any good flowing from disclosure of the information cannot be considered, merely any harm that might be caused. Moreover, no express defence of prior publication is provided; the only means of putting forward such argument would arise in one of the categories in which it was necessary to prove the likelihood that harm would flow from the disclosure; the prosecution might find it hard to establish such a likelihood where there had already been a great deal of prior publication. Thus, the Act was unlikely to have a liberalising impact on the publication of information allowing the public to scrutinise the workings of government.

The Public Interest Disclosure Act 1998 is also far from being a likely source of greater freedom of information; although, in principle, it affords a defence of 'public interest' disclosure to those facing the OSA disciplinary proceedings, full protection only exists where the disclosure is made in good faith to an employer or regulatory body. Thus, disclosure to the media is still a risky method and will be justified only where the malpractice is exceptionally serious or the whistleblower acts to avoid victimisation or a cover-up or an inept official investigation has occurred.

The OSA 1989 works in tandem with other measures designed to ensure secrecy. Sections 1 and 4(3) work in conjunction with the provisions of the Security Services Act 1989 to prevent almost all scrutiny of the operation of the security service. Even where a member of the public has a grievance concerning the operation of the service, it will not be possible to use a court action as a means of bringing such operations to the notice of the public – under s 5 of the Security Services Act, complaint can only be made to a tribunal and, under s 5(4), the decisions of the tribunal are not questionable in any court of law. Furthermore, the Act provides for no real form of parliamentary oversight of the security service, but this has, to some extent, been remedied by s 10 of the Intelligence Services Act 1994, which set up for the first time a Parliamentary Committee to oversee the operation of MI5, MI6 and GCHQ. However, since the Committee is not a Select Committee, its powers are limited. In a similar manner, s 4(3) of the OSA, which prevents disclosure of information about telephone tapping, works in tandem with the RIPA 2000. Under the 2000 Act, complaints can be made only to a tribunal (set up under the Act), with no possibility of scrutiny by a court.

Developments in the use of the common law doctrine of confidence as a means of preventing disclosure of information provide a further means of ensuring secrecy where information falls outside the categories covered by the OSA, or where it falls within one of them, but a prosecution is not undertaken. *AG v Guardian Newspapers* (1987), which concerned publication of material from *Spycatcher* by Peter Wright, demonstrated that temporary injunctions could be obtained to prevent disclosure of official information, even where prior publication has ensured that there is little confidentiality left to be protected. The House of Lords decided (relying on *American Cyanamid Co v Ethicon Ltd* (1975)) that temporary injunctions could be continued where there was still an arguable case for permanent injunctions. However, the House of Lords eventually rejected the claim for permanent injunctions on the basis that the interest in maintaining confidentiality was outweighed by the public interest in knowing of the allegations in *Spycatcher*. Moreover, it was impossible to sustain a restriction based on confidentiality when the worldwide publication of the book meant that the information it contained was clearly in the 'public domain'. In *AG v Punch Ltd and Another* (2003), the House of Lords reaffirmed the doctrine that where a temporary injunction has been obtained on grounds of breach of confidence, it will be contempt if another newspaper knowingly publishes material covered by the injunction.

There are other methods of seeking to deter persons from publishing information relating to the security and intelligence services. In *AG v Blake* (2000), a former security services operative published his memoirs. The Attorney General did not seek an injunction on grounds of breach of confidence, because the information concerned was at least 30 years old and did not in itself prejudice national security. The House of Lords, however, held that the Attorney General was entitled to an account of any profits from the publication of the memoirs, because such publication involved a breach of a contractual duty on the part of the operative, dating from his employment by the security services, not to disclose any information about his work.

A restraint over obtaining an injunction or damages for breach of confidence is now to be found in s 12 of the HRA 1998. This requires any court considering such relief not to grant any interim injunction unless it is satisfied that the claimant is likely to be successful at trial. Moreover, it must have particular regard to the importance of freedom of expression and, in relation to journalistic, literary or artistic material, consider both the public interest and the extent to which the relevant information is, or is about to be, in the public domain. It therefore appears that, in future, courts will apply existing statutory and common law rules with a far greater focus upon the public right to know. In this respect, the case of *AG v Times* (2001) is significant. A former MI6 officer wrote a book, *The Big Breach*, about his experiences in MI6 which *The Sunday Times* intended to serialise. There had been a small amount of publication of the material in Russia. The Attorney General sought an injunction to restrain publication. It was found that he had failed to demonstrate why there was a public interest in restricting publication; therefore, no injunction was granted. The requirement to seek clearance should not, it was found, be imposed: the editor had to form his own judgment as to whether the material could be said to be already in the public domain. That position was, the court found, most consonant with the requirements of Art 10 and s 12. This decision suggests that, bearing in mind the requirements of the HRA, an injunction is unlikely to be granted where even a very small amount of prior publication has already taken place.

Apart from the action for breach of confidence, the government can seek to prevent the publication of some forms of information by means of a curious institution known as the 'DA' Notice system. This system, which effectively means that the media censor themselves in respect of publication of official information, may preclude the need to seek injunctions to prevent publication. The DA Notice Committee was set up with the object of letting the press know which information could be printed: it was intended that if sensitive political information was covered by a 'DA' Notice, an editor would decide against printing it.[1]

It is clear from the discussion so far that the government has a range of measures available to it to prevent publication of forms of State information, but that the measures have recently become somewhat more liberal. The 1989 Act is a narrower measure than its predecessor and the action for breach of confidence has a narrower application due to the impact of the HRA. However, the narrowing down of the measures available to the State to prevent disclosure of information does not in itself mean that access to official information is available. The mere fact that a Crown servant will not be prosecuted for disclosing information and is unlikely to face civil liability does not in itself mean that the citizen can obtain access to the information.

Information of historical interest may be obtainable via the UK Public Records Act 1958, as amended by the Public Records Act 1967 and the Freedom of Information Act 2000. However, under the 1958 Act, public records in the Public Records Office are not available for inspection until the expiration of 30 years, and longer periods can be prescribed for sensitive information. Some information can be withheld for 100 years or forever and there is no means of challenging such decisions. For example, at the end of 1987, a great deal of information about the Windscale fire in 1957 was disclosed, although some items are still held back. Thus, the 1958 Act, even after amendment, can hardly be viewed as equivalent to a statutory right of access to current information.

However, for the past decade, there has been a slow but progressive movement towards freedom of information legislation for the UK, culminating in the Freedom of Information Act 2000. The then Conservative government published a White Paper in July 1993 setting out its intentions in relation to freedom of information, which included the means of allowing citizens access to some government information. A voluntary Code allowing the citizen access to official information in certain specified areas was introduced in 1994. However, it is suggested that a voluntary Code cannot replace a statutory right of access. The promise to release information only related to 'useful' or 'useable information'. However, in countries that have freedom of information, the usefulness of the information is determined by the person who seeks it, rather than by government ministers or civil servants. Usefulness is not an objective quality, but depends on the purposes of the seeker, which only he or she can appreciate, and therefore it may be argued that this is an unwarranted limitation on the principle of 'openness'.

Challenge through an ombudsman cannot be as effective as challenge in a court.

Voluntary open government asks the citizen to trust the government to act against its own interests. Clearly, government departments may be prepared voluntarily to release some information which is innocuous, but they are less likely to do so where the information will cause political embarrassment and may enable the opposition to make a more informed and therefore more damaging attack on government. When the Labour government came to power, it promised to introduce a Freedom of Information Act in the White Paper, *Your Right to Know*, Cm 3818. This promise took shape in the form of the Freedom of Information Act 2000, which will be brought fully into force by 2005. Once in force, the Act will have a number of important consequences. Primarily, it places a general right of access to information on a statutory basis for the first time, in s 1. The new right will allow the public access to information held by a very wide definition of public authorities, including local government, the NHS, schools and colleges, and the police. An Information Commissioner has been appointed to supervise the new scheme and the public will be able to contact her directly. Public authorities must, on request, indicate whether they hold information required by an individual and, if so, communicate that information to him within 20 working days.

However, a number of forms of information will be exempt, including that relating to security matters or which might affect national security, defence or the economy. The exemptions proposed under the White Paper were relatively narrow and were subject to quite a strict harm test. They may be sharply contrasted with those that emerged under the Act. The harm-based exemptions under the Act are similar to those indicated in the White Paper: they require the public authority to show that the release of the information requested would, or would be likely to, cause prejudice to the interest specified in the exemption. However, this test for harm is less restrictive than that proposed under the White Paper. Further, a number of exemptions are class-based, meaning that in order to refuse the request, the authority only has to show that the information falls into the class of information covered by the exemption, not that its release would cause or be likely to cause harm or prejudice.

However, the Act provides a public interest test in relation to some, but not all, of the class exemptions, and almost all the 'harm exemptions'. The authority, having decided that the information is *prima facie* exempt (either because the information falls into the requisite class exemption, or because the relevant harm test is satisfied, as the case may be), must still then go on to consider whether it should be released under the public interest test set out in s 2. This requires the authority to release the information unless 'in all the circumstances of the case, the public interest in maintaining the exemption outweighs the public interest in disclosing the information'.

Section 32 provides a particularly controversial class exemption: it covers information *which is only held* by virtue of being contained in a document or record served on a public authority in proceedings, or made by a court or tribunal or party in any proceedings, or contained in a document lodged with or created by a person conducting an inquiry or arbitration, for the purposes of the inquiry or arbitration. The public interest test does not apply. It overlaps with the law enforcement exemption of s 31, which does include a harm test. The other major class exemption, under s 35, has been just as criticised. It amounts to a very broad exemption covering virtually all information relating to the formation of government policy. Section 36 contains a harm-based exemption which covers almost exactly the same ground.

The imprecise terms used to indicate the exempted information and the introduction of class exemptions may allow the government to exempt from the disclosure provisions much information which is merely embarrassing or damaging to its reputation. Some such information may also be subject to the ministerial veto, where it relates to central government, which means that it cannot be disclosed even if it is not exempt.[2] However, where the veto is not used, a right to appeal to the information tribunal is granted by the Act to complainants and much will depend upon future interpretations of the statute by the Commissioner and the courts. To an extent it remains to be seen whether the new Act will be a substantial step towards greater openness in central government. In relation to other public authorities operating in non-exempt areas, the Act clearly represents a significant further step in the direction of freedom of information. It is concluded that the developments described here do suggest that a movement away from the tradition of government secrecy has been occurring over the last two decades, culminating in the Act of 2000. Nevertheless, the existence of class exemptions in the Act and of the ministerial veto suggest that some aspects of that tradition are reflected, ironically, in that Act.

Notes

1 It could be pointed out that the system is entirely voluntary and in theory the fact that a 'DA' Notice has not been issued does not mean that a prosecution under the OSA 1989 is precluded, although, in practice, it is very unlikely. Press representatives sit on the committee as well as civil servants and officers of the armed forces.

2 The veto can be exercised if two conditions are satisfied under s 53(1): first, the notice which the veto will operate to quash must have been served on a government department, the Welsh Assembly or 'any public authority

designated for the purposes of this section by an order made by the Secretary of State'; secondly, the notice must order the release of information which is *prima facie* exempt but which the Commissioner has decided should nevertheless be released under the public interest test in s 2. The White Paper made no provision for such a power of veto, on the basis that to do so would undermine confidence in the regime. Such a veto clearly dilutes the basic freedom of information principle that a body independent from government should enforce the rights to information.

Question 13

'A comparison between the *Code of Practice on Access to Government Information* introduced by the Conservative government and the Freedom of Information Act 2000 demonstrates that the Act is inadequate since it provides very little more than the Code. It therefore appears that, although with the introduction of the Act, the UK has gone a little way down the path towards freedom of information, there is still a long way to go.'

Discuss.

Answer plan

This is clearly quite a specific topic which calls for an answer confined to access to information rather than a general and wide-ranging answer looking at the whole area of government secrecy. In order to answer it, it is necessary to have detailed knowledge of both the Code and the key provisions of the Act of 2000.

Essentially, the following areas should be considered:

- the *Code of Practice on Access to Government Information* – exceptions and enforcement;
- comparison between the Code and the statutory right of access to government and public authority information under the 2000 Act;
- other freedom of information measures – the Data Protection Acts 1984 and 1998 and statutory access rights to manual files;
- conclusions as to stage reached in freedom of information terms.

Answer

The then Conservative government published a White Paper in July 1993, which set out its intentions in relation to freedom of information. Instead of freedom of information legislation, the Major government favoured the introduction of an unenforceable Code of Practice on access to government information. It came into effect in 1994 and the second edition was published in 1997. In contrast to the voluntary Code, the Labour government promised a statutory right of access to official information and this was established with the introduction of the Freedom of Information Act in 2000, although it will not be fully in force until 2005. In the following discussion, certain key features of the Code will be identified and these will be contrasted with the provisions of the Act. When the Code is compared with the Freedom of Information Act, it is found that both exhibit features which are found in freedom of information Codes or Acts abroad but, in almost every instance, where various possibilities are available, the Code chooses the course which disadvantages the seeker after information and undermines the principle of 'openness'. The picture that emerges under the Act is more mixed. Four particular key features of the Code will be considered in order to emphasise the contrasts between the Act and the Code. The argument will be that the Act creates a superior freedom of information scheme, but that it also displays a number of weaknesses.

The Code provides that non-exempted government departments will publish a range of information and will also provide information on receipt of specific requests. The presumption is in favour of disclosure; after the 1997 revision, the Code provided that information should be disclosed, unless the harm likely to arise from disclosure would outweigh the public interest in making the information available: Pt II. The 2000 Act is based on similar principles, but, in strong contrast to the unenforceable Code, it will give UK citizens, for the first time, a statutory right to non-exempt official information enforceable by an independent Information Commissioner, who, in the final resort, can enforce his or her orders through invoking the courts' power to punish for contempt of court.

One of the weaknesses of the Code is that it only provides for release of information as opposed to documents (Pt I, para 4). As the Campaign for Freedom of Information has pointed out, this is: '... a potentially overwhelming defect: the opportunities for selective editing are obvious.' In contrast, the right conferred under s 1(1)(b) of the Freedom of Information Act covers original documents as well as 'information'. Section 84 defines information broadly to cover information 'recorded in any form', and in relation to matters covered by s 51(8) this includes unrecorded information. In this respect, the Act is clearly an improvement on the Code.

The implied and express exemptions from the Code are extremely wide. Certain matters set out in Sched 3 to the Parliamentary Commissioner Act 1967 are excluded from the investigation by the Parliamentary Commissioner for Administration (PCA). These include the investigation of crime by, or on behalf of, the Home Office; security of the State; and personnel matters of the armed forces, teachers, the civil service or police. A very large number of matters are excluded from the Code, although the majority of these – after the 1997 revision – are subject to a harm test. They include defence, security and international relations; internal discussion and advice; law enforcement and legal proceedings; immigration and nationality; effective management of the economy and of the public service; research, statistics and analysis; privacy of an individual; information given in confidence. Of these restrictions, those attracting the most criticism have been the exclusion of contractual and commercial matters and of public service personnel matters.

In relation to major policy decisions (Pt I, para 3(i)), the Code relates only to information considered relevant by the government. In countries which have freedom of information legislation, the usefulness or relevance of documents containing information is determined by the person who seeks it rather than by government ministers or civil servants. Usefulness is not an objective quality but depends on the purposes of the seeker, which only he or she can appreciate.

The introduction of harm tests, which mirror some of those under the Official Secrets Act (OSA) 1989, is to be welcomed since it limits the width of the exemption in question, but the tests are so wide and imprecise that they are unlikely to have much impact in narrowing the exemptions. The harm tests are varied and some are more complex than others, but none of them provide a precise explanation of the meaning of 'harm'. Thus, in relation to defence, security and international relations, part of the harm test is concerned with 'information whose disclosure would harm national security or defence'. Exemption 2 covers 'information which would harm the frankness and candour of internal discussion'.

The exceptions under the Act of 2000 will be, on the whole, less wide-ranging than those under the Code, taking into account the limitations of the PCA's remit – the fact that the PCA does not cover many of the bodies who are covered by the Act and therefore the question of exemptions does not arise. In certain respects, however, the Code is, on its face, more generous. In particular, the total exemption under s 21 does not appear in the Code in as broad a form (para 8 of the Code refers to information obtainable under existing statutory rights) and the exemption under s 35 is broader than the equivalent exemption under the Code in para 2. The exemptions under the Act rely on the key distinction between 'class' and 'harm-based' exemptions. The harm-based exemptions under the Act are similar to those indicated in the White Paper: they require the public authority to show that the release of the information requested would, or would be likely to, cause prejudice to the interest specified in the exemption. However, a number are class-based, meaning that in order to refuse the request, the authority only has to show that the information falls into the class of information covered by the exemption, not that its release would cause or be likely to cause harm or prejudice.

The Act provides a public interest test in relation to some, but not all, of the class exemptions, and almost all the harm-based exemptions. However, where information falls into a class exemption, and an authority objects to disclosure even under the public interest test, it will be able not only to argue that the specific disclosure would have harmful effects, but also that the public interest would be harmed by any disclosure from within the relevant class of documents, regardless of the consequences of releasing the actual information in question.

This discussion cannot cover all of the Freedom of Information Act class exemptions but will consider some of the more controversial ones. Section 23(1) covers information supplied by or which relates to the intelligence and security services. The bodies mentioned in this exemption are not themselves covered by the Act at all. This exemption therefore applies to information which is held by *another public authority*, but which has been supplied by one of these bodies. Because it is a class exemption, it could apply to information which had no conceivable security implications, such as evidence of a massive overspend on MI5 or MI6's headquarters. The use of this class exemption unaccompanied by a harm test and not subject to the public interest test is likely to mean that sensitive matters of great political significance remain undisclosed, even if their disclosure would ultimately benefit those services or national security. Section 32 is another broad and controversial class exemption; it includes information *which is only held* by virtue of being contained in a document served on a public authority in proceedings or made in any proceedings. The public interest test does not apply.

Section 30(1) provides a sweeping class exemption, covering all information, whenever obtained, which relates to investigations that may lead to criminal proceedings. It represents a specific rejection of the recommendation of the Macpherson Report that there should be no class exemption for information relating to police investigations. This s 30 exemption extends beyond protecting the police and the CPS. Other bodies will also be protected: it will cover all information obtained by safety agencies investigating accidents. It is particularly hard to understand the need for such a sweeping class exemption when s 31 specifically exempts information which could prejudice the prevention or detection of crime, or legal proceedings brought by a public authority arising from various forms of investigation.[1]

A further major class exemption under s 35 has been just as criticised. It amounts to a very broad exemption covering virtually all information relating to the formation of government policy. This exemption is not restricted to Civil Service advice; it covers also the background information used in preparing policy, including the underlying facts and their analysis. Section 36 contains a harm-based exemption which covers almost exactly the same ground.[2] In contrast to the position under most other freedom of information regimes, s 35 allows the *analysis* of facts to be withheld. The Act is much more restrictive in this respect than the present, voluntary Code of Practice. The latter requires both facts and the analysis of facts underlying policy decisions, including scientific analysis and expert appraisal, to be made available once decisions are announced. Material relating to policy formation can only be withheld under a harm test. While information in the s 35 category is subject to a public interest test, it is important to note that, because, by definition, it will generally be information held by a government department, if the Commissioner orders disclosure on public interest grounds, the ministerial veto will be available to override him or her (see below).

The third feature of the Code to be considered relates to the role of the PCA (Ombudsman) in policing it. If a citizen fails to obtain information, or full information in a non-exempt area, he or she can complain to an MP who will probably pass the complaint to the Ombudsman. If the Ombudsman recommends that a department should reveal information and the department does not accept the recommendation, departments may be called upon to justify themselves before the Select Committee on the PCA. However, the Committee cannot compel a department to release information. Thus, the Ombudsman has no means of enforcing his recommendations unless he takes the means of redress into his own hands by disclosing the disputed information. No provision of the Code envisages that he might do this. He might be reluctant to take this course since it would probably damage relations between himself and the department in question, which would almost certainly have repercussions in relation to other aspects of his role. Thus, the Code is perhaps most open to criticism due to its lack of 'teeth'. Rodney Austin noted in 1994 in *The Changing Constitution* that 'Whitehall's record of compliance with the non-binding recommendations of the ombudsman is actually outstanding'. However, Austin goes on to note that governments will fight tenaciously to preserve secrets which matter to them and finds: 'there is little ground for optimism that in a crucial case the Government would not choose to defy the PCA ...' The Report of the PCA on the unprecedented refusal of the Home Office to supply information in November 2001 demonstrates that this contention is correct.

The enforcement review mechanism under the Act is far stronger than the mechanism established under the Code. The internal review of a decision to withhold information, established under the Code, was formalised under the Act and the role of the Ombudsman was taken over by the Information

Commissioner. The Commissioner's powers will be much more extensive than those of the Ombudsman: he or she will have the power to order disclosure of the information by means of an enforcement notice (s 52(1)) and can report a failure to disclose information to the High Court (s 52) which can treat it in the same way as contempt of court.[3] However, the ministerial veto weakens the enforcement of the access where government departments are involved. It is therefore another highly controversial aspect of the Act. The White Paper made no provision for such a power of veto, on the basis that to do so would undermine confidence in the regime. Such a veto clearly dilutes the basic freedom of information principle that a body independent from government should enforce the rights to information and, in cases where the release of information could embarrass ministers, it constitutes them judge in their own cause, which is objectionable in principle.[4] Thus, the enforcement mechanism under the Act, while stronger than that available under the Code, exhibits clear failures of commitment to the freedom of information ideal.

The final, and most fundamental, criticism of the Code is that, in principle, the case for a voluntary Code as opposed to a general statutory right of access to information is not a strong one, mainly because voluntary open government asks the citizen to trust government to act against its own interests. Clearly, government departments may be readily prepared to release voluntarily some information which is out of date or innocuous for some other reason, but this may be less likely where the information will cause political embarrassment and may enable the opposition to make a more informed and therefore more damaging attack on the governing party. The grace and favour nature of this scheme is, it is argued, inappropriate in relation to freedom of information, although the recommendatory nature of the PCA may be appropriate in relation to his or her main function. The fact that the PCA operates informally and privately has been thought to enhance her powers of persuasion. However, in relation to complaints under the Code, the lack of a power to award a remedy may in some situations appear to amount to a weakness in the PCA system. The fact that adherence to the Code is voluntary may mean that it is not taken seriously unless the PCA takes up a complaint.[5]

It is argued that the introduction of a statutory right of access to official information is clearly preferable to relying on a voluntary Code. However, it must be acknowledged that the Commissioner's power to force government to disclose information is weakened by the existence of the ministerial veto. This is one of the major concerns about the Act. The other is the great number and width of the exemptions it contains and the fact that many of these amount to class exemptions. It is concluded that the current *Code of Practice on Access to Government Information*, and the developments preceding it, represented a clear movement towards freedom of information, but an inadequate one. Despite the concerns expressed above, it is suggested that a far more significant step in that direction will be taken once the Act of 2000 is fully in force.

Notes

1   It could be pointed out that, where it has been decided that the information falls into the protected class, the authority must then go on to consider whether it should be released under the public interest test. Since most of the information above will not be held by a government department (discussed later in the essay), the Commissioner will be able to order disclosure if he or she thinks the information should be released under this provision, with no possibility of a ministerial veto.

2   The sole and very limited exception to this exemption appears in sub-s (2) of s 35; it applies only 'once a decision as to government policy has been taken' and covers 'any statistical information used to provide an informed background to the taking of the decision'.

3   Further discussion of the enforcement mechanism could be included. The Commissioner's powers are buttressed by powers of entry, search and seizure to gain evidence of a failure by the authority to carry out its obligations under the Act or comply with a notice issued by the Commissioner (detailed in Sched 3). However, the Commissioner's decisions are themselves subject to appeal to the Tribunal, and this power of appeal is exercisable upon the broadest possible grounds notice (s 57(2) and (3), s 58(1)). The Tribunal is empowered to review any finding of fact on which the Commissioner's notice was based and, as well as being empowered to quash decisions of the Commissioner, may substitute any other notice that she could have served. It may also be noted that no civil liability is incurred if a public authority does not comply with any duty imposed by the Act (s 56).

4   For the veto to be exercisable, two conditions must be satisfied under s 53(1): first, the notice which the veto will operate to quash must have been served on a government department, the Welsh Assembly or 'any public authority designated for the purposes of this section by an order made by the Secretary of State'; secondly, the notice must order the release of information which is *prima facie* exempt, but which the Commissioner has decided should nevertheless be released under the public interest test in s 2.

5   A survey published in March 1997 (see the journalists' magazine, *UKPG*, 7 March 1997, para 9) showed that public bodies were not meeting the standards of openness laid down in the government Code. Fifty government departments were asked for information to which the public is entitled under the Code. Eleven gave wrong or inadequate information and three refused to reply at all. Among those showing poor practice were the Legal Aid Board and the Commission for Racial Equality. The Department for Education and Employment and the Office for National Statistics were among those which refused to reply.

CHAPTER 3

FREEDOM OF ASSEMBLY AND ASSOCIATION

Introduction

Freedom of assembly is a subject which almost invariably appears on examination papers in civil liberties, often, but not always, in the form of a problem question. The concern in such questions is with the conflict between the need on the one hand to maintain public order and, on the other, to protect freedom of assembly. Whether problem questions or essays are set, the concern in either case will be with those provisions of the criminal law most applicable in the context of demonstrations, marches or meetings. The common law power to prevent a breach of the peace is still extensively used. Students should be aware of recent decisions on this power. The Public Order Act 1986 is still the most significant statute, but it is also particularly important to bear in mind the public order provisions of the Criminal Justice and Public Order Act 1994. Freedom of association tends to be considered in an essay question which also covers freedom of assembly, but it sometimes arises as an independent essay topic.

Problem questions sometimes call on the student to discuss *any* issues which may arise, as opposed to considering criminal liability only, in which case any tortious liability incurred by members of an assembly or by police officers may arise, as well as questions of criminal liability. The possibility of judicial review of police decisions may also occur.

At the present time, the Human Rights Act (HRA) 1998 is of course especially important and is relevant in all problem questions on public protest and assembly. Examiners will expect some discussion of its relevance and impact. Articles 10 and 11 of the European Convention on Human Rights (ECHR), which provide guarantees of freedom of expression and of peaceful assembly respectively, were incorporated into UK law once the HRA came fully into force in 2000. (Note that Art 10 protects 'expression', not merely 'speech', thus covering many forms of expressive activity, including forms of public protest.) Therefore, Arts 10 and 11 and other Convention Articles relevant in this area are directly applicable in UK courts, and should be taken into account in interpreting and applying common law and statutory provisions affecting public protest. Section 3(1) of the HRA requires: 'So far as it is possible to do so, primary and subordinate legislation must be read and given effect in a way which is compatible with the Convention rights ...' Section 3(2)(b) reads: 'this section does not affect the validity, continuing operation or enforcement of any incompatible primary legislation.' Section

3(1) goes well beyond the pre-HRA obligation to resolve ambiguity in statutes by reference to the Convention. All statutes affecting freedom of assembly and public protest, therefore, have to be interpreted so as to be in harmony with the Convention if that is at all possible.

Under s 6, Convention guarantees are binding only against public authorities; these are defined as bodies which have a partly public function. In the context of public protest, this will normally mean that if the police, local authorities or other public bodies use powers deriving from any legal source in order to prevent or limit peaceful public protest, the protesters can bring an action against them under s 7(1)(a) of the HRA relying on Art 11, probably combined with Art 10. It also means that, if the protesters are prosecuted or sued, they can rely on those Articles as providing a defence and/or reinterpretation of the legal provision involved. Depending on the interpretation afforded to those Articles, including the exceptions to them, the protesters might be successful unless a statutory provision absolutely unambiguously supported the limitation or banning of the protest. Where a statute limiting/affecting public protest is applied, the court is likely to rely on s 3 of the HRA; where a common law provision creating such a limitation is relevant, the court will rely on s 6. (For further discussion, see Chapter 9.)

Checklist

Students should have general knowledge of the background to the Public Order Act (POA) 1986 and the public order provisions of the Criminal Justice and Public Order Act (CJPOA) 1994 and, in particular, should be familiar with the following areas:

- freedom of assembly, association and public protest jurisprudence under Arts 10 and 11 of the ECHR;
- the HRA 1998, especially ss 3 and 6;
- notice requirements under s 11 of the POA 1986;
- conditions which can be imposed under ss 12 and 14 of the POA 1986 on processions and assemblies;
- banning power under ss 13 and 14A of the Act;
- liability under ss 5, 4, 4A and 3 of the Act;
- liability for assault on, or obstruction of, a police officer under s 89 of the Police Act 1996;
- common law power to prevent a breach of the peace;
- public nuisance;
- obstruction of the highway under s 137 of the Highways Act 1980;

- public order provisions of Pt V and s 154 of the CJPOA 1994;
- s 2 of the POA 1936;
- Pt II of the Terrorism Act 2000.

Question 14

How far does UK law afford recognition to freedom of association?

Answer plan

A fairly common and quite straightforward essay question. It requires a sound knowledge of the key provisions in the area and of the influence of Art 11 of the European Convention on Human Rights (ECHR).

Essentially, the following matters should be considered:

- lack of legal recognition of freedom of association;
- s 2 of the POA 1936;
- Pt II of the Terrorism Act 2000;
- Art 11 of the ECHR;
- *Council of Civil Service Unions v Minister for the Civil Service* (1984).

Answer

In general, there are no restrictions under UK law on the freedom to join or form groups which do not constitute conspiracies, although, equally, there is little likelihood of legal redress if a person is excluded from a group or prevented from joining one. However, in two areas, freedom of association is subject to constraints.

A number of specific statutory provisions place limits on the freedom to join or support groups associated with the use of violence for political ends. The most general restriction arises under s 2 of the Public Order Act 1936, which prohibits the formation of military or quasi-military organisations. Few prosecutions have been brought under this provision. The last successful one was in *Jordan and Tyndall* (1963). The defendants were both members of a fascist group called Spearhead. They engaged in various activities, which included practising foot drill and storing sodium chloride, with the probable aim of using it to make bombs.

Under s 2(1)(a), a group organised, trained or equipped in order to allow it to usurp the function of the army or police would fall within this prohibition against quasi-military groups, thus possibly catching vigilante groups, such as the Guardian Angels (a group organised with the object of preventing crime on underground railways).

By far the most important restrictions on political association relate to the proscription powers in Pt II of the Terrorism Act 2000 (which develop powers originally found in the Prevention of Terrorism Acts). The Secretary of State has a power to proscribe groups that he or she identifies as being 'concerned in terrorism'. This is a wide power. 'Concerned in' is a loose phrase: an organisation need not engage in terrorism itself; it is enough if it promotes or encourages it. Also, the term 'terrorism' is widely defined. It involves intimidating threats or actions aimed at political, religious or ideological ends and, though the types of threat include the use of serious violence against persons, they can also include non-violent means such as computer hacking. Proscribed groups are listed in Sched 2 to the Act. At first they were limited to paramilitary groups connected to the politics of Northern Ireland, but the list is now dominated by international terrorist groups including Al-Qa'ida. Part II of the 2000 Act then goes on to create a range of offences defined in respect of proscribed organisations; these include membership and various forms of supportive activity.

The decision to proscribe is not, itself, subject to judicial review (*R (Kurdistan Workers Party) v Secretary of State for the Home Department* (2002)). However, the 2000 Act introduces for the first time (it was not available under predecessor legislation aimed mainly at Northern Ireland) a right of appeal against the Secretary of State's refusal to 'deproscribe' an organisation. Under s 5 of the Act, appeals will go to a specially constituted Proscribed Organisations Appeal Commission (POAC) and from thence on a point of law to the Court of Appeal. There will, therefore, now be some judicial control over this area, in which the courts have in the past shown reluctance to become involved. In *McEldowney v Forde* (1971), for example, an order was made under statutory instrument banning republican clubs or any like organisation, thus potentially outlawing all nationalist political parties. Nevertheless, the House of Lords preferred not to intervene, Lord Diplock stating that he would do so only if proscription were extended to bodies obviously distanced from republican views.

Proscription has been seen as providing a means of channelling expressions of outrage at initially IRA, now international, terrorist activities, thereby tending to prevent illegitimate expressions of public anger. It may discourage supporters of terrorist organisations and may signal political strength. On the other hand, it has been argued that these benefits are minimal and essentially cosmetic and are, in fact, 'counter productive, as it impedes criminal investigation and political discussion'. Lord Jellicoe's review of proscription under the Prevention of Terrorism Act 1989 doubted the value of proscription, considering that its value might be outweighed by its detrimental effects in terms of constraining the free expression of views about Northern Ireland. It should also be noted that membership or support for a proscribed organisation is not a necessary element in respect of many anti-terrorist offences or powers such as, for example, the detention without trial for foreign terrorist suspects under Pt IV of the Anti-Terrorism, Crime and Security Act 2001.

Under the HRA, decisions to proscribe and not to de-proscribe an organisation will be subject to Art 11 of the ECHR in Sched 1. The POAC, for instance, will need to take this provision, along with all the other scheduled Articles, into account. A ban will be an interference with the freedom in Art 11(1) and so the issue will be whether the ban can be upheld under the provisions of Art 11(2). The interests of national security, the prevention of crime and protecting the rights of others are purposes that such a ban is likely to serve. There may be issues about whether the width of the definition of 'terrorism' allows the proscription provisions in the Act to meet the 'prescribed by law' test in Art 11(2); though, in line with *Brogan v UK* (1989), the Court of Human Rights may find that the test is satisfied in so far as, in any particular case, terrorism is used to describe activities which can be identified with some precision and which are offences.

Convention issues are most likely to arise in relation to the proportionality of any ban – broadly speaking, whether it can be said to be necessary in the sense of serving a pressing social need in a way which minimises the consequential impact on individual rights. Here, much depends upon the particular facts of any case. There are some pointers from the Court of Human Rights. Cases involving both freedom of association and of expression (Art 10) show the Court upholding these freedoms most strongly in the context of political speech. *United Communist Party of Turkey v Turkey* (1998) is an example of a case in which the Court stresses the importance of political pluralism, freedom of political association and expression, in an effective democracy. On the facts of the case, this seems to require States, through their law, not to ban political organisations which are seeking radical and constitutional changes and which, whilst not inciting violence, advocate their cause against a background of violence. Banning organisations which incite violence is, however, likely to be compatible with the provisions of Art 11(2). Furthermore, any genuine 'terrorist' organisation will find it difficult to mount a human rights case given Art 17, which prohibits using the Convention to uphold a freedom to abuse the rights of others. Whether the organisation does incite violence will depend upon the particular facts and how they are assessed. One issue, which has recently divided the Court, concerns the extent to which a court's focus should be on the literal meaning of the words, etc, that a person or organisation uses, or whether it is the context in which words are read and understood that should be mainly in issue (see, for example, *Baskaya and Okçuoglu v Turkey* (2001), where the dissenting judges stressed the latter approach). Such issues will need to be taken into account by the POAC as it determines the proportionality of any refusal to de-proscribe.

The decisions of the POAC can be appealed, on a point of law, to the Court of Appeal, not only by the applicant but also by the government. In the context of the detention of foreign terrorist suspects without trial, the Court of Appeal has overturned, in the government's favour, a decision by the Special Immigration Appeal Commission and the same could be done in respect of decisions by the POAC. It is possible that the Court of Appeal will adopt a more cautious, executive-friendly approach to anti-terrorism cases than the specialist body established to deal with the cases at first instance. A right of appeal, at least by the applicant, may, however, be necessary to ensure that the procedures satisfy Art 6 of the Convention.

Under s 13 of the Terrorism Act 2000, it is an offence to wear any item which arouses a reasonable apprehension that a person is a member or supporter of a proscribed organisation. This provision is obviously aimed at preventing such organisations arousing public support. A previous version of this offence was invoked in *DPP v Whelan* (1975) against leaders of a provisional Sinn Fein protest march against internment in Northern Ireland, all of whom wore black berets, while some wore dark glasses, dark clothing and carried Irish flags. It was found that, first, something must be 'worn' as apparel and, secondly, that it must be a uniform. Something might amount to a uniform if it was worn by a number of persons in order to signify their association with each other or it was commonly used by a certain organisation. By this means, the third requirement that the uniform shall signal the wearer's association with a particular political organisation can also be satisfied. Alternatively, it may be satisfied by consideration of the occasion on which the uniform was worn without the need to refer to the past history of the organisation. The justification for retention of these provisions is doubtful as they clearly overlap with those under s 1 of the POA 1936. These powers have, in effect, been enhanced by s 60AA of the Criminal Justice and Public Order Act 1994, introduced by the Anti-Terrorism, Crime and Security Act 2001, which gives police, in circumstances where serious violence is apprehended, the power to order removal of clothing being worn in order to conceal identity; of course such clothing may, simultaneously, be clothing with political significance or expressing political or religious affiliation.

Non-violent, constitutional politics takes place through the agency of political parties. Under the Political Parties, Elections and Referendums Act

2000, political parties that want to participate in elections are now subject to restraints on their freedom of association. They must register with the Electoral Commission, adopt a certain form of organisation and accept significant restraints on their powers to raise money and spend it on election campaigns. These restraints are aimed at eliminating corruption and ensuring the fairness of elections. They are likely to be compatible with Convention rights.

Apart from groups associated with violence, restrictions on freedom of association have been at issue in relation to trade union membership. Three issues arise in this context: freedom not to join a trade union; freedom to choose between unions; and the limits of the basic freedom to belong to a union. The first has been very controversial in British politics as it involves the closed shop. The issue was considered by the European Court of Human Rights (ECtHR) in *Young, James and Webster v UK* (1981), which involved a challenge to the closed shop agreement between British Rail and the unions. The applicants disagreed with the political activities of trade unions, refused to join the union stipulated under the agreement and were dismissed. They claimed that their dismissal constituted an infringement of Art 11 of the ECHR.

The ECtHR was careful not to say that all closed shop agreements would violate Art 11. The right to join a trade union in Art 11(1) did not import a similarly weighted negative right not to join a union. However, under UK law at the time, there was only one ground, a refusal based on religious belief, for not joining a union under a closed shop agreement. Confining itself to the specific facts of the case, the Court held that the existence of only one narrow ground to refuse membership meant that an individual's freedom of choice had been so abridged that a violation of Art 11 had occurred. UK law has now changed considerably so that, today, dismissal for refusal to join a union will be unlawful whatever the grounds on which the refusal is based (s 152 of the Trade Union and Labour Relations (Consolidation) Act 1992).

On the issue of whether an employee may join the union of his choice, the ECtHR has again emphasised that States have a wide margin of appreciation over the practices that are permitted, so long as the essence of the right to freedom of association is preserved and some element of real choice is maintained for the applicant. So long as there is no stark choice between continuing employment or union membership, detrimental arrangements, such as requiring a person to work at a different depot, which are consequences of the applicant's choice of union, are unlikely to violate Art 11 (see *Sibson v UK* (1993)). The flexible position under the Convention may be compared with that under the International Covenant on Economic, Social and Cultural Rights, which asserts (though, for some commentators, as an aspiration rather than 'hard' law) a 'right to join the trade union *of his choice*'.

Any outlawing of trade union membership as such would constitute a clear breach of Art 11. However, the Conservative governments of 1979 to 1997 took a range of measures that restricted union rights in various ways including, for example, on their internal organisation, on the need to elect all senior officials and on the use of funds for political purposes. There were also significant and complex restrictions on their ability to call their members out on strike. These restrictions have not generally been challenged under Art 11, and it can be noted that in recent cases, the ECtHR has emphasised the wide margin of appreciation enjoyed by States over the regulation of union membership given the basic right of freedom of association (see *Gustafsson v Sweden* (1996) and *AB Kurt Kellermann v Sweden* (2003)).

Certain bodies, such as the army under Queen's Regulations, the police under s 64 of the Police Act 1996 and certain public officials, have traditionally been debarred from union membership, but this group was enlarged when civil servants working at GCHQ were de-unionised. The Minister for the Civil Service, the Prime Minister, Margaret Thatcher, gave an instruction by means of an Order in Council to vary the terms of service of the staff at GCHQ, with the effect that staff would no longer be permitted to join national trade unions. The ban was challenged on the ground that she had been under a duty to act fairly by consulting those concerned before issuing it.

In the GCHQ case (*Council of Civil Service Unions v Minister for the Civil Service* (1984)), the House of Lords held that previous practice had created a legitimate expectation of prior consultation before altering the terms of service. However, they refused a remedy on the grounds that the government had acted in the interests of national security and this outweighed the duty to act fairly. The decision was challenged at Strasbourg as a breach of Arts 11 and 13. However, the Commission of Human Rights found against the union primarily on the basis of the second sentence of Art 11(2), which permits 'lawful restrictions on the exercise of freedom of association by members of the administration of the State'.

Article 11 has been similarly unhelpful to the thousands of civil servants, local government officers, police officers and other officials who are banned by their terms of employment or by statute from various forms of political activity, mainly taking an active role in political parties or becoming a member of legislative assemblies and local councils. Such restrictions on freedom of association and political freedom are said to be justified in order to maintain the impartiality of the public service and the proper functioning in the public interest of elected legislative assemblies. They have been widely criticised as wide-ranging and disproportionate restrictions on political freedom, which include far too many officials than is necessary. In *Ahmed v UK* (1999), however, the ECtHR accepted the legitimacy and proportionality of the statutory ban imposed on certain types of local government officers and found there was no violation of Art 11.

In conclusion, it is clear that the extent to which the UK 'affords recognition' to freedom of association has been subject to major change. Most importantly, as we have seen, the courts and other relevant public bodies must now approach the matter in terms of the rights to freedom of association and expression found in Arts 11 and 10 of Sched 1 to the HRA 1998. Prior to the Act, in a case such as *McEldowney v Forde* (1971), the basic question was whether the minister, in banning the Republican Clubs, had adopted a policy which was within the range of actions that were reasonably available to him. Under the Act, where there has been a restriction of such a freedom, there is now a clear burden on the State to satisfy the court that the restriction is justified in terms of it having a proper legal basis, being for a legitimate purpose and, on its individual facts, being a proportionate restriction. This should mean that the judicial (and quasi-judicial, applying such a term to the POAC) scrutiny should be much more intense and more capable of being grounded in the independent, rights-aware judgment of the court than before. This applies to the trade union issues as much as to the anti-terrorism issues. Regarding the latter, however, there is evidence (for example, in the detention without trial case, *A v Secretary of State for the Home Department* (2002)) that the courts are showing considerable deference to the State on the question of the extent of a threat to national security and this may, perhaps, show itself in proscription cases too. Similarly, the trade union cases mentioned and also political restriction cases such as *Ahmed v UK* (1999) demonstrate that, compatibly with the Convention, States enjoy a wide margin of appreciation in respect of freedom of association.

Question 15

Citizens of Southton are very concerned about plans to build a nuclear power station on the outskirts of the town. On Saturday morning, Brenda, a citizen of Southton, holds a meeting in Southton Town Hall in order to discuss the matter, which is attended by 100 Southton residents. The meeting becomes heated and Brenda suggests that they should all march at once to the town square (half a mile away at the head of the main road through the town, which leads to the shopping centre) in order to gain more publicity for their cause. The group sets off, Brenda leading. Brenda asks Philip to bring up the rear of the procession.

As the group moves down the main road and nears the town square, two police officers, Elaine and George, approach Brenda and tell her that she must disperse part of the group because it is holding up traffic and may cause other pedestrians to move off the pavement into the road. Brenda does not comply with the request. The procession arrives at the town square and Brenda begins to address the meeting. George again asks Brenda to disperse half the group and, further, to re-site the meeting on the outskirts of the town. She refuses, and George then informs her that he is arresting her for failing to comply with his orders. Brenda calls on Philip to continue the meeting and he moves towards the front of the group.

Seeing the arrest of Brenda, the group becomes angry. Encouraged by Philip, the group spreads out across the road, largely blocking the road and the pavement. Philip, with some of its members, calls on shoppers entering the main road not to go on, but to join the demonstration. George calls on Philip to disperse part of the group, but is ignored. Some shoppers join in, but others attempt to push past the demonstrators. One of the demonstrators, Roger, shouts and swears at the shoppers who are attempting to push past. He waves his fists threateningly at them and calls on other members of the group not to allow them to pass. Elaine and George move to arrest Philip and Roger.

Consider the criminal liability (if any) incurred by Brenda, Philip and Roger.

Answer plan

This question is confined to criminal liability incurred by members of the assembly; therefore, other possible issues, such as the lawfulness of any of the arrests and the question of breach of the peace, need not be considered. This question raises a large number of issues which typically appear on exam papers.

The essential matters to be discussed are:

- notice requirements under s 11 of the Public Order Act (POA) 1986;
- 'triggers' under ss 12 and 14 of the Act;
- conditions which can be imposed under ss 12 and 14 on processions and assemblies;
- liability which may arise under ss 5 and 4 as amended;
- public nuisance;
- obstruction of the highway under s 137 of the Highways Act 1980;
- relevance of Arts 10 and 11 of the European Convention on Human Rights (ECHR) as incorporated into UK law under the HRA 1998; relevant Strasbourg jurisprudence.

Answer

Liability in this case arises mainly under the POA 1986 (hereinafter 'the Act'), but common law provisions will also be highly relevant. The possible criminal liability incurred by Brenda, Philip and Roger will be considered in turn. The effect of Arts 10 and 11 of the ECHR, as incorporated into UK law under the HRA, will be taken into account at relevant points.

Under s 11 of the Act, advance notice of a procession must be given if it falls within one of three categories. The march from the town hall falls within s 11(1)(a), as it is intended to demonstrate opposition to the building of the power station. As no notice of the march was given, Brenda may have committed an offence under s 11(7)(a) of the Act, as she is the organiser of the march. However, the notice requirement does not apply under s 11(1) if it was not reasonably practicable to give any advance notice. This provision was intended to exempt spontaneous demonstrations such as this one from the notice requirements, but is defective due to the use of the word 'any'. This word would suggest that a phone call made five minutes before the march sets off would fulfil the requirements, thereby exempting very few marches. Although the march sets off suddenly, it is possible that Brenda had time to make such a phone call; on a strict interpretation of s 11, she is therefore in breach of the notice requirements, as it was reasonably practicable for her to fulfil them.

However, it can be argued that the word 'any' should not be interpreted so strictly as to exclude spontaneous processions where a few minutes was available to give notice, because to do so would defeat the intention behind including the provision. If read in combination with the requirements as to giving notice by hand or in writing, it should be interpreted to mean any written notice. If it were not so interpreted, it might be argued that s 11 breaches the guarantee of freedom of expression or freedom of assembly under Arts 10 or 11 of the Convention since it fails to exempt spontaneous marches from liability – even including peaceful ones. Since s 3 of the HRA requires that, where it is possible to do so, statutes should be interpreted so as to conform with the UK's Convention obligations, s 11 should be interpreted in so far as possible in accordance with Arts 10 or 11. Following this argument, liability will not arise under s 11.

Brenda may further incur liability under s 12(4) of the Act, as she was the organiser of a public procession, but failed to comply with the condition imposed by Elaine to disperse part of the group. Elaine can impose conditions on the procession only if one of the four 'triggers' under s 12(1) is present. The third of these, that the police officer in question must reasonably believe that 'serious disruption to the life of the community' may be caused by the procession, may arguably arise. The group of 100 citizens was marching down the main street of the town; Elaine's fear that traffic may be obstructed or passers-by forced into the road may found a reasonable apprehension that the life of the community will be disrupted, and it is arguable that such disruption may be termed serious. On this argument, Elaine is entitled to impose conditions on the march.

The condition imposed must relate to the disruption apprehended. This may be said of the requirement to disperse half the group; Brenda will therefore incur liability under s 12(4), unless she can show that the failure arose due to circumstances outside her control. Although the powers of an organiser to disperse members of a march are limited, it is clear that Brenda made no effort at all to fulfil the condition. It is therefore argued that she has committed the offence under s 12(4).

Brenda may further incur liability under s 14(4) of the Act, as she was the organiser of a public assembly, but failed to comply with the condition imposed by the most senior police officer present at the scene (who can be a constable) to re-site the assembly and disperse part of the group. It should be noted that as the group was in a public place and comprised more than 20 persons, it constituted a public assembly under s 16 of the Act. George can impose conditions on the assembly only if one of four 'triggers' under s 14(1) is present. These are identical to those arising under s 12(1) and the third of these will again be considered as the easiest to satisfy in the circumstances. It will be argued that, at the point of imposing the condition, the behaviour of the assembly did not fulfil the terms of the 'trigger', although it may have done so at a later stage. Unlike the march, there is no evidence that, at this stage, the assembly held up traffic. In the case of *Reid* (1987), it was determined that the 'triggers' should be strictly interpreted: the words used should not be diluted. In the instant case, a group of 100 citizens were gathered on the street in the morning on a Saturday; although it could be argued that such a circumstance might cause some disruption in the community (in terms of blockage of the pavement), it is less clear that a reasonable person would expect the disruption to be serious. Such a strict interpretation would appear to accord with the demand that the guarantee of peaceful assembly under Art 11 should only suffer interference where that can be justified as necessary in a democratic society – a demand that has been strictly interpreted (see *Ezelin v France* (1991)). On this argument, George had no power to impose conditions on the assembly; no liability therefore arises under s 14(4). The question of whether the failure to comply with the condition imposed arose due to circumstances beyond Brenda's control need not, therefore, be addressed.[1]

Brenda may, however, have incurred liability under s 137 of the Highways Act 1980, which provides that a person will be guilty of an offence if he 'without lawful authority or excuse in any way wilfully obstructs the free passage of the highway'. In *Nagy v Weston* (1966), it was held that a reasonable user of the highway will constitute a lawful excuse and that, in order to determine its reasonableness or otherwise, the length of the obstruction must be considered, its purpose, the place where it occurred and whether an actual or potential obstruction took place. In *Arrowsmith v Jenkins* (1963), it was determined that minor obstruction of traffic can lead to liability under the Highways Act. The assembly in question was held in a certain street which linked up two main roads, with the result that the street was completely blocked for five minutes and partly blocked for 15 minutes. The organiser was convicted. However, the question of the purpose of the obstruction, mentioned in *Nagy v Weston*, was given greater prominence in *Hirst and Agu v Chief Constable of West Yorkshire* (1986) – it was said that courts should have regard to the freedom to demonstrate. On that basis, the purpose of an assembly as a means of legitimate protest may suggest that it can amount to a reasonable user of the highway.[2] Some support for this approach is to be found in the House of Lords' decision in *DPP v Jones* (1999), where two members of the majority specifically held that there is a right of peaceful assembly on the public highway, so long as the assembly is peaceful and provided it does not obstruct the public's primary right of passage. The interpretation in *Hirst* appears to be in accord with the demand that peaceful protest should only be interfered with where that is necessary to serve a legitimate aim under Arts 10 and 11 of the ECHR. The police and courts must abide by that demand under s 6 of the HRA. The level of obstruction caused by Brenda's procession may well, therefore, be the crucial factor in deciding on her liability.

Brenda may also have incited the group to commit a public nuisance by blocking the highway. However, according to *Clarke* (1964), the disruption caused must amount to an unreasonable use of the highway in order to found liability for public nuisance. Thus, once obstruction has been shown, the question of reasonableness arises. However, as has already been pointed out, it is arguable that to cause a minor disruption for a legitimate purpose does not constitute an unreasonable use of the highway. It is unlikely that a user of the highway could be reasonable under the Highways Act but, nevertheless, able to amount to a public nuisance. This seemed to be accepted in *Gillingham Borough Council v Medway Dock Co* (1992). On this argument, liability for public nuisance will not arise.

Philip's possible criminal liability will now be considered. He may incur liability under s 12(4) in respect of his part in organising the march. The Act does not define the term 'organiser' and there is no post-Act case law on the issue; therefore, the issue as to the meaning of the term cannot be settled with certainty. However, it is submitted that, on the dictionary definition of the term, Philip is an organiser. This contention is supported by the ruling from

Flockhart v Robinson (1950) that a person who indicated the route to be followed should be designated an organiser as well as the person who planned the route. Thus, it appears likely that the term includes stewards. (If, in the alternative, it could be argued that Philip's role is too uncertain to allow him to fall within the term 'organiser', he could nevertheless incur liability under s 12(5) as a member of the march, subject to the argument below.) Therefore, the argument for liability on Brenda's part under s 12(4) will also apply to Philip, unless he was unaware of the condition imposed. It appears that Philip was at the back of the group when the condition was imposed and therefore it seems possible that he may have been unaware of it, in which case, he will not attract liability under s 12(4) of the Act.

On the assumption that Philip is a co-organiser, the above arguments as to Brenda's liability arising under s 137 of the Highways Act 1980 or for public nuisance will be relevant, but it is argued that they will fail to establish liability on the basis that, although the demonstration does partly block the road and shoppers are impeded, the demonstration may still be termed legitimate and therefore not unreasonable. Philip's actions in trying to persuade shoppers to join the demonstration may be viewed as in keeping with the aims of a legitimate protest.

Philip may incur liability under s 14(4) as an organiser of an assembly which is in breach of a condition imposed. When Philip took over leadership of the assembly, the situation changed; he encouraged the group to block the street and stop passers by. It is arguable that the fourth 'trigger', arising under s 14(1)(b), may have been fulfilled. It consists of an evaluation of the purpose of the assembly rather than an apprehension that a particular state of affairs may arise. The senior police officer present must reasonably believe that the purpose of the assembly is 'the intimidation of others with a view to compelling them not to do an act they have a right to do or to do an act they have a right not to do'.

Possibly the third 'trigger' could also apply to this situation, but that point need not be considered because the fourth 'trigger' seems to be most clearly indicated: the group are trying to prevent some persons entering the road leading to the shopping centre and are therefore trying to prevent persons doing something they have a right to do (presumably in the sense that there is a right to pass along the highway). The question is whether their actions have gone beyond what might be acceptable as part of a legitimate demonstration and could suggest an intention to intimidate. As noted above, it was determined in *Reid* (1987) that the 'triggers' should be strictly interpreted. In *Reid*, the defendants shouted, raised their arms and waved their fingers; it was determined that such behaviour might cause discomfort, but not intimidation, and that the two concepts could not be equated. In *News Group Newspapers Ltd v SOGAT* (1982), it was held that mere abuse and shouting did not amount to a threat of violence for the purposes of intimidation under s 7 of the Conspiracy and Protection of Property Act 1875. In the instant case, it could be argued that the group's behaviour in merely shouting at the shoppers could not amount to intimidation, but that in attempting to impede their passage, the behaviour crossed the boundary between discomfort and intimidation. On that basis, it appears that George had the power to impose conditions on the assembly.

Philip made no effort to comply with the condition imposed and will therefore incur liability under s 14(4). He may also incur liability under s 14(6) as inciting others to commit the offence under s 14(5) of taking part in a public assembly and knowingly failing to comply with the condition imposed. However, this point cannot be settled, as it is unclear from the facts whether or not other members of the group were aware of the condition imposed.

Following the above argument, Roger may incur liability under s 14(5). Moreover, he may incur liability under s 14(6) as an organiser, in that he calls on other members of the group to impede shoppers. He may be said to have taken on the role of organiser at this point. However, these points cannot be settled, as it is unclear from the facts whether or not Roger was aware of the condition imposed.

Roger may further incur liability under s 5(1) of the Act in respect of his behaviour towards the shoppers. In order to show this, his behaviour must amount to 'threatening, abusive or insulting words or behaviour or disorderly behaviour' which takes place in the hearing or sight of a person likely to be caused harassment, alarm or distress thereby. The three terms used must be given their ordinary meaning (*Brutus v Cozens* (1973)). The word 'likely' imports an objective test into the section: it is necessary to show that a person was present at the scene, but not that he or she actually experienced the feelings in question. Had Roger confined himself to abuse, it could be argued that his behaviour would be likely merely to irritate the shoppers. However, his use of threatening gestures might be likely to cause the stronger emotion connoted by the concept of harassment. Moreover, Roger appears to satisfy the *mens rea* requirement under s 6(4); it appears probable that he is aware or intends that his words or behaviour are threatening, although possibly not abusive or insulting.

However, a defence under s 5(3)(c) is available to Roger if it can be argued that his behaviour was reasonable. An argument for giving a wide interpretation to the term 'reasonable' can be supported on the basis that in so far as possible s 5 should be interpreted in accordance with Art 11 of the Convention. As already noted, a statute should be interpreted in conformity with the Convention if at all possible (s 3 of the HRA 1998). Whether a forceful demonstration which included some disorderly behaviour could fall within the terms of Art 11, which extend only to peaceful protest, is, however, debatable. Possibly the same could be said of Art 10; Art 10 was used in *Percy v DPP* (2002) under s 6 of the HRA to argue that liability should not arise under s 5 in respect of an entirely peaceful protest. However, it may be argued that Roger is not acting in an entirely peaceful manner. Thus, even if the term 'reasonable' is widely interpreted, it is arguable that it would not appear wide enough to encompass the behaviour in question which, it seems, went beyond persuasion and became coercion. It is submitted that this defence would fail. It appears then that Roger may incur liability under s 5.

It might be argued that Philip will also incur liability under s 5, but this argument would probably fail; his behaviour may cause discomfort or inconvenience to the shoppers, but it is argued that the words of s 5 connote a higher level of distress, especially when interpreted in conformity with Art 10 (see *Percy v DPP* (2002)).

Roger's behaviour may also support an argument that he has committed an offence under s 4, which is couched in the same terms as s 5, except for the omission of 'disorderly behaviour' and with the added need to show that somebody was likely to apprehend the use of immediate violence by Roger or another, or that he intended to arouse such an apprehension. Both these possibilities may be present. The behaviour in question must be specifically directed towards another person. Following *Ambrose* (1973), rude or offensive words or behaviour may not necessarily be insulting, while mere swearing may not fall within the meaning of 'abusive'. However, Roger's behaviour in waving his fists may fall within the meaning of the term 'threatening'. Possibly, in the circumstances – two police officers were present and Roger does not seem directly to approach the shoppers – they might be unlikely to apprehend immediate violence. However, it seems that Roger intended his words to provoke the rest of the group into using some force against the shoppers. Following the ruling in *Horseferry Road Metropolitan Stipendiary Magistrate ex p Siadatan* (1991), 'violence' in this context must mean immediate and unlawful violence. This was confirmed in *Winn v DPP* (1992). It is concluded that Roger's behaviour does not satisfy this strict test,[3] although it may fall within s 4A (inserted by s 154 of the CJPOA 1994), which creates liability for intentionally causing harassment, alarm or distress.

Notes

1   Had the argument under s 14(4) been resolved differently, Brenda might have fallen within the provision under s 14(6), as she called on Philip to take over as leader, thereby arguably inciting him to commit the offence under s 14(5) of taking part in an assembly and knowingly failing to comply with a condition imposed.

2   This argument is supported by the provisions of the POA; Pt II of the Act recognises the existence of marches and processions and therefore by necessary

implication permits them so long as its provisions are complied with. On this basis, the brevity of the obstruction and its purpose as part of a legitimate protest suggest that the march amounted to a reasonable use of the highway.

3   It may be worth considering whether members of the group, including Philip and Roger, may incur liability in respect of the offence of affray under s 3 of the Act. In order to establish an affray, it must first be shown that the defendant used or threatened unlawful violence towards another and, secondly, that his conduct was such as would cause a person of reasonable firmness present at the scene to fear for his personal safety. As Roger uses threatening gestures, it may be argued that the first limb of s 3(1) is fulfilled, but a strong argument can be advanced that the second is not; due to the fact that the gestures are part of a demonstration, it is probable that a person of reasonable firmness would not fear unlawful violence, even though such a person might feel somewhat distressed. In *Taylor v DPP* (1973), Lord Hailsham, speaking of the common law offence, said 'the degree of violence ... must be such as to be calculated to terrify a person of reasonably firm character'. The Act of course refers to 'fear', as opposed to terror, but this ruling suggests that 'fear' should be interpreted restrictively. On this argument, no liability will arise in respect of s 3.

Question 16

Clare is a member of the City Youth Club. She and 40 other teenagers attend the youth club on Friday evening and are told that it has to close down that night due to sudden drastic cuts in funding imposed by the Council. All the teenagers immediately walk out of the club in protest and assemble on the pavement outside it. While they are angrily discussing the closure of the club, Edwin and Fred, two police officers in uniform, approach the group.

Clare begins to address the group, telling them that they must remain peaceful in order to air their grievances more effectively. Edwin tells her that she must disperse part of the group if she wants to hold a meeting. She asks some of the teenagers to leave but takes no action when they make no attempt to do so. The meeting continues and becomes more heated. Clare then suggests that they should march through the town.

The group sets off, Clare leading. Traffic is held up for 10 minutes as the group enters the town. Edwin asks Clare to disperse half the group of marchers. Clare asks two of the teenagers to leave but takes no further action when they fail to comply with her request. Edwin then says that she will have to give him the names and addresses of the members of the group. She refuses, and Edwin then informs Clare that he is arresting her for failing to comply with his orders.

Consider the criminal liability (if any) incurred by Clare.

Answer plan

This is a fairly typical problem question dealing with issues which arise mainly, but not entirely, under the Public Order Act (POA) 1986 in respect of marches and assemblies. It also requires an awareness of the provisions of Arts 10 and 11 as interpreted at Strasbourg, and of their potential impact on UK law under the HRA 1998. If any of the statutory provisions considered leave open any room at all for a different interpretation (not only on the grounds of ambiguity), they should be interpreted in harmony with Arts 10 and 11 of the European Convention on Human Rights (ECHR).

It is very important to note that the answer is confined to the question of possible criminal liability incurred by Clare. Possible tortious liability incurred by Clare or the police officers is, therefore, irrelevant, as is the possibility that Clare could seek to challenge the police decisions by way of judicial review. The demands of Arts 10 and 11 as received into UK law under the HRA will be relevant at a number of points.

The essential matters to be discussed are:

- introduction – mention of need to consider the HRA and the demands of Arts 10 and 11;
- notice requirements under s 11 of the POA (hereinafter 'the Act'); s 3 of the HRA;
- 'triggers' under ss 12 and 14 of the Act; s 3 of the HRA;
- conditions which can be imposed under ss 12 and 14 of the Act on processions and assemblies;
- liability which may arise under ss 12 and 14;
- public nuisance; s 6 of the HRA;
- obstruction of the highway under s 137 of the Highways Act 1980; s 3 of the HRA;
- conclusions – dependent on interpretation of statutory provisions based on demands of Arts 10 and 11 as received into UK law under the HRA.

Answer

Liability in this case arises mainly, but not exclusively, under the POA 1986 (hereinafter 'the Act'). Since the question demands consideration of possible restrictions on protest and assembly, the requirements of Arts 10 and 11 as incorporated into UK law under the HRA 1998 must be taken into account. The liability of both possible defendants will be considered in turn, beginning with Clare.

Under s 11 of the Act, advance notice of a procession must be given if it falls within one of three categories. This march falls within s 11(1)(a) as it is intended to demonstrate opposition to the action of the local authority in closing the youth club. As no notice of the march was given, Clare may have committed an offence under s 11(7)(a) of the Act as she is the organiser of the march. However, the notice requirement does not apply under s 11(1) if it was not reasonably practicable to give any advance notice. This provision was intended to exempt spontaneous demonstrations such as this one from the notice requirements, but is defective due to the use of the word 'any'. This word would suggest that a phone call made five minutes before the march sets off would fulfil the requirements, thereby exempting very few marches. Although the march sets off suddenly, it is possible that Clare had time to make such a phone call; on a strict interpretation of s 11, she is, therefore, in breach of the notice requirements as it was reasonably practicable for her to fulfil them. However, it can be argued that notice was informally and impliedly given to the police officers already on the scene or, alternatively, that the term 'reasonably practicable' should be interpreted, under s 3 of the HRA, so as to exempt spontaneous processions from liability even where a few minutes was available to give notice, because to fail do so would be out of harmony with Art 11, which protects freedom of peaceful assembly (*Ezelin v France* (1991)). Thus, on either argument, liability will not arise under s 11.

Clare may be liable under s 14(4) of the Act as she was the organiser of a public assembly but failed to comply with the condition imposed by the most senior police officer present at the scene (Edwin) to disperse part of the group. (It should be noted that, as the group was in a public place and comprised more than 20 persons, it constituted a public assembly under s 16 of the Act.) Edwin can impose conditions on the assembly only if one of four 'triggers' under s 14(1) is present. The third of these, and arguably the easiest to satisfy, provides that the police officer in question must reasonably believe that 'serious disruption to the life of the community' may be caused by the assembly. In the case of *Reid* (1987), it was determined that the 'triggers' should be strictly interpreted: the words used should not be diluted. Clearly, it would be in accordance with Art 11, and indeed Art 10 (see *Steel v UK* (1998)) to adopt such an interpretation, under s 3 of the HRA, since otherwise an interference with assemblies outside the legitimate aims of Arts 10 and 11, para 2 might be enabled to occur. In the instant case, a group of over 40 teenagers are gathered on the street, in the evening; even if it could be argued that such a circumstance might cause some disruption in the community (in terms of noise or blockage of the pavement), it is less clear that a reasonable person would expect the disruption to be serious. On this argument, Edwin had no power to impose conditions on the assembly; no liability, therefore, arises under s 14(4). The question whether the failure to comply with the condition imposed arose due to circumstances beyond Clare's control need not, therefore, be addressed.

Will Clare incur liability under s 12(4) of the Act, as she was the organiser of a public procession but failed to comply with the conditions imposed by Edwin to provide the names and addresses of the group or to disperse part of it? Edwin can impose conditions on the procession only if one of the four 'triggers' under s 12(1) is present. The triggers are identical to those under s 14(1). The third of these may possibly arise. The group of teenagers was marching through the town; in such circumstances, it may be more readily argued that serious disruption to the life of the community may reasonably be apprehended. Such disruption could be argued for either on the basis that passers-by may be jostled by the group, especially if it has grown more excitable, or on the basis that traffic may be seriously disrupted. The fact that traffic has already been held up for 10 minutes may support a reasonable belief that such disruption may occur. Serious obstruction of the traffic might arguably amount to some disruption of the life of the community. Both possibilities taken together could found a reasonable apprehension that the life of the community will be seriously disrupted. However, courts are required under both ss 6 and 3 of the HRA to determine that the nature of the risk anticipated is one which would constitute one of the legitimate aims for limiting the primary rights under Arts 11 and 10. The vague and ambiguous phrase 'serious disruption to the life of the community' could be reinterpreted under s 3 of the HRA by reference to Art 11(2) and Art 10(2) of the Convention. The grounds for imposing the conditions would have to be justified, either on the basis of protecting 'the rights of others' or because the 'serious disruption' feared amounted to 'disorder' for the purposes of those second paras. Alternatively, the discretion as to the imposition of the conditions in s 12 could be viewed narrowly (possibly on ordinary principles of statutory construction). It could be argued that the restrictions are necessary in order to protect the rights of others. However, arguably, they are disproportionate to that aim, bearing in mind the importance of freedom of assembly (*Ezelin*). In particular, a requirement to provide names and addresses appears disproportionate to the aim in view, since it is unclear that it could serve that aim. In order to avoid breaching Arts 10 and 11, a court which took this view could adopt a strict interpretation of s 12, finding either that the behaviour in question is not serious enough and/or that the conditions could not be viewed as 'necessary' (s 12(1)(b)).

On the other hand, a court could rely on *Christians Against Racism and Fascism v UK* (1980), in which a ban on a peaceful assembly was not found to breach Art 11. *A fortiori*, a mere imposition of conditions might be found to be proportionate within the terms of Art 11(2). Following this argument, Edwin would be entitled to impose conditions on the march. The conditions imposed would have to relate to the disruption apprehended; this may be said of the requirement to disperse half the group but not of the order that Clare should disclose the names and addresses of the group. Thus, liability may arise only in respect of the failure to comply with the former condition. Clare made some attempt to comply with it but did not succeed; she would, therefore, following this argument, incur liability under s 12(4) unless she can show that the failure arose due to circumstances outside her control. Although the powers of an organiser to disperse members of a march are limited, it may be argued that, in approaching only two members of the group, Clare made in any event a token effort only; it is therefore arguable that she has committed an offence under s 12(4).

Clare may further have incurred liability under s 137 of the Highways Act 1980, which provides that a person will be guilty of an offence if he 'without lawful authority or excuse in any way wilfully obstructs the free passage of the highway'. In *Nagy v Weston* (1965), it was held that a reasonable user of the highway will constitute a lawful excuse, and that, in order to determine its reasonableness or otherwise, the length of the obstruction must be considered, its purpose, the place where it occurs and whether an actual or potential obstruction took place. There is no evidence to suggest that the group assembled outside the youth club caused obstruction; however, the march did cause a brief obstruction of the highway. In *Arrowsmith v Jenkins* (1963), it was held that minor obstruction of traffic can lead to liability under the Highways Act. However, the question of the purpose of the obstruction, mentioned in *Nagy*, was given greater prominence in *Hirst and Agu v Chief Constable of West Yorkshire* (1986): it was said that courts should have regard to the freedom to demonstrate.

This approach was to an extent confirmed by *DPP v Jones* (1999), where the House of Lords recognised that a demonstration should not be treated as an improper use of the highway unless it causes undue disruption to other users. Such an approach is, of course, given added weight by the need for the courts to give appropriate weight, by virtue of s 3 of the HRA, to the rights of freedom of expression and assembly in Arts 10 and 11 of the Convention. One possibility would be to interpret the uncertain term 'excuse' in order to seek to ensure harmony between s 137 of the Highways Act and Arts 10 and 11 under s 3 of the HRA, since otherwise s 137 would allow interferences with peaceful, albeit obstructive, assemblies, arguably contrary to the findings of the ECtHR in *Steel* and in *Ezelin*. On this basis, the brevity of the obstruction and its purpose as part of a legitimate protest suggest that the march amounted to a reasonable use of the highway. The stronger argument seems to be that liability under the Highways Act for inciting the group to obstruct the highway will not be established.[1]

Clare may also have incited the group to commit a public nuisance by blocking the highway. However, according to *Clarke* (1964), the disruption caused must amount to an unreasonable use of the highway in order to found liability for public nuisance. Thus, once obstruction has been shown, the question of reasonableness arises. In this instance, there has been some obstruction of the highway for 10 minutes. However, as has already been pointed out, it is arguable that to cause such a minor disruption for a legitimate purpose does not constitute an unreasonable use of the highway. It is unlikely that a user of the highway could be reasonable under the Highways Act but nevertheless able to amount to a public nuisance. This seemed to be accepted in *Gillingham Borough Council v Medway Dock Co* (1992). This argument is strengthened by consideration of the duty of the court and the police officers under s 6 of the HRA to abide by the Convention rights which includes the right to freedom of assembly. On this argument, liability for public nuisance will not arise.

Thus, in conclusion, Clare is most likely to attract liability under s 12(4) of the Act, but this depends on the interpretation afforded to the term 'serious disruption' in s 12(1)(a) under s 3 of the HRA.

Note

1   It could be argued further that Clare's conduct could not be described as 'wilful', in the sense that, at the point when the obstruction is caused, Edwin appears to be giving some sanction to the march and Clare may be relying on his official connivance. Such a restrictive interpretation would offer a further means, under s 3 of the HRA, of limiting the application of s 137 to protesters.

Question 17

The Asian community in Northton become increasingly concerned about apparent racism in Northton City Council employment practices. A number of council workers have recently been made redundant; a disproportionate number of them are Asians. A group of 40 Asians decides to hold a demonstration outside the Civic Centre on the lawns and courtyard in front of it. On the day appointed, they assemble, appoint Ali and Rashid as their leaders, and shout at workers going into the Centre telling them not to go in but to join the demonstration. When the workers do not respond, some of the Asians, including Ali, become angrier; they shout and wave their fists threateningly at some of the workers but make no attempt to impede them physically. Some of the workers appear to be intimidated.

One of the Asians, Sharma, tries to persuade workers not to enter the Civic Centre and to support the anti-racist protest, but eventually becomes involved in a heated argument with a group of the white workers. He continues more angrily to attempt to persuade them not to enter; they threaten to beat him up if the Asian group continues with its efforts.

Three police officers arrive on the scene. One of them, John, arrests Sharma, stating that this is for breach of the peace since the group of white workers is about to become violent. Sharma tries to leave, pushing John aside in the process; John seizes Sharma's arm. Belinda, one of the police officers, orders Ali to disperse half of the group; when he makes no effort to comply, she says that she is arresting him for failing to comply with the order. She also orders Rashid to leave the area. He fails to do so.

Discuss.

Answer plan

This question is partly concerned with liability which may arise in respect of assemblies under the Public Order Act (POA) 1986 (hereinafter 'the Act') and under ss 68 and 69 of the Criminal Justice and Public Order Act (CJPOA) 1994. The common law power to prevent a breach of the peace is significant in the question. The statutory provisions considered should be interpreted in harmony with Arts 10 and 11 of the ECHR (and any other relevant Articles) under s 3 of the HRA; the common law doctrine of breach of the peace, which is relevant, must be interpreted and applied in accordance with the duty of the court under s 6 of the HRA. It should be borne in mind that the problem concerns an assembly only, and not a march. Further, the assembly is not taking place on the highway. Therefore, liability particularly associated with marches and with assemblies on the highway will not arise. Note that a broad, wide-ranging discussion is called for due to the use of the word 'discuss'.

Essentially, the following matters should be discussed:

- introduction – mention of the need to consider the HRA; demands of Arts 10 and 11 as received into UK law under the HRA;
- 'triggers' under s 14 of the Act;
- conditions which may be imposed under s 14; s 3 of the HRA;
- liability under ss 5, 4, 4A and 3 of the Act; s 3 of the HRA (ss 3 and 4 covered in the Notes);
- liability under ss 68 and 69 of the CJPOA 1994; s 3 of the HRA;
- arrest for breach of the peace; s 6 of the HRA; liability under s 89(1) of the Police Act 1996;
- liability in tort;
- conclusions.

Answer

Liability in this case may arise mainly, but not exclusively, under the POA 1986. Since the question demands consideration of possible restrictions on protest and assembly, the requirements of Arts 10 and 11 as received into UK law under the HRA must be taken into account. Article 14, which provides protection from discrimination in the context of another right, will also be considered, briefly.

Ali may attract liability under s 14(4) of the POA, as he was the organiser of a public assembly but failed to comply with the condition imposed by the most senior police officer present at the scene (where the officers are of equal rank, this condition will be fulfilled when one of them issues an order) to disperse half of the group. It should be noted that, as the group was in a public place and comprised more than 20 persons, it constituted a public assembly under s 16 of the Act. Belinda can impose conditions on the assembly only if one of four 'triggers' under s 14(1) is present. Under s 14(1)(a), the police officer in question must reasonably believe that serious public disorder, serious damage to property or serious disruption to the life of the community may be caused by the assembly. The fourth 'trigger', arising under s 14(1)(b), consists of an evaluation of the purpose of the assembly rather than an apprehension that a particular state of affairs may arise. The senior police officer present must reasonably believe that the purpose of the assembly is 'the intimidation of others with a view to compelling them not to do an act they have a right to do or to do an act they have a right not to do'.

Possibly the third 'trigger' could apply to this situation, but that point need not be considered because the fourth 'trigger' seems to be most clearly indicated: the Asians are trying to prevent persons entering the Civic Centre and are, therefore, trying to prevent persons doing something they have a right to do (presumably in the sense that there is a right to pass along the highway to a place of work); the question is whether their actions have gone beyond what might be acceptable as part of a legitimate demonstration and could suggest an intention to intimidate. In the case of *Reid* (1987), it was determined that the triggers should be strictly interpreted: the words used should not be diluted. In *Reid*, the defendants shouted, raised their arms and waved their fingers; it was determined that such behaviour might cause discomfort but not intimidation and that the two concepts could not be equated. In *News Group Newspapers Ltd v SOGAT* (1982), it was held that mere abuse and shouting did not amount to a threat of violence for the purposes of intimidation under s 7 of the Conspiracy and Protection of Property Act 1875. In the instant case, it could be argued that the Asians' behaviour in merely shouting at the Civic Centre workers could not amount to intimidation, but that, in making threatening gestures with their fists, it crossed the boundary between discomfort and intimidation.

However, since the imposition of conditions, the arrest of Ali and (potentially) the imposition of criminal liability under s 14 creates interferences with the rights under Arts 11 and 10 of assembly and expression (*Steel v UK* (1998)), it must be asked whether the demands of s 14 as applied in this instance are in accordance with those rights. One possibility is that s 14(1)(b) could be reinterpreted under s 3 of the HRA by reference to Arts 10 and 11 of the Convention. The interference it represents (since it allows for the imposition of conditions) would have to be justified on the basis of protecting 'the rights of others'. It could be argued that the restriction is necessary in order to protect the rights of others since that is precisely what s 14(1)(b) is aimed at and that the requirements of s 14 in terms of applicability to this situation are proportionate to that aim. In *Ezelin v France* (1991), the ECtHR considered the issue of proportionality under Art 11 and found that the freedom to take part in a peaceful assembly is of such importance that it cannot be restricted in any way, so long as the person concerned does not himself commit any reprehensible act. It may be argued that the intimidation of others is reprehensible and that therefore the tests under Art 11(2) (and Art 10(2)) are satisfied by the application of s 14 in this instance, without requiring its reinterpretation under s 3 HRA.

On that basis, it appears that Belinda had the power to impose a condition on the assembly and the condition itself appears to relate quite closely to the mischief in question – the intimidation.[1] Ali made no effort to comply with the condition imposed. The question whether the failure to comply with it arose due to circumstances beyond his control need not, therefore, be addressed. Ali's arrest therefore appears to be justified under s 14(7) and he is likely to incur liability under s 14(4). Other members of the Asian group who were aware of the condition may commit the offence under s 14(5).[2]

Ali, Rashid and possibly other members of the Asian group may also incur liability under s 68 of the CJPOA 1994. The section requires, first, that the defendant has trespassed. This seems to be satisfied since Ali, Rashid, etc, appear to have exceeded the terms of an implied licence to be in the courtyard, and the courtyard is not excluded from s 68, since it is arguably 'land in the open air' – it is clearly not part of the highway (s 68(5)(a)). Secondly, it must be shown that the defendant intended to disrupt or obstruct a lawful activity or intimidated persons so as to deter them from that activity. This last requirement may also be satisfied by the Asians' behaviour in shouting at the workers entering the Civic Centre. It may perhaps be inferred that Ali and others did intend to intimidate the workers since they make threatening gestures towards them. Rashid (and possibly other Asians aware of John's order that members of the assembly should disperse) may also commit the offence under s 69 of failing to leave land after a direction to do so is given, founded on a reasonable belief that the offence under s 68 is being committed. Belinda tells Rashid to leave the land and he refuses to do so.

However, these possibilities of liability under ss 68 and 69 must be considered in relation to the HRA. The ECtHR made a clear finding in *Steel* (1998), confirmed in *Hashman v UK* (2000), that protest which takes the form of physical obstruction nevertheless falls within the protection of Art 10 – and presumably Art 11. Thus, it is necessary to decide whether the interference with Ali's and others' Convention rights is justifiable under the second paragraphs of those Articles. If not, s 68 may require reinterpretation under s 3 so as to exclude behaviour such as that of Ali and Rashid, or possibly a declaration of incompatibility may eventually have to be made between s 68 and Arts 10 and 11 under s 4 of the HRA. In *Steel*, the Court appeared to be readily convinced of the necessity and proportionality of the interferences with the two direct action protests complained of by the first two applicants. In contrast, the Court in *Ezelin* (1991) found that it was impossible to justify interferences with the freedom of peaceful assembly unless the person exercising the freedom himself committed a 'reprehensible act'. In order to reconcile the two decisions, therefore, it must be assumed either that obstructive protest, while it does fall within at least Art 10, does not constitute that class of purely 'peaceful' protest which, according to *Ezelin*, 'cannot be restricted in any way' or that any restriction is more readily justifiable. It seems clear from the findings in *Steel* as to the first and second applicants, and from the Commission decision in *G v FRG* (1980), that where a protester is engaged in obstructive, albeit non-violent activity, arrest and imprisonment are in principle justifiable under the Convention. It is arguable therefore that s 68 is Convention-compliant under s 3 and that the imposition of liability in this instance is compatible with the duty of the court under s 6 of the HRA. On this basis, liability under s 69 would also be established, since it is dependent on establishing a reasonable belief that the offence under s 68 has been committed; this appears to be the case, bearing in mind that it has not been found necessary to reinterpret s 68 by reference to s 3 of the HRA.

It could also be argued that, in shouting and waving his fists at the Civic Centre workers, Ali and the other demonstrators may incur liability under s 5 of the POA. Their behaviour must amount to 'threatening, abusive or insulting words or behaviour or disorderly behaviour' which take place in the hearing or sight of a person likely to be caused harassment, alarm or distress thereby. These three terms must be given their ordinary meaning following *Brutus v Cozens* (1973). The word 'likely' imports an objective test into the section: it is necessary to show that a person was present at the scene but not that he or she actually experienced the feelings in question. They shout and gesture aggressively; this behaviour may clearly be termed disorderly, or even threatening, and it is arguable, given the width of the concept of harassment, that it would be likely to cause feelings of harassment, although probably not of alarm, to the workers. It appears then that the demonstrators may incur liability under s 5 subject to argument below as to the *mens rea* requirement under s 6(4). On the same argument, liability under s 4A of the POA may be established, assuming that they *intended* to cause harassment, etc, and did cause it.

However, it is necessary to consider whether ss 4A and 5, interpreted as covering the behaviour in question, are compatible with Arts 10 and 11 under s 3 of the HRA (see *Percy v DPP* (2001)). Compatibility may be achieved by affording a broad interpretation to the defence of reasonableness in both sections (s 5(3)(c) and 4A(3)(b)). It was determined in *DPP v Clarke* (1992) that the defence is to be judged objectively, and it will therefore depend on what a bench of magistrates considers reasonable. In that case, the behaviour of the protesters outside an abortion clinic was not found to be reasonable. The use of pictures and models of aborted foetuses appeared to contribute to this conclusion. This decision does not give much guidance to protesters seeking to determine beforehand the limits or meaning of 'reasonable' protest. As a deliberately ambiguous term, it obviously leaves enormous discretion to the judiciary to adopt approaches to its interpretation under s 3 of the HRA in accordance with Arts 10 and 11 as interpreted in *Steel*. Offensive words used by protesters could be found to fall within this defence on the basis that in the context of a particular demonstration which had a legitimate political aim, such behaviour was acceptable and therefore reasonable (*Percy v DPP* (2001)). However, in the context under discussion, the demonstrators appear to have intended to intimidate others, rather than to make points which others could find offensive. It is arguable that the instant behaviour would fall outside the meaning of 'reasonable', even bearing the requirements of Arts 10 and 11 in mind.

Under s 6(4), it must be established in respect of s 5 that the defendant intended his words, etc, to be threatening, abusive or insulting or was aware that they might be. Under s 4A, intent to cause harassment, etc, alone is needed. In *DPP v Clarke* (1992), it was found that to establish liability under s 5, it is insufficient to show only that the defendant intended or was aware that he might cause harassment, alarm or distress; it must also be shown that he intended his conduct to be threatening, abusive or insulting, or was aware that it might be. Both mental states have to be established independently. Thus, showing that the defendant was aware that he might cause distress was not found to be equivalent to showing that he was aware that his speech or behaviour might be insulting. Applying this subjective test, the magistrates acquitted the defendants and this decision was upheld on appeal. Using this test, it was found that anti-abortion protesters had not realised that their behaviour in shouting anti-abortion slogans, displaying plastic models of foetuses and pictures of dead foetuses would be threatening, abusive or insulting. This decision allows those who believe fervently in their cause, and therefore fail to appreciate that their protest may insult or offend others, to escape liability. It therefore places a significant curb on the ability of s 5 (and to an extent, impliedly of s 4A) to interfere with Art 10 and Art 11 rights. Persons participating in forceful demonstrations may sometimes be able to show that behaviour which could be termed disorderly and which might be capable of causing harassment to others was intended only to make a point and that it had not been realised that others might find it threatening, abusive or insulting. This does not appear to be the case here since the threats appear to be used, not in order to make a point forcefully, but to intimidate.

Sharma may have committed a breach of the peace or his behaviour might have given rise to a reasonable belief that a breach of the peace was threatened; breach of the peace is not in itself a criminal offence but it would justify the arrest of Sharma by John. If the arrest was lawful, Sharma's action in pushing John away would be an assault on an officer in the execution of his duty, an offence under s 89(1) of the Police Act 1996. In *R v Howell* (1981), the court said that a breach of the peace will arise if a positive act is done or threatened to be done which either harms a person or, in his presence, his property, or is likely to cause such harm, or which puts a person in fear of such harm. In *Nicol v DPP* (1996), it was found that a natural consequence of lawful conduct could be violence in another only where the defendant rather than the other person could be said to be acting unreasonably and, further, that, unless rights had been infringed, it would not be reasonable for those others to react violently. However, in *Redmond-Bate v DPP* (1999), it was found that, taking Art 10 into account, the court should ask where the threat was coming from; the person causing the threat should be arrested. In the instant case, following *Nicol*, a court might take the view that Sharma was acting unreasonably in attempting to dissuade the workers from entering their place of work, and that the workers' rights were infringed. On the other hand, the threat would appear to be coming from the white workers. Therefore, it may be argued that the police breached their duty under s 6 of the HRA in arresting Sharma since they did not comply with Art 10 (and arguably the Art 14 right to non-discrimination which arises in the context of another right). Further, the court's findings in *Steel v UK* (1998) may be taken to suggest that the power to prevent a breach of the peace may infringe Arts 10, 11 and 5 when used against an entirely peaceful protester. In the instant case, Sharma may have remained peaceful, if 'heated' and angry. On this interpretation, therefore, which would accord with the court's duty to shape the common law in accordance with the Convention under s 6 of the HRA, Sharma should not have been arrested; therefore, he has not committed the offence under s 89(1) of the 1996 Act. He could sue John in tort for assault if the arrest is found to be unlawful. Following this argument, it is therefore possible that if the protesters who used intimidatory tactics had been arrested for breach of the peace, their arrests would not have breached Art 10.

In conclusion, therefore, it appears that Ali may incur liability under ss 5, 4A and 14 of the 1986 Act and under s 68 of the 1994 Act; Sharma appears not to have committed a breach of the peace and not to have incurred liability under s 89(1) of the 1996 Act and he may have a tort action for assault against John; Rashid will be likely to incur liability under ss 4A and 5 of the 1986 Act and under s 69 of the 1994 Act.[3] Other members of the Asian group, including Rashid and Sharma, may have committed the offence under s 14(5) of the POA and possibly under s 68 of the 1994 Act.

Notes

1   In finding that the imposition of the condition in question did not itself breach Art 11, a court could rely on *Christians Against Racism and Fascism v UK* (1980) in which a ban on a peaceful assembly was not found to breach Art 11. *A fortiori*, a mere imposition of conditions might be found to be proportionate within the terms of Art 11(2). As indicated, the conditions imposed must relate to the mischief apprehended or occurring, following both s 14(1)(b) (the condition must appear 'necessary' to prevent the intimidation) and the test of proportionality in Art 11(2); both are arguably satisfied by the requirement to disperse half the group.

2   Following the above argument in relation to s 14, Rashid and Sharma may be liable under s 14(5) of the 1986 Act for taking part in a public assembly and knowingly failing to comply with the condition imposed. However, this point cannot be settled as it is unclear from the facts whether or not they were aware of the condition imposed or, following *Vane v Yiannopoullos* (1965), were wilfully blind as to its existence.

3   It might be worth considering the argument that a number of the Asians, including, of course, Ali and Rashid, also incur liability in respect of the offence of affray under s 3 of the POA. In order to establish an affray, it must first be shown that the defendant used or threatened unlawful violence towards another and, secondly, that his conduct was such as would cause a person of reasonable firmness present at the scene to fear for his personal safety. As the Asians use threatening gestures, it may be argued that the first limb of s 3(1) is fulfilled, but a strong argument can be advanced that the second is not; due to the fact that the gestures are part of a demonstration, it is probable that a person of reasonable firmness would not fear unlawful violence, even though such a person might feel somewhat distressed. In *Taylor v DPP* (1973), Lord Hailsham, speaking of the common law offence, said 'the degree of violence ... must be such as to be calculated to terrify a person of reasonably firm character'. The Act of course refers to 'fear' as opposed to terror but this ruling suggests that 'fear'

should be interpreted restrictively. On this argument, no liability will arise in respect of s 3. Section 4 of the POA could also be considered, but for similar reasons liability is unlikely to be established, especially taking into account the need for a restrictive interpretation in this context (of a public protest) under s 3 of the HRA.

Question 18

Section 3 of the HRA 1998 requires that statutes should be interpreted, if possible, so as to accord with the demands of the European Convention on Human Rights. Is it fair to say that the restraints on assemblies of ss 11–14C of the Public Order Act 1986, as amended, create a balance between the public interest in freedom of assembly and in the need to maintain order, which is in harmony with Arts 10 and 11 of the Convention, and that therefore no reinterpretation of those provisions under s 3 is necessary?

Answer plan

The Public Order Act (POA) 1986 remains the central statute in this area but its amendment by the Criminal Justice and Public Order Act (CJPOA) 1994 created a significant new area of liability. The general public order scheme now created by the two statutes is very likely to appear on examination papers. This essay question requires a sound knowledge of certain key POA provisions which are particularly relevant to public assembly and protest. It also requires an awareness of the provisions of Arts 10 and 11 as interpreted at Strasbourg, and of their potential impact on this area of UK law under the HRA 1998. It is suggested that a distinction should initially be drawn between prior and subsequent restraints contained in the POA as amended. The provisions in question operate largely as prior restraints.

Essentially, the following matters should be considered:

• value of freedom of assembly;

• the provisions of Arts 10 and 11 as interpreted by Strasbourg;

• provisions aimed specifically at processions and assemblies under ss 11, 12, 13, 14, 14A, 14B and 14C of the 1986 Act (as amended by the 1994 Act);

• need for further protection of assembly by reinterpretation of the provisions under s 3 in accordance with the demands of Arts 10 and 11 as received into UK law under the HRA;

• conclusions.

Answer

The State and citizens have a legitimate interest in maintaining order, but citizens also have a legitimate interest in the protection of the freedoms of expression and assembly. The restraints available under ss 11–14C of the POA 1986, as amended by the CJPOA 1994, affect demonstrations, marches and meetings. To an extent, the number of restraints available is unsurprising because the range of State interests involved is wider than any other expressive activity would warrant: they include the possibilities of disorder, of violence to citizens and of damage to property. Clearly, the State has a duty to protect citizens from the attentions of the mob. The need to give weight to these interests explains the general acceptance of freedom of assembly as a non-absolute right, even though it may be that violent protest is most likely to bring about change.

Public protest is tolerated in free societies due to its close links with freedom of speech; in particular, it fosters participation in the democracy. One aspect of this is the use of protest as a means of demonstrating to the government that it has strayed too far from the path of acceptability in policy making. The question is where the balance is to be struck: what is the proper middle way between allowing free rein to the riotous mob on the one hand and on the other imposing an absolute prohibition on public meetings? The middle way clearly involves the use of controls; the need is to apply them sensitively in order to avoid arbitrary suppression of freedom of assembly. Articles 10 and 11 of the ECHR, afforded further effect in domestic law under the HRA, seek to avoid such suppression in providing guarantees of freedom of expression and of peaceful assembly, subject to exceptions under Arts 10(2) and 11(2), which may prevail only if they are prescribed by law, have a legitimate aim and are 'necessary in a democratic society'. The ECtHR has found that the right to organise public meetings is 'fundamental' (*Rassemblement Jurassien Unite Jurassienne v Switzerland* (1979)) and that the protection of free speech extends equally to ideas which 'offend, shock or disturb' (*Handyside v UK* (1976)). All forms of protest that can be viewed as the expression of an opinion fall within Art 10 according to the findings of the Court in *Steel v UK* (1998). In *Ezelin v France* (1991), the Court found that Art 11 had been violated; it found that the freedom to take part in a peaceful assembly is of such importance that it cannot be restricted in any way so long as the person concerned (whose freedom of assembly has suffered interference through arrest, etc) does not himself commit any reprehensible act.

This essay will ask whether the UK controls under ss 11–14C of the POA 1986 as amended are in harmony with Arts 10 and 11, taking into account the above Strasbourg jurisprudence. In so doing, it will consider the varying effects of these prior restraints on freedom of assembly, taking into account their very significant extension under the 1994 Act. In particular, it will be borne in mind that prior restraints are especially restrictive since their use may mean that the whole purpose of the assembly – to express a point of view – is lost.

The POA 1986, as amended by ss 70 and 71 of the CJPOA 1994, contains various prior restraints on assemblies which may mean that they cannot take place at all or can take place only under various limitations. These restraints are contained in ss 12, 13, 14, 14A, 14B and 14C of the Act. Sections 12 and 13 are underpinned by s 11, which provides that the organisers of a march (not a meeting) must give advance notice of it to the police. This statutory national notice requirement was imposed for the first time under the 1986 Act, although, in some districts, a notice requirement was already imposed under local Acts. The notice must specify the date, time and proposed route of the procession and give the name and address of the person proposing to organise it. Under s 11(7), the organisers may be guilty of an offence if the notice requirement has not been satisfied or if the march deviates from the date, time or route specified. Clearly, s 11 may have some deterrence value to organisers; such persons obviously bear a heavy responsibility in ensuring that any deviation does not occur. It can be argued that the word 'any' should not be interpreted so strictly as to exclude spontaneous processions where a few minutes was available to give notice, because to do so would defeat the intention behind including the provision. If read in combination with the requirements as to giving notice by hand or in writing, it should be interpreted to mean 'any written notice' under s 3 of the HRA. If it were not so interpreted, it might be argued that s 11 breaches the guarantees of freedom of assembly under Art 11 and of expression under Art 10, since it could lead to the criminalisation of the organisers of a peaceful, spontaneous march. Such an interpretation would seem to be in accordance with the findings in *Ezelin v France* (1991).

Sections 12 and 13 grew out of the power under s 3 of the POA 1936, allowing the Chief Officer of Police to impose conditions on a procession or apply for a banning order if he apprehended serious public disorder. The power to impose conditions on public assemblies under s 14 was an entirely new power. The power to impose conditions on processions under s 12 is much wider than the old power as it may be exercised in a much wider range of situations. It is identical to the power under s 14 and can be exercised in one of four situations: the senior police officer in question must reasonably believe that serious public disorder, serious damage to property or serious disruption to the life of the community may be caused by the procession. The fourth 'trigger' condition, arising under ss 12 and 14(1)(b), consists of an evaluation of the purpose of the assembly rather than an apprehension that a particular state of affairs may arise. The senior police officer must reasonably believe that the purpose of the assembly is 'the intimidation of others with a view to compelling them not to do an act they have a right to do or to do an act they have a right not to do'.

'Serious disruption to the life of the community' is a very wide phrase and clearly offers the police wide scope for interpretation. It may be interpreted broadly where police officers wished to cut down the cost of the policing requirement for an assembly because the conditions then imposed, such as requiring a limit on the numbers participating, might lead to a reduction in the number of officers who had to be present. The fourth 'trigger' requires a police officer to make a political judgment as to the purpose of the group in question. It must be determined whether the purpose is coercive or merely persuasive. Asking police officers to make such a judgment clearly lays them open to claims of partiality in instances where they are perceived as out of sympathy with the aims of the group in question.

The conditions that can be imposed if one of the above 'triggers' is thought to be present are very wide in the case of processions: *prima facie* any condition may be imposed which appears necessary to the senior police officer in order to prevent the mischief envisaged occurring. Obviously, they are not completely unlimited; if the condition imposed bears no relationship to the mischief it was intended to avert, it may be open to challenge. The conditions which may be imposed under s 14 are much more limited in scope, presumably because it was thought that marches presented more of a threat to public order than meetings. The scope for challenging the conditions was very limited in the pre-HRA era: there was no method of appealing from them; it was only possible to have them reviewed for procedural errors or unreasonableness in the High Court. It was made clear in *Secretary of State for the Home Department ex p Northumbria Police Authority* (1987) that such a challenge would succeed only where a senior officer had evinced a belief in the existence of a 'trigger' which no reasonable officer could entertain: no presumption in favour of freedom of assembly would be imported. In the post-HRA era, a challenge could be mounted under s 7(1)(a) of the HRA, relying on Arts 10 and 11. The very fact that such an avenue of challenge is now available and that the police as a public authority under s 6 of the HRA should take Arts 10 and 11 into account in imposing the conditions provides an implied limitation on them, possibly obviating the necessity of reinterpretation of the condition-imposing powers of ss 12(1) and 14(1) under s 3.

Under s 13, a ban must be imposed on a march if it is thought that it may result in serious public disorder. This reproduces the old power under s 3 of the POA 1936. Assuming that a power was needed to ban marches expected to be violent, this power was, nevertheless, open to criticism in that once a banning order had been imposed, it prevented all marches in the area it covered for its duration. Thus, a projected march likely to be of an entirely peaceful character would be caught by a ban aimed at a violent march. The Campaign for Nuclear Disarmament attempted to challenge such a ban after it had had to cancel a number of its marches (*Kent v Metropolitan Police Commissioner* (1981)), but failed due to the finding that an order quashing the ban could be made only if there were no reasons for imposing it at all. It is arguable that the 1986 Act should have limited the banning power to the particular marches giving rise to fear of serious public disorder, but this possibility was rejected by the government at the time on the ground that it could be subverted by organisers of marches who might attempt to march under another name. It would, therefore, it was thought, have placed too great a burden on the police who would have had to determine whether or not this had occurred. However, in making this decision, it is arguable that too great a weight was given to the possible administrative burden placed on the police and too little to the need to uphold freedom of assembly.

Originally, the 1986 Act contained no power to ban assemblies, possibly because it was thought that such a power would be too draconian, but provision to allow for such bans was inserted into it by s 70 of the CJPOA 1994. The banning power, arising under s 14A, provides that a Chief Officer of Police may apply for a banning order if he reasonably believes that an assembly is likely to be trespassory and may result in serious disruption to the life of the community or damage to certain types of buildings and structures. If an order is made, it will subsist for four days and operate within a radius of five miles around the area in question. Apart from these restrictions, this is a much wider power than that arising under s 13, since it is based on the very broad and uncertain concept of 'serious disruption to the life of the community'. Since it uses the same trigger as that operating under ss 12 and 14, it appears to leave a complete discretion to the police as to whether to ban or to impose conditions. Section 14A is backed up by s 14C (inserted into the 1986 Act by s 71 of the 1994 Act). Section 14C provides a very broad power to stop persons within a radius of five miles from the assembly if a police officer reasonably believes that they were on their way to it and that it is subject to a s 14A order. Thus, this power operates before any offence has been committed and hands the police a very wide discretion.

The meaning and ambit of s 14A were considered in *Jones and Lloyd v DPP* (1999), which concerned an assembly on the road leading to Stonehenge, at a time when a s 14A order was in force. The key finding of the House of Lords was that, since *the particular assembly in question* had been found by the tribunal of fact to be a reasonable user of the highway, it was therefore not trespassory and so not caught by the s 14A order. Their conclusion was that the demands of this 'right' to assemble are satisfied provided merely that an assembly on the highway is not invariably tortious. This interpretation did little, it is suggested, to ensure that s 14A is compatible with Arts 10 and 11, since it allows interferences with peaceful assemblies.

In general, it is argued that ss 12–14A appear to be out of accord with the demands of Arts 10 and 11 of the Convention. Sections 12 and 14 allow for the imposition of conditions on the basis of serious disruption of the life of the community – an aim not recognised in Arts 10 and 11. Sections 13 and 14A allow for the possibility of imposing blanket bans. Under all of those provisions, it is possible that those organising or taking part in protests and demonstrations can be subject to criminal penalties and hence to an interference with their Arts 10 and 11 rights, even though they themselves were behaving wholly peacefully. (For example, a march might be peaceful and yet arguably disruptive of the 'life' of the community under s 12; it might fall foul of a s 13 ban imposed due to the concerns generated by the projected march of a violent group.) Thus, the effects of ss 12 to 14A appear to be contrary to the statement of principle set out in *Ezelin* above, since the arrest and conviction of demonstrators under them cannot be seen to be directly serving one of the legitimate aims of preventing public disorder or ensuring public safety under para 2 of Arts 10 and 11. It is therefore arguable that the use of bans or conditions always constitute breaches of Arts 10 and 11, when they catch entirely peaceful protesters, since the 'legitimate aim' test is unsatisfied. Even if this is not accepted, on the basis that ss 12 to 14A have a more general aim in preventing disorder, it might be argued that the arrest of peaceful protesters is disproportionate to this legitimate aim.

On the other hand, there is a consistent line of case law from the Commission which indicates that bans – and therefore, *a fortiori*, the imposition of conditions – on assemblies and marches are in principle compatible with Art 11 even where they criminalise wholly peaceful protests (*Pendragon v UK* (1999); *Chappell v UK* (1989)) or prevent what would have been peaceful demonstrations from taking place at all (*Christians Against Racism and Fascism v UK* (1980)).[1] A court which preferred the *Ezelin* stance and formed the view that blanket bans *per se* were essentially incompatible with the Convention could enforce this view through a radical reinterpretation of s 14A under s 3(1) of the HRA. It would entail reading into s 14A(5) the requirement that a given assembly, as well as being trespassory and within the geographical and temporal scope of a subsisting s 14A order, also must itself pose a threat of disorder, or otherwise satisfy one of the exceptions to Art 11. Since such an interpretation would mean that s 14A effectively ceased to bestow a power to impose blanket bans and is only doubtfully necessary under the Convention, it is, however, unlikely to be adopted.[2]

Under s 14A, attention will therefore probably focus upon scrutiny of the risk of 'serious disruption to the life of the community' in granting the original ban. This method could also be used to bring ss 12 and 14 into line with the Convention. Courts could be required to determine that the nature of the risk anticipated is one which would constitute one of the legitimate aims for limiting the primary rights under Arts 11 and 10. This vague and ambiguous phrase could be reinterpreted under s 3 of the HRA by reference to Art 11(2) and Art 10(2) of the Convention. Given the terms of these criteria, the grounds for the ban/imposition of conditions would have to be justified, either on the basis of protecting 'the rights of others' or because the 'serious disruption' feared amounted to 'disorder' for the purposes of Arts 11(2) and 10(2). If those aims were established, the ban/conditions would also have to be necessary and proportionate to them, on the basis that disruption that could be curbed without imposing a ban/conditions could not be viewed as 'serious'. Thus, s 3 would be used to limit and structure the tests allowing for the use of these curbs on protest.

Section 13 could be reinterpreted under s 3 in order to achieve compatibility with Arts 10 and 11 in various ways. For example, it could be argued that a power to seek an order to ban all marches could be interpreted as a power to ban all *at the most*, using s 3 of the HRA creatively as the House of Lords did in *R v A* (2001). Alternatively, the words 'or any class of public procession' used in s 13(1) could be utilised to afford leeway to include potentially disruptive marches (using 'disruptiveness' as the method of defining their membership of the class) and therefore to exclude marches expected to be entirely peaceful.

It is concluded that the far-reaching nature of the public order scheme under discussion argues strongly for establishing further protection for freedom of assembly under the HRA, by reinterpretation of a number of the provisions under s 3. To say this is not to argue that the scheme is completely out of harmony with Arts 10 and 11. The scheme is, to an extent, pursuing legitimate aims – the prevention of disorder and crime – under those Articles, but, in so far as certain of its provisions allow for interference with peaceful assemblies, it appears, as indicated, that in certain respects it goes further than is necessary in a democratic society. However, ironically, the very fact that the scheme employs imprecise phrases such as 'serious', possibly in an attempt to afford maximum discretion to the police, works against it, in favour of freedom of protest, since it renders the task of reinterpretation under s 3 of the HRA relatively straightforward.

Notes

1   The alternative argument could be pursued here: it would therefore be open to a court to follow the Commission case law on the basis that it is more directly applicable to ss 12–14A, since it deals directly with prior restraints, unlike *Steel* and *Ezelin*. On such an approach, the imposition of conditions under s 12 or 14

or of bans under s 13 would be substantively unaffected by the HRA since the police assessment of the need to impose the condition or seek the ban would be deferred to. In relation to s 14A, this approach would probably require the court to satisfy itself that there was some risk of disorder or property damage to justify the making of the original s 14A order.

2   There would be strong grounds to justify a departure from *DPP v Jones*, on the basis that it affords too precarious a level of protection to a fundamental right in allowing peaceful, non-obstructive protests to be interfered with merely because a magistrates' court has found the assembly to be 'unreasonable'. The question would then be how far a court wished to go in establishing a new approach to s 14A. The civil trespass finding could be modified: a court could find that if an assembly is peaceful and non-obstructive, it must *always* be termed reasonable, therefore non-trespassory, and so outside the terms of any s 14A order in force.

CHAPTER 4

PRIVACY

Introduction

Examiners tend to set general essays in this area, rather than problem questions. The emphasis is usually on the degree to which a balance is struck between the interest of the State and other bodies in intruding on the individual, or in obtaining and publishing personal information, and the interest of the individual in maintaining personal privacy and the privacy of personal information. These two areas of privacy can be broken down into bodily and sexual privacy, the privacy of the home, access to personal information and the protection of personal information.

Questions are often asked which concern the balance struck between privacy and freedom of expression. There have been various government proposals for reform, including the introduction of a tort of privacy, but these have been now been overtaken by a debate about the extent to which the Human Rights Act (HRA) 1998 will lead to the courts developing a common law right to privacy. This is an issue which has been the subject of a number of high profile cases involving celebrities and the media. Another important topic concerns the needs of national security and crime control which clearly conflict with privacy in a range of ways arising from the provisions of a certain group of statutes: the Security Services Act 1989, the Intelligence Services Act 1994, the Police Act 1997 and the Regulation of Investigatory Powers Act (RIPA) 2000 (which repealed the substantive provisions of the Interception of Communications Act 1985). Essay questions may ask you to consider the conflict between those public interest needs and the individual's interest in maintaining personal privacy and the privacy of the home. The HRA will also be relevant to discussions of this area.

There is some overlap between the areas of freedom of information and privacy, since the principle that citizens should be able to gain access to their own personal information which is held by various bodies may fall under either head. However, the question of how far people should have access to their own personal information may be viewed most readily as a privacy issue, since the access is sought in order to ensure, *inter alia*, that the confidentiality of the information is maintained, not that it should be made freely available.

Checklist

Students should be familiar with the following areas:

- breach of confidence;
- defamation and malicious falsehood;
- trespass and nuisance;
- proposals for a tort of invasion of privacy;
- the developing role of the HRA 1998 and, in particular, Art 8 of Sched 1;
- the Data Protection Act 1998 and the Freedom of Information Act 2000;
- the Official Secrets Act 1989, the Security Services Act 1989, the Intelligence Services Act 1994, Pt 3 of the Police Act 1997, the RIPA 2000 and Pts 3 and 11 of the Anti-Terrorism, Crime and Security Act 2001.

Question 19

'The law of confidence has developed so far that it can now confidently be said that it provides adequate protection for personal information; therefore, a statutory tort of invasion of privacy is not needed.' Do you agree?

Answer plan

A fairly demanding essay question, which requires familiarity with the law of confidence. The statement made in the title should be questioned as follows. First, does confidence provide adequate protection for personal information? Secondly, assuming that it does, is it better, in terms of preserving media freedom, to protect such information through the doctrine of confidence or through a new tort? Essentially, the following points should be considered:

- development of doctrine of confidence – relationship between the parties may be informal;
- obligation of confidentiality may be imposed on third parties;
- the public interest defence;
- ambit of the proposed tort;
- comparison between the proposed tort and breach of confidence: impact on media freedom;
- Arts 8 and 10 of the European Convention on Human Rights (ECHR) and the impact of the HRA 1998.

Answer

No tort of invasion of privacy exists in the UK as in the US to control the activity of the media in obtaining information regarding an individual's private life and then publishing the details, possibly in exaggerated, lurid terms. However, certain legal controls arising from the law of confidence do exist, although they are not aimed directly at the invasion of privacy, they can be used against the media when private information is published. However, it will be argued that this control is still fairly limited in scope and, to some extent, aimed at the protection of other interests, arguably making it ill-suited to the protection of privacy. Further, it will be suggested that extension of confidence with a view to providing greater protection for personal information should be viewed with caution, due to the threat which would be posed to media freedom.

The Younger Committee, which reported on the legal protection of privacy in 1972, considered that confidence was the area of the law which offered most effective protection of privacy. It has a wider ambit than defamation, in that it prevents truthful communications and, furthermore, cases such as *Woodward v Hutchins* (1977) or *Lennon v News Group Newspapers Ltd* (1978) suggest that it protects confidential communications, whether or not their unauthorised disclosure causes detriment to the reputation of any person. However, it must be remembered that confidence, while quite closely associated with it, is protecting a somewhat different interest from that of privacy. The current concern of the courts, found in cases such as *Douglas v Hello!* (2003), is whether an action for breach of confidence, along with other statutory and common law remedies, provides sufficient protection for privacy so that a new tort is unnecessary or, at best, merely residual.

Breach of confidence will be established, according to Lord Greene MR, in *Saltman Engineering Co Ltd v Campbell Engineering Co Ltd* (1963), if information which has a quality of confidence about it, as it is not in the public domain, is transmitted in circumstances importing an obligation of confidence, and there is then unauthorised use of that information, usually, but not necessarily, involving detriment to the complainant. As *Duke of Argyll v Duchess of Argyll* (1965) demonstrated, these ingredients may arise when confidential information is imparted in a relationship of trust not of a contractual nature and, therefore, personal information is clearly covered. However, that ruling was delivered in the context of a formal relationship – marriage – and, combined with other rulings such as that in *Thompson v Stanhope* (1774), suggests that breach of confidence is relevant only where a formal relationship can be identified.

In *Stephens v Avery* (1988), however, which concerned information communicated within a close friendship, it was not found necessary to identify a formal relationship between the parties at the time when the information was communicated, thus suggesting that the confidential nature of the information was the important factor: '... it is unconscionable for a person who has received information on the basis that it is confidential subsequently to reveal that information. No particular pre-existing relationship is needed.' This general contention has been widely supported by later rulings.

These comments might appear to cover a communication of confidential information by one complete stranger to another so long as the communicator informed the recipient that the information was confidential. If so, *Stephens v Avery* dramatically points the way to a broader use of breach of confidence as a means of protecting privacy. However, it may be going too far to suggest that this ruling would support the use of confidence in relation to secrets passed between strangers. The *ratio* of the case would seem to be merely that no pre-existing formal relationship is needed; as the information was passed within a close friendship, it was not necessary for the decision to state that there was no need to identify any relationship at all. The comment to that effect was therefore only *obiter*, and so it was not certain that courts in future would be prepared to accept that confidences passed between slight acquaintances or strangers should be protected. Perhaps they would not, since the betrayal of trust for which the law of confidence has traditionally sought to provide a remedy would be less apparent, or perhaps completely absent, in such instances.

Stephens v Avery also demonstrated that a newspaper which was not a party to the original relationship, but was directly involved, in that it had been approached by one of the parties, could have obligations associated with a relationship of trust imposed upon it. *AG v Guardian Newspaper Ltd* (1987) (the *Spycatcher* case) took this a stage further, in making it clear that if an editor of a newspaper is not directly approached, but has merely acquired the information, he or she can be held to be under the same duty of confidence if he or she is aware that the information is confidential. Breach of confidence has been the basis of an action against the press in a number of cases. In *A v B plc* (2002), for example, a Premier League footballer failed to prevent the publication of a 'kiss and tell' story, and in *Campbell v Mirror Group Newspapers* (2002), Naomi Campbell similarly failed to obtain damages regarding a story that she was receiving medical treatment for drug addiction. In *Douglas v Hello!* (2003), on the other hand, damages were awarded against Hello! magazine for the unauthorised publication of photographs of the wedding of Michael Douglas and Catherine Zeta-Jones. Outside the celebrity world, breach of confidence was relied on, in *Venables v News Group Newspapers* (2001), to impose an injunction preventing the publication of the new identities of two men convicted when they were children of murdering a toddler.

Though these cases are not brought directly under the HRA, the Act, and in particular the right to private life under Art 8, seems to influence the development of the common law. In *Douglas v Hello!* (2001), the Court of Appeal refused to uphold a temporary injunction preventing publication of the claimants' wedding photographs. Sedley LJ, however, suggested that the time had come for the courts to protect privacy, as such, without needing to establish a prior relationship of confidentiality. This suggestion has been doubted by the Court of Appeal (*A v B plc* (2002) by Lord Woolf) and in *Douglas v Hello!* (2003) (the action for damages), Lindsay J expressly declined to hold that a law of privacy, distinct from breach of confidence, existed. The judge recognised that situations might arise in which media publication offended privacy without being in breach of confidence or in any other way unlawful. In such a situation, the law would need to develop appropriately to guarantee Convention rights, but this was seen as a matter for Parliament rather than for the courts to construct a new tort. A possible example of such a gap in the law is *Peck v UK* (2003). The European Court of Human Rights (ECtHR) held that the applicant had no sufficient remedy for the violation of his Convention right to private life when a local council distributed CCTV footage of his suicide attempt, made in a public place, to the media. It is unclear that the action of the council or the media could be the basis of a breach of confidence, despite the flexibility of the doctrine. An overarching right of privacy has been expressly denied by the House of Lords in *Wainwright v Home Office* (2003).

It does not follow that, just because there has been a breach of confidence, the courts will give a remedy – injunctive relief or damages. For example, in *Douglas v Hello!* (2001) (the injunction case), an injunction was refused. Since the claimants had sold the rights to their wedding pictures to another magazine, what was predominantly in issue was not confidentiality regarding private life, but the protection of a valuable commodity: their public image. In that circumstance, an action for damages was the appropriate remedy. Similarly, an injunction should only be issued if the public interest requires. The question of the public interest in the context of media disclosures about the lives of celebrities was considered by the Court of Appeal in *A v B plc*. A married Premier League footballer sought to prevent a Sunday newspaper from publishing accounts by two women of their brief, if tempestuous, adulterous relationships with him. In discharging the High Court's injunction, the court laid down guidelines for such cases. In particular, the court stressed that press freedom was, in itself, a matter of public interest and that privacy claims were easy to make. It followed from this that an approach which allowed restraints on the press unless a significant public interest in the story could be shown was wrong. It is legitimate for the press to publish stories the public are interested in. The proper approach was that it was the restraints on the press that needed specific justification in terms of the strength of the arguments for confidence and privacy. Public figures, for example, had to accept a greater degree of media interference than ordinary persons and confidentiality about transient relationships was likely to be weaker than about married or long-term relationships. In other cases, such as *Woodward v Hutchins* (1977), the courts have refused injunctions where the claimants had used the media to promote a particular image of themselves and then tried to prevent the publication of stories which countered that image. *Campbell v Frisbee* (2002), for example, involved a story about Naomi Campbell's relationship with a film star, which was published, possibly in breach of confidence. The Court of Appeal held that it was arguable that a remedy should be refused in so far as the story was true and showed the claimant in a less favourable light than through the image she had been promoting of herself.

The courts accept that a claimant cannot obtain a breach of confidence injunction to cover up his or her own wrongdoing or iniquity. In such circumstances, the public interest in disclosure will prevail. Despite *obiter* in *British Steel Corp v Granada Television* (1981), the public interest defence of disclosure is not limited to matters of iniquity and wrongdoing. In *Lion Laboratories v Evans* (1985), it was accepted by Stephenson LJ that there are a number of reasons justifying disclosure of otherwise confidential matter, and iniquity is merely one instance.

Nor should it be thought that the existence of an important public interest will necessarily justify public disclosure in the media. In *Lion Laboratories v Evans*, it was made clear that even in cases of iniquity the public interest may sometimes be best served by reporting to the police rather than public disclosure in the media. In *X (HA) v Y* (1987), a newspaper wished to publish information deriving from confidential hospital records which showed that certain practising doctors were suffering from the AIDS virus. In granting an injunction preventing publication, Rose J took into account the public interest in disclosure, but weighed it against the private interest in confidentiality and the public interest in encouraging AIDS patients to seek help from hospitals, which would not be served if it was thought that confidentiality might not be maintained. Similarly, the manner in which the information was obtained may be relevant. If the means used to obtain it suggest a gross breach of trust, such as the use of a telephone tap, the law of confidence may be successfully invoked. In *Francome v Mirror Group Newspapers* (1984), reporting of breaches of the rules of racing might not have attracted a remedy due to the iniquity defence, but the use of telephone tapping in order to obtain the story may have persuaded the Court of Appeal to allow a remedy.

In deciding whether to grant an injunction, a court must, of course, give full weight to freedom of expression as provided for under Sched 1, Art 10 of the HRA. Of course, an injunction will be compatible with Art 10 if it is lawful and proportionate and aimed at protecting the rights of others, such as the right to confidentiality. Section 12 of the HRA goes further and requires the courts to give full weight to freedom of the press when deciding whether to make an order restricting expression. Since the balancing of Art 8 by Art 10 is inherent in Convention jurisprudence anyway, it is unclear that s 12 adds much. Section 12 also requires the courts to have regard to any Code of Practice. The Press Complaints Commission's Code is accepted as a relevant provision. This, of course, just leads the debate back to the public interest question since, regarding privacy, the Code permits a public interest justification.

An important point that has been emphasised in recent cases is that confidentiality, in relation to information, may be protected under the Data Protection Act 1998. However, in *Campbell v Mirror Group Newspapers* (2002), s 32 of the Act was interpreted by the Court of Appeal to give the press wide scope to publish personal stories, again so long as they believed the public interest would be served.

The statutory tort proposed under the 1993 Green Paper would cover the publication of personal information without authorisation, which causes substantial distress. Such information has been defined as those aspects of an individual's personal life which a reasonable person would assume should remain private. Use of the word 'substantial' would limit the ambit of the tort; confidence might sometimes be available, although liability under the new tort would not be. The tort would not be subject to a general defence of public interest.

It would be a defence under the proposals to show that the act was done: for the purpose of preventing, detecting or exposing the commission of a crime; or for the purpose of preventing the public from being misled by some public statement or action of the individual concerned; or for the purpose of informing the public about matters directly affecting the discharge of any public function of the individual concerned; or for the protection of public health or safety; or under any lawful authority. Clearly, these defences are more tightly drawn than the broad public interest defence under the law of confidence.

Even if there are gaps in the protection offered to privacy by the common law doctrine of confidence, it does not necessarily follow that general measures to protect it should be adopted. Gaps, such as in *Peck v UK* (2003), if identified, might be best filled by context specific statutory provisions rather than the general tort that has been proposed. On the one hand, the tort might provide greater certainty than is provided by the uncontrolled and perhaps unpredictable development of confidence. In identifying the particular grounds of the public interest defence, the tort might also provide clearer protection for freedom of speech, though, on the other hand, the more flexible common law approach might, in fact, be more sensitive to the demands of the media. At present, it seems that the exposure of seriously anti-social conduct would not fall within the defences under the proposed tort, although it probably would fall within the defence under the law of confidence.

In conclusion, it is suggested that the continuing development of breach of confidence is preferable to the introduction of the new tort. In terms of protection of privacy, breach of confidence, especially when linked to data protection, has now developed to the point where personal information will be protected in a wide range of situations. There will, of course, be gaps, but it is suggested these are better dealt with by specific reform and regulation and do not need a new tort. The important point is that the reasonableness of any privacy claim must be capable of being weighed against the public interest, including press freedom, in disclosure, and that process is central to breach of confidence. The HRA now provides both substantive rights and the background to the development of the law. Article 8 provides a basic right to privacy which the courts, even when dealing with private law, must follow; and at the same time the courts must balance Art 8 with freedom of expression under Art 10. Breach of confidence cases decided under the influence of the Convention, such as *A v B plc* and *Campbell v Mirror Group Newspapers*, suggest that media freedom is fully recognised, though further cases will be needed before a proper judgment can be made as to whether the balance is being struck in the right place. Such developments, it is suggested, make a new tort unnecessary.

Question 20

'Not one of the various proposals for further press regulation succeeds in creating a proper balance between freedom of the press and privacy.' Discuss.

Answer plan

A reasonably straightforward essay question. It is important to concentrate on the various proposals, rather than undertaking a general review of the law relating to privacy. Obviously, the question could be 'attacked', in the sense that it could be argued that no balance at all should be struck between freedom of expression on the one hand and the protection of certain forms of private information on the other: freedom of expression should always prevail. This might be argued in relation to private information bearing on the public life of public figures. Alternatively, it might be argued that the balance to be struck should differ depending on the public interest value of the information. Essentially, the following matters should be considered:

- methods of self-regulation and proposals for their improvement;
- a statutory tribunal to regulate the press;
- proposals for a statutory tort of invasion of privacy;
- defences under the new tort;
- proposals to remedy various kinds of intrusion made with the intent to obtain personal material for publication.

Answer

Given the HRA 1998's enactment, the debate on how best to create a satisfactory right to respect for private and family life (in compliance with Art 8 of the European Convention on Human Rights (ECHR)) has re-opened. Proposals for further press regulation can be divided into three main areas, which will be considered in turn. Considered first will be the various experiments with methods of self-regulation and proposals for their improvement, or for a statutory tribunal to regulate the press; secondly, the proposals for a statutory tort of invasion of privacy; and thirdly, proposals to remedy various kinds of intrusion made with the intent to obtain personal material for publication.

Self-regulation by the press in respect of the protection of privacy has been and remains the preference of successive governments. A self-regulatory body, the Press Council, was created in 1953 and it aimed to regulate the press by issuing guidelines on privacy and adjudicating complaints. It could censure a newspaper and require its adjudication to be published. In practice, however, a number of deficiencies became apparent: the Council did not issue clear enough guidelines; its decisions were seen as inconsistent, and in any event, ineffective – it had no power of prior restraint nor could it fine or award an injunction. Moreover, it was seen as too lenient: it would not interfere if the disclosure in question could be said to be in the public interest and what was meant by the public interest was uncertain.

Its inefficacy led the Younger Committee, convened in 1972, to recommend a number of proposals offering greater protection from intrusion by the press. These proposals were not implemented, but the perception that further measures might be needed to control the tabloid newspapers remained, although, at the same time, there was concern that they should not prevent legitimate investigative journalism. This perceived need led eventually to the formation of the Committee on Privacy and Related Matters (hereafter 'Calcutt I') in 1990, which considered a number of measures, some relevant to actual publication and some to the means of gathering information. The Committee decided that improved self-regulation should be given one final chance and recommended the creation of the Press Complaints Commission (PCC).

After the Commission had been in place for a year, Sir David Calcutt (hereafter 'Calcutt II') reviewed its success and determined that it 'does not hold the balance fairly between the press and the individual ... it is in essence a body set up by the industry ... dominated by the industry'. He therefore proposed the introduction of a statutory tribunal which would draw up a Code of Practice for the press and would rule on alleged breaches of the Code; its sanctions would include those already possessed by the PCC and, in addition, the imposition of fines and the award of compensation. The proposal was rejected by the National Heritage Select Committee in 1993 and not implemented by the government.

The Commission agreed a Code of Practice, which the newspapers accepted. It can receive and pronounce on complaints of violation of the Code and can demand an apology for inaccuracy, or that there should be an opportunity for reply. Intrusion into private life is allowed under the Code only if it is in the public interest; this is defined as including 'detecting or exposing seriously anti-social conduct' or 'preventing the public being misled by some statement or action of that individual'. Harassment is not allowed. The Code makes special mention of hospitals and requires that the press must obtain permission in order to interview patients. The Commission does not require the complainant to waive any legal right of action as the Press Council was criticised for doing. However, it has the same limited sanctions as the Press Council. Self-regulation by the Commission remains the government's preferred approach. In 2002, for example, the Lord Chancellor decided not to legislate on the issue of press payments to trial witnesses, preferring to leave it to the Commission. A revision to the Code came into force in March 2003.

The Broadcasting Standards Commission (BSC) took over in 1996 from the Broadcasting Complaints Commission (BCC) the similar role of trying to ensure that broadcasters avoid the unwarranted infringement of privacy in the making and broadcast of radio and television programmes, and dealing with complaints in this area. (Under the terms of the Communications Act, its functions are transferred to Ofcom, the new general regulator, from the end of 2003.) It issues a Code with which broadcasters are expected to comply. The term 'privacy' will receive quite a wide interpretation according to the ruling in *Broadcasting Complaints Commission ex p Granada Television Ltd* (1993). Granada Television challenged a finding of the BCC that matters already in the public domain could, if re-published, constitute an invasion of privacy. In judicial review proceedings, it was found that privacy differed from confidentiality and went well beyond it, because it was not confined to secrets; the significant issue was not whether material was or was not in the public domain, but whether, by being published, it caused hurt and anguish. There were grounds on which it could be considered that publication of the matters in question had caused distress and, therefore, the BCC had not acted unreasonably in the *Wednesbury* sense in taking the view that an infringement of privacy had occurred. Under the HRA, the courts will apply Convention standards to such decisions. However, the courts will be reluctant to limit a domestic right to privacy merely on the grounds that it is more extensive than the Convention right (*R v BSC ex p BBC (Liberty Intervening)* (2000)).

Support for a statutory tort of invasion of privacy has been far from unanimous in the relevant Committees. Thus, while the Younger Committee recommended the introduction of a tort of disclosure of information unlawfully acquired, Calcutt I decided against recommending a new statutory tort of invasion of privacy relating to publication of personal information, although the Committee considered that it would be possible to define such a tort with sufficient precision. Calcutt II recommended only that the government should give further consideration to the introduction of such a tort, but the Heritage Select Committee made a more positive recommendation and this view was adopted by Lord Mackay in his Green Paper, published in July 1993. However, the Paper did not suggest that legal aid should be available to those seeking redress under the new civil privacy liability. If the proposal was to be implemented without the provision of legal aid or being brought within the contingency fee scheme, the new provisions might merely be used – as, arguably, defamation has been – by powerful figures to protect their activities from scrutiny, while the ordinary citizen might be unable in practice to obtain redress for invasions of privacy.

Turning now to the substantive merits of such a tort, it may be noted that the possible definition put forward by Calcutt I was designed to relate only to personal information which was published without authorisation. Such information was defined as those aspects of an individual's personal life which a reasonable person would assume should remain private. The main concern of the Committee was that true information, which would not cause lasting harm, was already known to some and was obtained reputably, might be caught by its provisions. The Green Paper, however, proposed a broader area of liability: the tort would cover any invasion of privacy causing substantial distress.

Calcutt I did not consider that liability should be subject to a general defence of public interest, although it did favour a tightly drawn defence of justified disclosure. The difficulty here is that it might not always be possible for a journalist trying to investigate corruption in public life to show that there was a clear justification for gathering the relevant information if the investigation was still at an inchoate stage; in order to be effective in protecting worthwhile journalism, any defences would have to require only an honest belief by the journalist that his or her investigations had one of the justificatory purposes. The Green Paper suggested a defence of public interest, which would cover the same areas as will be discussed below in relation to criminal liability. In particular, it would be a defence to show that the act in question was done: for the purpose of preventing, detecting or exposing the commission of a crime or other seriously anti-social conduct; or for the purpose of preventing the public from being misled by some public statement or action of the individual concerned. However, under the Green Paper, it was suggested that the defences should be narrowed down to exclude 'seriously anti-social conduct'. If the UK were to enact a right to privacy without including such a defence, which would afford protection to the freedom of the press, the detriment caused might outweigh the value of such a right. On the other hand, if the proposed tort were subject to a very wide-ranging defence, it might be emasculated. Thus, in the US, the scope of privacy rights is limited by a general defence of 'newsworthiness'. This allows stories disclosing embarrassing and painful personal facts to be published without the need for a justifying public interest. This perhaps suggests that there is little value in looking to the US for a model if a UK right to privacy is to have any efficacy.

At present, proposals for reform seem to be faced with two extremes: on the one hand, a claim of invasion of privacy might be met by such a general defence of public interest or newsworthiness that it has, in most instances, very little chance of success, while, on the other, a narrow defence of public interest or 'justified publication' might allow invasion of privacy too much scope. Arguably, an acceptable middle way forward may be to enact very specific and narrowly defined areas of liability relating to particularly intrusive invasions of privacy, which differentiate between the lives of ordinary citizens who happen to come into the public eye and the lives of public figures. It is to consideration of proposals for such measures that I will now turn.

The kinds of particularly clear invasions of privacy which arguably require some kind of statutory response are as follows: physical intrusion by reporters both onto the individual's own property or onto other private property where he or she happens to be, as in *Kaye v Robertson* (1990); the taking of photographs for publication without the subject's consent; and the use of bugging devices. The Younger Committee proposed the introduction of a tort and crime of unlawful surveillance by means of a technical device, and both Calcutt Committees recommended the creation of a specific criminal offence providing more extensive protection – a recommendation which was backed by the National Heritage Select Committee when it considered the matter. The clause proposed by Calcutt II creating the offence would also offer the individual whose privacy had been invaded the possibility of obtaining injunctions in the High Court to prevent publication of material gained in contravention of the clause provisions; damages would also be available to hold newspapers to account for any profits gained through publication of such material.

Criminal liability under the clause would be made out if the defendant did any of the following with intent to obtain personal information or photographs, in either case with a view to their publication: entering or remaining on private property without the consent of the lawful occupant; placing a surveillance device on private property without such consent; using a surveillance device whether on private property or elsewhere in relation to an individual who is on private property without his or her consent; and taking a photograph or recording the voice of an individual who is on private property without his or her consent and with intent that the individual should be identifiable. This offence seems to specify the forbidden acts fairly clearly and to be aimed at preventing what would generally be accepted to be undesirable invasions of privacy; it is worth noting that France, Germany, Denmark and the Netherlands all have similar offences on the statute books. It should be noted that the offence would not cover persistent telephoning, or photographing, interviewing or recording the voice of a vulnerable individual, such as a disaster victim or a bereaved relative, in a public place.

It would be a defence to any of the above to show that the act was done: for the purpose of preventing, detecting or exposing the commission of a crime or other seriously anti-social conduct; or for the purpose of preventing the public from being misled by some public statement or action of the individual concerned; or for the purpose of informing the public about matters directly affecting the discharge of any public function of the individual concerned; or for the protection of public health or safety; or under any lawful authority. *Prima facie*, the defences seem to range widely enough to prevent public figures from being able to use the offence to stifle legitimate investigative journalism. The defences might not cover exposures of salacious aspects of the private lives of celebrities, where the aim is merely to satisfy public prurience and curiosity, unless the celebrity's behaviour indicates hypocrisy. The defences relating to anti-social conduct and misleading statements were added by Calcutt II and, it is submitted, are essential to draw a clear distinction between the private citizen and the public figure, and to ensure the accountability of the latter. The interpretation given to the defences would of course be crucial in ensuring that this distinction was maintained,[1] but it is suggested that the proposed offence should be cautiously welcomed as an addition to self-regulation; it provides a remedy against some unjustifiable invasions of privacy, without risking the deterrence of serious journalism and the concomitant loss of public accountability vital to a healthy democracy.

Some of the ground covered by the above proposals has been covered to a limited extent by the Protection from Harassment Act 1997. This makes it an offence to pursue a course of conduct which amounts to harassment of another, where the harasser knows or ought to know that this will be its effect. It also provides for a civil remedy in the form of damages or a restraining order. The primary target of this legislation was 'stalking', however, and it has severe limitations as a weapon against press intrusion on privacy. Most significant is the requirement of a 'course of conduct', which means that a single intrusion would not engage the Act's provisions (see *Sai Lau v DPP* (2000)). Exceptionally, the Act has been used in respect of harassment by the press in *Esther Thomas v News Group Newspapers* (2001), though privacy was not directly involved.

In conclusion, it is by no means certain that the various proposals that have been put forward in this area would achieve the right balance between privacy and press freedom. In any case, it seems that there is no political will in government to legislate. Self-regulation by the PCC is preferred; indeed the courts, in cases such as *A v B plc* (2002), will, after laying down basic principles, defer to the regulatory body for the detailed policing of standards. The legal position is now dominated by the HRA. Section 12 requires the courts to give proper weight to freedom of expression in considering restraints on publication. Recent celebrity cases, such as *A v B plc* (2002), suggest that the courts see the terms of an action for breach of confidence as sufficient to deal with most privacy claims, and the case shows a willingness to uphold a wide conception of the public interest in freedom of the press. Likewise, the PCC and Ofcom (successor to the BSC), as public authorities, will have to act compatibly with the Convention in exercising their powers. The way in which these regulatory bodies strike the balance between Arts 8 and 10 and, in relation to the PCC, the extent to which, as a self-regulator, confidence in the independence of its judgments is maintained may well determine whether pressure for further statutory control increases.

Note

1   It could be pointed out that the defences would offer reasonable protection to journalists if an honest belief in the factor in question was required. If a reasonable belief was required, this might stifle investigative journalism since, at an early stage in the investigation, such a belief could not be formed.

Question 21

How far, if at all, does the law protect bodily and sexual privacy? Is reform in this area needed?

Answer plan

A fairly tricky essay question since, unlike access to personal information, there is no obvious and coherent body of law which is relevant. It is probably a good idea to begin by considering what is meant by bodily and sexual privacy.

Essentially, the following areas should be considered:

- possible ambit of bodily and sexual privacy;
- bodily privacy and crime control: police powers in this area;
- corporal punishment;
- bodily privacy in the medical context;
- personal autonomy as to the expression of sexuality – legal restraints;
- Art 8, Sched 1 of the HRA 1998 and relevant European Court of Human Rights (ECtHR) decisions – *Laskey* (1997), *Lustig-Prean* (1999), *ADT* (2000) and *Goodwin* (2002);
- White Paper on sexual offences: *Protecting the Public* (2002) and the Sexual Offences Act 2003.

Answer

Bodily and sexual privacy may be seen as encompassing two main interests. First, individuals have an interest in preventing actual physical intrusions on the body. This interest consists of a negative right to be 'left alone' in a physical sense, but may also encompass a positive claim on the State to ensure that bodily integrity is not infringed. However, the main concern here is with the extent to which the State allows such infringement. Secondly, an individual has an interest in retaining autonomy as regards freedom of choice in decisions as to the disposal or control of his or her own body. Usually, the individual is, in effect, asking the State to leave him or her alone to make such decisions in order to preserve autonomy. In some instances, however, the individual will be requiring the assistance of the authorities in ensuring that he or she is able to exercise autonomy. Thus, personal privacy at its simplest level may be defined as the freedom from physical intrusion, but, arguably, the concept may be expanded to encompass individual autonomy, thereby allowing a variety of interests to be considered under this head.

The law determines that, in certain circumstances, bodily privacy may give way to other interests. Thus, s 55 of the Police and Criminal Evidence Act (PACE) 1984 allows intimate strip searches, but recognises that the violation they represent may occur only in well-defined circumstances. Examination may occur only if there is reasonable suspicion that Class A drugs or implements which might be used for self-harm or to harm others may be found. The examination may only be carried out by a nurse (or a medical practitioner in respect of drugs or a weapon) or, if that is not practicable, it can be carried out by a police officer who must be of the same sex as the person to be searched. Customs officers have similar (and slightly stronger) rights.

The question as to how far clothing could be removed on instruction of State officials has been considered in *Lindley v Rutter* (1980), where a general order to remove the bras of all female detainees in the police station was challenged. It was found that such treatment constituted an affront to human dignity and therefore could not be standard practice, but needed a clearer justification which could be derived only from the specific circumstances of the arrestee. In *Wainwright v Home Office* (2003), the House of Lords accepted that the voluntary strip search of a prisoner's visitor, which was done in a humiliating and unseemly manner, was a breach of the prison's regulations. However, the House refused to give a remedy in tort and would not create a remedy by recognising a general right of privacy. Under the HRA, intimate searches, strip searches and other matters such as the taking of bodily samples clearly engage Art 8(1) and so will require justification in terms of legal basis, purpose and proportionality under Art 8(2). In *Wainwright*, it was suggested that any remedy under the Act would require the violation of privacy to be intentional rather than simply negligent.

Certain forms of punishment may be seen as an unjustified intrusion onto bodily integrity. Corporal punishment was outlawed in State schools after the decision of the ECtHR in *Campbell and Cosans v UK* (1982), and the ban was extended to private schools by the Schools Standards and Framework Act 1998. *Campbell and Cosans v UK* (1982) was determined not on the basis of Arts 3 or 8, but under Art 2 of the First Protocol, which protects the right of parents to have their children educated according to their own philosophical convictions. In *R (Williamson) v Secretary of State for Education* (2003), where a group of Christian parents and teachers challenged the ban applying to private schools, the Court of Appeal accepted that philosophical convictions about education, sufficient to engage Art 2 of the First Protocol, could, in principle, include beliefs in the virtue of reasonable corporal punishment. However, the Court denied that the statutory ban involved a violation of the

Art 2 right, since parents could always uphold their philosophical convictions by administering corporal punishment at home when their children broke school rules. In *Costello-Roberts v UK* (1993), the ECtHR found that the UK had a positive duty that schools, of whatever kind, used punishments that were compatible not only with Art 3 of the ECHR (which requires a sufficient level of severity) but also with Art 8. The latter, in certain circumstances, might afford a broader protection to physical integrity than that afforded by Art 3. In the most recent case to deal with this area, however, *A v UK* (1999), the ECtHR showed itself willing to interfere in family life in order to protect the rights of a child. A nine-year-old boy had been repeatedly beaten with a cane by his stepfather. The stepfather was acquitted of assault, having relied on the defence of reasonable chastisement. The ECtHR held that, by leaving the question of reasonableness to a jury and thus failing to protect the boy from ill-treatment, the UK was in breach of Art 3. To this extent, the Convention will protect bodily integrity, and this raises the possibility of the English courts further developing this area under the HRA.

Personal autonomy has been clearly recognised for some time in the US as a legitimate privacy interest – in *Doe v Bolton* (1973), Douglas J said:

> The right to privacy means freedom of choice in the basic decisions of one's life respecting marriage, divorce, procreation, contraception, education and upbringing of children.

Personal autonomy connotes an interest not in preventing physical intrusion by others, but in the extent to which the law allows an individual a degree of control over his or her own body. Recognition of the need to allow such self-determination has become more prominent this century. Thus, abortion and suicide are no longer crimes under the Abortion Act 1967 and the Suicide Act 1961. However, limits as to self-determination are represented by the Prohibition of Female Circumcision Act 1985 and the Surrogacy Act 1985 (although it should be noted that surrogacy is only curbed by the Act, not outlawed: it only prevents commercial surrogacy arrangements). Such measures may suggest that the 20th century placed greater value on bodily self-determination: the presumption is that, in this matter, the individual should apply his or her own moral standards, except when this allows something particularly abhorrent in British society to occur, such as female circumcision. Then, the law will impose the wider social standard on the particular individual.

The question of the ambit of self-determination has arisen most frequently in the context of medical treatment. In *Sidaway v Board of Governors of the Bethlem Royal Hospital* (1985), a professional standards test was upheld as regards the extent of information that patients should be given about the risks of any treatment. There would be no breach of a duty of care so long as the doctor had acted in accordance with practice accepted as proper by a body of medical practitioners (the test deriving from *Bolam v Friern HMC* (1957)) with regard to disclosure of risks. It may be argued that this stance fails to accord sufficient weight to the personal autonomy of the patient. Consent to medical treatment can involve the weighing of highly subjective factors such as, for example, life expectancy against a likely reduction in the quality of life. Arguably, it is the patient who will best know which of the options fits with his or her own aspirations and lifestyle, and certainly it is the patient who must live with the decision. Autonomy requires that he or she must be fully informed as to the options in order to take it effectively.[1]

Recent decisions of the courts indicate a greater willingness to accept adult patient autonomy. There are a number of cases in which the right of patients to refuse treatment has been upheld even though doctors believe the treatment is in the patient's best interests. It is, for example, unlawful for a hospital not to respect a pregnant woman's refusal of a Caesarean birth (*St George's Healthcare NHS Trust v S* (1998)) or a person's refusal of amputation of a gangrenous leg (*Re C (Adult: Refusal of Medical Treatment)* (1994)). The leading authority is *Re B (Consent to Treatment: Capacity)* (2002), in which the Court of Appeal upheld the right of a mentally alert but seriously ill woman to choose to have her life support machine turned off and, consequently, to die. What the law still will not permit is assisted suicide: where a seriously ill person wants to die but can only do so if others take positive steps. That the person assisting could be prosecuted for murder was confirmed in *R (Pretty) v DPP* (2002), and the ECtHR has held that there is no right to die inherent in Art 2 of the ECHR although, on the issue of dignity in death, Art 8 might be engaged (*Pretty v UK* (2002)).

Self-determination as regards the body in areas relating to sexuality may be regarded as a related interest, because it raises questions as to the extent to which individuals have the power of choice in relation to the expression of sexuality. Until recently, the criminal law continued to prohibit or restrict certain forms of sexual activity even though they were undertaken by consenting adults and did not involve harm to others. The justification for such prohibitions or restrictions was the need to use the criminal law to 'enforce morality' and uphold certain moral standards. Whether, in the absence of convincing arguments about harm to others, the criminal law should interfere in the private lives of citizens in order to enforce a particular pattern of behaviour, has been vigorously contested. The tendency of the law is now clearly set against prohibiting harmless conduct by consenting adults and this principle is embodied in the new law of sexual offences enacted during 2003.

Male homosexual acts, which could otherwise be crimes such as buggery or indecency between men (s 13 of the Sexual Offences Act 1956), were made legal by the Sexual Offences (Amendment) Act 1967 so long as they were undertaken in private. Indeed, the outright criminalisation of male homosexual acts involves an interference with private life, under Art 8(1) of the ECHR, that a State would find hard to justify under Art 8(2), even though States have a wide margin of appreciation on moral matters. In *Dudgeon v UK* (1981), the continuation of the threat of prosecution for private homosexual acts in Northern Ireland (to which the 1967 Act did not apply) was held to be disproportionate: it involved a grave interference with the applicant's private life despite, on the other hand, little evidence of damage to morals.

The 1967 Act set the age of consent at 21 and this was finally reduced to 16 by the Sexual Offences (Amendment) Act 2000, thus ending decades of discrimination between heterosexuals and homosexuals on the issue. Legal discrimination remained, particularly because the narrow conception of privacy in the 1967 Act meant that the criminal law could still be applied if, for example, there were more than two people present even in a private dwelling. Such discrimination may well be an unjustified intrusion into the right to private life in Art 8 of the ECHR, as was held in *ADT v UK* (2000).

The Sexual Offences Act 2003 introduces comprehensive reform. The Act redefines and creates a whole new range of sexual offences; it includes the abolition of the offences of buggery and indecency for both men and women. In general terms, the new offences are defined to deal with non-consensual (therefore harmful) sexual acts or to criminalise sexual acts involving children, or which are based on the exploitation of a relationship of trust or which involve other forms of sexual exploitation such as trafficking. With the exception of rape, a guiding principle is that sexual offences should not be gender specific. In so far as these reforms mean that the law on sexual behaviour is no longer based on moral disapproval and removes residues of discrimination based on gender and sexual orientation, it is to be welcomed as a necessary reform. Intercourse with an animal and the sexual penetration of a corpse are offences, and these can be sufficiently justified on the grounds of lack of consent, even if they also involve an expression of moral disapproval. Initial proposals for widespread restrictions on sexual activity in public places were toned down after parliamentary opposition during the passage of the Bill.

Some types of sado-masochistic behaviour are held to be unlawful whether or not the participants consent to it. The level of behaviour which will be unlawful despite consent is of a surprisingly minor nature; in *Donovan* (1934), it was defined as 'any hurt or injury calculated to interfere with health or comfort ... it need not be permanent, but must be more than merely transient or trifling'. However, such interference may be justified as in the public interest, thus exempting blows given in the course of friendly athletic contests which, following the ruling in *Coney* (1882), are seen as being for 'good reason'.

In *Brown* (1993), a group of sado-masochistic homosexuals had regularly, over 10 years, willingly participated in acts of violence against each other for the sexual pleasure engendered in the giving and receiving of pain. It was found that the inflicting of injuries amounting to actual bodily harm could not fall within the category of 'good reason' and therefore, despite the consent of all the participants, the defendants were convicted of actual bodily harm under the Offences Against the Person Act 1861. In *Laskey, Jaggard and Brown v UK* (1997), the ECtHR unanimously found that there had been no violation of Art 8, since it was within the State's competence to regard the convictions as necessary for the protection of health within Art 8(2).

This decision may be criticised for its subjectivity; it is unclear why it is acceptable that boxing contests may be carried out which can result in serious permanent injury or even death, while activities such as those in *Brown* are criminalised, although they may result in a lesser degree of harm. The activities in question were carried on privately and there was no suggestion that any of the 'victims' were coerced into consenting to them: all had chosen freely to participate and none seemed to be in a more powerful position than the others. The inescapable inference appears to be a moral-based objection to homosexual sado-masochism. Further, the domestic law appears to discriminate in favour of married couples (*Wilson* (1997), where a man branding his wife on the bottom was not considered a serious assault due to her consent). Such discrimination in private life should be difficult to continue to justify now that Art 14 of the ECHR is to be read into UK criminal law. The new legislation will not specifically deal with this issue, but, given its emphasis on consent, it perhaps indicates that the law should take a more tolerant view.

The rights of transsexuals have been a matter of concern. In a number of cases, the ECtHR allowed States to discriminate in law and administrative practices. However, the Court did note changing European standards. In *Goodwin v UK* (2002), it altered its position and has now held that discrimination against transsexuals can violate Art 8 and Art 12 (the right to marry). The restrictive British position was then made subject to a declaration of incompatibility by the House of Lords in *Bellinger v Bellinger* (2003). The government intends to bring forward proposals to deal with existing discrimination on matters such as birth certificates.

Similarly, the legal position of homosexual men and women was improved with, for example, the ending of administrative discharge from the armed forces following adverse rulings from the ECtHR (*Lustig-Prean v UK* (1999)). Major improvements are likely to follow through, for example, the introduction of the Civil Partnership Registration Scheme, which creates a range of family rights for same-sex couples which broadly place them in the same position as married or unmarried heterosexual couples. Discrimination in employment was, at last, outlawed in late 2003 under the terms of regulations designed to give effect to the Equal Treatment Framework Directive.

It is concluded that, until recently, the law had failed to give proper protection to bodily and sexual privacy and had permitted discrimination in a number of contexts. There is no question, however, that, in terms of the law, the situation is being transformed and, in most areas, non-discrimination and equality is now recognised as the policy of the law. The recognition of autonomy in consent to treatment cases, comprehensive new legislation relating to sexual offences which concentrates on lack of consent, abuse and exploitation rather than on immorality, and the major improvements in the position of homosexuals, transsexuals and same-sex couples which are being introduced suggest that legal protection is now improving greatly (though the arguably unreasonable assertion of moralism by the courts in the context of consensual sado-masochism still remains). These are, of course, recent changes in the law whose effects, not only on the law but also on attitudes in society, will need to be assessed in the fullness of time.

Note

1   It could be noted that medical consent forms are now, however, more detailed than they were 10 years ago, which suggests that respect for patient wishes is now seen as a priority.

Question 22

Consider the extent to which UK law maintains a reasonable balance between the freedom from infringement of privacy by agents of the State and the need to maintain internal security.

Answer plan

This is clearly quite a general and wide-ranging essay which requires knowledge of a number of different areas. It is mainly concerned with the power of the agents of the State to enter private property or to interfere with private property in furtherance of crime control and national security. The following areas should be considered:

- the Security Services Act 1989, the Intelligence Services Act 1994, the Police Act 1997, the Regulation of Investigatory Powers Act (RIPA) 2000 – safeguards against unreasonable intrusion;

- the influence of the European Court of Human Rights (ECtHR) in this area;
- ss 17 and 18 of PACE 1984 – safeguards in respect of the search and seizure power;
- Code of Practice B made under PACE (revised March 2003);
- comparison between powers of the security services to enter premises and those of police officers;
- the Terrorism Act 2000 and Pt 3 of the Anti-Terrorism, Crime and Security Act 2001.

Answer

Before addressing this question, it is necessary to consider what is meant by 'infringement of privacy' by State agents. It should not merely connote physical intrusion, but could clearly occur in a number of ways. Apart from entry to property, search and seizure, it could include the use of long-range surveillance devices, telephone tapping and the planting of surveillance devices on property. It would seem to include any form of violation of the privacy of the home. A number of private persons, such as reporters, might wish to undertake such intrusion, but the concern here is with intrusion by the agents of the State, with the aim of promoting internal security. Such an aim is clearly legitimate; the question is whether the safeguards against unreasonable intrusion are adequate.

The first point to be made is that the citizen may not even be aware that intrusion is taking place. This is particularly true of telephone tapping and the use of surveillance devices. Public awareness of the use of such devices is severely curtailed by the operation of the Official Secrets Act 1989, the Security Services Act 1989 and the RIPA 2000. In addition to preventing information as to the operation of the security services reaching the public domain, these statutes provide wide grounds on which the powers of the security services and the power to tap can be invoked.

The ECtHR in, for example, *Klass v Germany* (1979) has accepted that surveillance for national security purposes may be compatible with Art 8. Non-national security cases such as *Malone v UK* (1984) and *Kopp v Switzerland* (1999) confirm that surveillance must be regulated by law and the circumstances in which it is likely to be used be made reasonably foreseeable, and that there must be appropriate protection built into the regulatory scheme, albeit such protection is bound to reflect the secrecy of the process.

In Britain, the Home Secretary may issue warrants for the interception of communications by the security services under wide powers found in s 5 of the RIPA 2000, the successor to the Interception of Communications Act 1985.

The purposes for which warrants may be issued include that the warrant is necessary 'in the interests of national security' and 'for the purpose of safeguarding the economic wellbeing of the UK'. An important restriction on the Home Secretary's powers, in line with ECHR requirements under Art 8(2), is that an interception warrant 'shall not' be issued unless the Home Secretary believes that the conduct it authorises 'is proportionate to what is sought to be achieved'.

Public scrutiny is weak. Complaints can be made only to a tribunal set up under the Act with no possibility of scrutiny by a court. Whether the tribunal meets the requirements of independence and impartiality required by Art 6 is unclear. Tribunal decisions are not published and, although an annual report giving some information on the number of intercept warrants issued must be made available, it is first subject to censorship by the Prime Minister. The courts have, in the past, shown a reluctance to have their jurisdiction totally ousted even over national security matters (see, for instance, *Secretary of State for Home Affairs ex p Ruddock* (1987) where the right of the court to review whether legitimate expectations aroused by government statements on surveillance was asserted). The current tendency, post-11 September 2001, seems to be greater deference by the court to the government on national security claims (see *Rehman v Secretary of State for the Home Department* (2002)). In any case, there is a statutory bar to disclosure in court of information indicating that warranted telephone interceptions had been made (ss 17 and 18 of the RIPA 2000), and the danger of unaccountable State actions seriously affecting the liberty and private lives of citizens is real.

The Convention requirement that restrictions on the right to private life in Art 8(1) must, *inter alia*, be 'in accordance with the law' led, following an adverse Commission finding in *Harman and Hewitt v UK* (1986), to the Security Services Act 1989. The Act places MI5 on a statutory basis and it has been accepted by the Commission (*Esbester v UK* (1993)) as satisfying the legality test. In *Harman and Hewitt v UK* (1986), there was also held to be a breach of Art 13, the right to a remedy. Whether the 1989 Act resolves this issue is questionable, since the Act prevents almost all effective scrutiny of its operations. If a member of the public has a grievance concerning its operations, complaint to a court is not possible: under s 5 of the Act, complaint can only be made to a tribunal and, under s 5(4), the decisions of the tribunal are not questionable in any court of law. (It should be noted that the remedy under Art 13 need not be from a 'judicial authority' but it must be effective in the context: *Silver v UK* (1983).) Citizens may often be unaware that surveillance is taking place; service personnel who feel that they have been required to act improperly in bugging or searching a person's property are not permitted to complain to the tribunal and need to rely on internal reporting procedures for dealing with their concerns (*R v Shayler* (2002)).

Furthermore, parliamentary oversight of the security service is limited. The Intelligence Services Act 1994 followed the 1989 Act and placed MI6 and GCHQ on a statutory basis. Section 10 sets up a Parliamentary Committee to oversee the administration and policy of MI5, MI6 and GCHQ. Though this is a welcome move, the Committee cannot compel the disclosure of information against the wishes of the secret services or the Secretary of State and any report it makes is subject to censorship by the Prime Minister.

Given the width of the powers conferred on members of the security services under this legislation, the lack of accountability is disturbing. Any private individual can have surveillance devices placed on his or her premises, or can be subject to a search of the premises, even though engaged in lawful political activity which is not intended to serve any foreign interest. If the security services wish to enter or interfere with property, the Secretary of State can issue a warrant under s 5 of the 1994 Act. The warrant can be issued so long as the Secretary of State thinks it is 'necessary' for 'assisting' the various secret services in the discharge of their functions. The safeguards are internal and hard to challenge: the Secretary of State must be satisfied that the issue of a warrant is 'proportionate' to what is to be achieved, that this could not be achieved by other means and that there are adequate procedures to prevent improper disclosure of information gained. The functions of the Security Service are widely defined in s 1 of the 1989 Act and include 'the protection of national security and, in particular, its protection from ... actions intended to overthrow or undermine parliamentary democracy by political, industrial or violent means'.

The ease with which warrants may be obtained and the concomitant disregard for individual privacy may be contrasted with the position in Canada. The Canadian Security Intelligence Service (CSIS) can only be granted warrants on the authorisation of a judge, thus ensuring a measure of independent oversight. Moreover, the warrant will not be issued unless the facts relied on to justify the belief that a warrant is necessary to investigate a threat to national security are set out in a sworn statement. Clearly, the Canadian system places greater emphasis on the privacy of the citizen and therefore appears to strike a fairer balance between privacy on the one hand and the security of the State on the other.

The two statutes mentioned will work in tandem with the Official Secrets Act 1989, s 1(1) of which prevents members or former members of the security services disclosing anything at all about the operation of those services. All such members come under a lifelong duty to keep silent, even though their information might reveal serious abuse of power by the security services. There is no 'public interest' defence available under the Act (*R v Shayler* (2002)). These provisions also apply to anyone who is notified that he or she is subject to the provisions of the sub-section. Similarly, s 4(3) of the

Act prohibits disclosure of information obtained by or relating to the issue of a warrant under the RIPA 2000 or the Intelligence Services Act 1994. The wide grounds on which intrusion may be authorised, the secrecy surrounding the issuing of intercept warrants and burgling warrants, and the lack of an effective complaints procedure suggest that the balance has tipped too far away from concern for the privacy of the individual.

Warrants for the interception of communications under s 5 of the RIPA 2000 can be issued to the police (through the National Criminal Intelligence Service in England and Wales) for purposes including the detection of serious crime. The Security Service also has jurisdiction regarding serious crime. In a surveillance context and generally, the increasing involvement of security services in the traditional police function (against organised crime and terrorism, for example) is a matter for concern because of the far weaker legal regulation that applies to the security services.

For general purposes, the police may only enter premises in certain carefully defined circumstances and must follow a procedure, once there, designed to allow the citizen a reasonable chance of making a complaint if he or she wishes to do so. The basis of the procedure is in PACE and these powers are subject to more detailed requirements found in Code of Practice B, which was revised and reissued in March 2003.

First, the power to enter premises conferred by ss 17 and 18 of PACE can be exercised either where an officer wants to arrest a person suspected of an arrestable offence, or where a person has been so arrested and the intention is to search the person's premises immediately after arrest. Searching of premises other than under ss 17 and 18 can only occur if a search warrant is issued by a magistrate. A warrant will only be issued if there are reasonable grounds for believing that a serious arrestable offence has been committed and where the material is likely to be of substantial value to the investigation of the offence. The warrant must identify the articles to be sought, although once the officer is on the premises, other articles may be seized under s 19 if they appear to relate to any other offence. Further, the warrant authorises entry to premises on one occasion only. Important privacy issues can arise in respect of various types of confidential material and information. Police may not search for legally privileged material and other forms of confidential material, including journalistic material, cannot be searched for but require a disclosure order made by a judge usually on the basis of a hearing. A disclosure order can be refused on public interest grounds. These restrictions do not apply to warrants obtained by the security services, discussed above. The Criminal Justice and Police Act 2001 allows police to remove documents in order to see whether they come within one of the forbidden or restricted categories.

Under paras 5 and 6 of Code B, the subjects of all searches, consensual or otherwise, must receive information about the search in the form of a Notice of Powers and Rights and, under para 6.8, where a search has taken place but the occupier is absent, the Notice should be endorsed with the name of the officer and the date and time. Revised Code B retains the peculiarity that an officer need only identify her or himself where there is a non-consensual search (compare 5.2 with 6.5). It is suggested that protection for consensual searches should be as strong as for non-consensual searches since, despite the provision in Code B, para 5.2 that a person must be informed that they are not obliged to consent, many people may, nevertheless, believe they have little effective option.

These provisions suggest some determination to strike a reasonable balance between the perceived need to confer on the police a general power to search property and the need to protect the citizen. If the powers are exceeded, an action for trespass will lie. However, it may be argued that, although the provisions governing the power to enter premises show a respect for privacy, the provisions governing seizure, particularly s 19 of PACE, come too close to allowing a general ransacking of the premises once a lawful entry has been effected.

The Police Act 1997 put bugging and surveillance (other than searches) on a statutory footing for the first time. A warrant in respect of private premises can only be granted if the independent Commissioner has been consulted first. Complaints are to the surveillance tribunal, discussed above, and the same problems of lack of judicial oversight apply, but the Act allows unauthorised surveillance to be admitted as evidence in a later trial and, hence, has attracted much negative criticism.

The RIPA 2000 has extended the Police Act approach to 'directed' and 'intrusive' surveillance by the police and the security services. An example of directed surveillance would be where a 'bugging' device is placed in the hallway of a block of flats, thus providing information of a lesser quality than if the device was inside one of the flats. Intrusive surveillance would occur, for example, where a bugging device is placed in a car parked near a private house, thus providing information of the same quality as if the device was inside the house. The difference between the two types of surveillance is also indicated by the level of authority required to authorise it. As far as the police are concerned, for example, directed surveillance must generally be authorised by a superintendent; intrusive surveillance, on the other hand, must generally be authorised by the Chief Constable. Moreover, unless the case is urgent, approval for intrusive surveillance must generally be obtained in advance from an independent Surveillance Commissioner. It has been argued that this 'twin-track' approach to the different types of surveillance is unsatisfactory and, in particular, that the scheme for directed surveillance demonstrates little respect for individual privacy.

Serious issues have arisen in respect of anti-terrorism legislation. For example, s 37 of and Sched 5 to the Terrorism Act 2000 allow the police to seek a search warrant if it could lead to obtaining material of substantial value to a 'terrorist investigation'. The latter term is very widely defined and is not confined to activities which, in themselves, are criminal offences. The police have an additional power in the terrorist context, which is to demand an explanation from an occupier for any material produced by the search. Anti-terrorism legislation can also have an impact on normal rights of privacy in other ways. Part 3 of the Anti-Terrorism, Crime and Security Act 2001, for instance, drastically loosens the rules governing the circumstances in which public authorities holding personal information for a particular purpose can disclose it to other bodies, including the police, to assist in the investigation of crime.

Although it is to be welcomed that the statutory controls over surveillance now encompass both the police and the security services, it is not clear that the balance between personal privacy and the needs of internal security has been struck in the right place. There may well be challenges to the operation of these powers under the HRA and the desire to forestall such challenges clearly explains much of the legislation. Provided that there is a statutory scheme, that the question of the 'proportionality' of any action can be addressed (both of which are dealt with by the RIPA), and that the target's rights are recognised by some form of judicial-type scrutiny, albeit secret, the ECtHR has accepted the need for intrusive actions by the police and security services to deal with both national security and 'ordinary' serious crime. Thus, the general terms of the current law may well be compatible with the Convention so long as the tribunal is accepted as being capable of dealing with proportionality and, in context, providing an adequate remedy (Art 13) and a fair trial in so far as Art 6 is engaged. On national security, however, recent UK cases, post-11 September 2001 (for example, *Rehman v Secretary of State for the Home Department* (2001) and *A v Secretary of State for the Home Department* (2002)), suggest a willingness to defer to the executive on the issue of the existence and significance of a threat, and this will make any claim that an act of surveillance or other interference with privacy is disproportionate, very difficult to establish. The conclusion must be that the balance, particularly regarding national security, is still in favour of the police and security services as opposed to the privacy of the individual.

Question 23

Does Art 8 in Sched 1 to the Human Rights Act 1998 provide the basis for sufficient legal protection for legitimate claims to privacy that are not otherwise met by English law?

Answer plan

This question requires a critical assessment of Art 8 and its likely impact in English law under the HRA 1998. The invitation in the question is to focus on the case law, the jurisprudence, developed by the European Court of Human Rights (ECtHR) as it has applied Art 8 in different situations. There also needs to be an awareness of the circumstances in which Art 8 will be relevant under the terms of the 1998 Act. Above all, the focus of the answer should be on a critical assessment of the effectiveness of Art 8, by bringing out points of criticism and difficulty.

Essentially, the following areas should be considered:

- inadequacies, in general terms, with the protection of privacy under English law;
- the HRA, especially ss 3, 6 and 7;
- the terms of Art 8(1) and (2) of the European Convention on Human Rights (ECHR);
- the conception of private life developed by the ECtHR;
- issues involving respect for private life that relate to the terms of Art 8(2) such as 'in accordance with the law', 'margin of appreciation' and 'deference';
- case law dealing with the balance between private life and freedom of expression such as *A v B plc* and *Douglas v Hello!*.

Answer

The lack of a comprehensive, legally protected right to privacy in English common law has often been attested to by the judges (see *Kaye v Robertson* (1990) and more recently, *Wainwright v Secretary of State for the Home Department* (2003)). Privacy is the right, justified by dignity and autonomy, of an individual to be left alone and to decide and act as she or he sees fit. Aspects of privacy are legally protected by, for example, particular rules of common law or equity, such as breach of confidence; or by Act of Parliament, such as the Data Protection Act 1998. However, there remain major gaps. In

Wainwright, for example, the claimants had been subjected to an illegal strip search by prison officers but their claim for damages could not succeed in trespass. The judge at first instance took the view that it might have succeeded had there been a general right to privacy, giving rise to effective remedies, available in the law; this was doubted in the Lords.

Article 8 of the ECHR may, under the terms of the HRA 1998, go a long way towards providing such a general right. The first paragraph of Art 8 provides that 'everyone has the right to respect for his private and family life, his home and his correspondence'. The second paragraph lays down the exclusive circumstances under which this right may be interfered with by a public authority.

Under the terms of the HRA, the courts must now interpret Acts of Parliament, so far as it is possible to do so, to be compatible with Art 8; under ss 6 and 7, they are required to give a remedy against any public authority, including any person exercising public functions, which has violated Art 8. Where neither Act of Parliament nor public authority is involved, the courts, as public authorities themselves, are still required to act compatibly with the Article when, for example, developing the law or exercising discretion over remedies. In such circumstances, the courts are not required to create a new general right to privacy, but can use Art 8 to influence the way existing legal rights and remedies, such as breach of confidence, develop.

Given that, under the HRA, Art 8 will apply in the ways suggested, the next issue is to consider what the Article requires in terms of substantive law. Article 8 has the same structure as Arts 9, 10 and 11. There are two paragraphs: the courts must consider, first, whether the issue before them comes within the protection of Art 8(1) and, second, if Art 8(1) is engaged, whether the interference with private life, etc, is justified; it can only be justified in terms of Art 8(2).

Article 8(1) covers a wide range of matters going way beyond the scope of protections offered by the main categories of the common law. In particular, the Convention concept of 'private life' has been inclusively and non-exhaustively interpreted by the ECtHR in a way that responds to developments in social life. The guiding principle is the concept of individual autonomy and Art 8(1) can be invoked in respect of matters which are central to individual self-respect and wellbeing. It includes not only physical and psychological integrity, but also matters which are fundamental to a person's sense of identity such as gender, sexual orientation and sexual behaviour. In *Gaskin v UK* (1989), for example, Art 8(1) supported a right to have access to personal information about the applicant's childhood which was held by a social services department. Such information was necessary for the applicant's sense of identity and social development. The link between private life and autonomy, self-directedness, was indicated in *Pretty v UK*

(2002), where a right to die with dignity was accepted by the ECtHR as coming within the ambit of Art 8(1). The link between private life and the sense of wellbeing means that Art 8 can apply in the environmental context: it includes a right to a clean and quiet environment and can be invoked over issues such as night flying from Heathrow Airport (*Hatton v UK* (2003)).

The wide scope of Art 8(1) means that many reasonable privacy claims are likely to come within the scope of the Article. There will, of course, remain arguments at the margins. The extent to which persons have rights of privacy against being photographed or followed even though they are in a public place, is a good example. The law is developing in this area, but in *Peck v UK* (2003), which involved the improper use by the media of CCTV footage of the applicant's failed suicide attempt made in a town centre, it was made clear that there can still be certain reasonable expectations of privacy in such circumstances.

Doubts about the effectiveness of Art 8 are predominantly directed towards Art 8(2), which describes the exclusive circumstances under which a matter of private life, etc, can be interfered with by a public authority. Although Art 8(2) refers to interferences by a 'public authority', it is well-established that respect for private life, etc, is a State responsibility in the sense that, although the interference complained of may be directly caused by a private organisation (a company polluting the air, for example), Art 8(2) is engaged because the State has a duty to regulate social and economic life in such a way as to secure persons' Art 8 rights. It is in terms of Art 8(2) that the balancing between the claims of individuals to be left alone and the claims of society to pursue matters in the public interest despite their impact on individuals is undertaken.

First, any such interference must be 'in accordance with the law'. This means that State agents undertaking actions which interfere with private life, etc, must act on the basis of promulgated rules. This requirement has had a major impact on UK law, particularly in the context of privacy. State surveillance, for example, used to be conducted on the doubtful basis of prerogative or other administrative discretion. Cases such as *Malone v UK* (1985) and *Halford v UK* (1997) showed that this was not an adequate legal basis and there are now statutes in terms of which surveillance by various agencies can be authorised. 'In accordance with the law' also means that the promulgated law should be sufficiently detailed and precise to enable individuals who might be affected to foresee, by themselves or with professional advice, the circumstances in which they might be at risk from interference. It is arguable, particularly in the context of State surveillance, that Art 8 promises much more than it delivers in this matter. The legal regime on surveillance in the UK provides little, if any, scope for individuals to know about the uses of surveillance against them (there is a tribunal to complain to, but its dealings are largely secret); yet given past case law, the system is unlikely to violate Art 8. The foreseeability requirement of 'in accordance with the law' is, it seems, easily met.

Secondly, interferences with private life, etc, can only be for one or more of the purposes listed in Art 8(2). Similar to Arts 9(2), 10(2) and 11(2), these purposes are wide-ranging. They include 'the protection of the rights and freedoms of others' which can be invoked in a wide range of circumstances. Again, it will not normally be difficult for a public authority to show that it has restricted private life for a legitimate purpose under the Convention.

Two purposes are of particular interest in the context of private life. Again, arguably, they indicate that the balance in Art 8 between individual and State favours the latter, and may make reasonable privacy claims hard to sustain. First, privacy (as with the freedoms protected by Arts 9, 10 and 11) can be restricted 'for the protection of morals'. There is a good question, sounding in liberal theory, whether the State can legitimately restrict activities which are harmless to others but which violate some moral standard supposedly upheld in society. Classic liberal theory insists that autonomy (essential to private life) means that individuals should be free to pursue their chosen tastes and pursuits subject only to the requirement that they do not harm others. If 'harm' is to be a significant standard then it cannot be a wholly open-textured, merely subjective, term. Rather, 'harm' must be defined to exclude mere revulsion or disgust that people may feel at the thought of 'immoral' activities being performed. Article 8(2), however, permits restrictions which are illiberal in this sense. The issue was well-illustrated in *Laskey, Jaggard and Brown* (1997), in which the ECtHR refused to find a violation of Art 8 in respect of the conviction of a group of sado-masochists for actions undertaken voluntarily. Part of the Court's reasoning was that the crime for which the applicants had been convicted had the legitimate purpose of protecting morals. Article 8(2) is, secondly, unique in that it allows restrictions on private life 'in the interests of ... the economic wellbeing of the country'. This is an open-ended and permissive purpose, which, again, makes it easy for the State to show that its objectives are legitimate. In *Hatton v UK* (2003), it was accepted as a purpose justifying restriction on private life in the context of noise from night flying at Heathrow Airport; there could be concern that it can play a role in restricting the development of Art 8 in the context of environmental rights.

By far the most important issue concerning Art 8(2) is that any interference with private life, etc, must be 'necessary in a democratic society'. This has been taken to mean that any restriction must be a proportionate means of meeting a pressing social need. Thus, a court dealing with an Art 8 claim must make a detailed examination of the arguments put forward by the State for restricting private life and ensure that a fair balance has been made, given the strength of the privacy claim and the strength of the public interest in the legitimate purpose invoked. Proportionality imposes upon UK courts dealing with Art 8 issues a greater responsibility than before to assess the need for the restriction in the light of the legitimate purpose and the possibility of using other, less restrictive, means (*R (Daly) v Secretary of State for the Home Department* (2001)).

The 'margin of appreciation' doctrine applies to Art 8(2). It allows governments to decide proportionality issues on the grounds that they are better placed in terms of knowledge and understanding of the issues than an international court can ever be. The doctrine is variable and context-dependent: on some moral issues, such as in the sado-masochism case, it has a decisive role which reinforces the illiberalism of the Court's position, as discussed above. There are, however, examples of how the ECtHR has restricted the margin of appreciation in line with its sense of a developing Europe-wide consensus, even on a moral issue. The position of transsexuals is a good example. In *Goodwin v UK* (2002), the ECtHR has altered its position, greatly narrowed what had been a wide margin of appreciation and, in consequence, found that most, if not all, forms of legal discrimination against transsexuals involved an unjustified interference with their private life.

Domestic courts do not invoke the margin of appreciation. Its place is taken by the concept of 'deference' by which the courts will defer to the State authorities. Deference is context-dependent but it does mean that on some issues, particularly national security and anti-terrorism, a high degree of deference can be (and is) shown on, for example, the genuineness of threats; the greater degree of deference the courts feel is appropriate to a situation, the less assistance Art 8 can be to those who feel victimised by State action.

The desire of people to protect their privacy against media intrusion means that Art 8 can come into conflict with Art 10 (freedom of expression). English law on breach of confidence illustrates the problem well. Nothing in the Convention indicates how Arts 8 and 10 are to be compromised with each other. This is a matter for the courts seeking a balance appropriate to the individual facts. In the breach of confidence case *A v B plc* (2002), for example, the balance was in favour of freedom of expression, whilst in *Douglas v Hello!* (2003), it favoured private life. Section 12 of the HRA requires the UK courts to 'have particular regard to the importance ... of freedom of expression' in cases involving free speech, but the courts have resisted an interpretation of this section which appears to give a priority to Art 10 over Art 8 (*Douglas v Hello!* (2001)).

In conclusion, it can be seen that Art 8 is of great importance and, under the HRA , is capable of creating legal rights in a number of areas where, prior to the Act, there were few legal rights despite strong, arguable, privacy claims. However, the importance of Art 8 should not be overstated. It is subject to important limitations in its effects which derive from, amongst other things, the undemanding test of 'in accordance with the law', the wide range of purposes for which privacy can be legitimately restricted and the concept of the margin of appreciation and deference which, sometimes in areas in which privacy is most vulnerable to State interference, allow the State and its agents considerable freedom.

Question 24

You have been asked to research whether the UK requires a new privacy law in order to comply with its obligations under the Human Rights Act 1998. Present the findings of your research.

Answer plan

A slightly more inventive way of presenting a reasonably straightforward essay question, which requires consideration of the current law of privacy and of means of developing it to ensure that there are no gaps in its protection of the right to privacy. Since the essay is so wide-ranging, it will be necessary to be selective in the coverage of topics; otherwise, it will be too superficial. Since protection of personal information is seen as a key privacy issue at present, the coverage below has largely concentrated on that area.

Essentially, the following areas should be considered:

- breach of confidence;
- defamation and malicious falsehood;
- trespass and nuisance;
- development of existing remedies;
- possible incompatibility with the European Convention on Human Rights (ECHR);
- proposals for a new tort of invasion of privacy;
- recent controversial legislation such as the Regulation of Investigatory Powers Act (RIPA) 2000.

Answer

Since the ECHR has been incorporated into UK law, a right to respect for private and family life has for the first time become part of domestic law due to Art 8. It should be noted that this is not, strictly speaking, a right to privacy, but merely a right to 'respect', which is a lesser measure. Further, UK law by no means ignores privacy rights, but rather has a strange, sketchy and complicated way of protecting them. Thus, in order to decide whether and how reform is necessary, the present law must first be considered and then compared with relevant European Court of Human Rights (ECtHR) case law.

Privacy may be said to encompass two broad interests, which may be termed control over intrusions and control over personal information. At present, UK law recognises no general rights to privacy, although there is some evidence, as will be seen, that judges consider it to be an evil which should be remedied. It can be argued that the various heads of tort or equity such as trespass, breach of confidence, copyright and defamation are instances of a right to privacy, but the House of Lords, confirming cases such as *Kaye v Robertson* (1991), made clear in *Wainwright v Secretary of State for the Home Department* (2003) that these areas and others must be treated as covering specific and distinct interests which may only incidentally offer protection to privacy. The courts have often repeated that there is no general right to privacy in the common law. In cases involving a claim to privacy, it will be found that a recognised interest such as property actually formed the basis of the ruling. It will be argued that UK law currently offers a somewhat piecemeal protection to privacy and so reasonable privacy claims may be unmet if they cannot be brought within the terms of a particular tort or other form of action. In *Wainwright v Secretary of State for the Home Department*, two people visiting a prison were, prior to the HRA coming into effect, subject to an unlawful strip search which represented a gross invasion of their privacy. An action for damages against the prison authorities failed because, in the absence of an intention by prison officers to harm, the search could not be brought within the definition of the tort of trespass to the person. The HRA will fill some, but not all, of the 'gaps' in the law of privacy. It does not necessarily follow that even further measures are necessary if other 'gaps' remain.

Traditionally, the law has regarded intrusions on property as being less serious than physical intrusion on the body and therefore remedies are found in the civil, rather than the criminal law. A number of private persons, such as reporters, as well as agents of the State, might wish to undertake such intrusion and therefore the right to be left alone to enjoy one's property may impose positive obligations upon the State. The term 'intrusion' as used here is being given a wide meaning; it is intended to connote not just physical intrusion, but any activity which results in diminishing the privacy of the home. In this sense, many methods of invasion of the home may be seen as intrusion: trespassing, harassing, photographing, watching or lurking, or snooping using long-range, electronic surveillance devices. Many sophisticated devices are now available to someone who wants to place a person's home under surveillance and these remove the need for the snooper or watcher to enter the target's property. It can be argued that the law has not caught up with the new technology. The use of surveillance devices was not covered by the Interception of Communications Act 1985, and is not prevented by the RIPA 2000.

Limited protection from such intrusion is afforded by actions for the torts of trespass or nuisance. Trespass is defined as entering onto land in the possession of another without lawful justification. It is confined to instances in which there is some physical entry; neither prying with binoculars nor electronic eavesdropping from outside the target's land is covered. Surveillance from the highway could give rise to a legal remedy if the observer is not on the highway by right. As a matter of right the public may pass and re-pass along the highway and may also perform incidental activities and, perhaps, other reasonable activities as discussed by the House of Lords in *DPP v Jones* (1999). Surveillance activities may be incompatible with this right and so someone conducting surveillance would be vulnerable to an action for trespass from the person in possession of the land over which the highway ran. As *Hickman v Maisey* (1900) demonstrates, this person may be the object of the surveillance, though is more likely to be a public authority with no particular interest in preventing the surveillance.

Bernstein v Skyviews (1978) illustrates another limit to the ability of trespass to protect privacy. The defendants flew over the plaintiff's land in order to take photographs of it. The question arose whether the plaintiff had a right in trespass to prevent such intrusion. It was held that either he had no rights of possession over the air space in which the aeroplane flew or, alternatively, if he did have such rights, s 40 of the Civil Aviation Act 1942 exempted reasonable flights from liability. The court was not prepared to find that the taking of one photograph was unreasonable and a remedy could not be based solely on invasion of privacy as, of course, there is no such tort. How far can the tort of nuisance provide a means of protecting privacy? Nuisance involves disturbing a person in the enjoyment of his or her land to an extent that the law regards as unreasonable. There is a dearth of authority on the issue of surveillance. *Dicta* in an Australian case (*Victoria Park Racing Co v Taylor* (1937)) suggested that there would, in general, be no remedy in nuisance for looking over another's premises. However, *dicta* in *Bernstein* favoured the possibility that grossly invasive, embarrassing surveillance would amount to a nuisance and in *Khorasandjian v Bush* (1993), the Court of Appeal held that harassment could amount to nuisance. However, the House of Lords in *Hunter v Canary Wharf* (1997) restricted the range of plaintiffs in nuisance cases to those with a proprietary interest in the land affected. 'Harassing' behaviour of the kind which occurred in *Bush* is now easiest dealt with under the terms of s 1 of the Protection from Harassment Act 1997. The

1997 Act makes it an offence to pursue a course of conduct which amounts to harassment of another, where the harasser knows or ought to know that this will be its effect. It also provides for a civil remedy in the form of damages or a restraining order. The primary target of this legislation was 'stalking', however, and it has severe limitations as a general weapon against intrusion on privacy. Most significant is the requirement of a 'course of conduct', which means that a single intrusion would not engage the Act's provisions (see *Sai Lau v DPP* (2000)).

Common law actions in trespass and nuisance seem to offer only limited protection from invasions of privacy. Since 1972, there have been repeated recommendations, not so far heeded, that surveillance would become a crime when surreptitious, and that information collected by these means should be banned from publication.

These days, surveillance is often conducted by CCTV. There is surprisingly little regulation, although the Information Commissioner has produced a Code of Practice dealing with the requirements of the Data Protection Act 1998 as regards CCTV in public places. The use of CCTV in public places may not, in itself, raise major privacy questions in the eyes of the law. Article 8 of the ECHR, for example, does not provide for a right not to be photographed in the street (*Freidl v Austria* (1996)). However, misuse of the resulting film will raise privacy issues. In *Peck v UK* (2003), the applicant's suicide attempt was recorded on CCTV and distributed to the media by the local council involved. There was held to be a violation of Art 8, and this should now influence, for example, any judicial review by the English courts of local council decisions about the use of CCTV.

Intrusion on property may be with a view to obtaining and then publishing personal information. Various areas of the law exist aimed specifically at the dual invasion of privacy which is involved in such activity and therefore they control, to an extent, the activity of the media in obtaining information regarding an individual's private life and publishing the details, possibly in exaggerated terms. These controls may affect both the publication of information and the methods used to obtain it. Control over the publication of personal information is to be found in the laws of confidence, copyright, defamation and malicious falsehood. However, it will be argued that these controls are limited in scope and are aimed at the protection of other interests, making them ill-suited to the protection of privacy. The law of defamation is often thought to be closely linked to the protection of privacy. The difficulty with the use of defamation, however, is that the defence of justification means that it will not usually affect the situation where true facts are revealed. Moreover, the interest protected by defamation – the interest in preserving reputation – is not synonymous with the interest in preserving privacy. A reputation may not suffer, but private facts may nevertheless be spread abroad, which is, in itself, hurtful for the individual affected. It can also be very difficult to obtain an injunction to restrain publication on the basis of a likely defamation. In *Kaye v Robertson and Another* (1990), a well-known actor suffered serious injuries in a car crash and was photographed and interviewed in his hospital bed by two journalists. Due to his injuries, he did not object to their presence and shortly after the incident had no recollection of it. The Court of Appeal accepted that the article's implication that Mr Kaye had consented to a first 'exclusive' interview for a 'lurid and sensational' newspaper would lower him in the esteem of right-thinking people. However, the success of the claim was not inevitable and so it could not warrant the grant of an interim injunction. The court accepted that defamation and other forms of action did not deal directly with the 'monstrous invasion of privacy', which was his real grievance. An injunction founded on malicious falsehood, restraining the defendants until trial from publishing anything which suggested that the plaintiff had given an informed consent to the interview or the taking of the photographs, was substituted for the original order. However, this was a limited injunction, which allowed publication of the story with a certain number of the photographs. Thus, it seemed that no effective remedy was available for the plaintiff.

A further possible candidate for the development of a common law remedy for privacy is breach of confidence. This will protect some confidential communications, and its breadth has supported the view that it could afford a general means of protecting personal information. The Younger Committee, which reported on the legal protection of privacy in 1972, considered that confidence was the area of law which offered the most effective protection of privacy. It has a wider ambit than defamation, in that it prevents truthful communications and appears to protect confidential communications, whether or not their unauthorised disclosure causes detriment to the reputation of any person. However, it must be remembered that confidence, while quite closely associated with it, is, strictly speaking, protecting a somewhat different interest from that of privacy; it is concerned with the preservation of confidentiality and therefore may not be apt to cover all possible circumstances in which private life is laid bare.

At one time it was thought that breach of confidence was actionable only where there was a prior relationship implying confidentiality, such as between master and servant, husband and wife, medical practitioner and patient or secret service agent and the government. However, cases such as *Stephens v Avery* suggest that a relationship of confidence can be found, despite the absence of a formal relationship, and the concept of breach of confidence is clearly approaching the provision of a remedy to protect a general right of privacy to protect information about oneself being made public. An important point about breach of confidence is that any remedy requires a consideration of the public interest – whether, on balance, the public interest favours disclosure over secrecy; the law will not protect infamous conduct from disclosure. In *R v Chief Constable of North Wales ex p AB* (1999), for example, the disclosure by the police of confidential information about the whereabouts of child sex offenders was upheld on public interest grounds.

The extent to which breach of confidence, with the HRA as a catalyst, has developed into a comprehensive means for protecting privacy is hard to judge. In *Douglas v Hello!* (2002), in which the Court of Appeal was considering whether or not to confirm an interlocutory injunction preventing the unauthorised publication of photographs of the wedding of Catherine Zeta Jones and Michael Douglas, it was suggested by Sedley LJ that common law breach of confidence could be developed so that it would protect reasonable privacy claims without the need to establish the breach of a duty of confidentiality. In *Venables v News Group Newspapers* (2001), breach of confidence was applied in a new area to protect, in essence, a right of privacy. In this case, two young men who were serving sentences for the murder of a young boy sought injunctions restraining the media from revealing information which would enable them to be identified once they were released from prison and given new identities. Granting the injunctions on the basis of confidentiality, the judge made specific reference to the *Douglas* case. She also considered directly the extent to which it was possible to justify such an injunction in the light of Art 10 of the ECHR; she felt that it was, because it fell within the restrictions on freedom of expression allowed by Art 10(2). The claimants' lives might be at risk if their identities were revealed, so the injunction had the effect of protecting their right to life under Art 2 of the Convention.

However, Sedley LJ's suggestion that breach of confidence was developing into a general right to privacy did not find favour with a different Court of Appeal in *A v B plc* (2002). A Premier League footballer failed to obtain an injunction to prevent the publication of 'kiss and tell' stories in a Sunday newspaper. The development of breach of confidence, with its emphasis on balancing confidentiality with the public interest, was, rather than a general right to privacy, the basis of the decision. Also, when the substantive issue in *Douglas v Hello!* came before the High Court, the case was decided on the basis of breach of confidence and the development of an independent right to privacy was expressly avoided. What is not clear is whether the Court of Appeal takes the view that all reasonable privacy claims involving personal information can be met through a flexible interpretation of the rules of breach of confidence, or whether they still tolerate the position that some such claims can still not be remedied by the law. *Peck v UK* (2003) demonstrates that not all cases which raise a reasonable claim of privacy about personal information can also be brought within the confines of breach of confidence; and *Wainwright v Secretary of State for the Home Department* (2003) shows that, in a different context, a general remedy for breach of privacy is, arguably, needed. Both cases involved the actions of public authorities and, following the bringing into effect of the HRA, would today be decided with regard to Art 8.

As well as the common law, the impact of statute on the protection of privacy should also be noted. The Data Protection Act 1998 provides a statutory regime governing the holding of personal information. It applies to both public and private organisations and has its principal effect on the keeping of personal information in a systematic, record-based way (though when the Freedom of Information Act 2000 is brought into effect, the 1998 Act will apply to all personal information held by public authorities whether in record form or not). Such information must be processed in accordance with the data protection principles and this is enforced through the offices of the Information Commissioner and a tribunal; data subjects also have legal rights enforceable in the courts, for example, a right to have errors corrected. Privacy rights over personal information are limited, however, not only because of the wide range of exemptions in the Act, but also because the Act allows a wide exemption to the media, confirmed in *Campbell v Mirror Group Newspapers* (2002).

Two other recent statutes have also had a big impact in the field of privacy: the Freedom of Information Act 2000 and the RIPA 2000. The Freedom of Information Act 2000 creates a right of access to government information. It includes many exemptions and one of these is over personal information which cannot be disclosed under the terms of the Act, but must be dealt with under the terms of the Data Protection Act 1998. The RIPA 2000 has already been the subject of much controversy since, rather than aiming merely to regulate the exercise of police-type powers such as surveillance and interception of communications, it actually extends them in some cases, such as the powers of employers to intercept communications made by their employees at work. Though employers will risk court action if they intercept messages without lawful authority, that term is widely defined in a business context. A matter of recent controversy relates to the powers the Secretary of State has, under the RIPA 2000, over so called 'communications data' – information about communications (time and destination, etc) which telecommunication providers and others can be required to disclose to various public bodies. The Secretary of State can add to the organisations that are authorised to request such information from providers. In 2003, public opposition, including from the Information Commissioner, led to the withdrawal of a draft order which would have given a large range of public bodies power to obtain such data.

In conclusion, then, it seems that the common law currently offers only a partial protection of privacy and it no longer seems likely that the concept of breach of confidence will, as indicated by *Douglas v Hello!* (2003), develop into a general right to privacy. Article 8 of the ECHR may be the most satisfactory way forward. It gives each individual a right to respect for his or her private and family life, and the ECtHR has developed these rights fairly broadly. For example, the State has a positive duty to ensure respect for individuals' private and family lives (*X and Y v The Netherlands* (1986)); searches of the home or office are open to special scrutiny (*Niemietz v Germany* (1993)); there is a right to peaceful enjoyment of the home (*Sporrong and Lonnroth v Sweden* (1983) and *Powell and Rayner v UK* (1990)); and surveillance of the home by police or others is at least open to question (*Khan v UK* (2000)). However, the effect of Art 8 is limited. Article 8(2) allows public authorities to invade or limit privacy for a number of reasons, including the interests of national security and protecting the rights and freedoms of others. These exceptions could be interpreted broadly. The ECtHR has, for example, been particularly cautious in cases related to personal information (see *Leander v Sweden* (1987)). Thus, much depends upon the attitude taken by future courts and governments.

Article 8 applies directly in English law only through the provisions of the HRA. The main point here is that the direct impact will be on the interpretation of statutes and the actions of public authorities, identified by s 6 of the Act. The latter means that cases such as *Wainwright* and *Peck* should now be decided with proper reference to privacy. Whether Art 8 will have a major impact on privacy questions that do not involve public authorities will depend on the extent to which the Article is interpreted as imposing positive duties on the State to change the law affecting private parties, and the extent to which the 'horizontal effect' of the Act means that the courts, as public authorities themselves, will use the Convention as a source of values inspiring the development of the common law. Of great importance also will be the way Art 8 is related to Art 10, freedom of expression, including media freedom. This will show how the courts will undertake the difficult task of balancing the right of access of the press to information of public interest against the rights of public figures to some degree of privacy in their lives. Where Art 8 exposes gaps in the legal protection of privacy (such as in *Peck v UK* regarding CCTV, for example) the way forward, it is suggested, is by specific regulation; given Art 8, a general tort protecting privacy is unnecessary.

CHAPTER 5

POLICE POWERS AND THE RIGHTS OF SUSPECTS

Introduction

Examiners often set problem questions in this area since the detailed rules of the Police and Criminal Evidence Act (PACE) 1984 and the Codes of Practice made under it lend themselves to such a format. Note that the Codes were amended quite significantly in 2003; you must refer to the up-to-date provisions. The questions usually concern a number of stages from first contact between police and suspect in the street up to the charge. This allows consideration of the rules governing stop and search, arrest, searching of premises, seizure of articles, detention, treatment in the police station and interviewing. (It must be borne in mind that interviews do not invariably take place in the police station; an important area in the question may concern an interview of the suspect which takes place in the street or in the police car.) You need to be aware of ss 34–37 of the Criminal Justice and Public Order Act (CJPOA) 1994, as amended by s 58 of the Youth Justice and Criminal Evidence Act 1999, which curtail the right to silence in certain circumstances and therefore affect police interviewing. You should also be aware of the extension of police powers in the public order context contained in Pt V of the 1994 Act. The common law power to arrest to prevent a breach of the peace is still extensively used and may need to be considered.

The rules governing obstruction and assault on a police officer in the execution of his duty under s 89 of the Police Act 1996 may be relevant as necessitating analysis of the legality of police conduct in order to determine whether or not a police officer was in the execution of his or her duty. Finally, the question may call for an analysis of the forms of redress available to the suspect in respect of any misuse of police power. If essay questions are set, they often tend to place an emphasis on the balance struck by PACE between the suspect's rights and police powers.

Articles 5 and 6 of the European Convention on Human Rights (ECHR), which provide guarantees of liberty and security of the person and of a fair trial respectively, were incorporated into UK law once the Human Rights Act (HRA) 1998 came fully into force in 2000. It should be noted that Art 6 protects a fair hearing in the civil and criminal contexts, but our concern is with the criminal trial, and in particular with pre-trial procedures which may affect the fairness of the trial and which, therefore, may need to be considered under Art 6 (*Teixeira v Portugal* (1998)). Now that the 1998 Act is fully in force, Arts 6 and 5 and other Convention Articles relevant in this area, such as Art 8 (which provides a right to respect for private life and for the home), are directly applicable in UK courts; they should also be taken into account in interpreting common law and statutory provisions affecting the powers of State agents, including the police. Section 3 of the HRA requires that: 'So far as it is possible to do so, primary and subordinate legislation must be read and given effect in a way which is compatible with the Convention rights ...' Section 3(2)(b) reads, 'this section does not affect the validity, continuing operation or enforcement of any incompatible primary legislation'. All statutes affecting this area, in particular PACE, therefore have to be interpreted so as to be in harmony with the Convention, if that is at all possible.

Under s 6 of the HRA, Convention guarantees are binding only against public authorities. These are defined as bodies which have a partly public function. In this context, this will normally mean that if the police or the security services use powers deriving from any legal source in order to interfere with the liberty or privacy of the citizen, the citizen may be able to bring an action against them under Art 5, 6 or 8 (and/or any other relevant Article). Within the criminal process, citizens are able to rely on Art 6 in order to ensure the fairness of the procedure under s 7(1)(b) of the HRA. Exam questions now reflect this development and expect awareness of the Arts 5, 6 and 8 jurisprudence and of the likely impact of the HRA in this area.

This area concerns the balance struck by the law between the powers conferred on the police and the maintenance of individual freedom and of due process. That balance has been affected to an extent by the HRA, and the relevant HRA jurisprudence is gradually becoming a significant part of the law in this area.

Checklist

Students must be familiar with the following areas:

- provisions under PACE and the Codes of Practice (2003) which affect the areas mentioned above;
- provisions under the CJPOA 1994 relevant to police powers, especially ss 34, 36, 37 and 60;
- s 58 of the Youth Justice and Criminal Evidence Act 1999 – inserts s 34(2A) into the CJPOA 1994;
- obstruction and assault on a police officer in the execution of his or her duty under s 89 of the Police Act 1996;
- issues raised by the revisions of the Codes of Practice made under PACE;
- the PACE rules governing exclusion of evidence, particularly s 78;

- relevant tortious remedies;
- the police complaints mechanism under Pt IV of the Police Act 1996;
- the Security Services Act 1989, the Intelligence Services Act 1994 and the Interception of Communications Act 1985;
- Arts 5, 6 and 8 of the ECHR;
- the HRA, especially ss 2, 3, 6, 10 and 19.

Question 25

Toby, who has a history of mental disorder and has two convictions for possessing cannabis, is standing on a street corner at 2 am on Sunday when he is seen by two police officers in uniform, Andy and Beryl. Andy says: 'What are you up to now, Toby? Let's have a look in your pockets.' Toby does not reply, but turns out his pockets and produces a quantity of cannabis. Andy and Beryl then ask Toby to come to the police station; he agrees to do so.

They arrive at the police station at 2.20 am. Toby is cautioned, informed of his rights under Code C by the Custody Officer and told that he is suspected of dealing in cannabis. He asks if he can see a solicitor, but his request is refused by Superintendent Smith, on the ground that this will lead to the alerting of others whom the police suspect are involved. Toby is then questioned for two hours, but makes no reply to the questions. He then has a short break; when the interview recommences, he is re-cautioned and reminded of his right to legal advice although he is again told that he cannot yet exercise the right. After another hour, he admits to supplying cannabis. The interviews are tape-recorded. He is then charged with supplying cannabis.

Toby now says that he only confessed because he thought he had to in order to get home.

Advise Toby as to any means of redress available to him.

Answer plan

This question is fairly demanding and quite tricky, since it covers the problem of apparently voluntary compliance with police requests and the particular difficulty created when the police are dealing with a mentally disordered person. The most straightforward approach is probably to consider the legality of the police conduct at every point. Once this has been done, the applicability of the possible forms of redress in respect of each possible breach can be considered. As special problems arise in respect of each, they should be looked at separately. It should be noted that the examinee is merely asked to 'advise Toby as to any means of redress'; therefore, all relevant possibilities should be discussed. It is important to remember to consider whether adverse inferences are likely to be drawn at trial from Toby's silence under ss 34 and 36 of the Criminal Justice and Public Order Act (CJPOA) 1994, as amended. If a silence was excluded or if, although it was admissible, it could be argued on Toby's behalf that no adverse inferences could be drawn from it, that could be viewed as a form of redress. Essentially, the following issues should be considered:

- legality of the search under s 23(2) of the Misuse of Drugs Act 1971 and Code A of PACE;
- a voluntary detention or an arrest under s 24 of PACE? Legality of the arrest;
- access to legal advice under s 58 of PACE – exceptions under s 58(8) – legality of the refusal of advice;
- failure to ensure that an appropriate adult was present during the interview as required under para 11.14 of Code C;
- exclusion of evidence under ss 76 and 78 of PACE – relevance of s 36 of the CJPOA 1994; Art 6 of the European Convention on Human Rights (ECHR) under the HRA; *Khan v UK* (2000);
- inferences to be drawn at trial from Toby's silence under s 34 of the CJPOA 1994; relevance of ss 34(2A) and 36 of the CJPOA 1994; Art 6 of the ECHR;
- relevant tortious remedies;
- police complaints and disciplinary action.

Answer

The legality of the police conduct in this instance will be considered first; any possible forms of redress open to Toby will then be examined. In both instances, the impact of HRA 1998 will be taken into account.

The first contact between the police officers and Toby appears to be of a voluntary nature: the officers are entitled to ask questions; equally, Toby can refuse to answer them (*Rice v Connolly* (1966)). No adverse inference can be drawn from his silence at this point since he is not under caution (s 34(1)(a) of the CJPOA 1994) and he has not had the opportunity of having legal advice (s 34(2A)). When Toby is asked to turn out his pockets, this appears to be a request which he could refuse. It may therefore be characterised as part of a voluntary search. However, the 2003 version of Code A (para 1.5) banned consensual searches: officers may no longer ask members of the public to consent to a search where no power to search exists.

Thus, the search should not have taken place unless the police officers can show reasonable suspicion as the basis for the exercise of the power. In order to do so, it must be shown that the police officers complied with the provisions of s 23(2) of the Misuse of Drugs Act 1971 and of Code A. Under s 23(2), a police officer may search for controlled drugs if he or she has reasonable grounds for believing that he or she will find such articles. The necessary reasonable suspicion is defined in paras 1.6 and 1.7 of Code A. There must be some objective basis for it, which might include various factors which are mentioned in para 1.6, including the time and place and the behaviour of the person concerned. In the instant situation, the lateness of the hour might give rise to some suspicion, but it is apparent that the suspicion does not relate specifically enough to the possibility that Toby is in possession of drugs (*Black v DPP* (1995)). Following this argument, no power to stop and search arises; the seizure of the cannabis is therefore unlawful. It should further be noted that the procedural requirements of s 2 are breached (see *Osman v DPP* (1999), in which it was found that s 2 is mandatory). There are therefore two bases on which the search is unlawful.

The request made to come to the police station appears to assume that Toby will come on a voluntary basis; Andy and Beryl are not under a duty at this point to explain that he can withhold consent (see s 29 and Code C, para 10.2) and, on that basis, as Toby accedes to the request made, no breach of PACE appears to have arisen. However, he appears to be mentally disordered and so belongs to one of the vulnerable groups who may not be capable of giving consent to a voluntary search at all under Code A, Note 1E. As the police know him, they may be aware of this fact. Even if they are not aware that he has a specific mental disorder, they may recognise him as a person incapable of giving a genuine informed consent to the detention; if so, it is arguable that the detention is unlawful. Arguably, since the police must abide by Art 5 of the ECHR under s 6 of the HRA, this is the better view, on the ground that where there is a doubt as to consent to a deprivation of liberty, a strict view should be taken giving the emphasis to the primary right (*Murray v UK* (1994)).

If this assumption is correct, it is necessary to consider whether a power to arrest arises. Toby is presumably arrested for possessing cannabis, an offence arising under s 5(3) of the Misuse of Drugs Act 1971. It is an arrestable offence under s 24(1)(b) of PACE, as it carries a sentence of five years or more (Sched 4 to the Misuse of Drugs Act). In order to arrest under s 24, it is necessary to show that Andy and Beryl had reasonable grounds for suspecting that Toby was in possession of the cannabis. Clearly, this is the case. However, the cannabis is discovered during the course of an illegal stop and search. It may appear strange that an illegal stop and search could provide the reasonable suspicion necessary to found a lawful arrest. However, nothing in PACE provides that it cannot do so. Nevertheless, even assuming that reasonable suspicion is present, the 'arrest' (if it may be characterised as such) is clearly rendered unlawful due to the failure to state the fact of the arrest and the reason for it as required under s 28 of PACE and Art 5(2).

At the police station, Toby is not afforded access to legal advice. Delay in affording such access will be lawful if one of the contingencies envisaged under s 58(8) will arise if a solicitor is contacted. In this instance, the police will wish to rely on the exception under s 58(8)(b) allowing delay where contacting the solicitor will lead to the alerting of others suspected of the offence. Leaving aside the lack of any substantial evidence that others are involved at all, it will be necessary for the police to show, following *Samuel* (1988), that some quality about the particular solicitor in question could found a reasonable belief that he or she would bring about one of the contingencies envisaged if contacted. There is nothing to suggest that the police have any basis for this belief, especially as Toby has not specified the solicitor he wishes to contact. He may well wish to contact the duty solicitor. A further condition for the operation of s 58(8) is that Toby is being detained in respect of a serious arrestable offence. He is in detention at this point in respect of possession of cannabis. This is an arrestable offence under s 24, although he has not been arrested for it. Whether or not the offence can be termed a serious arrestable offence depends on the provisions of s 116. The section, as amended, includes as serious arrestable offences under sub-s (2)(a) 'offences mentioned in paras (a) to (f) of s 1(3) of the Drug Trafficking Act 1994'. As supplying cannabis is included in this section, this condition is fulfilled. However, the lack of any basis for the necessary reasonable belief under s 58(8) means that there has been a breach of s 58. This strict approach to s 58 is supported by the approach of the European Court of Human Rights (ECtHR) to the right of access to legal advice. It has placed considerable importance on the right in cases such as *Murray (John) v UK* (1996) and *Averill v UK* (2000). It has held that delay in access where the defendant faces the possibility that adverse inferences may be drawn from silence is likely to amount to a breach of Art 6 of the Convention. This strict approach should be followed by the police, since they are bound to abide by Art 6 under s 6 of the HRA.

Since Toby is mentally disordered, he should not have been interviewed except in the presence of an 'appropriate adult', as required under para 11.14 of Code C. Therefore, a further breach of PACE has occurred, unless it could be argued that the officers were not aware of his disorder; if so, following *Raymond Maurice Clarke* (1989), no breach of the Code provision has occurred. The behaviour of Andy suggests, however, that the officers were aware of Toby's condition.[1]

Having identified a series of illegal acts on the part of the police, it will now be necessary to consider any redress available to Toby in respect of them. The first such act was the search in breach of Code A and the seizure of the cannabis.[2] Toby could seek to claim damages in respect of the unlawful search either on the basis that it amounted to false imprisonment or possibly on the basis that the police violated Art 8 (and possibly Art 5) in conducting an unlawful search, and that therefore damages can be claimed against the police relying on ss 7(1)(a) and 8 of the HRA. However, it is arguable that he consented to the search and although voluntary searches are banned under Code A, para 1.5, no civil liability arises for breach of the Codes. If consent is present, false imprisonment cannot occur, although it is still arguable that a breach of Art 8 and possibly Art 5 has arisen.

Is the cannabis likely to be excluded from evidence under s 78 since it was obtained during an unlawful search? It could be argued, following *Edward Fennelly* (1989), that the products of the search should be excluded from evidence on the basis that there was no power to search in the circumstances. According to *Thomas* (1990) and *Effick* (1992), however, there is a narrow discretion to exclude physical evidence, which will be exercised only exceptionally. The pre-PACE ruling of the House of Lords in *Fox* (1986) would also lend support to this contention. Following the decision of the House of Lords in *Khan* (1997), evidence, other than involuntary confessions obtained improperly, is admissible subject to a narrow discretion to exclude it. The House of Lords took Art 6 of the ECHR into account in reaching this conclusion. They found that Art 6(1) does not require that evidence should be automatically excluded where there has been impropriety in obtaining it, basing this finding on *Schenk v Switzerland* (1988). In *Khan* itself, it was found that the trial judge had properly exercised his discretion to include the improperly obtained evidence under s 78. This position has been unaffected by the reception of Art 6 into domestic law under the HRA (*AG's Reference No 3 of 1999* (2001)) on the basis that the admission or exclusion of evidence is largely a matter for the national courts. The courts have therefore taken the view that the position that has developed under s 78 regarding exclusion of non-confession evidence need not be modified. It may be concluded that the cannabis would not be excluded from evidence.

Toby could make a complaint under the provisions of Pt IV of the Police Act 1996, in respect of the illegal seizure of the cannabis, since it can be characterised as resulting from a non-consensual search in breach of s 23(2) of the Misuse of Drugs Act 1971 and of Code A, para 1.5. Breach of a Code provision can be a breach of the police disciplinary Code under s 67(8) of PACE.

Assuming that the arrest was unlawful (which cannot be determined with certainty), Toby could bring an action for false imprisonment for the whole period of his detention. There is also the alternative possibility of taking action under s 7(1)(a) of the HRA based on the infringement of his rights under Art 5 of the Convention. A further option might be to make a complaint in respect of the failure to observe the provisions of s 28 of PACE.

Can a reasonable argument be advanced that the admissions made by Toby will be excluded from evidence under s 76? Following *Alladice* (1988) and *Hughes* (1988), unless it can be shown that the custody officer acted in bad faith in failing to allow Toby access to a solicitor, it seems that s 76(2)(a) will not apply. However, following *Delaney* (1989), which was concerned with the operation of s 76(2)(b), if the defendant was in some particularly difficult or vulnerable position, the breach of PACE may be of special significance. Toby may be said to be in such a position due to the fact that he is mentally disordered. On this basis, it seems that s 76(2)(b) may be invoked to exclude the admissions from evidence.

The admissions may also be excluded from evidence under s 78, on the basis that the police breached s 58. If so, following *Samuel* (1988), it must be shown that the breach of s 58 was causally related to the admissions made in the second interview. It may be that Toby would have made admissions had he had advice. The advisor might have considered that he should make admissions, since a failure to account for the cannabis could be commented on adversely in court under s 36 of the CJPOA 1994, assuming that he had been afforded an opportunity to have access to legal advice. On the other hand, the advisor might have considered that he had not been offered such an opportunity in reality and that therefore no adverse inferences would be drawn from his silence, in which case the advisor would have advised him to remain silent. This seems the stronger argument, bearing in mind Toby's mental disorder. It appears that Toby may have needed such advice. This argument failed in *Dunford* (1990) and *Alladice* (1988) on the basis that the appellants in those cases were experienced criminals, aware of their rights. It appears that Toby did remain silent for some time; possibly, therefore, he would have made the admissions in any event. As he has convictions, he will be aware of police procedures and know that he can keep silent. It might be argued that access to legal advice would have added nothing to his understanding of the situation. On the other hand, given his mental condition, it is unlikely that he would fully understand the implications of silence; he was obviously more vulnerable than the appellant in *Dunford*. On this analysis, the requisite causal relationship exists and the admissions may also be excluded from evidence under s 78. This approach is given additional weight by the importance attached to access to legal advice by the ECHR in cases such as *Murray (John) v UK* (1996) and *Averill v UK* (2000). Under ss 6 and 2 of the HRA, these decisions will need to be taken into account in considering whether the evidence should be excluded; they would be likely to tip the balance in favour of exclusion.

It has further been argued that a breach of para 11.15 of Code C occurred, in that Toby was interviewed, although no appropriate adult was present.[3] Following *DPP v Blake* (1989), the judge would therefore be likely to use his discretion to exclude the interview under s 78 on the basis that it may be unreliable or because Toby would not have made the admissions at all had the adult been present.[4]

The breach of s 58 could also be the subject of a complaint, as could the breach of para 11.14 of Code C.

It follows from the above analysis that the first interview, which may be said to be causally related to the breach of para 6.6, may be excluded from evidence under s 78, since had Toby had legal advice he might *not* have decided to remain silent. The solicitor, weighing up the situation, might well have decided that he should offer his explanation of the facts rather than allow an adverse inference to be drawn at trial from a failure to do so. This would be in accordance with s 34 of the CJPOA 1994, which provides that, where a person fails to mention a fact which he subsequently relies on in his defence, adverse inferences can be drawn from such a failure. He has also failed to account for the presence of the cannabis. The solicitor might also have advised him to account for the presence of the cannabis since, under s 36 of the 1994 Act, an adverse inference can be drawn from a failure so to account if the suspect has had an 'opportunity' to have legal advice. If he has had no such opportunity, the restriction on drawing adverse inferences would apply (para 10.4 of Code C). So whether the requisite causal relationship for s 78 purposes exists would depend on the view a solicitor would be likely to take of the opportunity he has had. Exclusion of the first interview under s 78 would appear to accord with the duty of the court under s 6 of the HRA since the ECtHR has, as indicated above, held that delay in access where the defendant faces the possibility that adverse inferences may be drawn from silence is likely to amount to a breach of Art 6 of the Convention. Such a breach could be avoided by excluding the interview.

Since the possibility that the interview will not be excluded cannot be ruled out, it must be considered whether adverse inferences would be likely to be drawn from Toby's silence during it. Section 34(2A) of the CJPOA 1994, introduced in order to satisfy Art 6 of the ECHR under the HRA, applies. Under s 34(2A), inferences cannot be drawn if the defendant has not had the opportunity of having legal advice. This appears to apply to Toby, especially as he has been unlawfully denied the opportunity, as argued above. Thus, no adverse inferences can be drawn. *Murray (John) v UK* (1996) and *Averill v UK* (2000) would support a strict interpretation of the term 'opportunity' in this context, and further, following those cases, a court bound by Art 6 under s 6 of the HRA would probably take the stance that no adverse inferences should be drawn. Code C, para 10.4 supports this stance.

Notes

1 This point is strengthened by the provisions of Code C, Note 11C in respect of the likelihood that mentally disordered persons might make an unreliable confession.

2 The breach of para 11.15 could also be considered under s 76 but, if so, the argument would not differ from that in respect of the breach of s 58. Note that since Toby is mentally disordered, as opposed to mentally handicapped, the special provisions of s 77 in respect of the mentally handicapped do not apply. Nevertheless, as in *Delaney*, courts will be particularly vigilant when determining whether to exclude confessions of the mentally disordered under either s 76 or s 78. The ruling in *McKenzie* (1992) supports this point.

3 It could be pointed out that if the police deliberately failed to afford Toby access to an appropriate adult, s 76(2)(a) might be invoked to exclude the admissions; alternatively (following *Alladice* (1988)), s 78 would be invoked without needing to discuss the question of reliability or of the requisite causal relationship between the breach and the confession.

Question 26

The Police and Criminal Evidence Act 1984 and the Codes of Practice made under it were supposed to strike a fair balance between increased police powers and greater safeguards for the suspect. Taking the effect of the Human Rights Act 1998 and any other relevant provisions into account, how far would it be fair to say that such a balance is currently evident?

Answer plan

A reasonably straightforward essay question which is commonly set on PACE. It is clearly much more wide-ranging than the ones that follow it and therefore needs care in planning in order to cover provisions relating to all the main stages in the investigation. Essentially, the following points should be considered:

- the arrest provision under s 25; Art 5 of the European Convention on Human Rights (ECHR);
- stop and search provision under s 1 and Code of Practice A and the efficacy of the procedural safeguards;
- detention provisions under Pt IV; Art 5 of the ECHR;

- safeguards for interviews under Pt V and Codes C and E – relevance of ss 34–37 of the Criminal Justice and Public Order Act (CJPOA) 1994, as amended; Art 6 of the ECHR;
- brief overview of redress available for breaches of these provisions – tortious remedies, the police complaints mechanism, exclusion of evidence; impact of the HRA, especially Art 6 of the ECHR.

Answer

It will be argued that although PACE 1984 and the Codes of Practice contain provisions capable of achieving a reasonable balance between increasing the power of the police to detain and question, and providing safeguards for the suspect, that balance is not maintained in practice. This failure arguably arises partly because many of the safeguards can be evaded quite readily and partly because there is no effective sanction available for their breach. It will further be contended that while the relevant articles of ECHR, afforded further effect in domestic law under HRA 1998, are likely to have some impact in encouraging adherence to the rules intended to secure suspects' rights, they will not have a radical effect, especially in terms of encouraging the exclusion of evidence where the rules have not been adhered to. Certain key provisions will be selected in order to illustrate this argument.

Before the inception of PACE, the police had no general and clear powers of arrest, stop and search or entry to premises. They wanted such powers put on a clear statutory basis, so that they could exercise them where they felt it was their duty to do so, without laying themselves open to the possibility of a civil action. In s 1, a general power to stop and search persons is conferred on the police if reasonable suspicion arises that stolen goods or prohibited articles may be found. This general power is balanced in two ways. First, the concept of reasonable suspicion, which is now defined in paras 2.2–2.6 of Code A, allows it to be exercised only when quite a high level of suspicion exists. Secondly, the police must give the person to be searched certain information, including the object of the search and the name of the police station to which the officer in question is attached (s 2 of PACE). These safeguards can be evaded if the search is made on an apparently voluntary basis. However, Code A para 1.5 now bans voluntary searches and the new ban should go some way towards addressing this problem,[1] although no sanctions are provided if para 1.5 is breached. It should also be pointed out that s 1 of PACE may be undermined in any event by s 60 of the CJPOA 1994, which, in certain circumstances, allows stop and search without reasonable suspicion if authorisation to do so has been given by a superintendent.

However, the HRA may tend to encourage a stricter adherence to the rules providing safeguards for suspects, since the police are bound under s 6 of the HRA to adhere to the Convention requirements and under s 3 of the HRA, PACE and other relevant provisions must be interpreted compatibly with those requirements if it is possible to do so. Article 5, contained in Sched 1 to the HRA, provides a guarantee of 'liberty and security of person'. It appears that the short period of detention represented by a stop and search may be sufficient to constitute a deprivation of liberty (*X v Austria* (1979)). Deprivation of liberty can occur only on a basis of law and in certain specified circumstances, including, under Art 5(1)(b), the detention of a person in order to secure the fulfilment of any obligation prescribed by law and, under Art 5(1)(c), the 'lawful detention of a person effected for the purpose of bringing him before the competent legal authority on reasonable suspicion of having committed an offence'. Both these provisions may cover temporary detention for the purposes of a search, but since they provide exceptions to a guarantee of a fundamental right, they may tend to require a restrictive approach to the use of stop and search provisions, and to apparently voluntary stops, due to the duty of the police under s 6 of the HRA. Whether this is occurring in practice is, however, debatable.

The exercise of the powers under s 60 of the CJPOA may be of doubtful compatibility with Art 5(1)(c) since reasonable suspicion is not required, although the power may fall within Art 5(1)(b). In appropriate cases, bearing in mind the recent evidence of a police tendency to show racial bias in decisions to stop and search, violation of Art 5(1)(b) or (c) might be found when read with the Art 14 guarantee of freedom from discrimination in the enjoyment of the Convention rights. This possibility may be of less significance given the amendments made to the Race Relations Act 1976 in 2000, allowing claimants to bring actions against the police in respect of direct or indirect discrimination in policing decisions, including decisions to stop and search. However, a defendant would also have the option of raising an Art 5 and Art 14 argument during the criminal process. The use of force in order to carry out a stop and search is permitted under s 117 of PACE, but under Art 3, the use of force must be strictly in proportion to the conduct of the detainee. Under it, the use of extreme force is permissible if necessitated by the conduct of the detainee, but if the use of such force causes death, it would appear to breach Art 2, which permits the use of lethal force to 'effect an arrest', not to effect a detention short of arrest.

The police also acquired a general power of arrest under s 25. However, this power does not merely allow an officer to arrest for any offence so long as reasonable suspicion can be shown. Such a power would probably have been viewed as too draconian. It is balanced by what are known as the general arrest conditions, which must also be fulfilled. One of these conditions (s 25(3)(c)) consists of a failure to furnish a satisfactory name or address, so that the service of a summons later on would be impracticable.

The others concern the immediate need to remove the suspect from the street. The inclusion of these provisions implies that the infringement of civil liberties represented by an arrest should be resorted to only where no other alternative exists. The concept of reasonable suspicion, which should ensure that the arrest takes place at quite a late stage in the investigation, also limits the use of this power, although the concept tends to be flexibly interpreted. Article 5, as incorporated into domestic law under the HRA, may have some impact on the interpretation of the concept. This can be found if the leading post-PACE case on the meaning of the concept, *Castorina v Chief Constable of Surrey* (1988), is compared with the findings of the Strasbourg Court in *Fox, Campbell and Hartley v UK* (1990).

In *Castorina*, the grounds for suspicion regarding a burglary of a firm were that the suspect was a former employee who appeared to have a grudge and the burglary appeared to be an 'inside job'. However, the suspect was not considered by the victim to be likely to commit burglary and she had no criminal record. Nevertheless, the court found that reasonable suspicion had been established. In *Fox, Campbell and Hartley v UK* (1990), the applicants had been arrested in accordance with s 11 of the Northern Ireland (Emergency Provisions) Act 1978, which required only suspicion, not reasonable suspicion. The only evidence put forward by the government for the presence of reasonable suspicion was that the applicants had convictions for terrorist offences and that when arrested, they were asked about particular terrorist acts. The government said that further evidence could not be disclosed for fear of endangering life. The Court found that although allowance could be made for the difficulties of evidence gathering in an emergency situation, reasonable suspicion which arises from facts or information which would satisfy an objective observer that the person concerned may have committed the offence had not been established. The arrests in question could not, therefore, be justified. It is debatable whether the UK courts are in general applying a test of reasonable suspicion under PACE which reaches the standards which the European Court had in mind, especially where terrorism is not in question. The departure, which the HRA brings about, is to encourage stricter judicial scrutiny of decisions to arrest.

Prior to PACE, the police had no clear power to hold a person for questioning. Such a power was put on a clear statutory basis under s 41 and it was made clear under s 37(2) that the purpose of the detention is to obtain a confession. The detention can be for up to 24 hours. In the case of a person in police custody for a serious arrestable offence (defined in s 116), it can extend to 36 hours with the permission of a police officer of the rank of superintendent or above, and may extend to 96 hours under s 44 after an application to a magistrate's court. These are very significant new powers. However, they are supposed to be balanced by all the safeguards created by

Pt V of PACE and by Codes C and E. The most important safeguards available inside the police station include contemporaneous recording under para 11.7 of Code C, tape-recording under para 3 of Code E, the ability to read over, verify and sign the notes of the interview as a correct record under para 11.11 of Code C, access to legal advice under s 58, and notification of the right under para 3.1, the option of having the advisor present under para 6.6 and, where appropriate, the presence of an adult under para 11.15.

However, there are methods of avoiding these safeguards without actually breaking the rules. For example, in *Hughes* (1988), the detainee, disappointed of obtaining advice from his own solicitor, inquired about the duty solicitor scheme, but was informed, erroneously (but apparently in good faith), that no solicitor was available. Under this misapprehension, he gave consent to be interviewed and the Court of Appeal took the view that his consent was not thereby vitiated.

Further, access to legal advice and tape-recording can be evaded and rendered worthless if the suspect is interviewed outside the police station. There has been an attempt to address the problem of such evasion: under para 11.1 as revised, such interviewing can no longer occur unless the decision to arrest the person being interviewed has not been taken or the exchanges do not amount to 'the questioning of a person regarding his involvement or suspected involvement in a criminal offence or offences' (para 11.1A); or urgent interviewing is necessary to prevent various contingencies arising. This provision may have encouraged the police to take suspects to the police station to be questioned, where an arrest was likely to occur in any event, but it is unclear that the number of suspects questioned in the street has dropped significantly and in any event the number and width of the express or implied exceptions to the prohibition are likely to have lessened its impact.

The right of access to legal advice was intended to bolster the right to silence. However, that right, originally included in the PACE scheme under Code C, was severely curtailed by ss 34–37 of the CJPOA 1994, thereby disturbing the 'balance' which was originally created. However, s 34(2A) was inserted into the CJPOA by s 58 of the Youth Justice and Criminal Evidence Act 1999. The amendments provide that, if the defendant was at an authorised place of detention and had not had an opportunity of consulting a solicitor at the time of the failure to mention the fact in question, inferences cannot be drawn. This amendment is now reflected in Code C after its revision in 2003: where the detainee has not had an opportunity to have legal advice, the old caution must be used, reflecting the full right to silence under para 10.6. This is a very significant change to the interviewing scheme, which was introduced as a direct response to the findings of ECtHR in *Murray v UK*

(1996). Had this change not been made, ss 34-37 might have been found to be incompatible with Art 6, under s 3(2) of the HRA.

However, it need not be assumed, conversely, that Art 6 will necessarily be satisfied where a defendant has access to legal advice before being questioned under caution. Cases such as *Condron* (1997) or *Bowden* (1999), where the defendants had had legal advice and had acted on it in remaining silent, should be considered on their particular facts in relation to the Art 6 requirements. Such cases differ from *Murray* on the issue of the relationship between silence and legal advice. In *Condron*, the defendants acted on legal advice in refusing to answer questions; in *Murray*, a breach of Art 6(1) was found on the basis of inference-drawing in the absence of legal advice (not on the basis of inference-drawing *per se*). In *Condron*, the fact of having legal advice was not to the defendants' advantage, possibly the reverse, since in a sense they may have been misled into remaining silent. It is arguable that allowing adverse inferences to be drawn in that context – where the innocent explanation for silence was that it was on legal advice – could in certain circumstances be viewed as a breach of Art 6(1). For example, this might be argued where the advisor had failed to point out that adverse inferences might be drawn despite the advice, and/or where the defendant could not be expected – due to his or her low intelligence, youth or other vulnerability – to decide to speak despite the advice. To hold otherwise might be viewed as undermining the value attached in *Murray* to granting access to legal advice where adverse inferences would be drawn from silence.

It may appear that throughout PACE, a reasonable balance was originally struck between safeguards and increased police powers. However, as has been pointed out, the safeguards may be evaded, even though the powers may, of course, be used to their full. The HRA provides opportunities, as indicated, of seeking to restore the balance originally created. However, where it is clear, whether due to adoption of a stricter interpretation under s 3 of the HRA or otherwise, that evasion or breach of the safeguards has occurred, thereby destroying the balance, there will not always be an effective remedy available which could go some way towards restoring it. This may continue to be the case despite the inception of the HRA.

Damages will be available at common law in respect of some breaches of PACE. For example, if a police officer arrests a citizen where no reasonable suspicion arises under s 24 or 25 of PACE, an action for false imprisonment will arise. Equally, such a remedy would be available if the provisions governing time limits on detention were breached. The question whether damages are available in respect of property unlawfully seized was considered in *Chief Constable of Lancashire ex p Parker and McGrath* (1993). It was argued on behalf of the police that s 22(2)(a) of PACE, which allows the retention of 'anything seized for the purposes of a criminal investigation', would be superfluous, unless denoting a general power to retain unlawfully seized material. It was held, however, that the sub-section could not bear the weight sought to be placed upon it: it was merely intended to give examples of matters falling within the general provision of s 22(1). Therefore, the police were not entitled to retain the material seized. This decision re-affirmed the need to retain the balance between safeguards for the subject of the search and the police power to search, which might have been disturbed had the various issues been resolved differently.

However, tortious remedies were inapplicable to the provisions of the Codes under s 67(10), and seem to be inapplicable to the most significant statutory interviewing provision, the entitlement to legal advice. There is no tort of denial of access to legal advice: the only possible tortious action is for breach of statutory duty. Whether this tort lies is a question of policy in relation to any particular statutory provision, and so the application of this remedy was purely conjectural.[2] Under s 7(1)(a) of the HRA, it is possible to bring an action against the police for breach of the Convention rights. However, it is likely that this remedy is not available in relation to breaches of Art 6 (which would cover the legal advice scheme) on the basis that Art 6 is concerned with the trial as a whole and therefore potential breaches of Art 6 should be addressed within the trial itself.

The police complaints mechanism covers any breaches of PACE, including breaches of the Codes under s 67(8), but it is generally agreed that it is defective as a means of redress. It does not allow for compensation to the victim or for the victim to attend any disciplinary proceedings. In any event, most complaints do not result in disciplinary proceedings and it appears that no disciplinary proceedings have been brought in respect of breaches of the Codes. The suspect concerned might, in many instances, be unaware that a breach of the Codes had occurred and while, theoretically, another officer could make a complaint leading to disciplinary proceedings for such a breach, in practice, this appears to be highly unlikely. Furthermore, despite the involvement (albeit limited) of the Police Complaints Authority (PCA), the complaints procedure tends to be perceived as being administered by the police themselves. The police disciplinary system has been found to provide an insufficient remedy for Convention breaches, under Art 13, in *Khan v UK* (2000), which criticised both its lack of independence and its lack of real remedies. The HRA has gone some way towards redressing this problem by allowing Convention-related issues, including Arts 5 and 8 complaints against the police, to be raised in ordinary courts and to receive the normal range of remedies. The Independent Police Complaints Commission, which is currently being set up to take over from the PCA, may improve the complaints system since it is supposed to inject a more independent element into it.

The context in which many breaches of PACE have been considered is that of exclusion of evidence. Confessions may be excluded under s 76 if obtained by oppression or in circumstances conducive of unreliability. Any evidence may be excluded under s 78 if its admission would be likely to render the trial unfair. It must be borne in mind that the PACE mechanism for exclusion of evidence provides a means of redress for such breaches only in one circumstance – that the case is pursued to trial and the defendant pleads not guilty. In this one instance, they can be of great value, in that the defendant may be placed in the position he would have been in had the breach not occurred and the police may seem to be 'punished' for their non-compliance with the rules by being prevented from profiting from their own breach. In this sense, exclusion of evidence does provide an effective means of redress. For example, in *Canale* (1990), the police failed to record an interview contemporaneously in breach of para 11.3 of Code C; it was excluded as possibly unreliable under s 78. In *Samuel* (1988), the police unlawfully denied the appellant access to legal advice; the court took the view that if a breach of s 58 had taken place, which was causally linked to the confession, s 78 should be invoked. It could be said that in *Samuel*, the court succeeded in restoring the balance between the police power to detain and question, which had been used fully in the case, and the safeguards the detainee should have had, in the sense that the outcome was what it would have been had the proper safeguards been in place. However, the provisions of ss 34–37 of the CJPOA 1994, reflected in the caution introduced under the 1995 revision of Code C, make it less likely that advisors will advise silence, since adverse inferences may be drawn at trial from silence. Thus, it may be more difficult to establish the causal relationship in question relying on the method used in *Samuel*. Section 78 may become less effective as a means of maintaining the balance between police powers and suspects' rights. On the other hand, if legal advice is denied, a suspect has not had an opportunity of having advice as required by s 34(2A) of the CJPOA 1994. Therefore, adverse inferences could not be drawn from his silence.

Theoretically, the *Samuel* argument as to the causal relationship between an impropriety and a confession could be applied to non-confession evidence but, in practice, it appears that it will not be. According to *Thomas* (1990) and *Effick* (1992), physical evidence will be excluded only if obtained with deliberate illegality. Following the decision of the House of Lords in *Khan* (1997), evidence other than involuntary confessions obtained improperly is, nevertheless, admissible, subject to a narrow discretion to exclude it. The House of Lords took Art 6 of the ECHR into account in reaching this conclusion. They found that Art 6 does not require that evidence should be automatically excluded where there has been impropriety in obtaining it, basing this finding on *Schenk v Switzerland* (1988). In *Khan* itself, it was found that the trial judge had properly exercised his discretion to include the improperly obtained evidence under s 78. This position has been unaffected by the incorporation of Art 6 into domestic law under the HRA (*AG's Reference No 3 of 1999* (2001)) on the basis that the assessment of evidence is largely a matter for the national courts. The courts have therefore taken the view that the position that has developed under s 78 regarding exclusion of non-confession evidence need not be modified under the HRA.[3]

Thus, although exclusion of evidence can provide a means of redress when police have not complied with one of the PACE safeguards, it may be unavailable where the evidence obtained due to the breach is non-confession evidence. It may be unavailable in any event: first, even where a clear breach of PACE has occurred, the evidence may, nevertheless, be admissible; secondly, exclusion of evidence is irrelevant to the majority of defendants who plead guilty. Thus, the police had an incentive to break the rules by, for example, refusing a request for legal advice in the hope of obtaining admissions and a guilty plea. If, in such circumstances, a defendant did plead guilty, he or she had suffered denial of a fundamental right with no hope of redress apart from that offered by a complaint. Now, however, the HRA enables any person who believes his arrest or trial have been unfair due to the behaviour of the police to argue breaches of, *inter alia*, Art 5 or 6; and *Khan* (2000) makes it clear that an effect on the fairness of proceedings, viewed as a whole, can create a breach of Art 6. Thus, courts are able to monitor and sanction police powers to a greater extent, and the remedies for most PACE breaches have been expanded.

In conclusion, it appears that the balance between safeguards and police powers has not always been maintained, due to the ease with which certain of the domestic safeguards may be evaded or ignored. Clearly, if safeguards are not observed, the justification for increasing police powers to stop, arrest, search premises, detain and question is lost. It is possible that courts will use the HRA and the Convention to create stronger protection in these areas for individual rights, thus restoring the balance that has been lost, but it is too early to discern a consistent pattern in post-HRA decisions.

Notes

1   The problem of voluntary searches and provision for them could be considered in more detail. Note for Guidance 1E previously provided that certain persons – juveniles, the mentally handicapped or mentally disordered and any person who appears incapable of giving an informed consent – should not be subject to a voluntary search at all. As indicated, such searches are now banned. However, this provision is contained only in a Code, not the statute, and may therefore be likely on occasion to be disregarded. Of course, if an apparently voluntary search takes place, but its subject feels intimidated during it, he or she will find it hard to make a complaint, as the requisite information will not have been given.

2   Theoretically, use of a false imprisonment claim might be available; argument could be advanced at this point that where gross breaches of the questioning provisions had taken place, such as interviewing a person unlawfully held incommunicado, a detention in itself lawful might thereby be rendered unlawful. However, although the ruling in *Middleweek v Chief Constable of Merseyside* (1985) gave some encouragement to such argument, it now seems to be ruled out due to the decision in *Weldon v Home Office* (1991) in the context of lawful detention in a prison. It seems likely, therefore, that access to legal advice will continue to be unaffected by the availability of tortious remedies.

3   This important issue could be considered further. The first instance decision in *Edward Fennelly* (1989), in which a failure to give the reason for a stop and search led to exclusion of the search, appears, then, to be on the wrong track. Furthermore, even if the principles developed under s 78 with respect to confession evidence could properly be applied to other evidence, *Edward Fennelly* would still be a doubtful decision, as no causal relationship could exist between the impropriety in question and the evidence obtained.

Question 27

Albert and Bill, two policemen in uniform and driving a police car, see Colin outside a factory gate at 11.30 pm on a Saturday. Albert and Bill know that Colin has a conviction for burglary. Colin looks nervous and is looking repeatedly at his watch. Bearing in mind a spate of burglaries in the area, Albert and Bill ask Colin what he is doing. Colin replies that he is waiting for a friend. Dissatisfied with this response, Bill tells Colin to turn out his pockets, which he does. Bill seizes a bunch of keys which Colin produces and, still suspicious, asks Colin to accompany them to the police station. Colin then becomes abusive and when Bill takes hold of him to restrain him, Colin hits Bill in the mouth. Albert and Bill then bundle Colin into the police car and tell him that he is being arrested for 'assaulting a police officer in the execution of his duty'. They then proceed to Colin's flat and search it, despite his protests. They discover nothing relating to a burglary, but do discover an amount of cannabis, which they seize.

Albert and Bill then take Colin to the police station, arriving at 12.20 am. He is cautioned, informed of his rights under Code C by the Custody Officer and told that he is suspected of dealing in cannabis. Colin asks if he can see a solicitor, but his request is refused 'for the time being'. Colin is then questioned and eventually admits to supplying cannabis. The interview is tape-recorded. He is then charged with supplying cannabis and with assaulting a police officer in the execution of his duty.

Advise Colin.

Answer plan

This is a reasonably straightforward question, but it does cover a very wide range of issues. The most straightforward approach is to consider the legality of the police conduct at every point. Once this issue has been determined at each point, the applicability of the possible forms of redress can be considered. It should be noted that the examinee is merely asked to 'advise Colin'; therefore, all relevant possibilities should be discussed – albeit briefly due to the time constraint. European Court of Human Rights (ECtHR) cases should be considered in relation to the relevant Articles of the European Convention on Human Rights (ECHR), contained in Sched 1 to the HRA, and the effects of ss 3 and 6 of the HRA should be discussed.

Essentially, the following issues should be considered:

- legality of the search under ss 1 and 2 of PACE 1984 and Code of Practice A; Art 5 of the ECHR;
- assaulting a police officer in the execution of his duty under s 89(1) of the Police Act 1996;
- the legality of the arrest under s 25 of PACE;
- the legality of the search of premises and the seizure of the cannabis under ss 18 and 19 of PACE; Art 8 of the ECHR;
- access to legal advice under s 58 of PACE – legality of the refusal of advice; Art 6 of the ECHR;
- exclusion of evidence under ss 76 and 78 of PACE;
- free-standing action under s 7(1)(a) of the HRA relying on Art 8;
- relevant tortious remedies;
- police complaints procedure under Pt IV of the Police Act 1996.

Answer

The legality of the police conduct in this instance will be considered first; any possible forms of redress open to Colin will then be examined. The impact of the HRA 1998 which affords ECHR further effect in domestic law will be taken into account at a number of significant points.

The first contact between the police officers and Colin appears to be of a voluntary nature: the officers are, of course, entitled to ask questions, which Colin may answer if he wishes to (*Rice v Connolly* (1966)). It is not therefore necessary to ask whether Albert and Bill are invoking powers of stop and search under s 1 of PACE at this stage. When Colin is asked to turn out his pockets, this appears to be a request, which he could refuse. It may therefore be characterised as part of a voluntary search. It is not clear that Colin consented to the search, and in any event Albert and Bill were under a duty not to engage in a voluntary search (para 1.5 of Code A) and, on that basis, have clearly breached the requirements of Code A.

Further, the seizure of the keys does not appear to be done with Colin's consent and therefore will only be lawful if it is part of a lawful stop and search. Thus, it must be shown that the police officers complied with the provisions of ss 1 and 2 of PACE and of Code A. Under s 1(2), a police officer may search for stolen or prohibited articles if he has reasonable grounds (s 1(3)) for believing that he will find such articles. The necessary reasonable suspicion is defined in paras 2.2–2.6 of Code A. There must be some objective basis for it which will relate to the nature of the article suspected of being carried. Various factors are mentioned in paras 2.3, 2.4 and 2.6, which may be taken into account in arriving at the necessary reasonable suspicion. These include the time and place, the behaviour of the person concerned and the carrying of certain articles in an area which has recently experienced a number of burglaries. In the instant situation, the lateness of the hour and the fact that Colin is outside a factory in an area which has recently experienced burglaries, coupled with his nervous behaviour, might give rise to a generalised suspicion, but it may be argued that the suspicion does not relate specifically enough to a particular article, since there is very little to suggest that Colin is carrying any particular article. Following this argument, no power to stop and search arises; the seizure of the keys is therefore unlawful. In any event, even if it could be established that reasonable suspicion is present, taking new provisions under para 2.3 into account regarding the legitimacy of generalised suspicion, the search and seizure is still unlawful, since the procedural requirements of s 2 of PACE are breached.[1] This outcome would appear to be consistent with the demands of Art 5, which the police must abide with under s 6 of the HRA; while short detentions for stop and search purposes may be compatible with Art 5, this will only be the case – assuming that Art 5 does cover short detentions – if an exception, in this instance that under Art 5(1)(c), applies. The exceptions are strictly interpreted and it does not appear that Art 5(1)(c) applies since reasonable suspicion has not been established.

The request made to come to the police station appears to assume that Colin will come on a voluntary basis; therefore, it is not necessary at this point to consider whether a power to arrest arises. However, after Colin becomes abusive, Bill takes hold of him to restrain him. If this restraining is not part of a lawful arrest and therefore lawful under s 117 of PACE, it could be characterised as an assault on Colin. Have Albert and Bill a power to arrest at this point? Any such power would have to concern an arrest on suspicion of participation in burglary and therefore would arise under s 24, as burglary is an arrestable offence. However, in order to invoke the power under s 24, Albert and Bill would have to show reasonable suspicion that Colin is involved in burglary and, as already considered in relation to s 1, it is arguable that no such suspicion arises on the facts; Colin's abusiveness could not be said to add anything to the suspicion already present (this conclusion would appear to accord with the findings in the leading case on reasonable suspicion, *Castorina v Chief Constable of Surrey* (1988) since the need for an objective basis for suspicion, even if it is not of a very high level, is not met). Moreover, even if the level of suspicion is high enough for a stop and search, it may be argued that it is not high enough for an arrest. Therefore, no power to arrest arises; the restraint of Colin is unlawful. In any event, it seems that the restraint may not have been an integral part of an arrest; if not, following *Kenlin v Gardner* (1967), it was clearly unlawful. Either argument obviously produces the same result.

Albert and Bill then arrest Colin for assault on a police officer in the execution of his duty, an offence arising under s 89(1) of the Police Act 1996. Is this arrest lawful? There is no power to arrest under s 89 of the Police Act 1996 and the offence in question is not an arrestable offence under s 24. Therefore, the arrest power must arise, if it arises at all, under s 25 or at common law, on the basis that the assault amounted to a breach of the peace. If it is to arise under s 25, two tests must be satisfied. First, it must be shown that one of the general arrest conditions under s 25(3) was fulfilled. It may be argued that the arrest was necessary to prevent Colin causing further physical harm to Bill; in that case, the condition under s 25(3)(d)(i) would be satisfied. Secondly, Albert and Bill must have reasonable suspicion that the assault has been perpetrated. It can be argued that Bill was not at that point in the execution of his duty, as he had laid hands on Colin unlawfully; therefore, can Albert and Bill be said to have reasonable suspicion as to that aspect of the offence? It may be argued, following *Marsden* (1868) and *Fennell* (1970), that, since Bill had exceeded his authority in restraining Colin, Colin was entitled to resist by way of reasonable force; any such resistance would be lawful and therefore could not amount to an assault. Assuming that Colin's action amounted to no more than reasonable force, he has not committed an assault. Thus, it is arguable that no power to arrest arises; the arrest therefore appears to be unlawful. When Colin is bundled into the car, Albert and Bill are not therefore entitled to use reasonable force under s 117, as they are not in the exercise of an arrest power. Thus, the subsequent detention is presumably also unlawful.

It can further be noted that the reason given for the arrest, following *Christie v Leachinsky* (1947) and receiving some support from *Abassy v Metropolitan Police Commissioner* (1990), must ensure that the arrested person knows which act he has been arrested for, but that there is no need to be more precise than that. However, more recently, in *Mullady v DPP* (1997), where the arrest reasons were given as 'obstruction' (which is also not arrestable), it was held that where the reasons given to a suspect for his arrest are invalid or the wrong reasons, then the arrest itself is unlawful. The reason given in the instant case conveyed the fact that the arrest was for striking Bill; arguably, this was sufficient, but of course this conclusion does not affect the earlier finding that the arrest was unlawful. These findings as to the arrest would appear to accord with the demands of Art 5(1) and (2).

The search of Colin's flat also appears to be unlawful. Under s 18, a power to enter and search premises after arrest arises, but only in instances when the arrest is for an arrestable offence. As the arrest has been effected under s 25, this condition is not satisfied. It follows from this that the power of seizure under s 19(2) does not arise, as it may only be exercised under s 19(1) by a constable lawfully on the premises. The seizure of the cannabis is therefore unlawful. The search of the home also appears to breach Art 8 under the HRA.

At the police station, Colin is denied access to legal advice. Delay in affording such access will be lawful if one of the contingencies envisaged under s 58(8) of PACE will arise if a solicitor is contacted. Following *Samuel* (1988), the police must have a clear basis for this belief. In this instance, the police made no effort to invoke one of the exceptions and have therefore breached s 58 and para 6 of Code C, which provides that, once a suspect has requested advice, he must not be interviewed until he has received it.

Having identified a series of illegal acts on the part of the police, it will now be necessary to consider the redress, if any, available to Colin in respect of them. The first such act was the unlawful seizure of the keys. The appropriate tortious cause of action in this instance will be trespass to goods; damages will, however, be minimal.

In taking hold of Colin outside the context of a lawful arrest, Bill commits assault and battery and breaches Art 5 of the Convention. The facts of the instant case closely resemble those of *Collins v Willcock* (1984) or *Kenlin v Gardner* (1967) which established this principle. Further, the unlawful arrest and the subsequent unlawful detention will support a claim of false imprisonment. The entry of the flat was unlawful, as was the seizure of the cannabis; Colin could therefore sue the police authority for trespass to land and to goods. Alternatively, Colin could sue under s 7(1)(a) of the HRA, receiving compensation under Art 5(4) and under s 8 in respect of an arguable breach of Art 8 in respect of the entry of his home, but since the tort action is available, there would be no need to rely on the HRA.

Colin may hope that the cannabis will be excluded from evidence under s 78 of PACE, as it was found during the course of an unlawful search.

However, according to *Thomas* (1990) and *Effick* (1992) and confirmed in *Khan* (1997), real evidence is admissible subject to a very narrow discretion to exclude it. That discretion might be exercised if it was obtained with deliberate illegality. The first instance decision in *Edward Fennelly* (1989), in which a failure to give the reason for a stop and search led to exclusion of the search, is out of line with the other authorities. It may be that Albert and Bill merely misconstrued their powers in thinking that a power of entry to premises arose in the circumstances, rather than deliberately perpetrating an illegal stop and search. In any event, it may be very hard to show that they acted in bad faith. If so, it appears that no strong argument for exclusion of the cannabis from evidence arises, and this outcome appears to be in accordance with the demands of Art 6 under s 3 of the HRA. Section 78 must be interpreted in accordance with Art 6, but no change in the current interpretation appears to be required due to the findings in *Khan v UK* (2000). This position has been unaffected by the incorporation of Art 6 into domestic law under the HRA (*AG's Reference No 3 of 1999* (2001)).

Can a reasonable argument be advanced that Colin's admissions should be excluded from evidence under s 76? Following *Alladice* (1988) and *Hughes* (1988), unless it can be shown that the custody officer acted in bad faith in failing to allow Colin access to a solicitor, it seems that s 76(2)(a) will not apply. Following *Delaney* (1989), it is necessary to show under s 76(2)(b) that the defendant was in some particularly difficult or vulnerable position, making the breach of PACE of special significance. Since this does not appear to be the case here, it seems that s 76(2)(b) cannot be invoked.

On the other hand, Colin's admissions may be excluded from evidence under s 78 on the basis that the police breached s 58. Following *Samuel* (1988), it must be shown that the breach of s 58 was causally related to the admissions made in the second interview. It may be that Colin was aware that he could keep silent (although he was aware that this might disadvantage him at trial), but decided to make admissions and would have done so had he had advice. This argument succeeded in *Dunford* (1990) and *Alladice* (1988), on the basis that the appellants in those cases were experienced criminals, aware of their rights. It appears that Colin did remain silent for some time; possibly, therefore, he would have made the admissions in any event. It might be argued that access to legal advice would have added nothing to his ability to weigh up the situation.[2] On this analysis, the requisite causal relationship does not exist and the admissions might not, therefore, be excluded from evidence under s 78. On the other hand, the ECHR has placed considerable importance on the right of access to legal advice in cases such as *Murray (John) v UK* (1996) and *Averill v UK* (2000). It has held that delay in access where the defendant faces the possibility that adverse inferences may be drawn from silence can amount to a breach of

Art 6 of the Convention. These decisions may make the court more willing to exclude admissions obtained while access to legal advice was refused. It is concluded that, taking Art 6 into account, the admissions are likely to be excluded from evidence under s 78. There is also the possibility of Colin being able to bring an action against the police under s 7(1)(a) of the HRA, claiming infringement of his Art 6 rights. It may be noted that adverse inferences could not be drawn from his silence under s 34(2A) of the CJPOA 1994, as amended, since he did not have an opportunity to have legal advice.

A further possibility is that the actions of the police could be the subject of a complaint, as could the other unlawful actions mentioned. Under s 84, the complaint would go in the first instance to the chief officer of police of the force Albert and Bill belong to.

Finally, Colin may want to know whether the charge of assaulting a police officer in the execution of his duty will succeed. Clearly, it will fail on the argument that Colin's actions did not amount to an assault, as he was entitled to resist Bill. Moreover, it has been determined that Bill was outside the execution of his duty.

Thus, in conclusion, a number of tort actions are available to Colin, as well as the possibility of an HRA action, or of making a complaint in respect of Albert and Bill's behaviour. It further seems that the charge of assaulting a police officer will be unsuccessful. However, it remains in doubt whether Colin's admissions and the cannabis found will be admissible in evidence against him.

Notes

1   Had it been found that the stop and search was lawful, the seizure of the keys would be lawful on the basis that the keys fall into the category of articles which may be seized if discovered under s 1(6).

2   This argument could be explored in more detail. It could be argued that, despite his conviction, Colin may not be well-equipped to withstand questioning. Possibly, had his solicitor been present, he or she might have been able to help Colin to keep silent (if that appeared to be in his best interests, despite the provision of s 36 of the CJPOA 1994 that a failure to account for having a substance in his possession might lead to the drawing of adverse inferences at trial) even after the prolonged questioning.

Question 28

Taking the Human Rights Act 1998 into account, critically evaluate the current scheme under which a citizen can be arrested.

Answer plan

A fairly difficult question, since it asks you to concentrate only on the arrest scheme. Moreover, it is no good merely writing down everything you know about arrest: you need to probe the weaknesses in the scheme and the areas of uncertainty.

Essentially, the following matters should be considered:

* arrest under common law powers;
* arrest under ss 24 and 25 of PACE 1984;
* arrest under the Terrorism Act;
* procedural elements of a valid arrest;
* Art 5 of the European Convention on Human Rights (ECHR) and relevant cases.

Answer

An arrest may often be the first formal stage in the criminal process. However, any arrest represents a serious curtailment of liberty; therefore, use of the arrest power requires careful regulation. An arrest is seen as *prima facie* illegal, necessitating justification under a specific legal power. If an arrest is effected where no arrest power arises, a civil action for false imprisonment may lie. Despite the need for clarity and precision, such powers were, until relatively recently, granted piecemeal, with the result that, prior to PACE, they were contained in a mass of common law and statutory provisions. No consistent rationale could be discerned and there were a number of gaps and anomalies. The powers are now contained largely in PACE, but common law powers remain, while some statutes create a specific power of arrest which may overlap with the PACE powers. Arrest must also be compatible with Art 5 of the ECHR, a scheduled Convention right in the HRA 1998. In particular, any arrest for an offence must be 'lawful' and based on a 'procedure prescribed by law', must be with the intention of bringing the arrested person before a court and must be based on 'reasonable suspicion' that an offence has been committed.

PACE has not affected the power to arrest which arises at common law for breach of the peace. Factors present in a situation in which breach of the peace occurs may also give rise to arrest powers under PACE, but may extend further than they do due to the wide definition of breach of the peace. The leading case is *Howell* (1981), in which it was found that breach of the peace will arise if violence to persons or property, either actual or apprehended, occurs. Threatening words are not in themselves a breach of the peace, but they may lead a police officer to apprehend that a breach will arise. A police officer or any other person may arrest if a breach of the peace is in being or apprehended, but not when it has been terminated, unless there is reason to believe that it may be renewed. The general power to arrest for breach of the peace has been found to be compatible with Art 5 in *Steel v UK*, although, as in that case, the circumstances of particular arrests may render them a disproportionate exercise of power.

PACE contains two separate powers of arrest without warrant, one arising under s 24 and the other under s 25. Broadly speaking, s 24 provides a power of arrest in respect of more serious offences, while s 25 covers all offences, however trivial (including, for example, dropping litter), if certain conditions are satisfied apart from suspicion that the offence in question has been committed. Thus, s 25 operates to cover persons suspected of offences falling outside s 24. Obviously, had s 25 not contained special conditions, there would have been no need for s 24. The difference between s 24 and s 25 is quite important, because, once a person has been arrested under s 24, he or she is said to have been arrested for 'an arrestable offence' and this may have an effect on his or her treatment later on. An 'arrestable offence' is, therefore, one for which a person can be arrested if the necessary reasonable suspicion is present, without a need to show any other ingredients in the situation at the time of arrest.

A police officer can arrest for one of the offences covered by s 24 if he or she has reasonable grounds to suspect that the offence is about to be, is being, or has been committed. An ordinary citizen can arrest under s 24 in the same way, with the omission of the possibility of arresting where the offence is about to be committed. Offences for which a person can be arrested under s 24 may also be classified as 'serious arrestable offences' under s 116.

The police acquired the general power of arrest under s 25, which they had lacked previously. However, this power does not merely allow an officer to arrest for any offence so long as reasonable suspicion can be shown. Such a power would have been viewed as too draconian and a very severe threat to civil liberties. It is balanced by what are known as the 'general arrest conditions', which must also be fulfilled. Therefore, in order to arrest under s 25, two steps must be taken: first, there must be reasonable suspicion relating to the offence in question; and, secondly, one of the arrest conditions must be fulfilled. The need for both factors was emphasised in *Edwards v DPP* (1993). A police constable (but not an ordinary citizen) can arrest if he or she has reasonable grounds to suspect the person of having committed or having attempted to commit the offence or of being in the course of committing or attempting to commit it.

The general arrest conditions divide into two groups: those in which there is or appears to be a failure to furnish a satisfactory name or address so that the service of a summons later on would be impracticable; and those which concern the immediate need to remove the suspect from the street, which would make it inappropriate to serve a summons later. The inclusion of these provisions implies that the infringement of civil liberties represented by an arrest should be resorted to only where no other alternative exists.

Sections 24 and 25 both depend on the concept of reasonable suspicion; the idea behind it is that an arrest should take place at quite a late stage in the investigation. This limits the number of arrests, thereby ensuring that liberty is infringed only where there is a fairly pressing reason to justify the infringement; it also makes it less likely that a person will be wrongfully arrested. It seems likely that the concept of reasonable suspicion will be interpreted in accordance with the provisions as to reasonable suspicion under Code A, which deals with stop and search.

However, Annex B, para 4 of the original Code A stated that the level of suspicion for a stop would be 'no less' than that needed for arrest. This provision has been omitted from subsequent revisions, including that of 2003. Nevertheless, it would seem that, in principle, the Code A provisions should be relevant to arrests if the Codes and statute are to be treated as a harmonious whole. Moreover, it would appear strange if a more rigorous test could be applied to the reasonable suspicion necessary to effect a stop than that necessary to effect an arrest. If this is correct, it would seem that certain matters, such as an individual's racial group, could never be factors which could support a finding of reasonable suspicion.

Code A requires that for a suspicion to be reasonable, it must have an objective basis. This requirement, which has been strengthened in the 2003 revision, states that, normally, reasonable suspicion should be linked to specific 'accurate and current intelligence or information'. The need for objectivity is echoed in various decisions on the suspicion needed for an arrest. In *Dallison v Caffrey* (1965), Lord Diplock said the test was whether 'a reasonable man assumed to know the law and possessed of the information which in fact was possessed by the defendant would believe there were [reasonable grounds]'. A hunch is not enough; there must be a concrete basis for this suspicion, which relates to the particular person in question and could be evaluated by an objective observer. If an officer only has a hunch – mere suspicion as opposed to reasonable suspicion – he or she might continue to observe the person in question, but could not arrest until the suspicion had increased and could be termed 'reasonable suspicion'.

However, this still leaves a great deal of leeway to officers to arrest where suspicion relating to the particular person is at a low level, but they want to further the investigation by gathering information. At present, the courts seem prepared to allow police such leeway, and it should be noted that PACE endorses a reasonably low level of suspicion due to the distinction it maintains between belief and suspicion, suspicion probably being the lower standard. In *Ward v Chief Constable of Somerset and Avon Constabulary* (1986), for example, the grounds for suspicion were fairly flimsy and might have warranted further inquiries before arresting. Similarly, the Court of Appeal in *Castorina v Chief Constable of Surrey* (1988) appeared reluctant to take a rigorous approach to the question of reasonable suspicion. An ex-employee was arrested and detained for four hours by detectives investigating a burglary which they believed to be an 'inside job'. The basis of their suspicion was that the ex-employee had been recently dismissed and that the documents stolen would be useful to someone with a grudge. The ex-employee claimed damages for false imprisonment. The Court of Appeal held that the test applied by the judge at first instance was too demanding of the police. It was held that the question of honest belief was irrelevant; the issue of reasonable suspicion had nothing to do with the officers' subjective state of mind. The question was whether there was reasonable cause to suspect the plaintiff of burglary. Given that certain factors could be identified, including inside knowledge of the company's affairs and the motive of the plaintiff, it appeared that there was sufficient basis for the detectives to have reasonable grounds for suspicion. In *Castorina*, Purchas J ruled that, once reasonable suspicion arises, there is a further issue: officers have discretion as to whether to arrest or do something else, such as making further inquiries. This discretion can be attacked on *Wednesbury* principles, like any other discretion of a public body. Case law, influenced by the HRA, now suggests that the *Wednesbury* principles are being replaced by 'proportionality'. In *R (Daly) v Secretary of State for the Home Department* (2001), the House of Lords suggested that there will be circumstances in which proportionality delivers a different outcome from the *Wednesbury* principles. Proportionality may be more demanding in the sense that, where *Wednesbury* principles were likely to be satisfied if arrest was within the range of actions a reasonable officer in the circumstances could take, proportionality requires a more careful demonstration that arrest was necessary and that the purpose of arrest could not be better achieved in other ways.

Thus, the need to make further inquiries would be relevant to the first stage – arriving at reasonable suspicion – but probably not to the second – determining whether to make an arrest – unless proportionality required it. That it must be relevant to the first is axiomatic: an investigation passes through many stages, from the first, in which a vague suspicion relating to a particular person arises, up until the point when it is proved – if it is – that that person's guilt can be shown beyond reasonable doubt. At some point in that process, reasonable suspicion giving rise to a direction as to whether to effect an arrest arises; thus, there must be a point in the early stages at which it is possible to say that more inquiries should have been made and more evidence gathered before the arrest could lawfully take place. As the courts appear prepared to accept that arrest at quite an early stage in this process may be said to be based on reasonable grounds, and that even the application of proportionality leaves little leeway for challenge to the decision to arrest, it may be said that the interest of the citizen in his or her personal liberty is not being accorded sufficient weight under the current tests.[1]

'Reasonable suspicion' is a requirement of Art 5(1)(c) and the Strasbourg case law suggests that the UK approach is broadly compatible with the Convention. Thus, in *Fox, Campbell and Hartley v UK* (1992), the ECtHR accepted that what was reasonable would depend upon the circumstances and stressed the need for suspicion to have an objective basis; honest belief is not enough. However, a suspicion could be reasonable if the facts on which it was based only implied that the defendant may have committed the offence. In *Murray and Others v UK* (1995), the Court made it clear that the factual basis of reasonable suspicion was below that needed for bringing a charge or securing a conviction.

The power of arrest with warrant does not arise under PACE. There are a large number of statutory provisions allowing an arrest warrant to be issued of which the most significant is that arising under s 1 of the Magistrates' Courts Act 1980. Under this power, a warrant may be issued if a person aged at least 17 is suspected of an offence which is indictable or punishable with imprisonment, or where no satisfactory address is known allowing a summons to be served. This provision therefore limits the circumstances under which a warrant will be sought, as opposed to using the non-warrant powers under PACE and, as the police now have such broad powers of arrest under ss 24 and 25, it seems that arrest in reliance on a warrant will be used even less under PACE than it was previously.

If a statute creates an offence which is a serious offence falling within s 24, then, obviously, the arrest power under s 24 is applicable. If a statute creates a more minor offence, then equally, the arrest power under s 25 is applicable, so long as one or more of the general arrest conditions are satisfied. Section 11 of the Public Order Act 1986 and s 89 of the Police Act 1996 provide examples of such offences. However, certain statutes expressly create specific powers of arrest which are not dependent on ss 24 or 25, such as s 68 of the CJPOA 1994. In such cases, the procedure under s 28, which will be considered below, will still apply.

Almost all the indictable offences under the Terrorism Act 2000 carry a penalty of at least five years' imprisonment and are, therefore, arrestable offences under s 24 of PACE. There is also a power of arrest under ss 40 and 41 of the Act itself. This power has two limbs. The first empowers a constable to arrest for certain specified offences under the Terrorism Act 2000. As these offences are arrestable offences in any event, this power would seem to overlap with that under s 24. However, if an arrest is effected under the Terrorism Act as opposed to s 24 of PACE, this has an effect on the length of detention, as will be seen below. The second limb provides a completely separate power from the PACE power; it allows arrest without needing to show suspicion relating to a particular offence.

Instead, the constable needs to have reasonable grounds for suspecting that a person is concerned in the preparation or instigation of acts of terrorism. This arrest is not for an offence but, in practice, for investigation, questioning and general intelligence gathering which may be conducted for the purpose, as Lowry puts it, of 'isolating and identifying the urban guerillas and then detaching them from the supportive or ambivalent community'. Thus, this power represents a clear departure from the principle that liberty should be curtailed only on clear and specific grounds which connect the actions of the suspect with a specific offence under criminal law. There are potential Convention difficulties here. First, an arrest could be for activities that are not themselves offences and, secondly, an arrest could be for a purpose other than bringing the person before a court. Both of these would seem to violate Art 5(1)(c). It must be said, however, that the Strasbourg Court adopts an autonomous definition of the word 'offence' and in *Brogan v UK* (1988), it held that suspicion of 'terrorism' could amount to suspicion of an offence for Art 5 purposes (though in the instant case the suspects were arrested for terrorism, but immediately questioned about specific offences). In the context of anti-terrorism laws, the Strasbourg Court is, perhaps, less demanding than for 'ordinary' offences. On reasonable suspicion, for example, it accepts that confidential evidence need not be disclosed, but it insists that at least some evidence demonstrating its objective basis must be (*O'Hara v UK* (2002)).

For an arrest to be made validly, not only must the power of arrest exist, whatever its source, but the procedural elements must be complied with. The fact that a power of arrest arises will not on its own make the arrest lawful. These elements are of crucial importance, due to the consequences which may flow from a lawful arrest which will not flow from an unlawful one. Such consequences include the right of the officer to use force in making an arrest, if necessary, and the loss of liberty inherent in an arrest. If an arrest has not occurred, the citizen is free to go wherever he or she will and any attempt to prevent him or her doing so will be unlawful. It is therefore important to convey the fact of the arrest to the arrestee and to mark the point at which the arrest comes into being and general liberty ceases.

At common law, there had to be a physical detention or a touching of the arrestee to convey the fact of detention, unless he or she made this unnecessary by submitting to it; the fact of arrest had to be made clear (*Alderson v Booth* (1969)) and the reason for it had to be made known (*Christie v Leachinsky* (1947)). The common law safeguards have been modified and strengthened by s 28 of PACE. Under s 28, both the fact of and the reason for the arrest must be made known at the time or as soon as practicable afterwards. However, an ordinary citizen is not under this duty if the fact of the arrest and the reason for it are obvious. Conveying the fact of the arrest does not involve using a particular form of words, but it may be that reasonable detail must be given so that the arrestee will be in a position to give a convincing denial and therefore be more speedily released from detention. Given the infringement of liberty represented by an arrest and the need, therefore, to restore liberty as soon as possible, consistent with the needs of the investigation, it is unfortunate that s 28 did not make it clear that a reasonable degree of detail should be given.

However, the reason for the arrest need only be made known as soon as practicable. This is important for knowing the time from which an initially lawful arrest becomes unlawful. In *DPP v Hawkins* (1988), the question arose whether an officer was in the execution of his duty despite the fact that he had failed, at the time, to give the reason for the arrest. If the arrest was thereby rendered invalid, he could not be in the execution of his duty, as it could not include effecting an unlawful arrest. It was determined in the Court of Appeal that the arrest became unlawful from the time when it was practicable to inform the defendant of the reason, but he was not so informed. This occurred at the police station or perhaps in the police car, but did not occur earlier, due to the defendant's behaviour. However, the arrest did not become retrospectively unlawful and therefore did not affect acts done before its unlawfulness came into being, which thus left acts done in the execution of duty unaffected.

Thus, the police have a certain leeway as to informing the arrestee; the arrest will not be affected and nor will other acts arising from it, until the time when it would be practicable to inform of the reason for it has come and gone. However, if there was nothing in the behaviour of the arrestee to make informing him or her impracticable, then the arrest will be unlawful from its inception. Following this decision, what can be said as to the status of the suspect before the time came and passed at which the requisite words should have been spoken? Was he or she or was he or she not under arrest at that time? In *Murray v Ministry of Defence* (1988), soldiers occupied a woman's house, thus clearly taking her into detention, but did not inform her of the fact of arrest for half an hour. The question arose whether she was falsely imprisoned during that half-hour. The House of Lords found that delay in giving the requisite information was acceptable due to the alarm which the fact of arrest, if known, might have aroused in the particular circumstances – the unsettled situation in Northern Ireland. Article 5(2) requires an arrested person to be informed 'promptly' of the reason for their arrest and it is likely that s 28 of PACE meets this requirement – the Strasbourg Court accepts that promptness is context-dependent. Article 5(2) also requires that the person must be informed in a language they understand, which may have implications for the arrest of foreign suspects and the use of interpreters.

If a false arrest occurs, a remedy will be available. Where the procedural elements are not complied with, but no good reason for such failure arises, or if no power to arrest arose in the first place, the arrestee would have grounds for bringing an action for false imprisonment. Further, if a false arrest occurs and, subsequently, physical evidence is discovered or the defendant makes a confession, the defence may argue that the evidence should be excluded due to the false arrest. However, *Murray* has rendered the concept of a false arrest less clear-cut (though the case has been recently distinguished by the Court of Appeal to suggest it cannot be used to justify clearly unlawful acts by the police: *Chief Constable of Thames Valley Police v Hepburn* (2002)).

It seems that an arrest which does not comply with all the procedural requirements will still be an arrest, as far as all the consequences arising from it are concerned, for a period of time. It is therefore in a more precarious position than an arrest which, from its inception, complies with all the requirements, because it will cease to be an arrest at an uncertain point. Therefore, some departure has occurred from the principle that there should be a clear demarcation between the point at which the citizen is at liberty and the point at which his or her liberty is restrained.

It is to be hoped that one of the impacts made by the Convention will be to reduce the areas of discretion and uncertainty regarding the power of arrest. On general fundamentals, such as the need for reasonable suspicion and proper information, there may be little incompatibility between the requirements of English statute and common law and the Convention. In addition, however, the Convention requires that any arrest must be 'lawful' and here it may have an impact, not only in introducing proportionality into any decision to arrest, but also strengthening the existing common law commitment to the rule of law. This may work to reduce the scope of discretionary, ancillary and implied powers that the police may claim and which can so easily undermine reasonable certainty in the law. In *Chief Constable of Thames Valley Police v Hepburn* (2002), for example, the Court of Appeal held that the police, acting on the basis of a warrant to search premises for drugs, could not claim an ancillary power to stop and search persons on those premises. The detention and search of Hepburn, who had tried to leave the premises when the police entered, was, therefore, unlawful. This strongly worded assertion of the rule of law does not mention the Convention, but it is clearly compatible with it and with the spirit of 'legality' that pervades it.

Note

1   Section 24 permits a constable to arrest without reasonable suspicion, on a hunch, if an arrestable offence is, in fact, being committed or has been committed or is about to be committed. The point of this provision is because it might otherwise seem strange that a person who had committed an arrestable offence could, nevertheless, found an action for false imprisonment. However, if it cannot be established that the offence was committed or was about to be committed, it is not enough to show that reasonable grounds for suspicion did, in fact, exist although the officer did not know them (*Siddiqui v Swain* (1979)).

Question 29

'The interviewing scheme under the Police and Criminal Evidence Act 1984 is wholly inadequate as a means of preventing miscarriages of justice.' Do you agree?

Answer plan

It should be noted that the question is only concerned with the interviewing scheme under PACE 1984, not with other methods of addressing the problem of miscarriages of justice.

Essentially, the following matters should be considered:

* the nature of the safeguards available under Pts IV and V of PACE and Codes of Practice C and E;
* the provisions determining when the safeguards come into play – definition of an 'interview' – interviewing inside or outside the police station;
* the legal advice provisions;
* the recording provisions;
* the value of exclusion of evidence as a form of redress for breaches of the interviewing scheme – the relevance of ss 34–37 of the Criminal Justice and Public Order Act (CJPOA) 1994;
* the scope for miscarriages of justice which remains.

Answer

Our criminal justice process relies heavily on the use of confession evidence but, at the same time, is wedded to a system in which a suspect is interviewed by a body, the police, who have a strong interest in securing a conviction, under conditions which are entirely under police control. In such circumstances, what can be done to ensure that a confession so acquired can be relied on by a court?

A body of rules can be devised, intended first to alter the balance of power between interviewers and interviewee, reducing the vulnerability of the interviewee and secondly, to create confidence in the evidence of what was said, putting the jury as far as possible in the position they would have been in had they been there. Such rules will, however, tend to run counter to the concerns of those expected to apply them and therefore may not be observed or, more subtly, weaknesses and loopholes will be discovered and explored. Further rules may then be created to eradicate the loopholes. However, the pressure to find loopholes will remain unchanged and may become greater as the unwieldiness and complexity of the scheme creates greater frustration with it.

This process began in this country with the Judges' Rules, which were replaced by the more complex interviewing scheme under PACE and Code C. A revised Code C was introduced in April 2003 which replaced the 1995 revision. Code E (also revised in 2003) deals with audio recording. Visual recording of interviews was experimented with in 2002–03 and may be introduced throughout the country; they are subject to Code F. These developments notwithstanding, the pressure which originally led the police to circumvent the rules is still unchanged.

Is it possible in this situation to prevent such evasion? Some might argue that it is not and that the system will always be flawed until its central weakness is addressed. However, before coming to such a conclusion, it seems worth considering the extent to which the revisions to Code C have remedied loopholes. In particular, suspects could be encouraged out of having legal advice and suspects could be interviewed outside the police station, thereby evading the safeguards available within it. An inquiry into the means used to eradicate these loopholes and the likely impact in terms of confessions admitted may say something about the general use of rules in this situation.

These changes represent an attempt to obtain greater control of the interviewing process, to address the inherent limitations of police interviews. If an interview is conducted in compliance with sound interviewing rules, it should be possible to feel confident that a conviction based on it will be safe and therefore miscarriages of justice should be less likely. Of course, evidence of compliance with the interviewing scheme without more will not necessarily preclude exclusion of the confession from evidence. Compliance with a sound interviewing scheme is no more than the first, necessary step towards ensuring the reliability of admissions obtained and the integrity of a resultant conviction.

In order to place the changes in their context, the general nature of the interviewing scheme, which PACE brought into being, should be considered. It consists of a web of provisions which derive from three sources of differing legal status: the Act itself, Codes C and E made under it and the Notes for Guidance accompanying the Codes. The Notes aim at helping police officers to apply the Code provisions; they are not part of the Codes. The important issue is not so much the nature of the safeguards but the question of when they come into play. It will be argued that there is still too great a variation in the levels of protection available. The safeguards available are intended to ensure either that the suspect is not at an undue disadvantage in comparison with the interviewers, or to protect the integrity of the interview so that it can be used later on as evidence against the suspect if necessary. Of course, these functions flow from the other. In what follows, both functions are in question where levels of protection for interviews are referred to.

A radical change to the balance between police and interviewee was made by curtailment of the right to silence under ss 34–37 of the CJPOA 1994. This was reflected in the new and complex caution introduced under the 1995 revision of Code C. It meant that, even where all the safeguards are in place, there may be great pressure on the suspect to speak, bearing in mind the disadvantage which silence may create, and this may result in an increase in the number of false confessions. However, ECtHR cases make it clear that a suspect must not be compelled to speak (*Funke v France* (1993)), and that adverse inferences should not normally be allowed when the detainee was not allowed independent legal advice (*Murray v UK* (1996)), and that inferences may not be drawn from silence unless that silence 'could only sensibly be attributed to their having no answer or none that would stand up to cross-examination', as to the question originally asked (*Condron v UK* (2000)). So, any silence which can later be explained plausibly should no longer trigger inferences or Art 6 will be breached. These Convention requirements have been adopted into the law under s 34(2A) of the CJPOA 1994, and the 2003 revision to Code C makes appropriate changes to the caution in respect of interviews from which adverse inferences cannot lawfully be drawn. The old caution, maintaining the full right to silence, must be used where the suspect has not had an opportunity of having legal advice, under para 10.6. The 2003 revision, in line with Convention rights, emphasises the importance of the right to legal advice. There is still room for argument, however, as to the meaning of the term 'opportunity'. Also, it seems that adverse inferences can be drawn from silence in interviews under caution outside the police station, even though the suspect has had no opportunity to have access to legal advice and has not been notified that it will be available later.

The correct interpretation of the term 'interview' used in Code C as originally drafted was a matter of great importance, because the relevant safeguards only came into play once an exchange between police officer and suspect was designated an interview. The term 'interview' therefore tended to be given a wide interpretation and eventually the definition given to it by the Court of Appeal in *Matthews* (1990), 'any discussion or talk between suspect and police officer', brought within its ambit many exchanges far removed from formal interviews.

However, assuming that an exchange could be called an interview, the safeguards applying to it differed quite markedly, depending on where it took place. Those available *inside* the police station included contemporaneous recording or tape-recording; the ability to read over, verify and sign the notes of the interview as a correct record; notification of the right to legal advice; the option of having legal advice and of having the advisor present and, where appropriate, the presence of an adult.[1] In 'the field', however, it was only necessary to ensure that an accurate record of the interview was made and, where appropriate, an adult was present. In other words, a minimum level of protection only was available, thus creating greater scope for impropriety, including fabrication of confessions, in such circumstances. The arbitrary dividing line thus drawn between those suspects interviewed in or out of the police station was one of the main deficiencies of the original Code C.

Under the revised Codes, classifying an exchange as an interview will not be quite as crucial because, under para 11.13, any comments relevant to the offence made by a suspected person outside the context of an interview must be accurately recorded and then verified and signed by the suspect; or disagreements signified. However, such classification will still be important, because it remains the first, although not the only, step towards ensuring that the other safeguards mentioned above are available. A definition of the term 'interview' is now contained in para 11.1A, which reads: 'An interview is the questioning of a person regarding their involvement or suspected involvement in a criminal offence or offences, which, under paragraph 10.1 is required to be carried out under caution.'

Paragraph 10.1 of Code C requires a caution to be given where the answers to questions (or the suspect's failure to answer questions) may be given in evidence to a court in a prosecution. Questioning which is simply to establish a person's identity, or the ownership of a vehicle, or to assist in the conduct of a search of a person or property, will not, therefore, constitute an 'interview'. Questioning a person at port and border controls under the Terrorism Act 2000 is also excluded.

The definition, introduced in 1995, replaced one which had been criticised by the courts (*Cox* (1992)). It had tried, in a way that turned out to be impracticable, to distinguish questioning about a criminal offence from questioning aimed at obtaining information.

The hallmark of an interview is 'questioning', so if the conversation is instigated by the suspect, this may not be an interview (*Menard* (1995)). The current definition is in line with the approach taken in *Absolam* (1989), where an interview was defined as questions directed by the police to a suspect, and in *Maguire* (1989), where an invitation to the suspect to explain himself was not treated as amounting to an interview.

Once an exchange can be designated an interview, it will be of significance whether it takes place inside or outside the police station. The significance is not as great as it used to be. Paragraph 11 contains provisions in sub-para 11.11 for giving the suspect the record of the interview to verify and sign and this, unlike the situation prior to 1995, applies to all interviews, not just those that took place in the police station, since para 11.7(a) requires a record to be made of all interviews, wherever they take place. Further, under para 11.7(c), the interview must be recorded contemporaneously wherever it takes place unless, in the investigating officer's view, this would not be practicable or would interfere with its conduct. Thus, where an exchange is an interview, the new provisions do go beyond para 11.13. However, there is no change as far as notification of the right to legal advice is concerned. It is also, at present, unlikely that the interview would be recorded: neither Code E on audio recording nor Code F on visual recording envisage recording taking place anywhere but inside the police station, though the latter is not explicit on the point. Thus, an unsatisfactory distinction between suspects interviewed in or out of the police station is still preserved.

Since 1995, the problem has been addressed in a radical way by means of a prohibition under para 11.1 on interviewing outside the police station except in exceptional circumstances. It is, of course, only 'interviews' which must not occur outside the police station; other exchanges can take place because, in general, the need for them to be subject to the level of protection available inside it will not be so pressing. Any comments made relevant to an offence would need to be recorded and acknowledged by the suspect under para 11.13. However, courts have recently interpreted any questioning designed to incriminate the suspect as an 'interview': see *Bailey v DPP* (1998).

Even if an interview is taking place, para 11.1 will not apply if the decision to arrest has not yet been taken. Paragraph 11.1 requires a police officer to categorise a person either as someone who may possibly be involved in an offence or as someone who will clearly be arrested. Presumably, the para 11.1 prohibition was aimed at ensuring that suspects being interviewed were afforded the safeguards available once they were in the police station. It is therefore anomalous that persons suspected of an offence can be questioned away from it. This anomaly is created by the difference between the levels of suspicion denoted by para 11.1A and para 11.1: the level under para 11.1A appears to be the lower, giving scope for the argument that the decision to arrest had not yet been made because the level of suspicion was not high enough. This loophole could have been closed had the words 'suspected involvement' in an offence also been used in para 11.1 to determine the point at which an exchange would become an interview (as in 1995, the opportunity was not taken in 2003). The police may find it difficult where there are very strong grounds for suspicion to support a claim that interviewing could continue, because the decision to arrest had not been taken, but otherwise it will be difficult to be certain, in retrospect, on this point.

Under para 11.1(a), (b) and (c), interviewing can occur outside the station in order to avert certain specified risks. The first exception under para 11.1(a), allowing interviewing to take place at once where delay might lead to interference with evidence, could be interpreted very broadly and could apply whenever there was some likelihood that evidence connected with any offence, but not immediately obtainable, was in existence.[2]

It is clear that there is continuing variation in levels of protection for interviews; the change brought about by para 11.1 is far less radical than may at first appear. Wide but uncertain scope for interviewing outside the police station still remains. Thus, things stand as they did under the original Code: in order to bring certain safeguards into play, it must first be found that an exchange constitutes an interview and then that it took place within the police station. Taking access to legal advice, tape-recording and the provision for interviews under paras 11 and 12 as the main safeguards, it becomes apparent that there are three levels of protection available, which depend on the category into which the exchange falls.

Inside the police station, if the person in question is an arrestee or a volunteer under caution and the exchange is an interview, all the available safeguards will apply. If an interview takes place outside the police station, but falls outside the para 11.1 prohibition, the same verifying and recording provisions will apply, with the proviso that contemporaneous recording, tape-recording and, for the future, video-recording are likely to be impracticable. The most important difference is that no notification of the right to legal advice need be given.

If the person is suspected of involvement in an offence, but the level of suspicion is below that which would warrant a caution or *a fortiori* an arrest and the interview takes place in the police station, the lower level of protection described above will apply, but the person also has the right to have legal advice and, possibly, due to the provision of para 11.2, to be told of this right. The paragraph requires a reminder to be given of the entitlement to free legal advice before any interview in a police station. This provision may apply to the situation envisaged, although the use of the word 'remind' suggests that that was not the intention behind it, because the person in question will not already be aware of the right. Utterances relevant to the offence, outside the context of an interview, made by a suspected person (who could obviously be an arrestee or a volunteer under caution) are subject only to the basic level of protection, which obtains under para 11.13, though under para 11.4, 'significant statements' or silences made prior to the interview should, at the beginning of the interview, be put to the suspect for confirmation or denial.

The main objection to this scheme is that an arbitrary dividing line is still being drawn between suspects interviewed inside or outside the police station, although admittedly, interviewing outside it should now occur less frequently. The arbitrariness of this division is most clearly apparent in the distinction drawn between suspects who fall just outside and just inside the category of those who will clearly be arrested. Further, even where, formally speaking, all the safeguards should be in place, there may still be methods of evading them. As research conducted by Sanders in 1989 showed, the police have developed a number of means of subverting the legal advice scheme, with a view to discouraging suspects from obtaining access to legal advice. The 2003 revision of Code C, in note 6J, for example, emphasises the importance of legal advice.[3]

Disputes over the admissibility of confessions under s 78 will continue, because it will be necessary to put exchanges between suspect and police into the categories mentioned above; having done so, if one of the safeguards applicable to that category has not been made available, the confession may be inadmissible. The other category of confessions which may be inadmissible will be those which should not have taken place at all, because they occurred outside the police station, but fell within the para 11.1 prohibition. If one of the aims of para 11.1 is to reduce the scope for such disputes, it appears unlikely to fulfil it. Moreover, the scheme is unlikely to prevent miscarriages of justice, because it leaves open scope for evading certain of the key safeguards including tape recording and access to legal advice. Confessions obtained without such safeguards will only be subject to the s 78 test if the suspect pleads not guilty. Further, evasion of the rules must usually be characterised as a breach of the scheme in order to trigger off use of s 78. However, it may not appear that a breach has occurred, again leaving open the possibility that a potential miscarriage of justice will go unrecognised.

In conclusion, it is suggested that, whilst to say that the interviewing scheme in PACE and Code C is 'wholly inadequate' to prevent miscarriages of justice may be an exaggeration, the 1995 and 2003 amendments to the Code still do not prevent, as securely as they should, the questioning of suspects away from police stations and the safeguards therein, and this, given the pressures on the police, can increase the possibility of miscarriages. What of the Convention? Article 6 applies to pre-trial behaviour, including by the police (*Teixeira v Portugal* (1998)). The extent of its influence in providing protection from police abuses is hard to judge. Undoubtedly, it shifts attention away from the detailed classification of police actions towards an evaluation of the overall fairness of the process. Nevertheless, the UK courts have also recognised and utilised the fact that Art 6 rights are flexible and context-dependent and may well find, subject to the access to legal advice provisions mentioned above, that much of the interviewing scheme in Code C is compatible with Art 6. Other potential causes of miscarriages of justice, such as those flowing from inadequate disclosures of evidence to the defence, or from the continued use of public interest immunity, are, perhaps, more likely to change as a consequence of Art 6.

Notes

1   If the interview took place on 'other premises', all the safeguards outlined above would apply apart from the requirements to inform of the right to legal advice and to allow the suspect to verify and sign the record of the interview.

2   In support of this, it could be pointed out that, even if there were no others involved in the offence who had not been apprehended, it could be argued that the evidence was at risk from the moment of arrest, because news of the arrest might become known to persons with a motive for concealing the evidence. This argument could also apply to the exception under (c) in respect of hindering the recovery of property obtained in consequence of the commission of any offence, with the proviso that (c) will obviously apply to a narrower range of offences.

3   The 2003 revision of Code C also clarifies the time when the 'interview' ends and further questioning should cease. In particular, the interviewee is to be given the opportunity to give an innocent explanation (para 11.6).

Question 30

At 12.00 on Saturday night, Carl and Bert, two policemen in uniform and driving a police car, see Ali, an Asian youth, hurrying through the street. Bearing in mind a knife attack perpetrated at 11.50 pm by Asian youths in the area, they approach Ali and ask him where he has just been. He refuses to answer their questions and they ask him to get into the police car. Bert then says, 'We're going to search you. OK?'. Ali does not reply but makes no resistance to the search. Carl and Bert then search him and discover a knife. Carl cautions Ali, and then questions him as to the whereabouts of the others involved in the attack; Ali admits that he was with some other youths in the street where the attack took place at 11.50 pm. No notes are taken during the questioning. Bert then informs Ali that he is under arrest for wounding.

They arrive at the police station at 12.35 am. Ali is re-cautioned under para 10.5 of Code C and informed of his rights under Code C by the Custody Officer, Doris. He makes a request to contact his solicitor but Eileen, the investigating officer, is unable to contact the solicitor. Eileen then asks Ali whether he is prepared to go ahead with the interview without a solicitor and he reluctantly agrees to do so. A period of two hours elapses. He is then questioned and after half an hour he admits that he participated in the knife attack, although he says that he acted in self-defence. (The interview is tape-recorded.) He is asked to sign the notes (compiled later in the station) of the questions and answers in the police car and does so.

At 8 am on Sunday, he is charged with wounding and is remanded in custody.

Ali (who has no previous convictions but was cautioned for theft two years previously when he was 16) now alleges that his confession was untrue, that he knew nothing of the attack until informed of it by the police and was merely carrying the knife as a precaution. He says, 'I only confessed because I was desperate to get home. I wasn't even there; I only said I was because I was scared of them'.

Advise Ali as to whether the interviews and the finding of the knife will be admissible in evidence against him. Do *not* consider any other possible advice that could be given regarding aspects of the problem.

Answer plan

This is a fairly tricky problem question since it involves police behaviour that is close to rule bending as opposed to rule breaking. It is fairly narrowly focused: it is concerned only with the question of exclusion of evidence. It must first be established that breaches of PACE have occurred and then asked whether or not they are likely to lead to exclusion of admissions made during any interview affected. You should take into account the cautioning provisions under Code C. Note that the question *expressly* does not call for consideration of forms of redress available to Ali other than exclusion of evidence. Also, it does not ask you to consider whether adverse inferences will be drawn from his silence, assuming that it is not excluded from evidence.

Essentially, the following matters should be considered:

• the lawfulness of Ali's arrest under s 24 of PACE; Art 5 of the European Convention on Human Rights (ECHR);

- the legality of the stop and search; relevance of Art 5 of the ECHR;
- the applicability of the prohibition on interviews outside the police station under Code C, para 11.1, bearing in mind the exception under para 11.1(b);
- possible breach of Code C, para 11.5 in respect of the first interview (in the police car); impracticability of contemporaneous recording;
- exclusion of the first interview from evidence under ss 76 and 78 of PACE; Art 6 of the ECHR;
- possible breach of Code C, para 6 affecting the second interview in the station; admissibility of the second interview; relevance of Art 6;
- the likelihood that the second interview will be excluded from evidence; ss 76 and 78 of PACE; relevance of Art 6 of the ECHR under the HRA;
- the likelihood that the knife will be excluded from evidence under s 78; Art 6 of the ECHR.

Answer

Confessions may be excluded from evidence under s 78 or s 76 of PACE. Non-confession evidence, in this instance the knife, may be excluded from evidence under s 78 of PACE. A first step in the direction of exclusion from evidence of the admissions made by Ali and of the knife is to demonstrate that substantial and significant breaches of PACE or the Codes have occurred. The impact of the HRA 1998 which affords the ECHR further effect in domestic law will be taken into account at a number of significant points.

The facts of the instant case may support an argument that Ali was unlawfully arrested. If the arrest was unlawful, the subsequent detention would also be unlawful as his detention is dependent on the power to detain for questioning under s 37(2) of PACE, which is in turn dependent on an 'arrest', not an unlawful arrest. Ali is arrested for wounding, an offence arising under s 18 or s 20 of the Offences Against the Person Act 1861. Both offences are arrestable offences under s 24(1)(b) of PACE. In order to arrest under the section, it is necessary to show that Carl and Bert had reasonable grounds for suspecting that Ali had committed the wounding. Ali's proximity in time and place to the offence, coupled with his possession of the knife, is, it is submitted, sufficient to give rise to the necessary suspicion. This outcome would appear to be consistent with the demands of Art 5, which the police must abide with under s 6 of the HRA since it appears that the exception under Art 5(1)(c) applies.

The knife is discovered during the course of a stop and search of doubtful legality. Any illegality of the stop and search is significant. It may be argued that the stop and search was consensual. However, Carl and Bert were under a duty not to engage in a voluntary search (Code A, para 1.5) and, on that basis, have clearly breached the requirements of Code A. Thus, it must be shown that the police officers complied with the provisions of ss 1 and 2 of PACE and of Code A. Under s 1(2), a police officer may search for offensive weapons or prohibited articles if he has reasonable grounds (s 1(3)) for believing that he will find such articles. The necessary reasonable suspicion is defined in paras 2.22.6 of Code A. There must be some objective basis for it which will relate to the nature of the article suspected of being carried. Various factors are mentioned in paras 2.3, 2.4 and 2.6, which may be taken into account in arriving at the necessary reasonable suspicion. These include the time and place, the behaviour of the person concerned and the carrying of certain articles in an area, which has recently experienced a number of burglaries. The fact that Ali was Asian and was hurrying through the street near the scene of the attack only 10 minutes after it had taken place might be enough to give rise to the reasonable suspicion that a weapon was being carried required by Code A.[1] Arguably, since para 2 of Code A should be interpreted compatibly with Art 5 of the ECHR under s 3 of the HRA, the better view is that there are insufficient grounds for suspicion, on the ground that where there is a doubt as to consent to a deprivation of liberty, a strict view should be taken giving the emphasis to the primary right (*Murray v UK* (1994)). In any event, even if it could be established that reasonable suspicion is present, taking new provisions under para 2.3 into account regarding the legitimacy of generalised suspicion, the search and seizure is still unlawful, since the procedural requirements of s 2 of PACE are breached.[2] Nevertheless, nothing in PACE provides that evidence obtained from an unlawful search may not be used to fuel reasonable suspicion under s 24, allowing for an arrest. Further, if the above argument as to the reasonable suspicion is correct, there may be sufficient suspicion for s 24 purposes, even without the finding of the knife. Thus, on this argument also, s 24 would be satisfied. The possible consequence of the unlawful search in evidential terms will be discussed below.

The next question to consider is whether by questioning Ali in the police car, Carl and Bert breached the prohibition on interviews outside the police station under Code C, para 11.1. If para 11.1 is to apply, two conditions must be satisfied: the questioning must constitute an interview under Code C, para 11.1A; and the decision to arrest must have been made at the point when the questioning took place. It is apparent that the first of these conditions has been met, as questions were put to Ali which concerned his suspected involvement in the wounding. The second is less clearly satisfied: the police might argue that, until Ali admitted that he was in the street when the wounding took place, the level of suspicion was not high enough to justify an arrest. However, the stronger argument is that the other factors present (the finding of the knife and his proximity to the offence already observed by the officers) gave rise to a level of suspicion sufficient to justify an arrest, even before the admission in question was made. Therefore, the questioning falls within para 11.1 and should not have taken place at all until the police station was reached, unless the exception under para 11.1(b) can apply. The exception may be invoked if a delay in interviewing would be likely to 'lead to the alerting of other persons suspected of having committed an offence but not yet arrested for it'. The questions were directed to determining the whereabouts of the other youths involved in the attack who might be alerted by the news of Ali's arrest. It is only necessary to show a likelihood that such a contingency might arise, not a reasonable suspicion; therefore, it appears that this exception may be invoked. No breach of para 11.1 has therefore occurred.

If an interview takes place outside the police station but falls outside the para 11.1 prohibition, the verifying and recording provisions under paras 11.11 and 11.7 will apply, with the proviso that contemporaneous recording may be impracticable. The mere fact that an interview is conducted in the street or in a police car, as here, may not be enough to support an assertion that it could not be contemporaneously recorded. This seems to follow from the decision in *Fogah* (1989). What is impracticable does not connote something that is extremely difficult but must involve more than mere inconvenience (*Parchment* (1989)). Note taking while the suspect was dressing and showing the officers round his flat was held to be impracticable. However, Carl and Bert are in the police car at the time and Ali has shown no sign of violence. While it might have been inconvenient to record the interview in the police car, it would not have been difficult. It appears, then, that para 11.7 has been breached. It should be noted that Carl and Bert assumed wrongly that the minimum level of protection provided by para 11.13 for comments made outside the context of an interview applied: a written record was made at the police station of the interview and the notes were offered to Ali to sign.

Could it be argued that the interview should be excluded under s 76, as it was not contemporaneously recorded in breach of para 11.7? Under s 76(2)(a), the prosecution must prove beyond reasonable doubt that Ali's confession was not obtained by oppression. According to the Court of Appeal in *Fulling* (1987), 'oppression' should be given its dictionary definition: '... the exercise of authority or power in a burdensome, harsh or wrongful manner.' The breach of para 11.7 could fall within this definition on the basis that the police acted in a wrongful manner. However, the Court of Appeal in *Hughes* (1988) ruled that oppression could not arise in the absence of 'misconduct' on the part of the police; in the context of the case, 'misconduct' clearly meant bad faith. On that basis, and assuming that Carl and Bert merely misinterpreted the level of suspicion connoted by the wording of para 11.1, the holding of the interview in the police car could not be termed oppressive.

Under s 76(2)(b), it is necessary to show that something was said or done in the first interview in circumstances conducive of unreliability. Following the rulings of the Court of Appeal in *Delaney* (1989) and *Barry* (1991), it is essential under this head to identify some special factor in the situation (such as the mental state of the defendant or an offer made to him) which make it crucial that the interview should be properly recorded. In other words, a single breach of PACE cannot amount to both 'circumstances' and 'something said or done' under s 76(2)(b).

However, even if the first interview is admissible under s 76, the trial judge will still have a discretion to exclude it from evidence under s 78 if, due to the circumstances in which it was obtained, its admission would have a significantly adverse effect on the fairness of the trial. Can it be argued under s 78 that the first interview should be excluded from evidence as unreliable due to the lack of contemporaneous recording? Ali is not alleging that he did not make the admissions in question but that they are untrue. Presumably, he signed the interview record as a means of indicating his acceptance that he had made the admissions, although he intended to allege later that he had lied out of fear. Thus, admission of the first interview which was not recorded contemporaneously may not have the necessary adverse affect on the fairness of the trial: its recording under para 11.13 may be sufficient and therefore may not lead to its exclusion under s 78.[2]

It will now be considered whether the second interview would be excluded from evidence under s 76, on the basis that Ali's consent to be interviewed without legal advice must be treated as vitiated due to the failure to advise him of the duty solicitor scheme (this argument is considered fully below in relation to s 78). Unless it can be shown that Eileen acted in bad faith in failing to inform Ali of the duty solicitor scheme (which as argued below does not appear to be the case), s 76(2)(a) will not apply. As noted above, if argument under s 76(2)(b) is to succeed, it would have to be shown that Ali was in a vulnerable position in the interview. No specific factor can be identified which might support such argument. The courts appear to take the view (see *Canale* (1990)) that, when a defendant of ordinary ability to withstand questioning is interviewed in breach of one of the PACE provisions, s 78 should be considered rather than s 76(2)(b). Therefore, although it could be argued that the failure to afford him legal advice could amount to 'something said or done' conducive of unreliability, some special circumstance as identified in *Delaney* is missing.

It will now be considered whether a reasonable argument for the exclusion from evidence of the interview under s 78 can be advanced. Again, it will be necessary to identify some impropriety occurring in the police station. It will be argued that insufficient effort was made to comply with Ali's request for legal advice. Under para 6.6(d) of Code C, a suspect who has requested advice can change his mind and consent to the commencement of the interview even though he has not obtained it. However, it can be argued that the suspect should not be misled into giving such consent. Once she had failed in her effort to contact Ali's solicitor, Eileen failed to inform him that he could obtain the services of the duty solicitor; it could therefore be argued that his consent was vitiated as based on the misapprehension that, unless he obtained advice from his own solicitor, he could not obtain it at all. However, in the case of *Hughes* (1988), the Court of Appeal considered that a consent to go ahead with an interview after a suspect had been led to believe that the duty solicitor was unavailable could be treated as a genuine consent. The police had given this information in good faith although the duty solicitor was, in fact, available. In principle, there is little difference between leading a suspect to believe that the duty solicitor is unavailable and failing to inform the suspect of the duty solicitor scheme. Thus, following *Hughes*, Ali's consent to go ahead with the interview could be treated as genuine; on this analysis, para 6.6 has not been breached.[3]

On the other hand, even if Eileen acted in good faith, it could be argued that a requirement to inform of the duty solicitor scheme is implied in para 6 (rather than arising only from Note 6B which is not a Code provision according to Code C, para 1.3) and that, therefore, the instant situation is not analogous to that in *Hughes*. It is submitted that this is the better view, since it accords with the prominence given to legal advice in the PACE scheme. It is also in accordance with the need to interpret the Code provisions compatibly with Art 6 under s 3 of the HRA. The ECtHR has placed considerable importance on the right of access to legal advice in cases such as *Murray (John) v UK* (1996) and *Averill v UK* (2000). It has held that delay in access where the defendant faces the possibility that adverse inferences may be drawn from silence can amount to a breach of Art 6 of the Convention. Adoption of this interpretation is supported by the provision of Code C, para 6.4 that no attempt must be made to persuade the suspect to forgo advice: a failure to provide the requisite information could be characterised as part of such an attempt in the sense that it might have the effect of persuading the detainee to forgo advice. It is also supported by the first instance decision of *Vernon* (1988), which concerned a situation almost exactly in point with that of the instant case, and by the strict approach to the legal advice provisions taken in *Beycan* (1990) by the Court of Appeal.

On this argument, a breach of para 6.6 has occurred. However, this breach may not be causally related to the admissions made in the interview (see *Samuel* (1988)). It may be that Ali would have made the admissions had he had advice. This is suggested since the solicitor would be aware that under s 34 of the CJPOA 1994, recognised in the para 10.5 caution, it may be disadvantageous to a defendant to hold back a defence. On the other hand, his confession in the interview may suggest that he gave in eventually to pressure to confess and that the 'defence' he puts forward is just part of a false confession. A solicitor who believed him would probably still have advised him to remain silent. Moreover, if his consent to forgo legal advice is not treated as genuine, he should have been cautioned under para 10.6 since he had had no genuine opportunity to have advice. In that case, he would have been more likely to remain silent. On this analysis, it is possible that the requisite causal relationship exists, and the interview may therefore be excluded from evidence under s 78, following *Samuel*. Such an interpretation would appear to accord with the demands of Art 6(1) on the basis of the argument that where a detainee has not had access to legal advice and makes admissions, that fact may suggest that he or she is more vulnerable than a detainee who manages to remain silent. Had Ali remained silent, a breach of Art 6(1) would probably have been established if the interview was admitted into evidence and adverse inferences drawn from the silence (*Murray v UK*).

Will the knife be excluded from evidence under s 78? According to the analysis above, the stop and search could be characterised as non-consensual. On that basis, it would be possible to argue, bearing the breach of s 2 of PACE in mind, that following *Edward Fennelly* (1989), the products of the search should be excluded from evidence. According to *Thomas* (1990), however, physical evidence will rarely be excluded, although there is a narrow discretion to exclude it.

Following the decision of the House of Lords in *Khan* (1997), evidence, other than involuntary confessions, obtained improperly, is nevertheless admissible, subject to a narrow discretion to exclude it. The House of Lords took Art 6 of the ECHR into account in reaching this conclusion. They found that Art 6 does not require that evidence should be automatically excluded where there has been impropriety in obtaining it, basing this finding on *Schenk v Switzerland* (1988). In *Khan* itself, it was found that the trial judge had properly exercised his discretion to include the improperly obtained evidence under s 78. In general, the courts have been prepared to exercise the discretion under s 78 to exclude confessions (for example, *Scott* (1991)) or identification evidence (for example, *Payne and Quinn* (1995)), where a substantial and significant breach of PACE has occurred. They have been much less ready to exclude physical evidence and this position has been unaffected by the reception of Art 6 into domestic law under the HRA (*AG's Reference No 3 of 1999* (2001)), on the basis that the admission or exclusion of evidence is largely a matter for the national courts. The courts have therefore taken the view that the position that has developed under s 78 regarding non-confession evidence need not be modified by reference to s 3 of the HRA or to the duty of a court under s 6. Therefore, it is probable that a judge would exercise his or her discretion to include the knife in evidence under s 78, despite the breach of s 2.

In conclusion, the stronger argument seems to be that the second interview will be excluded from evidence under s 78. The first interview and the knife will, however, probably be admissible in evidence.

Notes

1   The question of the meaning of reasonable suspicion could be considered in more detail at this point, bearing in mind the provision of Code A, para 2.2, which states that reasonable suspicion cannot be supported on the basis of personal factors (including colour) alone. However, where colour is a genuinely identifying factor, as it appears to be in this instance, it would appear that it should be taken into account, although the extent to which it is identifying will depend on the racial mix of the persons in the area at the time in question.

2   However, if, at trial, the particular unfairness likely to arise from the improper recording is not specified, but the breaches of the recording provisions affecting this interview are pointed out, it may appear that it cannot be relied on; it will then be excluded from evidence under s 78. A similar situation arose in *Keenan* (1989); the Court of Appeal held that the admissions in question should have been excluded under s 78. In *Canale* (1990), the importance of contemporaneous recording was stressed; however, in those instances, the defendant had not signed the interview record. Thus, although these points might be raised, the conclusion will remain the same.

3   There are two arguments which could be used to escape from this conclusion. One is set out above; the other is indicated here. It might be possible to show that Eileen deliberately failed to mention the duty solicitor scheme in order to obtain a confession from Ali more readily. In *Hughes*, the consent in question would have been treated as vitiated had the police acted in bad faith. However, it may be that the failure to advise Ali of the duty solicitor scheme arose because Eileen mistakenly believed that he did not need to be specifically advised of it again after the notification of rights by Doris and the reminder before the third interview that advice was available. Eileen is not specifically required to remind a suspect, unable to obtain advice from his own solicitor, of the duty solicitor scheme before he gives consent to be interviewed, although this can perhaps be implied from the wording of Note 6B.

Question 31

Marcus, a journalist, is seen at 3 am outside a nightclub by two police officers who are responding to a report that a violent disturbance is occurring. He appears to be angry and hostile. The police officers stop Marcus, search his pockets and question him. They find a small knife which they believe has been used in an assault earlier that night. At this point, Marcus becomes angry and swears at the officers, then repeatedly kicks the police car. While Marcus is being taken to the police station, an officer visits Marcus's home and searches there for evidence related to the earlier assault. They find items which they believe are related to several other serious offences.

Advise Marcus as to the lawfulness of the behaviour of the police and as to the likelihood that the knife and the items found at his house will be admissible in evidence against him.

Answer plan

This is a reasonably straightforward, if broad-ranging, problem question which encompasses almost all of a defendant's rights under PACE 1984. Students should demonstrate detailed knowledge of PACE, the Codes and the relevant Notes. Case law should also be considered.

The key issues are:

- were the officers entitled to stop and search Marcus?;
- at which point were there sufficient grounds for arrest?;
- was the evidence found at Marcus's house obtained properly, and so is it admissible?

Answer

The first issue to be addressed is whether the officers were originally entitled to stop and search Marcus, and on which basis. Section 1 of PACE 1984 allows a valid stop and search of a person only when a number of conditions have been met. The search must be for stolen or prohibited articles, or offensive weapons, and the officer must be able to show that he had reasonable grounds for suspicion that any such article would be found. It is not clear why the decision to stop and search Marcus was made: it could have been on suspicion that he had been involved in the violent disturbance, or because he was on the street late at night, or because he fits the description of the man wanted for the earlier assault, or because the officers believe that he may have an offensive weapon.

Not all of these possibilities will fall within those acceptable under PACE. There is no general power to stop and search Marcus; it is only if there are reasonable grounds for suspicion that he has a weapon or stolen property on his person that the search is justifiable under s 1. The further conditions are in s 2 and include that the officer must identify himself as such, state the grounds and reasons for the search and, where practicable, keep a record of the search. If more than outer clothing is to be removed, then the suspect must be taken out of public view and the search must be conducted by a person of the same sex as the suspect. If the PACE rules are not followed, then any evidence found may be inadmissible and any later arrest may be groundless; hence, the safeguards have great importance. It is not known whether the officers have any reasonable grounds for suspicion that Marcus has a prohibited article on his person; if they were simply lucky in finding the weapon, then the search will not be justified under PACE and Code A, para 2. The reasonable grounds must exist prior to the search: in *King v Gardner* (1980), it was held that an officer must be able to demonstrate that he believed that there were reasonable grounds at the time of the search, and that 'reasonableness' is an objective term. Hence, the officers who carried out the search need to provide information as to the reasons why Marcus was searched and to demonstrate that they complied with Code A of PACE.

Those officers might argue that the search fell outside PACE, since it was carried out 'by consent'. A genuinely consensual search is not illegal and such searches used to be accepted under Code A. There seem, however, to have been many such 'consensual' searches where the suspect disputes ever having given his consent. Code A, as revised in 2003, now expressly states that a consensual search must not be undertaken unless the power for a non-consensual search, under Pt I of PACE, exists (para 1.5). Therefore, the officers would still be expected to show they had legal grounds even for a consensual search and as indicated above there do not appear to be reasonable grounds for suspicion as required in para 2 of Code A.

The second issue is whether and when there were sufficient grounds to justify arresting Marcus and whether he has been correctly cautioned. Once Marcus became angry and then kicked the police car, there is more than one basis on which to justify arresting him. Any arrest is unlawful unless justified at common law or under the two PACE methods: with or without a warrant. It is not clear whether Marcus was arrested at this stage, if at all. It is possible that he attends the police station voluntarily to 'help police with their inquiries'; however, it is more likely that he has been arrested, since it is hard to argue voluntary attendance by a man in an angry and violent state of mind.

There are three methods by which an arrest may validly be made: at common law for breach of the peace; or by two separate PACE methods, which will be discussed below. According to the leading case of *Howell* (1981), arrest at common law may be carried out where the constable (or other person) has actually witnessed a breach of the peace by the arrestee; or where, although no breach of the peace has occurred, the person making the arrest reasonably believes that one is imminent; or where a breach of the peace has already been committed by the person being arrested and the person making the arrest now has a reasonable belief that a further breach of the peace will occur. Any of these could be argued on the present facts, and so a common law arrest is justifiable from the moment that Marcus became angry and kicked the car.

If, however, Marcus has been arrested under either of the PACE methods, then matters are less straightforward. The first PACE method is under s 24 – without a warrant, where an arrestable offence is being, or has been, committed by the suspect. Depending upon the injuries inflicted in the earlier assault, that offence might justify arrest without warrant in this way, or the kicking of the car could be criminal damage. The arrest could also be under s 25 for these offences; swearing at the police officers is not, in itself, arrestable; however, it might justify arrest under the s 25 general arrest conditions, since it can be argued that Marcus's current state of mind makes him likely to injure another or damage property (s 25(3)(d)). Under PACE, the question of whether the arresting officer had reasonable grounds for his belief arises again. In *Castorina v Chief Constable of Surrey* (1988), it was stated that it is not necessary 'for the officer to conclude that the person was guilty of the offence; it was enough that a reasonable man would suspect that that was so'.

The third method of arrest is by warrant, which is not practicable and did not occur on the present facts, due to the time delay which would be involved.

Whichever the method of and grounds for arrest, Marcus must now be cautioned and informed of the reasons for his arrest (Code C, para 10.1; s 28(3) of PACE). The arrest is unlawful since these safeguards have not been carried out.

The next issue is whether the evidence found at his house was obtained properly and, hence, whether it is admissible in court against him. It does not appear that Marcus has given his consent to the search of his premises. Therefore, one of the two relevant PACE provisions must have been complied with: either s 8 (entry and search with a warrant) or s 18 (entry and search without a warrant after arrest). Under s 8, magistrates may issue warrants to enter premises to search them for evidence of serious arrestable offences if satisfied that there are reasonable grounds for belief that all five following grounds exist:

- that a serious arrestable offence has been committed;
- that there is material on the premises which is likely to be of substantial value to the investigation of that offence;
- that the material is likely to be relevant evidence;
- that the material is not subject to legal privilege (s 10), is not excluded material (s 11) or special procedure material (s 14); and
- that one of the conditions in s 8(3) applies: for example, it is not practicable to obtain consent of any person to the entry onto the premises, or that the purposes of the search might be frustrated unless entry is immediate.

Further, the safeguards for search warrants in s 15 of PACE and Code B, para 2 must be complied with. The warrant must specify which material is to be sought, and the entry and search of the premises will be unlawful if the terms of the warrant are not complied with, for example, if the police have conducted a 'fishing expedition' and the material which they have taken was not what they were looking for.

Under s 18, police may, after arresting a person for an arrestable offence, enter and search premises occupied or controlled by the arrestee if they have reasonable grounds to suspect that evidence may be found there which relates to that offence; any such evidence found may be seized under s 18(2). Since it appears that the evidence taken, or at least some of it, does not relate to the offence for which Marcus has been arrested, but to other serious offences, there is a problem here for the police in justifying its removal. In *Jeffrey v Black* (1978), a search was held to be unlawful, since the offence of arrest and the items found did not match. For s 18, written authorisation must have been given to the searching constable by an inspector. Again, s 32 allows searches of premises which an arrestee has left shortly before being arrested, but only for evidence related to the offence of arrest. The seizure of articles found in any of these manners is covered by s 19 and Code B, para 7; a constable who is lawfully on premises may seize any items found on the premises if he or she has reasonable grounds for belief that they were obtained through the offence, that they would otherwise be destroyed or disposed of, or that they are evidence relating to *any* offence *and* it is necessary to seize them in order to prevent them being disposed of (even if they are excluded material). The crucial question, then, is whether the entry was lawful in the first place, since otherwise the seizure cannot be justified.

Marcus is a journalist; hence, some of the material at his house is likely to be excluded material under s 11(1)(c), and so cannot be taken from the premises unless it was intended for publication or the s 19 power is used. Where the police have a power of seizure, the Criminal Justice and Police Act 2001 allows the removal of material in order for it to be sifted by police at a police station. Any privileged, excluded or special procedure material must be identified and returned under the provisions of the Act.

Every aspect of Marcus's treatment before, during and after arrest must be scrutinised and found to comply with PACE and its Codes, if the admissibility of the evidence so produced and of the knife is not to be challenged successfully at his later trial under s 78. The HRA may have some effect. Article 6 does not prescribe particular rules of evidence or require a ban on unlawfully obtained evidence (even of evidence obtained in breach of other rights such as under Art 8) (*Schenk v Switzerland* (1991)). It does, however, require the courts to look to the overall fairness of the trial process (*Teixeira v Portugal* (1998)) which includes the pre-trial process. The ability of Marcus, under s 78, to challenge admissibility on the grounds of overall fairness will be important (*R v Bailey* (2001)) in this respect. It would be possible to argue, bearing the breach of s 28 of PACE and the other breaches or improprieties identified in mind, that, following *Edward Fennelly* (1989), the products of the search should be excluded from evidence. According to *Thomas* (1990), however, physical evidence will rarely be excluded, although there is a narrow discretion to exclude it. Following the decision of the House of Lords in *Khan* (1997), evidence, other than involuntary confessions, obtained improperly is nevertheless admissible, subject to a narrow discretion to exclude it. The House of Lords took Art 6 of the ECHR into account in reaching this conclusion. They found that Art 6 does not require that evidence should be automatically excluded where there has been impropriety in obtaining it, basing this finding on *Schenk v Switzerland* (1988). In *Khan* itself, it was found that the trial judge had properly exercised his discretion to include the improperly obtained evidence under s 78. In general, the courts have been prepared to exercise the discretion under s 78 to exclude confessions (for example, *Scott* (1991)) or identification evidence (for example, *Payne and Quinn* (1995)), where a substantial and significant breach of PACE has occurred. They have been much less ready to exclude physical evidence and this position has been unaffected by the reception of Art 6 into domestic law under the HRA (*AG's Reference No 3 of 1999* (2001)), on the basis that the admission or exclusion of evidence is largely a matter for the national courts. The courts have therefore taken the view that the position that has developed under s 78 regarding non-confession evidence need not be modified by reference to s 3 of the HRA or to the duty of a court under s 6. Therefore, it is probable that a judge would exercise his or her discretion to include the knife and the products of the search in evidence under s 78.

Question 32

'The Police and Criminal Evidence Act 1984 provides important safeguards for the suspect during interviews in the police station, but no adequate means of redress is available if the police do not comply with them.' Discuss.

Answer plan

A reasonably straightforward essay question which is quite often set on PACE 1984. It is important to take the provisions of the Criminal Justice and Public Order Act (CJPOA) 1994 into account and to bear in mind the changes consequent to Code C. It should be noted that it is only concerned with the interviewing scheme and its applicability inside the police station. It is not concerned therefore with safeguards concerning, for example, stop and search. It is important to take the HRA into account in your answer, since it provides new possibilities of creating redress in relation to safeguards for police interviews.

Essentially, the following matters should be considered:

- the nature of the safeguards available under Pts IV and V of PACE and Codes of Practice C and E;
- the curtailed right to silence under ss 34–37 of the CJPOA 1994;
- relevant tortious remedies;
- the efficacy of the police complaints mechanism;
- the nature of the PACE scheme for exclusion of evidence;
- the relevance of ss 34–37 of the CJPOA 1994;
- the value of exclusion of evidence as a form of redress;
- new possibilities under the HRA 1998.

Answer

It is generally accepted that the safeguards for interviews introduced by PACE, particularly access to legal advice and tape-recording, can reduce the likelihood that an interview will be unreliable. However, it will be argued that the forms of redress available in respect of breaches of these provisions are inadequate, either as a means of encouraging the police to comply with them or as a means of compensating the detainee if they do not. The HRA 1998 allows for ECHR arguments to be raised in any proceedings under s 7(1)(b) and provides for a free-standing cause of action where a public authority has breached a Convention right, under s 7(1)(a); remedies are available under s 8. Obviously, the extent to which the HRA can affect adherence to the interviewing rules depends on the relationship between the rules and the Convention Articles. This issue will be considered below. In general, it will be contended that while the relevant Articles of the ECHR afforded further effect in domestic law under the HRA, and are likely to have some impact in encouraging adherence to the interviewing rules, they will not have a radical effect, especially in terms of encouraging the exclusion of evidence where the rules have not been adhered to.

The most important safeguards available inside the police station include: contemporaneous recording under para 11.5 of Code C or tape-recording under para 3 of Code E; the ability to read over, verify and sign the notes of the interview as a correct record under para 11.10 of Code C; notification of the right to access to legal advice under s 58 and para 3.1 of Code C; the option of having the advisor present in the interview under para 6.6 and, where appropriate, the presence of an appropriate adult under para 11.14. The right to silence, encapsulated in the old Code C caution, has been viewed as a valuable safeguard, but it has now been greatly curtailed by ss 34–37 of the CJPOA 1994, which provides that in certain circumstances adverse inferences can be drawn from silence. These provisions were reflected in the much more complex caution introduced in the 1995 revision of Code C. No adverse inference can be drawn from silence unless the suspect is under caution (s 34(1)(a) of the CJPOA) and he has had the opportunity of having legal advice (s 34(2A)). Section 34(2A), inserted by s 58 of the Youth Justice and Criminal Evidence Act 1999, is therefore a significant new provision since it may tend to encourage adherence to the legal advice scheme. It was introduced to satisfy the demands of Art 6 of the ECHR. Section 34(2A) is now reflected in the changes made to the caution in the 2003 version of Code C; para 10.6 provides that the old caution – reflecting the full right to silence – must be used where the suspect has not had an opportunity to have legal advice.

The interpretation given to the legal advice provisions by the courts has meant that the circumstances in which non-compliance with a provision will be lawful have been narrowed down. In particular, in *Samuel* (1988), the Court of Appeal had to consider s 58(8), which provides that access to legal advice may be delayed, where, *inter alia*, allowing such access might alert others involved in the offence. It was determined that s 58(8) could not be fulfilled by an unsubstantiated assertion that this contingency would materialise if a solicitor was contacted. After this ruling, in order to fulfil s 58(8), the police must be able to demonstrate a reasonable belief in some particular quality of naivety or corruption possessed by the solicitor in question.

Equally, the courts have not been willing to accept that compliance with PACE was impracticable even in informal situations. In *Absolam* (1988), the Custody Officer questioned the detainee in the heat of the moment, without first advising him of his right to legal advice. At first instance, it was determined that the detainee was only entitled to his right to consult a solicitor as soon as it was practicable under para 3.1 of Code C and, further, that the questions and answers did not constitute an interview; therefore, para 3.1 did not apply. The Court of Appeal, however, held that the questions and answers did not constitute a formal interview, but were nevertheless an interview within the purview of para 6.3. Since the appellant's situation was precisely the type of situation in which the Code's provisions were most significant, there could be no question of waiving them. Paragraph 3.1 of Code C had been breached.

However, although the courts may be quick to find that a breach of PACE has occurred, this does not mean that redress will automatically be available to the detainee who has thereby been disadvantaged. What form of redress might such a detainee seek?

Tort damages will be available in respect of some breaches of PACE. For example, if a police officer arrests a citizen where no reasonable suspicion arises under ss 24 or 25 of PACE, an action for false imprisonment will be available. Equally, such a remedy would be available if the Pt IV provisions governing time limits on detention were breached. However, tortious remedies are inapplicable to the provisions of the Codes under s 67(10) and may not be available in respect of the most significant statutory interviewing provision, the entitlement to legal advice. There is no tort of denial of access to legal advice: the only possible tortious action would be for breach of statutory duty. Whether such an action would lie is a question of policy in relation to any particular statutory provision.[1] At present, the application of this remedy must be purely conjectural. Theoretically, an action for false imprisonment might lie; an argument could be advanced that where gross breaches of the questioning provisions had taken place, such as interviewing a person unlawfully held incommunicado, a detention in itself lawful might thereby be rendered unlawful. However, although the ruling in *Middleweek v Chief Constable of Merseyside* (1985) gave some encouragement to such argument, it now seems to be ruled out due to the decision in *Weldon v Home Office* (1991) in the context of lawful detention in a prison. It seems likely, therefore, that access to legal advice, like the rest of the safeguards for interviewing, will continue to be unaffected by the availability of the established tortious remedies. However, the HRA provides the possibility of redress under s 8, which may affect adherence to the safeguards where they reflect the demands of Art 6. Where pre-trial procedures have created unfairness, thus potentially causing a breach of Art 6, the trial or appeal judge should seek to negate the unfairness in accordance with the duty of a court under s 6 of the HRA by, for example, excluding evidence or even staying the trial.

Access to custodial legal advice can be viewed as an implied right under Art 6(1), where the detainee is aware that adverse inferences may be drawn from silence (*Murray v UK* (1996) and *Averill v UK* (2000)). However, at present it is very doubtful whether Art 6 can be viewed as providing free-standing rights. Breaches of Art 6 are clearly most likely to be addressed within the criminal process itself. The Strasbourg jurisprudence does not cover instances in which the pre-trial procedure is flawed in a manner which might be viewed, potentially, as infringing the Art 6(1) guarantee of a fair trial, but where no court action in fact occurs. However, given that certain of the rights, and in particular the implied right of access to custodial legal advice under Art 6(3)(c), clearly have value outside the trial context, an action based on s 7(1)(a) or on a breach of the statutory duty under s 58 of PACE, but raising Art 6(3)(c) arguments under s 7(1)(b), might resolve this issue in favour of the complainant, domestically. Other Convention Articles may have some impact on police interviewing practices and techniques and where those Articles are breached during detention and interviewing, a free-standing action will arise.

Where provisions of Art 3, 8, 5 or 14 are coterminous with Code safeguards, liability to pay damages under the HRA for breach of the Convention guarantees might provide the Code provisions with a form of indirect protection, as the more detailed embodiment of the Convention requirements. Certain aspects of the Convention guarantees, including aspects of the Art 3 requirements, have no domestic statutory basis, but are recognised only in certain Code provisions. In the *Greek* case (1969), the conditions of detention were found to amount to inhuman treatment owing to inadequate food, sleeping arrangements, heating and sanitary facilities, combined with overcrowding and inadequate provision for external contacts. It was also found that conduct which grossly humiliates may amount to degrading treatment contrary to Art 3. Such treatment may include racially discriminatory and, probably, sexually discriminatory questioning and treatment in detention (*East African Asians* cases (1973)). In *Lustig-Prean and Beckett v UK* (1999) and *Smith and Grady v UK* (2000), it was found that grossly humiliating, intrusive interrogation could, if of an extreme and prolonged nature, amount to a breach of Art 3. Possibly it could also fall within Art 8. Where discrimination is a factor, Art 14 would also be engaged. The creation of new tortious liability indirectly protective of the Code provisions, but also creating new safeguards for interviewing under the HRA would be a very significant matter, since it might lead to a regulation of police interviewing practices and techniques which has been largely absent from UK law.

The police complaints mechanism covers any breaches of PACE, including breaches of the Codes under s 67(8), but it is generally agreed that it is defective as a means of redress. It does not allow for compensation to the victim or for the victim to attend any disciplinary proceedings. In any event, most complaints do not result in disciplinary proceedings and it appears that no disciplinary proceedings have been brought in respect of breaches of the Codes. The suspect concerned might, in many instances, be unaware that a breach of the Codes had occurred and while, theoretically, another officer could make a complaint leading to disciplinary proceedings for such a breach, in practice, this appears to be highly unlikely. Furthermore, despite the involvement (albeit limited) of the Police Complaints Authority, the complaints procedure tends to be perceived as being administered by the police themselves, although the government under current proposals intends to introduce into it a somewhat greater independent element in the form of civilian investigators in certain cases. In *Khan v UK* (2000), the ECtHR found a violation of Art 13 of the ECHR, on the basis that the Police Complaints Authority does not provide a sufficient means of redress for Convention breaches. It was found to be insufficiently independent as a remedial procedure, since complaints can be handled internally, the Chief Constable of the area is able to appoint from his own force to carry out an investigation, and since the Secretary of State is involved in appointments to the Police Complaints Authority. Thus, reform was necessary. The Independent Police Complaints Commission is currently being set up with a view to creating greater confidence in the system. However, as indicated above, the HRA may divert some complaints to the courts under s 7(1)(a) where police malpractice also falls within the ambit of a Convention right (apart, probably, from Art 6 as discussed above) and so limit this problem.

The context in which breaches of Code C and of the entitlement to legal advice have been considered is that of exclusion of evidence. It must be borne in mind that the PACE mechanism for exclusion of evidence provides a means of redress for breach of the interviewing provisions only in one circumstance – that the case is pursued to trial and the defendant pleads not guilty. In this one instance, it can be of great value, in that the defendant may be placed in the position he would have been in had the breach not occurred (the approach taken in *Absolam* (1988)) and the police may seem to be 'punished' for their non-compliance with the rules by being prevented from profiting from their own breach.

The Act contains three separate tests, which may be considered after a breach of the interviewing rules has been shown and, in theory, all three could be considered in a particular instance. Under the 'oppression' test (s 76(2)(a)), once the defence has advanced a reasonable argument (*Liverpool Juvenile Court ex p R* (1987)) that the confession was obtained by oppression, it will not be admitted in evidence unless the prosecution can prove that it was not so obtained.[2] In *Fulling* (1987), the Court of Appeal proffered its own definition of oppression: 'The exercise of authority or power in a burdensome, harsh or wrongful manner.' The terms 'wrongful' and 'improper' used in this test could cover any unlawful action on the part of the police and would therefore mean that any breach of the Act or Codes could constitute oppression. This wide possibility has been pursued at first instance (in *Davison* (1988)), but the Court of Appeal in *Hughes* (1988) held that a denial of legal advice due not to bad faith on the part of the police, but to a misunderstanding could not amount to oppression. In *Alladice* (1988), the Court of Appeal also took this view in suggesting, *obiter*, that an improper denial of legal advice, if accompanied by bad faith on the part of the police, would certainly amount to 'unfairness' under s 78 and probably also to 'oppression'.

The test for oppression, then, does not appear to depend entirely on the nature of the impropriety, but rather on whether it was perpetrated deliberately. Thus, bad faith seems to be a necessary, but not sufficient condition for the operation of s 76(2)(a), whereas it seems that it will automatically render a confession inadmissible under s 78.

The test under s 76(2)(b), the 'reliability' test, is concerned with objective reliability: the judge must consider the situation at the time the confession was made and ask whether the confession would be likely to be unreliable, not whether it is unreliable. It is not necessary, under this test, to show that there has been any misconduct on the part of the police.[3] In *Delaney* (1989), the defendant was 17, had an IQ of 80 and, according to an educational psychologist, was subject to emotional arousal which would lead him to wish to bring a police interview to an end as quickly as possible. These were circumstances in which it was important to ensure that the interrogation was conducted with all propriety. In fact, the officers offered some inducement to the defendant to confess by playing down the gravity of the offence and by suggesting that, if he confessed, he would get the psychiatric help he needed. They also failed to make an accurate, contemporaneous record of the interview in breach of para 11.5 of Code C (now 11.7). Failing to make the proper record was of indirect relevance to the question of reliability, since it meant that the court could not assess the full extent of the suggestions held out to the defendant. Thus, in the circumstances existing at the time (the mental state of the defendant), the police impropriety did have the necessary special significance necessary.

Thus, it appears that the 'circumstances existing at the time' may be circumstances created by the police in breaching the interviewing rules; equally, following *Mathias* (1989), such a breach may amount to something said or done. However, a single breach of the interviewing rules, such as a denial of legal advice, in ordinary circumstances, would not, it seems, fulfil both limbs of the test.

Due to the need to find some special factor in the situation in order to invoke either head of s 76, breaches of the interviewing rules unaccompanied by any such factor are usually considered under s 78. The idea behind the section was that the function of exclusion of evidence after police misconduct must not be disciplinary, but must be to safeguard the fairness of the trial. The first question to be asked under s 78 is whether a breach of the rules has occurred at all and then whether it is significant and substantial (*Keenan* (1989)). Once such a breach is found, the next question to be asked will be whether admission of the confession gained during the improperly conducted interview will render the trial unfair. This might occur if, for example, as in *Canale* (1990), there has been a failure to make contemporaneous notes of the interview in breach of para 11.7 of Code C. The defence may then challenge the interview record on the basis that the police have fabricated all or part of it, or may allege that something adverse to the detainee happened during the interview which has not been recorded. The court then has no means of knowing which version is true, precisely the situation which Code C was designed to prevent. In such a situation, a judge may well exclude the confession on the basis that it would be unfair to allow evidence of doubtful reliability to go before the jury.[4]

Breaches of the recording provisions will normally be considered under s 78 as opposed to s 76(2). Allegedly fabricated confessions cannot fall within s 76(2), due to its requirement that something has happened to the defendant which causes him to confess; its terms are not therefore fulfilled if the defence alleges that no confession made by the defendant exists. Secondly, s 76(2)(b) requires that something is said or done in special circumstances; a breach of the recording provisions could amount to something said or done in the *Delaney* sense (see above), but unless special circumstances, such as the particular vulnerability of the defendant, exist, the other test under the section is unsatisfied. In *Canale* (1990), the police breached the recording provisions and allegedly played a trick on the appellant in order to obtain the confession. Ruling that the confession should have been excluded under s 78, the Court of Appeal took into account the fact that the appellant could not be said to be weak-minded; it was therefore thought inappropriate to invoke s 76(2)(b). Equally, such instances would not normally fall within s 76(2)(a), because it may not be apparent that the police deliberately breached the recording provisions. On the other hand, if the defence alleges that the police made threats or *deliberately* tricked the detainee into confessing, the prosecution might not be able to prove beyond reasonable doubt that the police had in fact behaved properly, due to the breach of the recording provisions. This line of argument could have been considered in *Canale*.

Moreover, a significant and substantial breach of the interviewing rules, although unaccompanied by bad faith, may have caused the defendant to confess and, on that basis, admission of the confession could be said to render the trial unfair, even though it appears that the confession is reliable. The difficulty here lies in determining whether the defendant confessed for other reasons. In *Samuel* (1988), the Court of Appeal determined that the police impropriety – a failure to allow the appellant access to legal advice – was causally linked to the confession: the appellant was not a sophisticated, hardened criminal able to handle the interview without advice. Conversely, in *Dunford* (1990), the Court of Appeal determined that the criminally experienced appellant had made his own assessment of the situation in deciding to make certain admissions and legal advice would not have affected his decision; the failure to allow legal advice was not therefore causally linked to the confession. Curtailment of the right to silence under ss 34–37 of the CJPOA 1994 means that legal advisors are less likely to advise silence and therefore the causal relationship in question will be more difficult to establish. Section 78 may therefore become less effective as a means of providing a form of redress where there is a failure to comply with the PACE provisions.[5] On the other hand, the importance attached to access to legal advice by the ECtHR in cases such as *Murray (John) v UK* (1996) and *Averill v UK* (2000) may encourage greater use of s 78, since the courts' duty under s 6 of the HRA 1998 means that these decisions should be taken into account in considering whether interviews should be excluded from evidence where breaches of the legal advice provisions have occurred.

Section 34(2A) of the CJPOA, reflected, as indicated above, in the 2003 version of Code C, may be likely to encourage the police to afford access to legal advice. Whether it does so in practice will depend on the interpretation of the term given to the provision. It provides essentially that adverse inferences shall not be drawn from a suspect's silence under caution before or after charge at an authorised place of detention if he has not been allowed an 'opportunity' to consult a solicitor before that point. Clearly, the term 'opportunity' may be taken to mean that, formally, an opportunity had been offered, but the suspect had not availed himself of it. This interpretation would not curb the use of ploys by the police discouraging the suspect from having legal advice. Such an interpretation would not appear to accord with Art 6(1) jurisprudence and therefore a broad interpretation of the term 'opportunity' could be adopted under s 3 of the HRA.

In conclusion, it is apparent that the courts are concerned to uphold the safeguards created by the PACE interviewing rules, but it must be questioned whether exclusion of evidence is an adequate or appropriate method of doing so. The majority of defendants plead guilty. Thus, the police have an incentive to break the rules by, for example, refusing a request for legal advice in the hope of obtaining admissions and a guilty plea. If, in such circumstances, a defendant does plead guilty, he or she has suffered denial of a fundamental right with little hope of redress, apart from that offered by a complaint. However, whilst not a direct remedy for breaches of PACE and its Codes, the incorporation of the Convention by the HRA has provided a separate method of redress for many situations which involve a PACE breach; if the pre-trial proceedings are unfair, viewing the trial process as a whole, then there will be a breach of Art 6 issue, for which any domestic court may provide any available remedy (s 8 of the HRA), including quashing any conviction obtained. Thus, the HRA may have some impact in making up for the deficiencies in the PACE remedial scheme.

Notes

1   The tone of the only relevant case (a 1985 unreported application to prevent a breach of s 58) was unpropitious: '... were I to make the order sought it would be unreasonable, a hindrance to police inquiries may be caused.'

2   The meaning of oppression could be considered in more detail. The only evidence given in the Act as to its meaning is the non-exhaustive definition contained in s 76(8): 'In this section, "oppression" includes torture, inhuman or degrading treatment, and the use or threat of violence (whether or not amounting to torture).' The word 'includes' ought to be given its literal meaning according to the Court of Appeal in *Fulling* (1987). Therefore, the concept of oppression may be fairly wide: the question is whether it could encompass breaches of the interviewing scheme unaccompanied by any other impropriety.

3   There are two limbs to the test as *Harvey* (1988) illustrates: the defendant, a mentally ill woman of low intelligence, may have been induced to confess to murder by hearing her lover's confession; the 'something said or done' (the first limb) was the confession of the lover, while the 'circumstances' (the second limb) were the defendant's emotional state, low intelligence and mental illness.

4   The question of any other available evidence as to what occurred could be pursued further at this point. In *Dunn* (1990), the defence had an independent witness to what occurred – a legal representative – and the judge admitted the confession as the defence had therefore a proper basis from which to challenge the police evidence.

5   For completeness, s 82(3), which preserves the whole of the common law discretion to exclude evidence, could be mentioned at this point, although it should be noted that, in practice, its role in relation to breaches of the interviewing rules is largely insignificant, due to the width of s 78.

CHAPTER 6

PRISONERS' RIGHTS

Introduction

Examiners tend to set both problem and essay questions in this area. Problem questions often concern the use of judicial review by prisoners to challenge disciplinary hearings which appear to have fallen below the standards demanded by natural justice. Essay questions often concern the use of judicial review and Arts 6 and 8 of the European Convention on Human Rights (ECHR) to uphold prisoners' rights.

Checklist

Students should be familiar with the following areas:

- Arts 6 and 8 of the ECHR;
- key decisions of the European Court of Human Rights (EctHR) on privacy, access to a court and standards in disciplinary hearings;
- recent decisions of the Court on Art 3 and the treatment of, in particular, ill, disabled and mentally ill prisoners;
- use of judicial review in this area, particularly the application of the principles of natural justice;
- key provisions of the Prison Rules 1999 (consolidated 2002);
- the Woolf proposals and Ramsbottom Reports;
- influence of private law remedies;
- proposals for prison reform, including potential privatisation.

Question 33

'Enjoyment of civil liberties no longer stops at the prison gates. Nevertheless, despite the influence of the European Convention on Human Rights, prisoners' rights are still in their infancy.' Discuss.

Answer plan

A reasonably straightforward essay question. It is necessary to identify the areas in which improvement has occurred and to consider how far the Convention has influenced those areas. It is also necessary to ask whether in certain instances the domestic courts have gone further in protecting prisoners' rights than the European Court of Human Rights (ECtHR). It should be asked in relation to the fundamental right to freedom from inhuman and degrading treatment whether reliance on the ECHR is the best method of improving basic living standards in UK prisons. The extent to which, in the various areas, improvement is still needed should be considered.

Essentially, the following matters should be considered:

- key decisions of the ECtHR on privacy, access to a court and standards in disciplinary hearings;
- use of judicial review in this area, particularly the application of the principles of natural justice: general influence of the ECtHR;
- *Deputy Governor of Parkhurst Prison ex p Hague; Weldon v Home Office* (1991);
- limitations of the ECHR, particularly in relation to improving basic living standards in UK prisons.

Answer

During the late 1970s and the 1980s, there was an increasing recognition that certain fundamental rights of prisoners should receive legal protection, even though the Prison Rules themselves allowed them to be unjustifiably infringed or seemed to provide only basic protection. It will be argued that greater protection has been achieved partly, but not solely, due to the influence of the Convention; improvement has also come about through the application of the principles of natural justice in judicial review proceedings. Of course, in some instances, UK judges may have been influenced by an expected ruling of the ECtHR while, in others, UK judges may have set out to ensure that UK law was in conformity with the Convention. However, use of the Convention may be of limited impact, in view of the application of the doctrine of the margin of appreciation; a particularly broad margin will tend to be allowed where positive obligations would be placed upon a State party by a decision under the Convention. It will be argued that in certain areas, such as the right to a fair hearing, progress has been made, and even where progress has been slow, such as regarding the right to freedom from inhuman or degrading treatment, matters are beginning to improve.

Until recently, a prisoner could receive a substantial 'loss of remission' after a hearing of the Board of Visitors in which he was not allowed to call witnesses or cross-examine prison officers. However, gradually, in judicial review proceedings, prisoners established the right to a fair hearing before punishment could be awarded. Such rights have been based predominantly on common law rules of natural justice. Under the HRA 1998, rights to a fair hearing must also satisfy Art 6; under the Article, procedural protections not required by natural justice may be necessary.

Natural justice includes two principles. First, there should be a fair hearing of the accused's case, in the sense that the proper procedural elements are in place and, secondly, there should be no bias.[1] Prison Rule 54 provides that the prisoner must be given a full opportunity of hearing the allegations against him and of presenting his own case and thus is clearly declaratory of natural justice, but it was uncertain what consequences would follow if it was breached, and in any event it did not detail the requirements of a fair hearing.

The law on fair procedures relating to disciplinary action against prisoners has gone through major changes in recent times, largely required by the impact of Art 6 of the ECHR. Under the old system, serious disciplinary offences were heard by the Boards of Prison Visitors. The rules of natural justice were applied to these hearings. In *Board of Visitors of Hull Prison ex p St Germain (No 1)* (1979), certain prisoners complained that the disciplinary proceedings which followed the Hull prison riots were not conducted in accordance with the principles of natural justice. The Court of Appeal, in the first such ruling since *Ridge v Baldwin* (1964), held that prisoners only lose those liberties expressly denied them by Parliament – otherwise, they retain their rights under the law. There was nothing in the Prison Act 1952 or the Prison Rules made under it to take away the jurisdiction of the courts, and the Board of Visitors was discharging a quasi-judicial function. Thus, it was found that the decision in question must be open to review and that Boards of Visitors must act in accordance with the rules of natural justice.[2]

An important issue was whether, given the application of the rules of natural justice, prisoners were always entitled to legal representation. The House of Lords refused, in *Secretary of State for the Home Department ex p Tarrant* (1985), to hold that legal representation was mandatory for Boards of Prison Visitors. It was a matter over which a Board was required to exercise discretion and representation was normally required for more serious charges.

Serious disciplinary hearings, however they are referred to in domestic law, are likely to be hearings that determine a 'criminal charge' given the way that term is determined in Convention law. As such, they should be conducted in line with the requirements of Art 6 of the ECHR. In *Campbell and Fell v UK* (1984), the ECtHR found that Art 6 of the Convention had been breached by a failure to allow legal representation to a prisoner in a disciplinary hearing. Breaches were found of Art 6(3)(b) and (c) concerning time and facilities to prepare a defence and availability of legal assistance; the applicants had had no assistance before the hearing or representation at it. This decision was, of course, prior to the HRA, and in *Board of Visitors of HM Prison, the Maze ex p Hone* (1988), the House of Lords continued to hold that legal representation was not, as a matter of domestic law, mandatory but remained a matter over which a Board was required to exercise discretion.

It became increasingly difficult to be satisfied that the disciplinary function of the Board of Prison Visitors could be exercised compatibly with the ECHR and in 1992 the function was abolished. Now serious disciplinary offences are dealt with as criminal offences by the ordinary courts, magistrates and Crown Courts, which are, of course, 'Article 6 compliant' and before which a prisoner has full rights of representation.

The less serious offences, called offences against prison discipline, are still dealt with within the prison service. Traditionally, the governor would determine such cases and had the power to punish in various ways including the imposition of up to 42 'additional days' imprisonment. In *Deputy Governor of Parkhurst Prison ex p Leech; Deputy Governor of Long Lartin Prison ex p Prevot* (1988), the House of Lords decided that it was impossible to find a principled basis for distinguishing hearings before a Board of Prison Visitors and disciplinary hearings before governors. It was held, therefore, that the rules of fairness and natural justice applied to the latter as much as to the former. In any case, what is now r 54 of the Prison Rules grants procedural rights to prisoners being disciplined, which may well be coterminous with the common law rules.

The rules of natural justice are context-dependent. We have seen, for example, that they do not necessarily require a right of representation and, regarding governor's hearings, it may be that a greater recognition of administrative convenience is acceptable. The question that arose after the introduction of the HRA was whether the procedural requirements for a fair trial applied to governor's hearings and, if they did, whether the application of natural justice was sufficient to satisfy Art 6. In *Ezeh v UK* (2002), two prisoners had been found guilty in disciplinary hearings in which neither was represented. Following *Tarrant*, the High Court, in judicial review proceedings, held that the governor's refusal to allow representation was neither irrational nor perverse and was, therefore, perfectly lawful. The ECtHR, however, decided that the seriousness of the charges and the severity of punishments open to the governor meant that disciplinary proceedings involved the determination of a criminal charge and thus the standard of a fair trial was set by Art 6. Failure to permit legal representation in these circumstances violated Art 6(1) and 6(3)(c). Since this decision was made after the coming into effect of the HRA, it would, under s 2 of that Act, normally be followed by English courts charged with interpreting Prison Rules. In 2002, following *Ezeh*, the Prison Rules were amended (see rr 51–61). Where a governor forms the view that an allegation is so serious that, if proved, it should be punished by the award of 'additional days', he or she must refer the matter to an adjudicator who alone can award the 'additional days' punishment. A prisoner is entitled to be represented before an adjudicator (r 54(3)). Adjudicators' hearings are intended to satisfy all the requirements of Art 6 on such matters as independence and impartiality.

In a succession of cases (for example, *Raymond v Honey* (1983) and *R v Secretary of State for the Home Department ex p O'Brien and Simms* (1999)), the courts have accepted that imprisonment does not mean that prisoners lose their fundamental rights. Unless fundamental rights are taken away expressly or by necessary implication of the fact of imprisonment, they are retained. There have been a number of significant improvements relating to prisoners' rights to privacy and to access to a court. The requirement, under r 34 of the Prison Rules, that the Home Secretary's permission was required before a prisoner could contact a solicitor, was challenged in *Golder v UK* (1975) in the ECtHR, the applicant alleging a violation of Art 8, which guarantees respect for private life and expressly mentions correspondence, and of Art 6, which governs the right to a fair hearing and from which a right of access to the court can be implied. The ECtHR took a rather cautious stance on this point and did not rule that prisoners have an absolute right of access to court. It ruled that, in this particular instance, given all the factors in the situation, including the fact that unpleasant consequences had already arisen from the alleged libel, Golder should have been able to go before a court. Thus, a breach of Art 6 had occurred.

The position has been strengthened by later cases which have emphasised rights of legal privilege and unimpeded access to legal advisors. Such principles are of such fundamental and constitutional importance that they can only be taken away by clear and express words in primary legislation. These principles are embodied in the Prison Rules (rr 38 and 39) and continue to be asserted and strengthened by the courts, particularly in the light of the HRA. In *R (Daly) v Secretary of State for the Home Department* (2001), the Home Secretary had imposed a blanket rule by which all prisoners had to be removed from their cells whilst their correspondence was examined. The House of Lords held that the blanket nature of the ban meant that it was a disproportionate interference with prisoners' rights, especially their right of privileged access to legal advisors. This right could only be taken away expressly and not on the basis of the Home Secretary's general power to make prison rules.

The improvement which has come about in relation to privacy of correspondence (see *Silver v UK* (1983)), the right of access to a court and in the standards of prison disciplinary proceedings may be contrasted with the failure of prisoners to use the courts to prevent cruel and degrading treatment in prisons. Once a prisoner is inside a prison, he or she may be subject to various punishments such as solitary confinement or withdrawal of privileges. Where formal punishment is not ordered, a decision may nevertheless be taken which subjects a prisoner to unpleasant conditions or even to violence from other prisoners. However, in contrast to their intervention in disciplinary hearings, the courts have not, at least on the basis of common law and statutory interpretation, shown much willingness to provide remedies where prisoners complain of punishment or of conditions in prison.

The applicability of the prohibition in the Bill of Rights 1688 of 'cruel and unusual' punishment has been accepted by the courts in this context (*Secretary of State for Home Department ex p Herbage (No 2)* (1987)). However, its scope was drastically limited by the decision in *Williams v Home Office (No 2)* (1982) that detention in the control unit at Wakefield prison which involved denial of association with other prisoners, little exercise, and constant surveillance and searches was not a breach of the Bill of Rights. It was found that a punishment had to be both cruel and unusual and that the control unit regime did not fall within either head: it was not cruel, because it did not fall below the minimum standard below which treatment would always be cruel, and it was not unusual, as a similar regime could be found in a number of prisons.

Prisoners have also explored private law remedies to challenge the use of certain punishments, but again, with limited success. If a punishment is imposed in a manner that is in breach of the Prison Rules, it would be unlawful, but in cases such as *Williams v Home Office (No 2)* (1982), the courts have refused to interpret the Prison Rules as conferring a right of action for damages on an individual prisoner.

In *Deputy Governor of Parkhurst Prison ex p Hague; Weldon v Home Office* (1991), the prisoners made a claim in the tort of false imprisonment. The Deputy Governor of Parkhurst prison ordered Hague to be transferred to another prison as a troublemaker and be segregated there for 28 days under r 43 of the Prison Rules. The House of Lords found that r 43 had not been complied with in determining the segregation but refused to give damages for breach of statutory duty, confirming the position in *Williams*. Weldon argued that he had been subjected to intolerable conditions in respect of confinement in a strip cell. Both prisoners argued that treatment within a prison, rather than the imprisonment itself, could amount to false imprisonment. They argued that prisoners, despite their confinement, possess a residual liberty, which can be infringed by an unlawful order or by intolerable conditions. This claim failed, because it was found that the notion of a species of freedom of movement within the prison, enjoyed as a legal right which prison authorities cannot lawfully restrain, is illusory: the prisoner is lawfully restrained by the fact of imprisonment; if he is segregated as opposed to being allowed into the company of other prisoners, this is merely the substitution of one form of restraint for another. In *Toumia v Evans* (1999), the Court of Appeal held that a prisoner could proceed with an action against a prison officer (the head of the Prison Service trade union) in an action for false imprisonment (when, due to industrial action, the prisoners were kept in their cells for long periods).

Hague and Weldon confines private law remedies to assault, negligence and misfeasance in public office and may be contrasted with the development in public law relating to fair procedure, considered above. Obviously, allowing prisoners a substantive cause of action against prison officers would be controversial, as it would alter the balance of power between the two parties. In contrast, insisting on procedural fairness is less contentious. However, it has not worsened the position of prisoners in private law terms, although it has closed off two possible avenues of argument. It means that a prisoner may be subjected to solitary confinement without any lawful basis and will have no remedy unless the prison authorities have acted with malice, in which case, the tort of misfeasance in public office applies.[3] Lord Bridge differed from Lord Goff in contemplating that liability for negligence might sometimes be appropriate, when intolerable conditions had been imposed, even where no physical harm had occurred, a possibility which would of course represent a departure from the traditional stance as to what may be termed harm within the meaning of damage in negligence.

The rules of statutory interpretation and common law principles which have been applied to the issue of whether prisoners have legal remedies in respect of decisions and actions taken in relation to their treatment now must be decided in the light of the HRA. In relation to the interpretation of statutes, the application of the law to public authorities such as the Prison Service and to the development of the common law, the 1998 Act is likely to have relevance. Schedule 1, Art 3 is relevant to the treatment of prisoners. Until recently, the Strasbourg Court was reluctant to find violations of the Article save for the most severe and unlawful forms of treatment such as brutal assaults or cruel punishments, for example, involving the deprivation of food. It remains the case, as UK courts recognise (see *R (Q) v Secretary of State for the Home Department* (2003), a case involving the duty of the State to provide welfare for asylum seekers) that the threshold for a breach of Art 3 is high. Nevertheless, recent Strasbourg decisions suggest that Art 3 has increasing relevance especially as regards the treatment of prisoners who are mentally or physically ill or disabled. In *McGlinchey v UK* (2003), for example, the treatment of a prisoner who was both a heroin addict and asthmatic was held to violate Art 3. In *Peers v Greece* (2001), where a prisoner was held in seriously unpleasant conditions in a regime which failed to distinguish remand from convicted prisoners, the Strasbourg Court found a violation of Art 3 despite the absence of any special responsibilities such as towards ill or disabled prisoners. Article 3, therefore, is likely to be of increasing significance in the development of the law on prison conditions. It should also be noted that, in *McGlinchey*, the lack of an effective means for prisoners and their families to inquire into and complain about treatment was a possible violation of Art 13 – the right to a remedy (not a scheduled Convention right).

Other scheduled Convention rights are having a significant impact on the law relating to prison conditions, especially through the application of 'proportionality'. Rules restricting or limiting contact with the media, for example, have been examined in the light of Art 10(2). In *R v Secretary of State for the Home Department ex p Simms* (2000), the House of Lords insisted that restrictions on contacts with the media should not be allowed to prevent prisoners being able to pursue and publicise their claims of innocence, and in *Hirst v Secretary of State for the Home Department* (2002), the High Court allowed regulated contributions to radio programmes on prison conditions.

Serious problems involving prisoners' rights remain. However, there have been significant developments and it is misleading to say that such rights, whilst by no means fully developed, are still in their infancy. Under the common law, there were significant developments regarding disciplinary procedures. Now we can see that the HRA is beginning to have considerable influence over a range of matters. This is not only because UK courts must take the Convention into account, but also because the ECtHR is interpreting the Convention in a way that gives greater recognition to the position of prisoners even as regards questions of their treatment. Serious problems in the prisons remain. Under the influence of the HRA, legal challenges are likely on issues such as the investigation of deaths in custody; overcrowding; medical treatment; treatment of disabled prisoners; the continued interceptions and censorship of mail; the parole process; the allocation of inmates to particular prisons and the legality of disciplinary adjudications. The status of the Prisons and Probation Ombudsman, who may need a new statutory footing and extended powers to compel the Prison Service to comply with his recommendations, is also an important issue. The result of such litigation, some of which will depend on how the Convention is interpreted, remains to be seen.

Notes

1 In *Ridge v Baldwin* (1964), the House of Lords held that when an administrative body takes a decision affecting the rights or legitimate expectations of citizens, that exercise of power is open to review by the courts. If there has been a failure to follow the principles of natural justice (procedural impropriety), a court can make an order under Pt 54 of the Civil Procedure Rules – usually a quashing order – which renders the decision void.

2 This point could be developed: it might be noted that these principles were confirmed in *Board of Visitors for Nottingham Prison* (1981); it was held that if it were established that a prisoner had asked for and been refused permission to call witnesses, that would, *prima facie*, be unfair. The refusal of witnesses and of cross-examination led to the quashing of six convictions in *St Germain (No 2)*.

3 It might be further argued that prison represents a deprivation of liberty, but not a complete deprivation, due to a degree of freedom in moving about within the prison. The curtailment of that remaining freedom is part of the essence of the punishment represented by segregation. Such deprivation of remaining freedom might be acceptable if it were within that which the relevant statute allows, but otherwise it is arguable that it should be tortious.

Question 34

Prisoners at Burham prison occupy the roof in an attempt to air their grievances. After the disturbance has been brought under control, Abel and Bert, two of the prisoners, are charged with various offences against discipline as laid down in the Prison Rules 1999. Abel is charged with attempting to assault an officer by throwing a slate from the prison roof. On an initial consideration of the evidence, the governor takes the view that 20 'additional days' would be the appropriate punishment if the allegation is proved. Bert is charged with intentionally obstructing an officer in the execution of his duty. He is dealt with by the governor, who imposes a punishment of 14 days' forfeiture of privileges and 28 days' stoppage of earnings.

Both Abel and Bert are allowed to appear in person at their respective hearings, but both are refused legal representation on the ground that the hearings must be dealt with swiftly. Abel is permitted to call one witness in his defence, but two others are refused on the ground that they have been dispersed to other prisons. Bert's request to call a witness is refused. Abel is allowed to remain present during his hearing while a prison officer gives evidence against him, but is refused permission to cross-examine him. The governor gives Bert a summary of the allegations made against him by a prison officer, but refuses to allow him to see the full statement. Bert is surprised by the content of the allegations, which appear to be more extensive than those appearing in the statement of charges given to him prior to the hearing. Despite this, the governor refuses to give him time to consider them.

Advise Abel and Bert as to any redress they might have.

Answer plan

This is a very straightforward question on the principles of natural justice and the impact of Art 6, Sched 1 to the HRA 1998. Answers must take into account recent changes to the Prison Rules required following decisions of the European Court of Human Rights (ECtHR) in Strasbourg and the need to ensure that the Prison Rules and practices are compatible with European Convention rights. It is very important to bear in mind that what is meant by a fair hearing will vary from hearing to hearing, and that the more serious the penalty, the higher should be the standards observed. Thus, it is probably a good idea to deal with both hearings separately. It must first be shown that the courts are prepared to review the decision in question on the ground of want of natural justice and, secondly, in relation to each hearing separately, that a breach (or breaches) of natural justice have taken place. Although one serious breach might lead to the quashing of the decision, you should strengthen your argument by considering as many as possible.

Essentially, the following matters should be discussed:

- the courts are prepared to review prison disciplinary decisions on the ground of want of natural justice (*St Germain* (1979));
- the courts are prepared to review decisions of governors in prison disciplinary hearings on the ground of want of natural justice (*Leech v Deputy Governor of Parkhurst Prison; Prevot v Deputy Governor of Long Lartin Prison* (1988));
- the new system for imposing the punishment of 'additional days', introduced following *Ezeh v UK* (2002) and incorporated into the Prison Rules;
- the discretion to allow the calling of witnesses;
- the discretion to allow cross-examination;
- whether there is a duty or merely a discretion to allow legal representation in the different types of disciplinary hearings;
- the right of a prisoner to a full opportunity of hearing the allegations against him and to present his case (r 54) and Art 6 of the ECHR.

Answer

Both Abel and Bert will wish to show that these decisions were made in breach of the principles of natural justice. First, it must be determined whether the rules of natural justice apply to the process in question. As Abel and Bert are involved in two separate hearings and the consequences for each differ in degree of seriousness, their cases will be considered separately.

It was determined in *Board of Visitors of Hull Prison ex p St Germain (No 1)* (1979) that prison disciplinary hearings were subject to the principles of natural justice. Certain prisoners complained that the disciplinary proceedings which followed the Hull prison riots were not conducted in accordance with the principles of natural justice. The Court of Appeal held that prisoners only lose those liberties expressly denied them by Parliament – otherwise they retain their rights under the law. This ruling was confined to Board of Visitors' hearings (who at that time dealt with the more serious disciplinary offences) who were dealt with as if they were an independent tribunal. Governors' hearings were excluded.

However, following *Leech v Deputy Governor of Parkhurst Prison; Prevot v Deputy Governor of Long Lartin Prison* (1988), the principles developed in relation to Boards of Visitors' hearings were applied to those of governors, on the basis that it was not possible to distinguish between the disciplinary function of the Board of Visitors and that of governors. Both should be conducted in accordance with the principles of natural justice. In *St Germain*, Shaw LJ said, *obiter dicta*, 'I do not find it easy, if at all possible, to distinguish between disciplinary proceedings conducted by a Board of Visitors and those carried out by a prison governor ... the essential nature of the proceedings ... is the same. So in nature if not in degree are the consequences to a prisoner'. Though it can be concluded that the rules of fairness and natural justice apply to all prison disciplinary hearings, the content of these rules is context-dependent and will vary according to circumstances such as the seriousness of the offence and likely penalty.

As well as the rules of natural justice, it is also important to realise that in Abel's case the impact of Art 6 has been important. Article 6 imposes a right to a fair hearing and other ancillary rights in respect of the determination of a 'criminal charge'. Whether or not a criminal charge is being determined is a matter of Convention jurisprudence and is not conclusively decided by how an issue is described in domestic law. The nature of the charge and the severity of the punishment are important factors. If a hearing can result in additional time in prison, then it is likely to be a hearing determining a 'criminal charge' and the rights in Art 6(1)–(3) will apply. In *Ezeh v UK* (2002), the ECtHR held that a governors' hearing which could impose 'additional days' as a punishment was covered by Art 6. As a result, the Prison Rules have been changed. Where an allegation is made against a prisoner, the governor, on an initial consideration of the evidence, must decide whether, if the facts alleged are proved, 'additional days' would be an appropriate punishment (r 53A). If so, the governor must pass the case over to an adjudicator to be 'inquired into' and only an adjudicator has the authority to punish by the imposition of additional days. Adjudicators' hearings must comply with the requirements of Art 6.

Given that the governor's initial assessment is that 20 additional days would be an appropriate punishment if the allegation against Abel is proved, this becomes a case for the adjudicator and is governed by Art 6, which will supplement and, where there is conflict, have priority over the rules of natural justice.

The first question in Abel's case is whether a disciplinary hearing requires the calling of all or any of the witnesses requested by the prisoner. Article 6(3)(d) gives the defendant the right 'to examine or have examined witnesses against him and to obtain the attendance and examination of witnesses on his behalf under the same conditions as witnesses against him'. This is not treated as giving an absolute right for a defendant to call any witness he or she pleases (see, for example, *Vidal v Belgium* (1992)). Article 6 does not impose specific procedural rules on Member States but is, rather, a standard against which the fairness of the particular rules and practices of domestic law can be judged. Regarding domestic law, it was held in *Board of Visitors of Hull Prison ex p St Germain (No 2)* (1979), that Boards of Visitors must be able to exercise a discretion to refuse a prisoner's request for witnesses if they feel that he is purposely trying to obstruct or subvert the proceedings by calling large numbers of witnesses or if, where the request is made in good faith, they feel that the calling of large numbers of witnesses is unnecessary. Such a principle is likely to be consistent with Art 6. However, mere administrative inconvenience would not support a decision to refuse such a request. In Abel's case, it appears that the only reason for the refusal was the inconvenience involved in recalling the witnesses from other prisons. If so, the adjudicator will have taken into account a factor he should have disregarded. Furthermore, given the fact that Abel was allegedly merely one of a group of prisoners on the roof, it would seem essential that he should be able to challenge evidence that he was present, that he threw the slate and that, in doing so, he was attempting to assault a prison officer. The failure to allow him to present his defence would violate Art 6. If Abel can demonstrate that calling more than one witness was necessary due to the nature of his defence, it would follow that he should have been allowed to call them. This is required not only by the rules of natural justice, but also as a Convention right. In *Board of Prison Visitors for Nottingham Prison* (1981), it was held that, if a prisoner had asked for and been refused permission to call witnesses, this would, *prima facie*, be unfair and require explanation.

The Prison Rules give Abel the right to present his own case but do not specify that he has a right to cross-examine witnesses. In *St Germain (No 2)*, it was made clear that the right to a fair hearing must include not only the right to know the nature of the charge, but also the opportunity to correct and contradict evidence given. In addition, Art 6(3)(d) gives a defendant to a criminal charge the right to examine witnesses against him. Although, under both the rules of natural justice and Art 6(3)(d), the right to cross-examine is not absolute (if the effect of cross-examination can be met in other ways, as in *R v Governor of HM Prison Swaleside ex p Wynter* (1998), for example), in this case, a fair trial requires that Abel be able to challenge the main prosecution evidence and, it is submitted, the failure to allow cross-examination is a breach of both Art 6 and natural justice.

Abel's final ground of complaint is that he received no legal representation. In *Secretary of State for the Home Department ex p Tarrant* (1985), it was accepted, following *Fraser v Mudge*, that a Board of Visitors was entitled to retain discretion as to whether a prisoner was entitled to representation. The court then suggested certain factors which a Board could properly take into account. These included the seriousness of the charge and of the penalty, the likelihood that points of law might be likely to arise, the ability of the prisoner to conduct his own case and the need for speed in making the adjudication. The House of Lords in *Board of Visitors of HM Prison, the Maze ex p Hone* (1988) considered the issue afresh, but determined that no absolute right to legal representation in prison disciplinary hearings could be created. This situation has now changed following *Ezeh v UK* (2002). The failure to permit legal representation in respect of a prison disciplinary hearing which, in terms of various factors including the potential penalty, was determining a criminal charge, violated Art 6(3)(c), which gives a right to a defendant to 'defend himself in person or through legal assistance of his own choosing ...'. Prison Rule 54 was amended to give a right to be represented in hearings before an adjudicator (who has power to award 'additional days' punishment). The refusal to allow Abel representation is, therefore, a breach of the Prison Rules.

Thus, proceedings in Abel's case seem to have breached the *Audi* rule, in that he was not allowed witnesses and probably in that he was not allowed an opportunity for cross-examination; they have also breached Art 6 and the Prison Rules in not allowing legal representation.

The requirements of a fair hearing in Bert's case will differ from those in Abel's, because the consequences for Bert are less serious than for Abel: he is losing privileges and earnings, rather than having additional days in prison added on. In *Aston University ex p Rothy* (1969), it was held that natural justice would apply, although there was no kind of legal right in question; it was necessary to look at all the circumstances – the expectation of a fair hearing and the serious consequences which would follow from the decision. Possibly, the loss of privileges might not alone be sufficiently serious to warrant the application of the principles of natural justice, but might be so if coupled with the loss of earnings – deprivation of a legal right – and on this ground natural justice may apply. On this argument, *Leech v Deputy Governor of Parkhurst Prison; Prevot v Deputy Governor of Long Lartin Prison* (1988) applies to Bert's hearing, which should therefore have been conducted in accordance with the principles of natural justice. The fact that the charges against Bert and the punishments are relatively less serious than for Abel (in particular, they do not involve the loss of liberty) also suggests that these hearings would be accepted as determining disciplinary rather than criminal matters and so it is less likely that Art 6 would apply.

Bert has four grounds of complaint: he was not allowed to call witnesses; have legal representation; see a full statement of the allegations against him; and it seemed that the allegations had been added to since he saw the statement of charges against him prior to the inquiry.

Once the principle is accepted that natural justice applies in proceedings before a governor, it follows that all the aspects of a fair hearing considered in decisions relating to Boards of Visitors' hearings may apply in governors' hearings. Before governors, however, especially as they may no longer award 'additional days', administrative inconvenience is likely to be allowed much more weight. Following *Secretary of State for the Home Department ex p Tarrant* (1985), it may be argued, in the instant case, that the triviality of the penalty involved, coupled with the need for speed in making the adjudication, outweigh other factors, such as the need to deal with points of law and therefore do not warrant the grant of legal representation.

However, it may be argued that the governor should have exercised his discretion in favour of allowing Bert to call a witness (and perhaps allowing cross-examination of the prison officer whose evidence is presented). The test from *St Germain (No 2)* seems to be satisfied: Bert appears to be making the request in good faith and there seems no sufficient reason for refusing it. The administrative inconvenience involved would be minor since the witness is presumably present in the prison.

Furthermore, Bert is denied the opportunity to see a full statement of the allegations. Rule 54 of the Prison Rules 1999 provides that a prisoner shall have a full opportunity of hearing what is alleged against him. It may be said that r 54 is declaratory of the principles of natural justice and indeed may represent, in that respect, a minimum standard. It was determined in *Tarrant* that a prisoner should be given sufficient time to understand what is alleged against him and prepare a defence. Clearly, if somebody is unaware of the extent of the charges against him, he will be unable to answer them; the inconvenience involved would have been very minor.

In *Board of Visitors of Gartree Prison ex p Mealy* (1985), Mealy alleged unfairness, because, when he came to answer the charges against him, he found that the order of the proceedings had been changed. This took him by surprise and, he believed, adversely affected his ability to defend himself. The Divisional Court found that Chairmen of Boards of Visitors should guide prisoners through the proceedings and not surprise them by sudden changes of format. This could apply to the instant case as Bert was upset by additional allegations which he had not expected. Of course, *Mealy's* case was in the context of proceedings before a Board of Visitors. However, in principle, the rule from *Mealy* could apply in governors' hearings; although the procedure is obviously more informal, it is still necessary to give the accused time to consider how to answer the charges. This is supported by the requirement under r 54 that prisoners should be given a full opportunity of presenting their case.

In general, what is required for a fair hearing will differ as between governors, who hear the more common, less serious offences, the adjudicators, who hear the more serious disciplinary offences and the courts, who deal with serious criminal allegations against prisoners. Although adjudicators and the courts will be expected to adhere to the highest standards, a reasonable standard must be observed in governors' hearings, even though loss of liberty is not in question. It does not appear that such standards have been observed here. Therefore, Bert may be able to show that the *Audi* rule has been breached with regard to all his complaints, apart from the denial of legal representation.

Thus, since both Abel and Bert are able to show breaches of the principles of natural justice, the decisions will be void. (In *Anisminic v FCC* (1969), the House of Lords held that a decision which breached the principles of natural justice would be void, not voidable.) Under the Civil Procedure Rules 1998, quashing orders will be issued to quash the decision in each instance.

Question 35

'Recent developments have made it apparent that prisoners must look to the European Convention on Human Rights in order to uphold their basic rights to privacy and to access to a court.' Do you agree?

Answer plan

This is a reasonably straightforward essay question. It should be noted that it is confined to two particular areas of prisoners' rights. Clearly, it is necessary to consider the general influence of the Convention, not merely the decided cases. It is also necessary to ask whether in certain instances the domestic courts have gone further in protecting prisoners' rights than the European Court of Human Rights (ECtHR). Finally, it might be asked whether domestic courts are now taking a more activist stance in these areas.

Essentially, the following areas should be considered:

- key provisions of the Prison Rules relating to correspondence;
- Arts 8 and 6 of the ECHR;
- key decisions of the ECtHR on privacy and access to a court;
- use of judicial review in this area – general influence of the ECtHR.

Answer

It is an inevitable concomitant of imprisonment that certain basic rights, such as freedom of movement, are removed from prisoners, while others are curtailed. Privacy is clearly curtailed, but this does not mean that a prisoner enjoys no privacy, while, on the other hand, the fundamental right of access to a court need not be abrogated at all. Articles 8 and 6 of the ECHR have been used successfully by prisoners to protect these fundamental liberties and recently the domestic courts have, it will be argued, adopted a more activist stance in these areas. Now that the HRA 1998 is in force, domestic opportunities for challenges of the Prison Rules 1999 have become far greater. In most cases, it is the authority of the Prison Rules 1999 (amended in 2000 and 2002) which are directly or indirectly in issue. At common law and (by implication) under the HRA, delegated legislation which is incompatible with fundamental rights or Convention rights can be held to be void, unless expressly authorised by primary legislation. Since s 47 of the Prison Act 1952, which authorises the making of the Prison Rules, is expressed in general terms, it is unlikely that a court would find that any incompatibility with Convention rights could not, because of s 47, be removed. Hence, declarations of incompatibility are unlikely to be necessary.

Cases brought under Art 6 of the Convention have led to greater protection for the right of free access to the court. Under r 34 of the Prison Rules, which related to correspondence (now r 39), the Home Secretary's permission was required before a prisoner could contact a solicitor. This provision was challenged in *Golder v UK* (1975) in the ECtHR. The applicant, at the time a prisoner, had wished to bring a libel action against a prison officer who had wrongly accused him of assault and, as a result, prevented him obtaining parole. Golder therefore wished to communicate with his solicitor but, under r 34 of the Prison Rules, had to obtain the Home Secretary's permission to do so. Permission was refused and therefore Golder could not initiate the libel action. On release from prison, he applied to Strasbourg, alleging a violation of Art 8, which guarantees respect for privacy, expressly mentioning correspondence, and of Art 6, which governs the right to a fair hearing. Golder's claim that he had been denied the right to a hearing could be considered only if Art 6 included a substantive right of access to a court, rather than merely providing guarantees of fairness once the hearing was in being. The ECtHR held that Art 6(1) could not be narrowed only to include procedural guarantees, because it would not be possible to benefit from such guarantees if access to a court itself could be denied. Thus, it was found that access to a court must be inherent in Art 6(1).

The Court did not rule that prisoners have an absolute right of access to court. It ruled that, in this particular instance, given all the factors in the situation, including the fact that unpleasant consequences had already arisen from the alleged libel, Golder should have been able to go before a court. Thus, a breach of Art 6 had occurred. In responding to this finding, the government modified r 34 of the Prison Rules, but in a fairly minimal fashion – only to the extent that prisoners could communicate with their solicitors freely, but complaints about the inner workings of the prison could not be communicated, unless the internal complaints machinery had first been exhausted. This was known as the prior ventilation rule and it was clearly still likely to inhibit access to a court. Not surprisingly, in *Silver v UK* (1983), the prior ventilation rule was found to be an unwarranted curb on correspondence. Prison orders regarding correspondence were again modified so that a solicitor could be contacted with matter relating to a complaint as soon as the complaint had been registered internally. This rule, known as the simultaneous ventilation rule, was itself challenged successfully in the domestic courts in *Secretary of State for Home Department ex p Anderson* (1984). It was found that if prisoners had to register a complaint internally before communicating with a solicitor, this would constitute an impediment to their right of access to the court; an inmate might hesitate to make an internal complaint, because he could lay himself open to a disciplinary charge. The court held that the restriction placed on him by the simultaneous ventilation rule was *ultra vires*, because it conflicted with this fundamental right – a right so fundamental that it could only be taken away by express language.

Anderson is an interesting case, because it provides an instance of a domestic decision going beyond the rights provided by the Convention, and the same may be said of *Secretary of State for the Home Department ex p Leech (No 2)* (1993), in which the Court of Appeal found that it was a principle of great importance that every citizen had an unimpeded right of access to a court, and that this was buttressed by the principle of legal professional privilege. Legal privilege, recognised by common law, could openly be taken away by subordinate legislation only where that was expressly authorised by the enabling legislation (s 47 of the Prison Act 1952). Section 47 might authorise some screening of correspondence, but it must be strictly construed in accordance with the presumption against statutory interference with common law rights. The point was emphasised by the House of Lords in *R (Daly) v Secretary of State for the Home Department* (2001). The Home Secretary imposed a policy that, without exceptions, prisoners should be removed from their cells during searches, even when the searches might involve the scrutiny of legally privileged material. Because of its lack of exceptions, the policy was held to be void and incapable of authorisation under s 47 of the Prison Act 1952; the House of Lords emphasised both the common law protection of legal privilege and the impact of Art 8 of the Convention. Such rulings, it is suggested, represent an example of judicial activism in using the common law and demonstrate that reliance on the ECHR, via the HRA, is not always necessary.

The area in which the ECtHR, as opposed to the domestic courts, has had a particular influence is that of privacy of correspondence under Art 8. In *Golder v UK*, it was found that prisoners' privacy of correspondence must be upheld; implied limitations on it due to detention were rejected. *Silver* was also concerned with privacy of correspondence generally; certain letters unconcerned with legal proceedings, including communications with journalists, had also been stopped. It was found that such interference with correspondence was in breach of Art 8, and certain changes were therefore made to standing orders in prisons. Prisoners were freer as to the contents of letters; previously, they could not make criticism of persons in public life or make complaints about the prison. They were also allowed greater freedom in their choice of correspondents; they were not confined to relatives or friends, but could correspond with others, including journalists.

However, under the old rules, all letters at non-'open' establishments could be routinely read, except for correspondence relating to legal proceedings to which the inmate was a party. Such correspondence could not be read or stopped unless the governor had reason to suppose that it contained matter not relating to the proceedings. However, other correspondence with a solicitor, including that in respect of proceedings to which the inmate was not already a party, could be read and stopped if objectionable. The latter rule was challenged successfully in *Campbell v UK* (1992) under Art 8, the applicant alleging that correspondence with his solicitor and with the European Commission had been opened without justification. Following the case, the Prison Rules 1999 have extended, under r 39, the scope of the confidentiality of prisoners' correspondence to all such correspondence with a legal advisor, whether or not legal proceedings have been commenced. However, such correspondence may still be opened under r 39(2) and (3) if the governor has reasonable cause to believe its contents to be illicit, illegal or a threat to security.

Although letters unrelated to legal proceedings may still be opened, read and stopped (under r 35A–D), routine censorship of correspondence generally has been abolished in open prisons and, since 1988, reduced at category C prisons and many closed Young Offender Establishments. Following the Woolf Report, the Home Secretary announced the end of routine censorship of most prisoners' letters. Thus, the categories of letters which may be routinely subject to restrictions and interference have steadily been reduced, while the categories of possible correspondents and of contents of correspondence have been widened.

The impact of Art 8 and also Art 10 has, for example, led the courts to invalidate blanket bans or restrictions on prisoners' contacts with the media. In *R v Secretary of State for the Home Department ex p Simms and Another* (1999), a refusal by the Prison Service to allow prisoners unrestricted access to journalists in order to further claims of wrongful conviction was overturned, and in *R (Hirst) v Secretary of State for the Home Department* (2002), a refusal to allow even conditional access of a prisoner, who was an advocate of prisoners' interests, to live radio shows was also invalidated.

Article 8 is beginning to have an impact in areas of privacy other than communications and correspondence although, from a prisoner point of view, this has not always been successful. Article 8(2) allows law-based restrictions on private and family life if they are a proportionate way of achieving one of the listed legitimate purposes. Restrictions that are consistent with the overall purposes of prison (incarceration, punishment and deterrence, for example) are, subject to proportionality in individual cases, likely to be upheld. For example, a refusal by the Prison Service to allow a prisoner to conceive a child with his wife by artificial insemination was upheld in *R (Mellor) v Secretary of State for the Home Department* (2001). Similarly, the policy of separating prisoner-mothers from their babies at eighteen months has been found to be compatible with Art 8(2), although proportionality requires the policy to be responsive to needs in particular cases – *R (P and Q) v Secretary of State for the Home Department* (2001) and *R (CD) v Secretary of State for the Home Department* (2003).

In conclusion, although the ECtHR has provided the impetus needed to ensure that rights to privacy and access to the court are upheld, improvement has also come about through the application of common law principles including natural justice in judicial review proceedings. It is clear that UK judges have set out to ensure that UK law is at least in conformity with and perhaps better than, the Convention. With the HRA, giving effect to the Convention is more straightforward than previously and it is to be hoped that courts will use their post-enactment powers to improve prisoners' human rights to embody and, where necessary, enhance the spirit of the Convention.

Question 36

Evaluate the recent proposals for reform of UK prisons and the government response to them. Is further reform needed?

Answer plan

This is a reasonably straightforward question, assuming that you are aware of the main proposals. You do need to keep specifically to the recent reforms and resist the temptation to write down everything about changes in prisoners' rights, which you have revised.

Essentially, the following matters should be discussed:

* the Woolf Report;
* the White Paper;
* a Code of Standards in prisons;
* issues raised by HM Inspectors of Prisons' reports;
* limitations of the government response, particularly in relation to improving basic living standards in UK prisons;
* the impact of the HRA and the European Convention on Human Rights (ECHR) case law.

Answer

Reform in prisons has concentrated on improving the quality of prison disciplinary hearings and on improving basic living standards, especially in the context of overcrowding and sanitation. As is discussed below, a range of other matters have also arrived on the reform agenda. It remains to be seen whether the changes in prison disciplinary hearings have gone far enough, and it is a matter of concern that the government response to proposals to improve standards is still too minimal.

Serious prison riots in 1990 were followed by an inquiry which led to the Woolf Report in 1991. Its recommendations (which had similarities with the Prior Report of 1987) included the suggestion that the disciplinary jurisdiction of governors be limited to minor offences, and that the more serious offences should be dealt with by the ordinary courts, no longer by the Board of Visitors. It is argued that the Woolf proposals created, on the whole, a sensible method of dealing with the situation. First, the Board of Visitors was increasingly being perceived as insufficiently independent of the prison administration and as conducting hearings in which proper procedural safeguards were not in place, despite decisions improving their quality. For example, it was still the case, despite decisions such as *Tarrant* (1985), that legal representation was very rarely granted. Unfair decisions may have contributed to unrest in prisons. Secondly, the disciplinary function of Boards of Visitors was perceived as incompatible with their other function as prison 'watchdog'. Boards of Visitors are meant to provide an outlet and a remedy for prisoners' grievances. Increasingly, they could not fulfil this central role because they were distrusted by prisoners. Again, this perception of the nature of Boards of Visitors may have contributed to unrest: prisoners may have perceived that a sufficient, legitimate outlet for grievances was lacking.

The government published a White Paper, *Custody, Care and Justice*, in 1991, dealing with the Woolf proposals, and the Prison Rules were amended to remove the disciplinary function of Boards of Visitors. Where offences by prisoners were also the more serious crimes, they were referred to the police and dealt with in the ordinary criminal system. Governors retained the disciplinary function for 'offences against discipline' and were able to award 28 'additional days' which was increased, in 1994, to 42. (The concept of additional days replaced loss of remission as an available punishment by s 42 of the Criminal Justice Act 1991.)

These changes were not entirely consistent with the Woolf proposals, which were based on reducing and eventually abolishing the use of extra days in prison as a punishment, and increasingly substituting loss of facilities and opportunities. Also, it is not clear whether the Woolf Report's distinction between those cases that should be dealt with by the police and courts and those that should be heard by governors reflects the old division between the jurisdiction of the Board of Prison Visitors and governors. The danger may be that the governors' disciplinary jurisdiction may extend to cover a part of that of the Board of Visitors', with only a small percentage of offences being dealt with in court. Given that procedural safeguards in governors' hearings are of a far more basic nature than those in Board of Visitors' hearings (and legal representation is unheard of), this may be a retrograde step. Arguably, both Woolf and the White Paper focused too exclusively on the deficiencies of

Board of Visitors' hearings, to the exclusion of concern with those of governors'.

The conduct of governors' hearings has been a matter for concern. In 1988, the Chief Inspector of Prisons reported that, 'Governors' adjudications were not always being carried out in accordance with the appropriate standard of justice'. Now that such hearings are open to judicial review, some improvement may come about, but it is unlikely to be very far-reaching. This is particularly a matter of concern because the government's proposals for reform in prisons will have little impact on governors' hearings. There may be a case for arguing that all adjudication of offences above a certain level (not only those which constitute serious criminal offences) should be placed in the hands of an independent body.

Arguably, second tier adjudication need not have been completely swept away, but should instead have been made entirely independent of the prison administration by entrusting it to a prison tribunal, which could sometimes meet externally to the prison or, where appropriate, could convene within it, and which would conduct its proceedings in a court-like fashion with a duty solicitor always on hand to conduct the defence. This has been partially met by changes made to the disciplinary system following *Ezeh v UK* (2002), which found that governors' hearings (at least those leading to an award of additional days) are subject to the fair trial protections in Art 6 of the Convention. Under these changes, governors lose the power to punish by awarding additional days. The governor must decide whether an allegation would, if proved, justify an award of additional days and if so the matter must be inquired into by an adjudicator. The adjudicator's procedure involves a right to representation, gives the defendant more time to prepare his or her defence and is likely to meet the requirement for independence found in Art 6. Of course, the issue about whether to refer the matter to the police or to the adjudicator is still decided by the governor, who may, in other than the most serious matters, prefer to deal with the matter expeditiously through a governors' hearing.

The Woolf Report also recommended that a Code of Standards in Prisons should be promulgated, influenced by the European Prison Rules 1987 and the United Nations Standard Minimum Rules for the Treatment of Offenders. The idea of legally enforceable prison standards is still resisted. Indeed, the best that might be hoped for is a Code of Practice similar to those produced under the Police and Criminal Evidence Act 1984. In respect of standards, there is some evidence that Art 3 of the ECHR may be developed to require certain minimum standards where, for example, conditions are very poor or in relation to prisoners with special needs. Though this development is welcome, it should not be forgotten that the threshold for a violation of Art 3 is high.

Compliance with standards is monitored by the Inspector of Prisons and the Board of Visitors. Individual complaints are dealt with within the prison service. There is no independent appeal – the governor reviews decisions taken by subordinates in his name. A major innovation has been the introduction of the independent Prisons and Probation Ombudsman. A prisoner who is dissatisfied with the way a complaint has been handled by the Prison Service can complain to the Ombudsman, who investigates and may make recommendations which the Prison Service will generally, but not always, accept. This is an important and increasingly used system based on the idea of investigation and reporting rather than enforcing legal standards. Though this is a welcome development, there is clearly a case for introducing a properly independent system to deal with appeals.

A number of other issues relate to the Prison Service which have been identified by, for example, HM Inspector of Prisons or the Committee administering the European Convention on the Prevention of Torture and Inhuman or Degrading Treatment who make visits every five years. The dominant problem is overcrowding, which flows from changes in penal policy and court practice. Resolving other issues largely involves administrative action by the Prison Service such as, for example, seeking to improve health care by transferring the Prison Medical Service to the NHS Trust model. There are, however, some developments that involve legal changes.

Racism, for example, is an acknowledged problem in British prisons. The Race Relations (Amendment) Act 2000, as well as making racial discrimination by a public authority such as the Prison Service illegal, also imposes a positive duty on scheduled authorities to take active steps to promote good race relations. The Home Office is amongst the scheduled authorities and so, through it, the Act should have an impact on the Prison Service.

Suicide and other deaths in custody are, particularly amongst young offenders, an increasing problem. Here Art 2 of the ECHR, the right to life, which is a scheduled Convention right in the HRA, has had a considerable effect. In particular, the jurisprudence on Art 2 not only places a duty on State agencies to take positive steps to protect life, but also places a duty on the State to have a full investigation which involves the deceased's family. The courts are involved in determining the detailed standards. In *R (Amin) v Secretary of State for the Home Department* (2003), which involved the death of an Asian prisoner at the hands of his racist cell mate, the House of Lords reversed the Court of Appeal's decision and held that the investigation into the prisoner's killing was neither sufficiently comprehensive nor sufficiently involving of the family to meet the UK's Convention obligations. Individual cases will indicate the extent to which this case has brought about changes in Prison Service policy.

The impetus for reform of UK prisons comes from a number of sources such as the government's responses to the Woolf Report, the reports of HM Inspectors and the impact of Convention rights and other international standards. As exemplified above, there have been a number of significant developments in which improvements have been made and been based on legally enforceable standards. The examples of racism and deaths in custody can be added to the beginnings of an Art 3 jurisprudence on treatment[1] as well as to the now well developed principles of fair disciplinary procedures based on fairness and natural justice and Art 6. However, major problems remain, many of which, as the HM Inspectors' reports suggest, are based on overcrowding. Without legally enforceable standards of treatment, the Prison Service still enjoys wide discretion and it is suggested that improvements in standards and in other practices, such as provision for visits and other contact with families, should be made legally enforceable. Without this, the UK remains unlikely to achieve the goal of providing the minimum standards set out in the United Nations Standard Minimum Rules for the Treatment of Offenders.

Note

1   Recourse to Strasbourg should not be seen as a substitute for government action. The ECtHR should not be placed in the position of having to determine domestic spending priorities. The Prison Reform Trust has produced a paper, *Strangeways – Ten Years On*, which is a retrospective of the last 10 years of prison reform in the light of the Woolf proposals.

CHAPTER 7

FREEDOM OF MOVEMENT

Introduction

Examiners usually set essay questions in this area, although a problem question on the effect of the European Court of Human Rights (ECtHR) on asylum and immigration law is becoming more common. The emphasis is usually on the degree to which a balance is struck between the interest of the State in national security and the individual's basic freedom to enter, move about within and leave the UK. Students should be aware that this is an area in which there have been repeated and relatively major changes recently; for example, the former power to make an exclusion order from the UK or Northern Ireland lapsed in 1998 and is not included in the new permanent Terrorism Act 2000, and wide-reaching changes to the asylum process, including to rights of appeal, are in the Nationality, Immigration and Asylum Act (NIAA) 2002.

Checklist

Students should be familiar with the following areas:

- relevant provisions of the European Convention on Human Rights (ECHR);
- deportation and administrative removal provisions under the Immigration Act 1971, as amended, and the Immigration and Asylum Act (IAA) 1999;
- the Geneva Convention of 1951 as amended by the 1967 Protocol;
- key provisions and effects of the IAA 1999 and the NIAA 2002 relating to asylum seekers;
- the appeals procedure under Pt IV of the NIAA 2002.

Question 37

'The law governing deportation is in need of further reform in order to create a fairer balance between individual civil liberties and the right of a sovereign State to determine who should come within its boundaries.' Do you agree?

Answer plan

In answering this question, it will be necessary not only to identify substantive and procedural aspects of the deportation procedure which have an adverse impact on civil liberties, but also to suggest what might be meant by a 'fairer' balance.

Essentially, the following matters should be discussed:

* deportation and administrative removal provisions under the Immigration Act 1971, as amended, and the Nationality, Immigration and Asylum Act (NIAA) 2002;
* the relevant provisions under the Immigration Rules 2003;
* procedure followed in making the decision to deport/remove;
* the impact on terrorism;
* infringement of civil liberties;
* the relevance of the European Court of Human Rights (ECtHR).

Answer

Deportation and its close relative 'administrative removal' represent the clearest infringement of freedom of movement and therefore should be used only where there is clear justification and where there are mechanisms allowing careful scrutiny of the decision to deport. Broadly speaking, a person who is not a UK citizen with rights of residence is liable to deportation only if the Secretary of State deems that person's removal to be conducive to the common good, or where a court has recommended it after a conviction for a serious offence, or for national security reasons, or where the person is a relative of someone deported on one of those grounds (s 3(5)(b) and 3(6) of the Immigration Act 1971). However, the Immigration and Asylum Act (IAA) 1999 also allows 'administrative removal' of a person who did originally have leave to enter or remain, but has failed to observe the conditions attached to his leave, overstayed or obtained leave by deception (s 10). Administrative removal is a controversial term, which is practically indistinguishable from deportation and formerly was a procedure which only applied to illegal entrants. An overstayer may apply for leave to remain under the new arrangements in s 9 of the 1999 Act and, if refused, may appeal to an adjudicator administered by the Immigration Appellate Authority; as soon as he has applied for leave to remain, he cannot be subject to administrative removal, but may be deported if his application and any appeal fail.

The deportation of family members of a deportee has caused concern, since the practice seems indirectly discriminatory: a wife will often find it harder to meet the criteria for not being deported than a husband. The wife will not, however, automatically be deported; r 367 of the Immigration Rules 2003 provides that various circumstances should be taken into account, including representations she makes and her ability to maintain herself. Any bland assumption that all husbands, whatever their actual circumstances, can be treated differently from all wives is unjustifiable, particularly after ECtHR cases such as *Abdulaziz* (1985).

In considering the decision to deport or administratively remove, r 364 provides guidance as to the factors to be taken into account: these include balancing the public interest against any compassionate circumstances of the case. While each case will be considered in the light of the particular circumstances, the aim is an exercise of the power to deport or remove which is consistent and fair as between one person and another, although one case will rarely be identical with another in all material respects. However, as will be seen, the HRA 1998 will complicate the situation somewhat, since the leading relevant cases have been decided on the basis of what is fair on those particular facts, rather than a scrutiny of the rules and procedures themselves.

Deportation due to conviction of a criminal offence is fairly readily resorted to, but, as the Court of Appeal held in *Nazari* (1980) (building on *Caird* (1970)), no court should 'make an order recommending deportation without full inquiry into all the circumstances. It should not be done, as has sometimes happened in the past ... as if by an afterthought at the end of observations about any sentence of imprisonment'. A number of factors were identified which a court might bear in mind when considering deportation: any criminal record of the accused; the seriousness and circumstances of the offence; the effect that an order recommending deportation (or now removal) will have on others who are not before the court, and who are innocent persons, in terms of hardship and breaking up of families. The court should not, however, take into account the nature of the regime to which the deportee will return. This is a matter for the Home Secretary at the time of deportation who must, of course, take into account the deportee's Convention right not to be sent to a country in which they might suffer death or torture, etc.

In *Serry* (1980), a single offence of shoplifting was found insufficiently serious, presumably because there were no particular aggravating circumstances. An important circumstance will be the likelihood of the repetition of the offence; where this factor is present, it may aggravate an otherwise trivial offence; where it is absent, it may have a mitigating effect on a serious offence. As *B v Secretary of State for the Home Department* (2000) (below) demonstrates, under the HRA, the proportionality test must be applied and this requires greater regard to all the individual circumstances of the case. In *Aramide v Secretary of State for the Home Department* (2000), the

Court of Appeal held that the seriousness of the criminal offence (to be judged by the sentence actually given, not in a general manner) must be carefully balanced against the applicant's family ties. In *R v Stefanski (Artur)* (2002), it was confirmed that a court should not be influenced by the defendant's immigration status but may need to make inquiries to ensure that prejudicial assumptions are not made.

The 'conducive to public good' ground for deportation can be used where a person is convicted of an offence, but the court does not recommend deportation in respect of persons who have engaged in criminal activity abroad (*Martinez-Tobon v IAT* (1988)). The use of this power to exclude people on political rather than criminal grounds has attracted the most criticism. For example, the former militant student leader, Rudi Deutschke, was deported in 1969 on the basis that he might 'become a focus for student unrest'. Similarly, the journalists Agee and Hosenball were deported on national security grounds, Agee presumably due to the damage he might have done to the CIA in writing books exposing certain of their activities (*Secretary of State for the Home Department ex p Hosenball* (1977)). Rather flimsy grounds were also, it seems, relied upon in making the decision to deport a number of Iraqi or Kuwaiti residents during the Gulf War in 1991, a policy apparently not followed during the Iraq War of 2003. Anti-terrorism policy is said to justify the deportation or, where this is not legally possible, the detention of foreign terrorist suspects. This is further discussed below.

An aspect of the controversial nature of this power is that it seems that it can be used as an alternative to extradition, where, for example, there is no power to extradite or to avoid the protections, such as they are, in the extradition process. In *Brixton Prison Governor ex p Soblen* (1963), a deportation order was challenged on the grounds that the Secretary of State had acted for an improper purpose – allegedly in order to comply with a request from the US for S's return, made in order to circumvent the non-availability of extradition proceedings which were not possible due to the nature of S's alleged offences (conspiracy to commit espionage). The Court of Appeal upheld the deportation order on the basis that the Secretary of State could act for a plurality of purposes, though these had to include a genuine belief that removal was necessary for the public good. It did not matter if the Minister's main motive for acting might have been to comply with the request from the US. Since the Home Secretary had (and still has) an unfettered discretion regarding where to deport a person to, he did not need to consider deporting S to Czechoslovakia (which was willing to take him).

The danger in this approach is clearly that the individual circumstances of the person in question may become much less significant than the political expediency of falling in with the wishes of particular governments. However, there have been indications that such an approach is no longer justifiable, especially since ECHR rights (particularly Arts 8, 3 and 5) must always be considered in relation to any proposed deportation. Any deportation decision must now meet the Convention test of proportionality. There is some uncertainty regarding the extent to which the court must make its own judgment on what proportionality demands in any particular case. In *B v Secretary of State for the Home Department* (2000), the Court of Appeal decided that the applicant had a right both to freedom of movement (he was an EU national) and to family life under the Convention, and that, in the particular circumstances, these rights outweighed any pressing need for deportation. In *R (Samaroo) v Secretary of State for the Home Department* (2001), on the other hand (a decision to deport a Guyanese man despite compassionate factors), the Court of Appeal, whilst reserving ultimate authority to itself, seemed most concerned to ensure that the Home Secretary had made a reasonable decision on proportionality; one that was fully aware and compliant with the range of human rights issues; arguably it focused more on the procedure by which the decision was taken than on the outcome.

The 'public good' head of deportation can cover a number of widely different factors, but it seems reasonably clear that the decision to deport should be based on all the circumstances relevant to the particular evil in question and the likely consequences flowing from any deportation. Thus, in *IAT ex p (Mahmud) Khan* (1983), the applicant successfully challenged the Immigration Appeal Tribunal (IAT)'s dismissal of his appeal against deportation, on the ground that the Tribunal's reason for its decision – that he had entered into a marriage of convenience – failed to show that it had properly considered whether the couple did intend to live as man and wife. In other words, grounds which might raise an inference that the marriage was merely one of convenience were not examined to see whether this was actually the case. Similarly, it is not enough to show that a person has behaved in an anti-social manner in the past; it must be considered whether future wrongdoing is likely (*IAT ex p Ullah* (1983)).

In considering consequences flowing from the deportation, it would appear that detriment flowing from it to the public or part of the public as well as the good may be considered: the two may be balanced against each other. Thus, in *Singh v IAT* (1986), the House of Lords held that the immigration adjudicatory authorities ought to have taken into account the detrimental effect on the Sikh community in the UK which deportation of the applicant would have. The applicant was a valued member of that community by virtue of his religious, charitable and cultural activities. In *Rehman v Secretary of State for the Home Department* (2001), the first case to be appealed from a decision of the Special Immigration Appeals Commission (SIAC), the House of Lords considered when deportation could be justified on the basis of national security grounds. The applicant had been refused indefinite leave to remain and a deportation order had been issued by the Home Secretary. The SIAC found that the Home Secretary had defined 'national security' too widely, and stated that a person could be said to have offended against national security if he had engaged in, promoted or encouraged violent activity which affected the security of the UK or its nationals, wherever they might be. Applying the test of a 'high civil balance of probabilities', the SIAC then found that the Secretary of State had not shown that the applicant was a threat to national security. The House of Lords upheld the Court of Appeal's decision and found that the security of all States is intertwined and so a threat against State B may justify a person's deportation from State A. The SIAC's approach had been too narrow: if a person had been engaged in violent activity which involved a real possibility of either direct or indirect adverse repercussions upon the security of the UK, then deportation was justified. It does not have to be shown to a high standard of probability that the person in question has performed any individual act which would justify the conclusion that he was a threat to national security. In the anti-terrorism context, it was appropriate for the reviewing court to show considerable deference to the executive on national security threats.

Appeal rights against deportation decisions have been developed over the years, but there have been major changes to the appeal system, introduced by the NIAA 2002, which may make appeals harder for some applicants. Under s 82, most deportation decisions can be appealed against to an adjudicator and then, if there are grounds, to a tribunal. An important change made by the 2002 Act is to increase the number of appeals that can only be made from outside the UK, which considerably increases the burden on applicants. Human rights violations are amongst the grounds for appeal (s 84(1)(c)) and so Arts 3, 5 and particularly 8 of Sched 1 to the HRA are likely to figure in future appeals. Human rights appeals can still be made from within the UK unless the Home Secretary certifies that the grounds are without foundation.

A person to be removed on public good grounds enjoys the right of appeal unless the decision was made by the Home Secretary on 'national security' grounds or on reliance on information which ought not to be disclosed in court. In those circumstances, there is a right of appeal to the SIAC before which the applicant has only the most limited rights. It can, for example, decide a case on the basis of evidence not disclosed to the applicant.

Where deportation is impossible because, following *Chahal v UK* (1996), the deportee might suffer torture, etc, in violation of Art 3, UK law (the Anti-Terrorism, Crime and Security Act 2001) permits a person to be detained indefinitely, without trial, if the Home Secretary certifies that he or she is suspected of being a non-British international terrorist. To facilitate this, the

UK has derogated from Art 5 of the ECHR in the context of the 'war on terrorism'. This is a highly controversial power but one that has been upheld, on appeal from SIAC, by the Court of Appeal.

The law on deportation has undergone significant change in recent years, especially in relation to asylum claims. The law and the administrative and appeal procedures are designed expressly to take account of the Convention rights (both refugee and ECHR) of potential deportees and in that respect it can be said that individuals are treated fairly. It is clear, however, that overall the balance between the individual and the State remains firmly weighted in favour of the latter – a matter which is most clearly illustrated where national security issues are involved.

Question 38

'The current arrangements for considering the claims of asylum seekers suggest that the UK respects the letter of the Geneva Convention, but not its spirit.' Do you agree?

Answer plan

This is a relatively straightforward essay question. It is particularly topical at a time when the number of asylum seekers is rapidly increasing, and there has been a great deal of recent statutory and case law on the subject.

Essentially, the following matters should be discussed:

* the Geneva Convention of 1951, as amended by the 1967 Protocol;
* key provisions of the Immigration and Asylum Act (IAA) 1999, the Nationality, Immigration and Asylum Act (NIAA) 2002 and the Immigration Rules relating to asylum seekers;
* the appeals procedure under the 2002 Act and 2000 Rules.

Answer

The UK accepts certain international obligations in respect of asylum seekers under the Geneva Convention of 1951, as amended by the 1967 Protocol relating to the Status of Refugees (which allowed the Convention to apply to those who became refugees due to events occurring after 1 January 1951). This is reflected in the Immigration Rules and the Asylum and Immigration Appeals Act 1993, although neither the Convention nor the Protocol have been enacted directly into the law of the UK. Rule 334 of the Immigration Rules provides that immigrants:

> ... will be granted asylum in the UK if the Secretary of State is satisfied that ... refusing his application would result in his being required to go (whether immediately or after the time limited by an existing leave to enter or remain) in breach of the Convention and Protocol, to a country in which his life or freedom would be threatened on account of his race, religion, nationality, political opinion or membership of a particular social group.

Section 2 of the Asylum and Immigration Appeals Act 1993 states that nothing shall be laid down in the immigration rules which would be contrary to the Geneva Convention.

The Convention and Protocol are concerned only with political asylum seekers and this is reflected in the ambit of r 334, so that those fleeing from famine or disaster are not covered. Sometimes, it may be hard to make this distinction when a person leaves a country which is in the middle of a civil war. The applicant must belong to a group which is likely to be persecuted and this will include a 'social group'. In *Islam v Secretary of State for the Home Department* (1999), the House of Lords found that a group of Pakistani women who had been falsely accused of adultery could claim refugee status under the Geneva Convention, since they were a group of people unprotected by their own State; there is no requirement of cohesiveness or indeed of minority status for persons to constitute a 'group'. In *Adan (Lul Omar) v Secretary of State for the Home Department* (2000), the House of Lords stated that, on a correct interpretation of the Convention, a well-founded fear of persecution could be based on the activities of non-State groups where the State was unable or unwilling to give adequate protection, though in *Horvath v Secretary of State for the Home Department* (2001), the need to show the failure of the State to give protection was emphasised.

The obligation not to remove or return refugees will not apply if either of two circumstances is present: the refugee may be reasonably regarded as constituting a threat to the security of the country he is in; alternatively, he may represent a danger to the particular community in that country, a finding that will be made if the refugee has been convicted of a grave crime. It should be noted that, under the Terrorism Act 2000, the definition of 'threats to national security' may stretch far beyond terrorist activity and may encompass environmental and political agitation.

A duty to grant asylum is not directly imposed, but if no safe alternative destination can be found for the asylum seeker, the country in question will have to grant asylum. Under the Convention, the refugee must be given time to find a safe third country. If a person seeks asylum, the case must be referred by the immigration officer to the Home Office for decision, even though it appears that the claim is unjustified. The Home Office will consider the case in accordance with the provisions of the Convention and Protocol relating to the Status of Refugees, and the claimant will not be removed until the Home Office has considered the case.

In making a decision, the Home Secretary may take into account guidance given by the advisory Executive Committee to the High Commissioner for Refugees, an office established in 1951 within the framework of the General Assembly of the United Nations, as to the interpretation of the Convention and Protocol (*Bugdaycay v Secretary of State* (1987); *IAT ex p Yassine* (1990)). If an interpretation of the Immigration Rules is adopted which does not conform with the Convention, the decision may be quashed for 'illegality' or 'irrationality' as happened in *Bugdaycay*; it may also now be quashed under s 2 of the 1993 Act.

In *Bugdaycay*, the applicant was a Ugandan refugee whose father and cousins had been killed by the secret police and who therefore feared for his life if he should return to Uganda. He had lived in Kenya and the Home Secretary, in rejecting his claim for asylum, determined to deport him there, regardless of the fact that Kenya had been known to return such refugees to Uganda. The House of Lords found that when the Immigration Rules were interpreted in accordance with Art 33 of the Geneva Convention, it was found that the decision to deport him would be a breach: although deportation to Kenya would not directly threaten his life, it might lead to such a threat, due to the probability that Kenya would deport the applicant.

Under the HRA and the developing principles of administrative law, the courts must apply a 'proportionality' test. This should involve a closer examination of the public good served by deportation when balanced with the interference with the applicant's liberty. This may involve the courts in being more demanding of the executive than under the old *Wednesbury* rule where the Home Secretary needed only to show that there was some evidence to support his findings (*R (Daly) v Secretary of State for the Home Department* (2001)).

The term 'persecution' in Art 1(A) of the Convention has been interpreted fairly restrictively by the English courts as meaning 'to pursue with malignancy', 'to oppress for holding a heretical opinion or belief' (*IAT ex p Jonah* (1985)). Under this strict interpretation, 'harassment' will not always be enough. The House of Lords in *Secretary of State for the Home Department ex p Sivakumaran* (1988) laid down the test for determining whether the fear of persecution is well-founded. Once it appears that the applicant genuinely fears persecution, the Secretary of State is required to ask himself, on the basis of all the available information, whether there has been demonstrated a 'real likelihood' or, as in *Fernandez v Government of Singapore* (1971), a 'reasonable chance' of persecution.

The applicant has the burden of proving that there are grounds for thinking that persecution may occur. However, information may be taken into account of which he or she is unaware. Thus, the fear must be based on reasonable grounds, objectively assessed and it appears that the question for a tribunal is whether a fear of persecution would have been felt by an objective observer in possession of all the available information.

The emphasis of this test differs from that put forward by the High Commissioner, which involves asking whether, subjectively, a real fear of persecution is present and then considering whether it is a fear no one would reasonably hold. The test put forward by the House of Lords therefore provided less protection for refugees and, moreover, the imprecise nature of expressions such as 'real likelihood' leaves considerable latitude for differences of opinion as to the severity of the risk of persecution.

The fact that all the available information must be considered may, of course, work to the advantage of the applicant, as it will mean that a court cannot disregard any piece of information: this will include what has happened in the past, which should be related to any current events, although the mere fact that an asylum seeker has been persecuted in the past will not raise a presumption in his favour that he is a refugee (*Secretary of State for the Home Department ex p Direk* (1992)). Recent cases seem to be applying a new, lower threshold for asylum. In *Karanakaran v Secretary of State for the Home Department* (2000), the Court of Appeal held that, when considering whether there was a serious possibility of persecution if an asylum seeker were returned, it was wrong to exclude matter totally from consideration simply because the decision maker did not consider that it had been proved on the balance of probabilities. In asylum cases, no such burden or standard of proof arises; the relevant question is simply whether, taking all relevant matters into account, it would be unduly harsh to return the asylum seeker. Similarly, the courts are stressing the importance of adjudicators making an all-round consideration of the facts rather than accepting a narrow, formalistic, interpretation of the rules. In *R (Sivakumar) v Secretary of State for the Home Department* (2003), for example, the evidence was that the applicant, a Tamil, had been horribly tortured by the Sri Lankan authorities as part of an investigation into terrorist acts. The Home Secretary contended that torture in furtherance of a terrorist investigation fell outside the protection of the Convention. This was rejected by the House of Lords, which held that the issue was whether, on a full view of the facts, the persecution might, in reality, be on Convention grounds such as race or membership of a social group.

One aspect of asylum claims, which has come into greater prominence in recent years, relates to the ECHR. Although refugees receive no direct protection under the main body of the Convention or under the HRA, asylum seekers' rights have been considered under a variety of Articles. Thus, Art 8, which imposes upon States an obligation to respect an individual's private and family life, might be used to show that family ties would be damaged by denial of an asylum claim when other members of the family are already within the UK. Most importantly, where an asylum claimant can show a risk of persecution or life-threatening conditions, the prohibition of torture and of inhuman or degrading treatment or punishment under Art 3 may arise. Thus, in *Hatami v Sweden* (1998), it was held that, although the right to political asylum is not within the scope of the Convention's protection, to remove an asylum claimant from the jurisdiction after finding his claim to be without foundation could constitute an Art 3 breach. This would be if there were substantial grounds for thinking that the claimant would face a real risk of being subjected to torture or inhuman or degrading treatment or punishment in the receiving country. In such circumstances, Art 3 includes an implied obligation not to expel the claimant to any such country. Further, the activities of the claimant cannot be a relevant consideration in a human rights claim, regardless of how undesirable or dangerous they may have been. *Soering v UK* (1989) and *Vilvarajah v UK* (1992) both confirm that the UK is covered by the implied obligation not to expel any person in such circumstances, although in the latter case, the applicants, a group of Tamils, failed to show a breach of Art 3, since there was only a possibility that they might be detained and ill-treated, rather than a substantial risk. Thus, it can be seen that, in some respects, the Convention is of weaker protection than the Geneva Convention, since the former requires greater likelihood of harm to the applicant.

Rights of appeal for asylum seekers have been revised, in a restrictive manner, under Pt V of the NIAA 2002. Appeal is to an adjudicator and there is a further appeal to the IAT, which has been reconstituted with improved status by the 2002 Act. Grounds of appeal can include that the Geneva Convention has not been followed or that the immigration decision was taken in violation of the applicant's human rights.

Section 92 of the 2002 Act reduces the range of appeals that can be heard in the UK. Some asylum seekers, in any case, have been removed to 'safe countries'. Under ss 11 and 12 of the IAA 1999, the Secretary of State can remove an asylum seeker to one of the Member States of the European Union (EU), all of which are deemed to be 'safe' under s 11(1). This runs counter to the decisions in *Besnik Gashi* (1999), *Lul Omar Adan* (1999) and *Aitseguer* (2000) that France and Germany were not 'safe' because they were not applying the Convention properly.

Section 92 exempts asylum claims where an appeal is made on human rights grounds. These can still be made from inside the UK (s 92(4)). Even here, however, the Secretary of State may certify (s 94(2)) that a claim of either kind is 'clearly unfounded', and again the applicant can only appeal from outside the UK. Since appeals from outside the UK are hard to mount, there may be an argument that an asylum seeker's rights under Art 13 of the ECHR (not a scheduled Convention right in the HRA) are violated. Furthermore, the right of an asylum seeker to mount an appeal from inside the UK is lost if, under s 94(3) and (4), the Home Secretary certifies that the applicant is entitled to reside in one of a list of designated safe countries. This is highly controversial since there is little opportunity to challenge the Secretary of State's judgment that the countries are safe.

Rights of appeal from within the UK are also restricted where the Home Secretary certifies that the appeal issue has already been settled or that its real purpose is delay (s 96).

Clearly, much depends on the certificates made by the Home Secretary, and it should be noted that these are not subject to appeal, though they are subject to judicial review. It remains to be seen whether the 2002 Act and the Rules are interpreted entirely in line with the Geneva Convention, although this is intended to be the case. There must clearly be concern that, given the power, in effect, of the Secretary of State to determine that many asylum appeals can only be mounted from outside the UK, the balance has shifted away from the applicant.

There have been a number of other important developments in the law and administrative practice, which arguably increase the difficulties faced by people wishing to pursue asylum claims in the UK. For example, detention of claimants for fast processing was held to be not incompatible with either the Immigration Act 1971 or Art 5 of the ECHR in *R (Saadi) v Secretary of State for the Home Department* (2002) and, under the NIAA 2002, asylum seekers can be required to reside at 'accommodation centres' in return for welfare support. The 2002 Act also reintroduced measures by which even minimal welfare support from the government could be denied to asylum seekers who did not make their claim as soon as reasonably possible on arriving in the UK. In *R (on the Application of Q and Others) v Secretary of State for the Home Department* (2003), the Court of Appeal held that what was reasonable must be related to the applicant's circumstances and found that some of the procedures used by officials were unfair. However, merely leaving an asylum seeker destitute would not, of itself, violate Art 3 of the ECHR. Government policy seems to be reflecting a degree of antipathy towards asylum seekers. Disproportionate measures in this direction could be incompatible with both the Refugee Convention and the ECHR.

It can be suggested, therefore, that, in formal terms, UK law respects the letter of the Geneva Convention. In particular, Convention rights can be argued on appeal. Nevertheless, there is clear evidence that aspects of asylum law and administrative practice, such as those relating to detention, rights of appeal and welfare, seem to have the effect of making asylum claims harder to make and pursue. In this respect, it may be said that the spirit of the Geneva Convention is being ignored.

Question 39

Miss Shia is a trained specialist gynaecological nurse. In the past, she resided and worked in Entriastan (a non-EU State), where she assisted in the carrying out of abortions. Whilst she was resident there, she was under repeated threats from religious fundamentalists opposed to abortion. When the fundamentalists came to power in a coup, she fled to France. From France, she entered the UK illegally, but is seeking political asylum. Her brother is a student at a UK university and intends to begin a PhD after he has completed his undergraduate studies. Miss Shia is under threat of being sent back to France, but is terrified that other fundamentalist groups unconnected with the Entriastan government may threaten her there. She is also worried that threatened health care cuts in Entriastan would not only cost her a job, but would limit her access to drugs which control her serious asthma.

Advise Miss Shia of her chances of being allowed to remain in the UK.

Answer plan

This problem question deals with a variety of issues relating to the grant of political asylum. Students must be aware of not only the relevant domestic law and practice, but also the Geneva Convention, as amended, and a number of key decisions of the European Court of Human Rights (ECtHR).

Essentially, students should discuss the following issues:

- is Miss Shia a political refugee entitled to asylum under the Geneva Convention 1951?;
- is she a member of a 'particular social group' (*Ouanes* (1998); *Islam* (1999))?;
- is France a 'safe third country' under the Dublin Convention 1990?;
- will ECtHR decisions as to Arts 8 and 3 give her a better chance of asylum or a right to remain in the UK?

Answer

The first question which must be answered is whether Miss Shia is in fact a political asylum seeker. In order to assess this, we must look to the definitions given in the Geneva Convention 1951, which is adopted into domestic law by the Immigration and Asylum Act (IAA) 1999. The Convention provides that a person is an asylum seeker when he:

> ... owing to a well founded fear of being persecuted for reasons of race, religion, nationality, membership of a particular social group or political opinion, is outside the country of his nationality and is unable or, owing to such fear, is unwilling to avail himself of that protection of that country; or who, not having a nationality and being outside the country of his former habitual residence or as a result of such events, is unable or, owing to such fear, is unwilling to return to it.

Hence, the key relevant elements of the test are a well-founded fear of persecution, and that the persecution feared must be on relevant grounds. Miss Shia may try to argue that she has a well-founded fear of persecution, either on a personal level due to any acts from which she had already suffered before she left Entriastan, or as a member of a 'particular social group'. In relation to the former, she is unlikely to succeed, particularly if Entriastan is now a violent country where human rights violations are likely to occur: see *Ward v Secretary of State for the Home Department* (1997), where an individual's torture was found to be 'nothing more than the sort of random difficulties faced by many thousands of people in Peru'. Further, 'solitary individuals do not exhibit cohesiveness, co-operation or interdependence', which were seen to be the requirements for a social group by Lord Justice Staughton in *Islam* (1998). But the fact that the threats which she suffered came from anti-abortion fundamentalists is not in itself a problem, since the persecution need not come from a State source: *R v Secretary of State for the Home Department ex p Bouheraoua and Kerkeb* (2000); the Convention provides protection from persecution by non-State agents, but only if the authorities of the State in question are unwilling or unable to give effective protection (see *Horvath v Secretary of State for the Home Department* (2001)). Thus, Miss Shia has an arguable claim of fear of persecution if she can show that Entriastan fails to offer her a reasonable level of protection. She may argue that she is a 'member of a particular social group' and fears persecution on that basis.

There is some debate as to the correct approach on which to determine this issue. In *Ouanes v Secretary of State for the Home Department* (1998), the claimant was an Algerian citizen who worked as a midwife for the Ministry of Health. Her job included providing contraceptive advice. She had received threats for not wearing a veil in public, and there had been incidents where other midwives similarly employed had been killed by fundamentalists. The

Court of Appeal found that 'government-employed midwives' lacked the degree of cohesiveness required in the earlier case of *Shah* (1997), and that the expression 'particular social group' does not ordinarily cover a body of people linked only by the work that they do. The characteristic which defines a 'particular social group' must be one which members should not be required to change, since it is fundamental to their 'individual identities or conscience'. So, if *Ouanes* is followed, Miss Shia would have great trouble in showing that she is a member of a 'particular social group'. However, there is also the rival approach adopted by the House of Lords in *Islam v Secretary of State for the Home Department* (1999), where Pakistani women were found to be a 'particular social group' within the meaning of Art 1A(2) of the Geneva Convention. The women claimants had both been falsely accused of adultery in Pakistan and feared that if they were returned, they would face criminal proceedings for sexual immorality and could be sentenced to either flogging or stoning to death. The House of Lords found that, although the general low status of women in Pakistan and the high level of violence against women in that society would not, in themselves, give rise to a claim to refugee status, the fact that the State tolerated and partly sanctioned discrimination against women, coupled with the fact that they were not granted the same rights as men, meant that they were a particular social group and so the claimants could satisfy the Geneva Convention test. There was not found to be any requirement of cohesiveness of a 'particular social group'. It is not clear whether a court would find Miss Shia's case sufficiently similar to the facts in *Islam* (1999) for the House of Lords case to be followed in preference to *Ouanes*.

Assuming that she is found to be a member of a relevant particular social group, the next issue to be determined is whether there is a 'safe third country' to which she may be returned under the Dublin Convention 1990. The 1990 Convention provides that the European country in which an asylum seeker first arrived should be the country to determine his application unless, under the 1951 Geneva Convention, that country would not be considered to be a safe third country. Since Miss Shia has travelled to the UK via France, we need to decide whether France could be considered to be a safe third country. In *Secretary of State ex p Aitseguer* (2000), the House of Lords held that France could not automatically be treated as 'safe' because it was not interpreting the 1951 Convention properly. In particular, it did not recognise that the threat of persecution could come from a source other than the State itself. However, under s 11 of the IAA 1999, all member countries of the EU are deemed to be 'safe' for the purposes of dealing with asylum applications and the courts, in cases such as *R (Benda) v Secretary of State for the Home Department (No 1)* (2002), treat this as authority whose effect is to overrule *Aitseguer*.

The only possibility of assistance to Miss Shia in this situation, therefore, comes from the ECHR and the HRA. Although there is no direct or implied right of asylum in either the Convention or the Act, a number of other Articles of the Convention have been employed in certain situations where the removal of an asylum seeker from the jurisdiction would cause exceptional hardship in his or her personal circumstances, or would show a lack of respect for his or her family or private life, or would risk him or her being tortured or otherwise ill-treated on return to his or her home country or to a 'safe' third country. Miss Shia has potential arguments based on each of these lines. First, she might argue under Art 3 that to return her to her home country or to France would risk torture, inhuman or degrading treatment or punishment contrary to Art 3. Cases such as *Chahal v UK* (1997) and *Hatami v Sweden* (1998) have shown that, where there are substantial grounds for believing that there is a real risk that the asylum seeker will be subjected to torture or inhuman or degrading treatment or punishment in the receiving country, then the State who currently has the asylum seeker within its jurisdiction falls under a positive obligation not to expel that person. Secondly, under Art 8, there must be respect for the claimant's right to a private and family life. Since Miss Shia has a brother at university in the UK who intends to be there for an extended period as a postgraduate student, it is arguable that she may have strong family ties within the UK which might be upheld under Art 8. The argument failed in *Ahmut v The Netherlands* (1996) but succeeded in *C v Belgium* (1996). Miss Shia's health could be in issue. Lack of medical treatment in her home country might lead to a violation of Art 3 if she was removed, though the threshold of severity is high (see *D v UK* (1997)). In *Bensaid v UK* (2001), Art 8 was considered in circumstances where continued bad health would undermine private and family life. Again, the threshold is high and the ECtHR accepted that immigration control is a valid reason for restrictions under Art 8(2). Neither argument would be effective if Miss Shia was to be returned to France, a country with adequate treatment for asthma.

There are clearly some uncertainties in the law, particularly the human rights points. Miss Shia may have to use the new appeal procedure under the Nationality, Immigration and Asylum Act (NIAA) 2002. This would allow her to pursue her human rights claim whilst remaining in the UK unless the Home Secretary certifies that her claim is clearly unfounded. The Court of Appeal, in *R (Razgar) v Secretary of State for the Home Department (No 2)* (2003), has said that such a certificate can be issued if, but only if, the Home Secretary is satisfied that the human rights claim will fail. The uncertainties in this case suggest that the Home Secretary could not be so satisfied in Miss Shia's case.

Question 40

In what ways can a person faced with an order for deportation from the UK challenge that decision? To what extent does the law in this area comply with the UK's international obligations?

Answer plan

The first part of this question requires you to explain the various procedures for appeal that exist at common law or under the immigration legislation. In particular, you will need to deal with:

- habeas corpus;
- judicial review;
- appeal under the Nationality, Immigration and Asylum Act (NIAA) 2002 and the Special Immigration Appeals Commission Act 1997;
- challenge under the HRA 1998.

As far as appeals under the immigration legislation are concerned, the special provisions relating to asylum seekers will need to be noted.

In relation to the second part of the question, the most obvious international obligations arise under:

- the Geneva Convention on the Status of Refugees 1951;
- the European Convention on Human Rights (ECHR).

The first of these is particularly relevant to the way in which appeals for asylum are treated; the Convention is, of course, more generally relevant, and the discussion of this area will obviously be closely linked to the section of your answer to the first part of the question which deals with the HRA.

Answer

All those who do not have a 'right of abode' in the UK, as defined by the Immigration Act 1971, are liable to deportation. The grounds on which such deportation can be ordered are to be found in s 3 of the 1971 Act, as amended by the Immigration and Asylum Act (IAA) 1999. They include being convicted of a criminal offence (this only applies to adults), having a family member who is subject to a deportation order, or where the Secretary of State deems that the deportation would be 'conducive to the public good'. Slightly more restricted grounds apply to citizens of Member States of the European Economic Area in order to give recognition to the rights of free movement within that area.

There are four possible methods for challenging deportation decisions – habeas corpus, judicial review, appeal under provisions contained in the immigration legislation and challenge under the HRA.

Where a person is being detained prior to deportation, then the action for the writ of habeas corpus might be used. This is the traditional common law remedy by which a person's release from detention by the executive can be achieved. It is sought by means of an application to the High Court, which takes precedence over all other actions. It is only concerned with jurisdiction, however, rather than the substance of a decision, so its use is limited. In *Secretary of State ex p Cheblak* (1991), for example, it was held that the Secretary of State did not need to give reasons for a decision that deportation would benefit 'national security'. Further, in *Secretary of State ex p Rahman* (1997), it was held that the Home Secretary was, in making his decision, entitled to rely on evidence which in ordinary legal proceedings would clearly amount to hearsay, and therefore would be inadmissible. Other methods of challenge rather than habeas corpus are therefore more likely to be effective.

A second possible route of challenge is by judicial review. The decision to deport and the procedures which have led to it are clearly administrative acts which are susceptible to such challenge. The broad wording of the statutory powers means that the decision will be subject to a 'proportionality' test (*R (Daly) v Secretary of State for the Home Department* (2001)), which requires particularly anxious scrutiny by the courts if there is a human rights challenge. However, it was said in *Daly* that 'context is all' and it remains likely that, especially where national security is in issue, the customary high level of deference shown by the courts to the executive (as in *Secretary of State ex p Hosenball* (1977), for example) will continue. In recent times, the point is best illustrated in the SIAC appeal cases which are mentioned later. Outside the national security context, the courts are prepared to judicially review executive decisions involving the deportation process. In *R (I) v Secretary of State for the Home Department* (2002), for example, the Home Secretary had detained the applicant under the Immigration Act 1971 pending deportation. Various factors, including the political impossibility of returning the applicant to Afghanistan, meant that deportation was becoming less and less likely. The Court of Appeal held that continued detention was unlawful, it was not reasonable to detain for the purpose of deportation.

The main route of appeal, however, will be to use the procedures set out in the immigration legislation. The NIAA 2002 gives a right of appeal to an immigration adjudicator and thence to the IAT. This does not apply, however, where the decision follows a recommendation of a court before which the applicant has been convicted of an offence (an appeal through the criminal process being the appropriate remedy), or where the decision is to deport on the basis that this would be conducive to the public good on grounds of national security (this being subject to a special procedure, outlined below). The adjudicator or the IAT can review the facts, the legality of the decision, and the way in which any discretion has been exercised. In other words, it is a full reconsideration of the substance of the decision, and not simply a review of the process (as with judicial review). The decisions of the adjudicator or IAT (unless appealed) are binding on the Secretary of State.

Deportations on national security grounds are not subject to these rights of appeal. Originally they could be reviewed by three 'advisors' in a secretive process that was strongly criticised by the ECtHR in *Chahal v UK* (1997). Such appeals now go to the SIAC, under the Special Immigration Appeals Commission Act (SIACA) 1997. The procedure still gives rise to major concerns. The SIAC has three members, including a judge and an experienced immigration adjudicator. The appellant may be excluded from seeing some evidence or being present at part of the proceedings on public interest grounds. If this happens, a 'special advocate' will be appointed by the Attorney General to represent the appellant's interests. The SIAC now has the full powers of the High Court and can review and overturn deportation decisions. However, an appeal on a point of law may be taken by either side to the Court of Appeal. In *Secretary of State for the Home Department v Rehman* (2001), the House of Lords, upholding the Court of Appeal's decision, took a broader view than the SIAC of what could be prejudicial to national security, holding that it could cover international terrorism which had no direct impact on the UK. Under the Anti-Terrorism, Crime and Security Act 2001, the SIAC can also review the indefinite detention of foreign 'terrorist suspects' who, for legal reasons such as the likely violation of their Art 3 rights in the receiving country, cannot be deported. In *A v Secretary of State for the Home Department* (2002), the SIAC was again overturned by the Court of Appeal, here on the issue of whether confining the detention power to foreigners was discriminatory.

Asylum seekers can appeal against deportation decisions or, if they have been given leave to stay, against the refusal of their asylum claim. Section 84 of the NIAA 2002 provides, as one of the grounds of appeal, that the deportation would be contrary to the applicant's human rights or rights under the Geneva Convention on the Status of Refugees 1951 (the 1951 Convention). Unlike many immigration appeals, asylum and/or human rights appeals can be made from within the UK (s 92(4)(a)). There are significant exceptions. Appeal from within the UK does not apply where the removal is to a 'safe' country, and all Member States of the EU are deemed to be 'safe' (even though the English courts have recently ruled that France and Germany were not applying the 1951 Convention properly, and were not therefore 'safe', for example, in *Lul Omar Adan* (1999)). A right to remain in order to appeal will also be lost if the Home Secretary certifies that any human rights or asylum claim being made is 'clearly unfounded' or that the applicant is entitled to reside in one of a number of so-called safe countries listed in s 94(4).

There are also provisions in the NIAA 2002 to ensure that consecutive appeals are not allowed, that all relevant grounds are introduced in one appeal and that the right of appeal is lost if the executive certifies that its real purpose is delay (s 96). The power of the authorities to restrict the right of appeal by issuing certificates on the matters mentioned are only subject to judicial review.

The fourth basis for an appeal against deportation would be by means of a direct challenge under s 7 of the HRA. The most likely Articles on which to rely would be Art 3 or Art 8. HRA arguments are likely to be raised in connection with an application for judicial review, or an appeal under the NIAA 2002 or the SIACA 1997. As has been noted, the NIAA 2002 allows the executive to certify a human rights claim as being clearly unfounded, thus forcing the appeal to be made abroad. The question of whether these are compatible with the UK's obligations under the ECHR is considered below.

Turning to the UK's international obligations in this area, there are two relevant treaties: the 1951 Convention and the ECHR. The obligation under the 1951 Convention is that a person should not be returned to a country where there is a well-founded fear that he or she would face 'persecution' for reasons of, for example, race, nationality, political opinion, or membership of a particular social group. 'Persecution' is a strong word meaning more than harassment or discrimination. As far as 'social group' is concerned, it was held in *Islam v Secretary of State for the Home Department* (1999) that 'women' could constitute a 'social group' in the context of their potential return to Pakistan, because of the institutionalised State-sanctioned discrimination against them, which might lead to their being flogged or stoned to death for adultery under Sharia law (areas of incompatibility between Sharia law and human rights have been highlighted in *Refah Partisi v Turkey* (2003)). The current UK law on immigration clearly does pay attention to this obligation, as indicated by ss 1 and 2 of the Asylum and Immigration Appeals Act 1993. As we have seen, special provisions exist to deal with the claims of asylum seekers. What must be open to question, however, are the current rules on what amounts to a 'safe' country to which to return an asylum seeker. As has been noted, under the IAA 1999, all Member States of the EU are deemed to be safe, despite the fact that there have been very recent court decisions holding that various of them are failing to implement the 1951 Convention properly. However, for the Court of Appeal, the critical point is not how the law is interpreted but whether, in reality, a person would be deported from a Member State to a country where they might be persecuted (*R (Yogathas) v Secretary of State for the Home Department* (2002)). The reforms to the appeal process are likely to maintain, if not make lower, the already very low success rate of asylum appeals.

A broader set of obligations is placed on the UK by the Convention, and these must, of course, now be taken into account by our courts under the HRA. The Articles which are most relevant to this area are Arts 3 and 8. In *Chahal v UK* (1997), for example, the applicant was a Sikh activist who had been ordered to be deported to India. It was held that there was sufficient evidence of the risk that the applicant would suffer treatment falling within Art 3 ('torture or inhuman or degrading treatment') to find that his deportation to that country would be contrary to his rights under the Convention. Moreover, the failure at that time to provide a proper route of appeal when the deportation was on grounds of national security was a breach of the right to challenge detention decisions (under Art 5(4)) and a right to a remedy under Art 13 (the SIAC, discussed above, was introduced following this decision). It must be remembered, however, that Art 3 only protects a person from actions with very severe consequences.

Article 8 requires the authorities to respect private and family life. Deporting someone who has lived in the UK for a long time and who is dependent on family here could amount to a breach of this Article. Article 8 can also be engaged by deportations of the seriously ill, which, by affecting physical and moral integrity, affect private life. Possibly a lower level of severity is required than under Art 3 (see *Bensaid v UK* (2001), followed by English courts in *R (N) v Secretary of State for the Home Department* (2003)). Of course Art 8, unlike Art 3, is qualified, in that certain legitimate grounds for infringement are recognised in Art 8(2). It may well be possible, therefore, for a deportation to be argued to be necessary in the interests of, for example, national security, preventing crime or in the interests of the economic wellbeing of the country.

Immigration officials, immigration adjudicators, the courts and the Home Secretary will, since they are all 'public bodies' for the purposes of the HRA, have to keep the above Articles in mind when dealing with deportation decisions. To that extent, the UK does now give proper attention to its obligations under the Convention. What is more difficult to justify is that although the NIAA 2002 specifically recognises the right to challenge decisions on the HRA, there are restrictions built in. There must be doubts, for example, that the executive's power to certify a human rights claim 'clearly unfounded' is compatible with Art 6 (right to a fair trial), since the consequent requirement of such certificates, that deportees can only pursue their appeals from outside the jurisdiction, must raise doubts as to whether a fair trial is being guaranteed.

In conclusion, there are various routes for appeal against deportation. Current UK law allows a claimed violation of either Convention as a ground of appeal that is still exercisable in the UK. As indicated above, however, important issues remain, particularly over the certification powers of the Secretary of State over matters such as 'safe' countries and whether Convention claims are well-founded. It may be expected that there will be further challenges to certain aspects of the system, either in the UK courts or, failing that, in Strasbourg.

Question 41

'A political refugee has a far greater chance of success in avoiding deportation under the European Convention on Human Rights 1950 than under existing domestic law.'

Discuss.

Answer plan

This question requires discussion of a variety of issues relating to the grant of political asylum. Students must be aware of not only the relevant domestic law and practice, but also the Geneva Convention as amended and a number of key decisions of the European Court of Human RIghts (ECtHR).

Essentially, students should discuss the following issues:

- when is a political refugee entitled to asylum under the Geneva Convention 1951?;
- the definition of 'particular social group' (*Ouanes* (1998); *Islam* (1999));
- the relevance of a 'safe third country' under the Dublin Convention 1990;
- will ECtHR decisions as to Art 8 and Art 3 give a better chance of asylum or a right to remain in the UK?

Answer

In any application for asylum, the first question is whether the applicant in fact falls within the definition of a political asylum seeker. This requires considering the definitions given in the Geneva Convention 1951, which is adopted into domestic law by the Immigration and Asylum Act (IAA) 1999. The Convention provides that a person is an asylum seeker when he or she:

> ... owing to a well founded fear of being persecuted for reasons of race, religion, nationality, membership of a particular social group or political opinion, is outside the country of his nationality and is unable or, owing to such fear, is unwilling to avail himself of that protection of that country; or who, not having a nationality and being outside the country of his former habitual residence or as a result of such events, is unable or, owing to such fear, is unwilling to return to it.

Hence, the key relevant elements of the test are a well-founded fear of persecution and that the persecution feared must be on relevant grounds. It is not sufficient that the applicant has a well-founded fear of persecution on a personal level, perhaps because they happen to come from a lawless country. What is required is, rather, that the applicant is likely to suffer persecution as a member of a 'particular social group'. Being a trade unionist threatened by right-wing paramilitary groups could, for example, be the basis of a claim (*R v IAT ex p Walteros-Castenda* (2000)).

Further, 'solitary individuals do not exhibit cohesiveness, co-operation or interdependence', which were seen to be the requirements for a social group by Staughton LJ in *Islam* (1998). The persecution need not come from a State source (*R v Secretary of State for the Home Department ex p Bouheraoua and Kerkeb* (2000)); the Convention provides protection from persecution by non-State agents if the authorities of the State in question are unwilling or unable to give effective protection. Persecuted Roma in Slovakia were not protected by the Convention, since the Slovakian authorities would offer protection (*Horvath v Secretary of State for the Home Department* (2001)). There is some debate as to the correct approach on which to determine the issue of what constitutes a 'particular social group'. In *Ouanes v Secretary of State for the Home Department* (1998), the plaintiff was an Algerian citizen who worked as a midwife for the Ministry of Health. Her job included providing contraceptive advice. She had received threats for not wearing a veil in public and there had been incidents where other midwives similarly employed had been killed by fundamentalists. The Court of Appeal found that 'government-employed midwives' lacked the required degree of cohesiveness for membership of a 'particular social group' and that the term does not ordinarily cover a body of people linked only by the work that they do. The characteristic which defines a 'particular social group' must be one which members should not be required to change, since it is fundamental to their 'individual identities or conscience'. However, the House of Lords adopted a more open approach in *Islam v Secretary of State for the Home Department* (1999), where Pakistani women were found to be a 'particular social group' within the meaning of Art 1A(2) of the Geneva Convention. The women claimants had both been falsely accused of adultery in Pakistan and feared that if they were returned, they would face criminal proceedings for sexual immorality and could be sentenced to either flogging or stoning to death. The House of Lords found that, although the general low status of women in Pakistan and the high level of violence against women in that society would not, in themselves, give rise to a claim to refugee status, the fact that the State tolerated and partly sanctioned discrimination against women, coupled with the fact that they were not granted the same rights as men, meant that they were a particular social group, and so the claimants could satisfy the Geneva Convention test. There was not found to be any requirement of cohesiveness of a 'particular social group'.

A welcome tendency is a recognition by the courts that they should avoid an overly legalistic approach and seek, rather, to give effect to the point of the Convention. Thus, in *R (Sivakumar) v Secretary of State for the Home Department* (2003), the applicant had been tortured as a suspected Tamil Tiger. The House of Lords held that, if all the realities of the situation were considered, what was, in a formal sense, persecution for being a terrorist suspect could in fact be seen as persecution for one of the Geneva Convention reasons.

The next issue to be determined is whether there is a 'safe third country' to which he or she may be returned under the Dublin Convention 1990. The 1990 Convention provides that the European country in which an asylum seeker first arrived should be the country to determine his application unless, under the Geneva Convention, that country would not be considered to be a safe third country. As far as Member States of the EU are concerned, that issue is now determined by s 11 of the IAA 1999, which deems all of them to be 'safe' for these purposes. Though the UK courts have held that France and Germany do not apply aspects of the refugee Convention properly (for example, *Adan (Lul Omar)* (2000)), the House of Lords has also held that it is reasonable to consider these countries as safe since, in practice, they will not return applicants to face persecution in the receiving country (*R (Yogathas) v Secretary of State for the Home Department* (2002)). As regards States which are not members of the EU, a judgment must be made in each case. A right, certified by the Home Secretary, to reside in one of a number of listed, allegedly safe, countries means that an asylum seeker suffers the disadvantage of being unable to appeal from inside the UK – s 94(3) of the Nationality, Immigration and Asylum Act (NIAA) 2002.

The final possibility of aid to a political asylum seeker comes from the ECHR and the HRA. Although there is no direct or implied right of asylum in either the Convention or the Act, Arts 3 and 8 in particular have been used to challenge asylum and deportation decisions. Following the HRA, of course, asylum legislation must, so far as it is possible to do so, be interpreted in a way which is compatible with the scheduled Convention rights, and the officials involved, including adjudicators and the tribunals, must, as public authorities, act compatibly with Convention rights. UK courts must take the approach of the Strasbourg Court into account.

A number of cases, such as *Chahal v UK* (1997), have shown that Art 3 (the right not to suffer torture or inhuman or degrading treatment or punishment) imposes an obligation of signatory States not to deport a person if there are substantial grounds for believing that they will suffer torture or some other violation of their Art 3 rights in the receiving State. In *Jabari v Turkey* (2000), the ECtHR held it would violate Art 3 to deport a woman to Iran where she would be subject to fierce and cruel laws on adultery and in *Hilal v UK* (2001), the applicant successfully challenged the view of UK courts that it was acceptable to return someone to a 'safe' part of a country even though they were at risk of death and torture in another part of the country. Article 3, however, is only violated in respect of the most severe conditions.

Claimants may also seek the protection of Art 8 (respect for private and family life). Respect for 'family life' has been invoked by deportees with strong family ties to the signatory State. There has been variable success: in *Ahmut v The Netherlands* (1996), the argument failed, but it succeeded in *C v Belgium* (1996). The deportation of the seriously ill to a country where any treatment will be inadequate can, in the most serious cases, violate Art 3 (*D v UK* (1997)). Less serious cases can try and invoke Art 8 where it has been held that the need to respect for 'private life' is, arguably, applicable in respect of proposed deportation of claimants who are physically or mentally ill (*Bensaid v UK* (2001)), and there may be a lower threshold of harm than required by Art 3. Of course, any claim brought under Art 8 is likely to meet a government argument that the interference with family and private life is lawful, for a legitimate purpose and proportionate in terms of the second paragraph. Immigration control is accepted by Strasbourg as a legitimate purpose for interfering with private life (if it is in the economic interests of the country, for example) and so the issue tends to be resolved on the issue of proportionality and the particular facts of any case.

Through its development of Arts 3 and 8 in particular, the ECHR increases the grounds on which a refugee may avoid deportation. In particular, returning someone to a country in which their Art 3 rights are violated is, itself, a violation of the Convention. Current immigration and asylum law in the UK aims to be compatible with both the Geneva Convention and the ECHR. That a deportation would violate the Geneva Convention or be incompatible with the ECHR is, for example, a ground of appeal under the NIAA 2002. The two sets of rules, from the Geneva Convention and from the ECHR, now operate in tandem. This may add to the confusion facing asylum seekers and professionals working in this field. Perhaps it is time for wide-ranging reform so that the Geneva Convention and the ECHR case law can be given a better degree of fit, so that the rights in the Geneva Convention and those in Arts 3 and 8 of the ECHR are more successfully related together.

CHAPTER 8

FREEDOM FROM DISCRIMINATION

Introduction

Examiners tend to set essays in this area which focus not only on the provisions of the Sex Discrimination Act 1975, the Race Relations Act 1976 and the Disability Discrimination Act 1995, but also on the relevant European Union (EU) provisions. The Sex Discrimination Act and the Race Relations Act have recently been amended as a result of the implementation of EU Directives, with a view to improving the position of individual applicants who are bringing claims. Discrimination on grounds of sexual orientation in employment is covered from December 2003 by the Employment Equality (Sexual Orientation) Regulations 2003 implementing European Council Directive 2000/78/EC. Discrimination in employment, but also in other spheres, on this ground can also be addressed in certain circumstances by using the Human Rights Act (HRA) 1998. The new Regulations and the use of the HRA in this way are new and very significant developments.

This area of law may also appear in employment law courses and such courses may tend to cover the Equal Pay Act 1970, as amended. Since the 1970 Act is solely concerned with the matter of pay in employment, it tends to arise on such courses, rather than as an aspect of civil liberties courses covering discrimination, whereas the other instruments mentioned cover matters going well beyond employment. The exception is the Employment Equality (Sexual Orientation) Regulations 2003, but since, as indicated, they represent such an important new incursion into tackling discrimination on grounds of sexual orientation, a question on them may well appear on civil liberties exams as part of a question concerning the limitations of the protection against such discrimination – a question which would also expect account to be taken of the impact of the HRA in this area (since by using the HRA, protection from discrimination in areas going outside employment, such as housing, may be available).

It is clear, then, that at the present time, discrimination on grounds of sex, race and disability is not the only concern. The emphasis in essay questions on sex and race discrimination is usually on the extent to which anti-discrimination legislation has been, or is likely to be, successful in combating discrimination, taking account of recent changes.

Checklist

Students should be familiar with the following areas:

- the Sex Discrimination Act 1975 as amended;
- the Race Relations Act 1976 as amended and the Race Relations Remedies Act 1994;
- the Disability Discrimination Act 1995, as amended;
- the Employment Equality (Sexual Orientation) Regulations 2003, implementing the 'Framework' Directive;
- the Equal Pay and Equal Treatment Directives;
- provisions in domestic law relevant to discrimination on grounds of sexual orientation;
- Arts 6, 8 and 14 of the European Convention on Human Rights (ECHR) scheduled in the HRA.

Question 42

'Despite recent changes to the Sex Discrimination Act and the Race Relations Act, applicants still face practical difficulties in bringing a case. Moreover, further improvement in the remedies available in respect of an anti-discrimination claim is still needed. It is still fair to say that an individual who attempts to gain redress under the legislation is entering a minefield.'

Discuss.

Answer plan

A fairly demanding essay question. Note that it is confined to the Sex Discrimination Act and the Race Relations Act. It does not ask for a general survey of the substantive law, but for consideration of recent relevant changes. It is then necessary to examine continuing practical difficulties and to consider why recent changes have not eased them. Changes to the remedies but continuing weaknesses must be considered. It is obviously important to ensure that your answer keeps firmly to the terms of the question.

Essentially, the following areas should be considered:

- recent changes to the scheme created by the Race Relations Act 1976 and the Sex Discrimination Act 1975: the Sex Discrimination (Indirect

Discrimination and Burden of Proof) Regulations 2001 (SI 2001/2660) and the Race Relations Act 1976 (Amendment) Regulations 2003 (SI 2003/1626) – implementing EU Directives; the Race Relations (Amendment) Act 2000;

- remaining practical difficulties, including coverage of tribunal procedure in discrimination cases;
- the role of the Equal Opportunities Commission (EOC) and the Commission for Racial Equality (CRE); proposals for change;
- remedies under the Race Relations Act 1976, as amended, and the Sex Discrimination Act 1975, as amended;
- conclusions as to the efficacy of the schemes and consideration of the possibility of moving away from a scheme based largely on individual action.

Answer

The anti-discrimination scheme created by the Race Relations Act (RRA) 1976 and the Sex Discrimination Act (SDA) 1975 has recently been improved as a result of the changes made by the Sex Discrimination (Indirect Discrimination and Burden of Proof) Regulations 2001 and the Race Relations Act 1976 (Amendment) Regulations 2003. The Race Relations (Amendment) Act 2000 inserted s 19B into the 1976 Act, thereby ensuring that discrimination (direct or indirect) by a public authority in carrying out its functions was brought within the ambit of the Act. These changes have, in the case of the 1976 Act, widened the reach of the scheme and, in the case of both statutes, eased the burden on applicants to an extent. However, as this essay will argue, applicants continue to face practical difficulties in bringing a case. Further, these changes have not in themselves created improvement in the remedies available in respect of anti-discrimination claims. Thus, applicants still face obstacles in bringing a claim and may not – even if they are successful – obtain an effective remedy.

One of the main difficulties facing applicants under both schemes is to show that the adverse treatment is discriminatory – that is, it is on grounds of race or sex and not on neutral grounds. In *Dornan v Belfast CC* (1990), it was found that once the woman has raised a *prima facie* inference of discrimination, the burden will shift to the employer to show that the differentiation occurred on non-discriminatory grounds. In other words, although the plaintiff began the case bearing the burden of proof, it could shift to the defendant once a certain stage was reached. Thus, the formal burden of proof remained on the plaintiff, but once it appeared that a minimum threshold of proof of discrimination was established, the burden shifted to the defendant. The position was clarified under the Sex Discrimination (Indirect Discrimination and Burden of Proof) Regulations 2001: the complainant need not prove her case, merely the facts of the case, from which the court or tribunal should draw inferences of discrimination if the employer does not provide a satisfactory explanation. Regulation 41 of the Race Relations Act 1976 (Amendment) Regulations 2003 inserts s 54A into the RRA, effecting a similar change in race cases. These amendments clearly benefit applicants and remove one of the main obstacles they used to face.

Indirect discrimination claims tend to be especially problematic. As McColgan has pointed out, judicial interpretation has exacerbated the technicalities of indirect discrimination under both statutes (in *Sceptical Essays on Human Rights*, 2001). However, a further obstacle has now been removed, affecting claims of indirect discrimination under both schemes. In such claims, according to *Perera v Civil Service Commission* (1983), it was for the applicant to show that an absolute condition had been applied to him or her. In *Perera*, this concerned a requirement that a candidate for the Civil Service had a good command of English. This requirement was sometimes waived; it was determined that it could not, therefore, amount to a 'requirement or condition' for indirect discrimination purposes. This decision placed a brake on claims of indirect sex and race discrimination, although the approach was being abandoned even prior to implementation of the Burden of Proof Directive in the Sex Discrimination (Indirect Discrimination and Burden of Proof) Regulations 2001. It was pointed out in *Meer v Tower Hamlets* (1988), by Balcombe LJ in the Court of Appeal, that it allows discriminatory preferences free rein, as long as they are not expressed as absolute requirements. In that case, a candidate who had previous experience working in the local authority was preferred, although such experience was not absolutely required, and this had a tendency to debar non-British applicants.

The CRE recommended that this interpretation should be abandoned so that non-absolute criteria could be considered (CRE, *Second Review of the Race Relations Act*, 1991). In *Falkirk Council v Whyte* (1997), the decision in *Perera* was found to be out of accord with the purposive approach to legislation that implements a Directive, which has been adopted in a number of equal pay cases. It was found that the term 'a requirement or condition' should not be afforded a restrictive interpretation; the proper test, it was said, was to ask whether the 'factor' hindered women as opposed to men in the particular context. Under the amendments made by the 2001 Regulations to the SDA 1975, this approach will prevail, since the terms used are 'provision, criterion or practice', which appear to cover non-absolute criteria. Once the Race Directive was implemented in the Race Relations Act 1976 (Amendment) Regulations 2003, it became reasonably clear that indirect discrimination could be found to exist where a non-absolute requirement was applied to the applicant. The Directive uses the same wording as that adopted in the Burden of Proof Directive.

These are significant improvements. Nevertheless, a number of aspects of the procedure which has to be used in bringing a discrimination claim still combine to deter applicants from engaging in it. It is notable that less than half of the applications are heard; there is obviously a strong tendency to give up a claim halfway through.[1] There may be a number of reasons why cases are not brought, why they are abandoned and why the success rate is so low. The very fact that the success rate is low may mean that applicants are deterred from ever bringing a claim in the first place. In other words, the number of applications may be self-limiting: only the very determined applicants will pursue cases all the way to a hearing. Obviously, the applicant is in a very vulnerable position; the position of the parties is usually unequal, especially if an applicant is bringing the claim against his or her employer. The applicant will be afraid of being labelled a troublemaker, perhaps of being sacked for reasons apparently unrelated to the claim, or of losing promotion prospects. There may be continual pressure not only on the applicant, but also on any workmates who have consented to act as witnesses in the claim, and they may withdraw their consent to act.

The weakness of the remedies is unlikely to encourage claims, and the complexity and technicality of the substantive law may also act as a deterrent. It may do so in any event but, coupled with the lack of legal aid, the task facing the applicant may appear overwhelming. These two factors are exacerbated by, and also contribute to, the lack of experience tribunal members have of discrimination cases. The legal rules bearing on claims of indirect discrimination in particular are so complex that the applicant may be especially vulnerable to pressure to withdraw or settle the claim. The lack of legal aid, meaning that many applicants are not legally represented, leads to a poor quality of decision making and to the charge that the employers' lawyers may manipulate the members of the tribunal, due to their lack of experience in the area. Thus, a vicious circle is set up. The tribunals need more experience in these cases, but do not receive it due to the factors mentioned here; when a tribunal does hear such a case, it may not deal with it satisfactorily, thereby having the effect of deterring future applicants and ensuring that tribunals do not gain more experience. Indeed, it may be argued that the tribunal procedure is simply unsuitable for discrimination claims, given the current highly technical and complex nature of the substantive law. The applicant may be aided by the EOC or the CRE, but these bodies have to refuse the majority of applications due to their lack of funds.

The CRE has proposed that there should be a discrimination division of employment tribunals dealing only with discrimination claims. Such tribunals would gather expertise in this very specialist area and could be equipped with powers to order higher levels of compensation. Legal aid could be made available in this specialist division, even though it remained unavailable in respect of other tribunal cases. So far this proposal has not been implemented.

The various remedies available which are applicable in race and sex discrimination cases have generally been perceived as inadequate. The means of enforcing them are still problematic. A court/tribunal can award a declaration which simply states the rights of the applicant and the respect in which the employer has breached the law. It can also award an action recommendation which will be intended to reduce the effect of the discrimination. However, the Employment Appeal Tribunal in *British Gas plc v Sharma* (1991) held that this could not include a recommendation that the applicant be promoted to the next suitable vacancy, as this would amount to positive discrimination. It might, however, be argued that this would merely be putting the person in the position he or she should have been in, rather than giving them a special preference due to race or sex.

A tribunal can also award compensation, which will be determined on the same basis as in other tort cases. It will be awarded for financial loss and injury to feelings; exemplary damages will not be available. For a number of years after the introduction of the two statutes, awards tended to be low, but they rose after the decision in *Noone* (1988) that a consultant who was not appointed on grounds of race should be awarded £3,000 for injury to feelings. In *Alexander* (1988), it was held that awards for injury to feelings should not be minimal, because this would tend to trivialise the public policy to which the Act gives effect. On the other hand, it was found that they should be restrained and therefore should not be set at the same level as damages for defamation. On this basis, £500 was awarded for injured feelings due to racial discrimination.

However, the decision of the European Court of Justice (ECJ) in *Marshall (No 2)* (1993) had a very significant impact on the level of awards. The ECJ found that the award of compensation in sex discrimination cases brought against organs of the State should be set at a level which would allow the loss sustained to be made good in full. In the *Von Colson* case (1984), the ECJ had held that any sanction must have a real deterrent effect. In order to ensure, after *Marshall (No 2)*, that applicants in race discrimination cases were placed on the same footing as those in sex discrimination cases, the Race Relations Remedies Act 1994 was passed to remove the existing limits on the level of compensation. It seems fairly clear that awards at the levels set prior to *Marshall (No 2)* did not encourage claims, did not deter employers from discrimination and were unlikely to affect deeply rooted discriminatory ideologies in institutions. However, the *Marshall* decision led to an improvement in the level of compensation payable in both race and sex discrimination cases, which is allowing the legislation to have some real bite. There is now no statutory limit on the compensation awardable for unlawful discrimination.[2]

It is fairly common for the other party to fail to comply with the award. The applicant must then return to court in order to enforce it. If an action recommendation has not been complied with, the tribunal will award compensation, but only if compensation could have been awarded at the original hearing. As this is unlikely to be the case in an indirect discrimination claim, there will be no remedy available, except to apply to the CRE and the EOC, alleging persistent discrimination.

It may be concluded that individuals have not been able to use the legislation very effectively in practice in order to bring about change, although possibly this situation may continue to improve as further EU Directives are introduced effecting further improvements to the scheme – of practical benefit to applicants. It is fair to say that the remedies available have improved greatly as a result of ECJ intervention and that, in itself, this encourages applicants to seek to overcome the obstacles of bringing a claim. Nevertheless, pitfalls – especially in relation to the tribunal system – still exist as indicated above and it may be argued that the whole system of bringing individual actions is flawed as a means of addressing discrimination. The EOC and CRE have proposed that they should be able to join in an individual's action in order to address institutionalised discrimination in an undertaking. By tackling such discrimination more effectively, this could both obviate to some extent the need for individuals to bring claims and would provide the support and expertise which is needed in order to allow individual claims to succeed. However, this would require a better level of funding from the government; the level of funding these bodies receive at present suggests that there is a lack of commitment to ending discriminatory practices.

Notes

1   The number of applications began to decline from 1976 onwards, although it began, in the 1990s, to rise again. The decline in the rate of applications may have been attributable in part to the initial rush to attack very blatant examples of sexism and racism, which died away as employers and others began to ensure that policies enshrining such values were either abolished or made less overt.

2   It might be pointed out that it was necessary for the same higher level of compensation to become available in race discrimination cases, since the 1975 and the 1976 Acts are intended to harmonise this.

Question 43

Evaluate the success of the Equal Opportunities Commission and the Commission for Racial Equality in curbing discrimination on grounds of race or sex in the UK.

Answer plan

A reasonably straightforward essay question. It is important to view the powers of these two bodies in the context of the individual method of using the legislation which they are supposed to complement.

Essentially, the following areas should be considered:

- power of the Equal Opportunities Commission (EOC) and the Commission for Racial Equality (CRE) to issue a non-discrimination notice;
- power to conduct a formal investigation;
- assistance to claimants;
- use of judicial review; relevance of the Race Directive;
- inherent limitations of the two bodies.

Answer

Apart from the individual method of bringing about change, the Race Relations Act 1976 and Sex Discrimination Act 1975 also contain an 'administrative method', which was included with the aim of relieving the burden on individual applicants. It may also represent a more coherent approach than the piecemeal method of bringing individual cases. The aim was to bring about general changes in discriminatory practices, rather than waiting for an individual to take on the risk and the burden of bringing a case.

Both the CRE and the EOC have two main powers. They can assist claimants and they can issue a non-discrimination notice in respect of discriminatory practices where there may be no known victim who wants to bring a claim.[1] This may be because the company or institution has effectively deterred certain people from coming forward with applications for a job. If indications of race discrimination appear – if, for example, it appears that very few of a certain group are employed – then, first, a formal investigation will be conducted.

This decision might be taken if, for example, the workforce was only 1% Afro-Caribbean, although the company was in a racially mixed area in which that ethnic group comprised about 30% of the population. It may be that the recruiting policy is indirectly discriminatory; for example, it may largely be by word of mouth and therefore the existing workforce may tend to reproduce itself. However, the CRE has had the power to issue a non-discrimination notice curbed by the House of Lords' decision in *CRE v Prestige Group plc* (1984). It was found that the CRE is not entitled to investigate a named person or company, unless it already has a strong reason to believe that discrimination has occurred.

Thus, after this decision, where the strong suspicion needed to bring a formal investigation is not already present (an investigation is needed in order to acquire it), the CRE and the EOC can embark on a general investigation only. This means that their powers are more limited: they cannot subpoena witnesses or issue a non-discrimination notice.

Thus, the CRE and the EOC now tend to be confined to a reactive approach; they can only react to very blatant forms of discrimination. They cannot investigate more subtle and insidious instances of discrimination which may be the more pernicious, and this clearly represents a limitation of their role. After the *Prestige* decision, the CRE had to abandon a number of investigations which it had already begun. There has therefore been a tendency for subtle institutionalised racism and sexism to continue unchecked, although more blatant examples of racism and sexism, such as the phrase 'no blacks', which used to appear in advertisements, have now disappeared.

Although the investigative powers of the EOC have been curbed, it may be able to bring about general changes in discriminatory practices by seeking a direct change in the law. In *Secretary of State for Employment ex p EOC* (1994), it was found that the EOC can seek a declaration in judicial review proceedings to the effect that primary UK legislation is not in accord with EC equality legislation. At the time, certain provisions of the Employment Protection (Consolidation) Act 1978 governed the right not to be unfairly dismissed, compensation for unfair dismissal and the right to statutory redundancy pay. These rights did not apply to workers who worked less than the specified number of hours a week. The EOC considered that since the majority of those working for less than the specified number of hours were women, the provisions operated to the disadvantage of women and were therefore discriminatory. The EOC accordingly wrote to the Secretary of State for Employment, expressing this view and arguing that, since the provisions in question were indirectly discriminatory, they were in breach of EC law.

The Secretary of State replied by letter that the conditions excluding part-timers from the rights in question were justifiable and therefore not indirectly discriminatory. The EOC applied for judicial review of the Secretary of State's refusal to accept that the UK was in breach of its obligations under EC law. The application was amended to bring in an individual, Mrs Day, who worked part-time and had been made redundant by her employers. It was found that Mrs Day's claim was a private law claim, which could not be advanced against the Secretary of State, who was not her employer and was not liable to meet the claim if it was successful.

The Secretary of State further argued that the EOC had no *locus standi* to bring the proceedings. However, the House of Lords found that, since the EOC had a duty under s 53(1) of the SDA 1975 to work for the elimination of discrimination, it was within its remit to try to secure a change in the provisions under consideration, and therefore the EOC had a sufficient interest to bring the proceedings and, hence, *locus standi*. The Secretary of State also argued that no decision or justiciable issue susceptible of judicial review existed. However, the House of Lords found that, although the letter itself was not a decision, the provisions themselves could be challenged in judicial review proceedings. In other words, the real question was whether judicial review was available for the purpose of securing a declaration that certain UK primary legislation was incompatible with EC law and, following *Secretary of State for Transport ex p Factortame* (1992), it would appear that judicial review was so available.

As regards the substantive issue – whether the provisions in question, while admittedly discriminatory, could be justified – the House of Lords thought that, in certain special circumstances, an employer might be justified in differentiating between full and part-time workers to the disadvantage of the latter, but that such differentiation, employed nationwide, could not be justified. Thus, the EOC, but not an individual applicant, was entitled to bring judicial review proceedings in order to secure a declaration that UK law was incompatible with EC law. Declarations were made that the conditions set out in the provisions in question were indeed incompatible with EC law.

This was a very far-reaching decision: it means that where UK legislation is incompatible with EC law, a declaration can be obtained to that effect more rapidly than if it was necessary to wait for an individual affected to bring a case against the particular person or body who was acting within the terms of the UK legislation in question. The decision did not directly have an effect on race discrimination at the time. However, now that the Race Directive has been implemented in the Race Relations Act 1976 (Amendment) Regulations 2003, it opens the possibility that the CRE could challenge any relevant provisions of UK law in the same manner. A further method has therefore been provided of seeking to ensure that provisions affecting sex and race discrimination are brought into harmony with EC equality provisions.

The CRE and the EOC have made a number of proposals for reform, which would strengthen the administrative method and allow it to work more closely in harmony with the individual method. The CRE wants to try to narrow the gap between individual cases and what can be achieved by a formal investigation and has proposed that, in order to do this, it should be able to join in the individual's case as a party to the action, so as to draw attention to the likelihood of further discrimination occurring. Thus, the individual would receive the remedy, but the general effect of discrimination in the defendant company would be addressed by issuing a non-discrimination notice at the same time. This may be supported on the ground that if one individual brings a successful case against an employer, it is probable that discrimination in that concern is quite widespread.[2] Both the EOC and the CRE want legislation to reverse the *Prestige* decision. They want to be able to launch investigations into a named person or company, even when there is no initial strong evidence of discrimination.

It may be argued, in conclusion, that both bodies have been set a task – the curbing of discriminatory practices – which they were always ill-fitted to undertake. Both have been subject to external pressures – lack of funding, lack of sympathy with their role evinced by the judiciary – which have undermined their purpose. Sacks argues that the EOC is also affected by its internal limitations, which spring from its status as a quango. She suggested that an internal contradiction inevitably arises from that status: it is supposed to have taken a stance independent of government and even in conflict with it, but it is at the same time at the mercy of government in terms of appointees to it and in terms of funding.

Notes

1   Further, it might be pointed out that if a non-discrimination notice is issued, the CRE or EOC can apply for an injunction to enforce it.

2   If an individual in an undertaking has been the victim of discrimination, it is likely that discrimination may be institutionalised within it and may recur in future if the remedy is confined to the individual applicant only.

Question 44

Critically evaluate the current legal protection from discrimination on the ground of sexual orientation in the fields of employment, housing and education.

Answer plan

This is a fairly tricky essay since a number of areas of law are relevant. Also, one finds in these fields that certain provisions outlaw discrimination while others enshrine it, subject to the possibility of an anti-discriminatory interpretation under the HRA 1998. The potential to use the HRA clearly renders this field complex. Discrimination on grounds of sexual orientation in employment was covered from December 2003 by the Employment Equality (Sexual Orientation) Regulations 2003, implementing European Council Directive 2000/78/EC. Discrimination in employment, but importantly also in the other spheres mentioned on this ground, can also be addressed in certain circumstances by using the HRA and relying on Arts 8 and 14. The HRA is significant in this field in three respects. First, a free-standing action could be brought under it, relying on s 7(1)(a), against a public authority allegedly discriminating on this ground. Secondly, any body, including private bodies allegedly discriminating on this ground in reliance on legislative provisions in, say, housing, could find that the use of s 3 of the HRA means that the discrimination is outlawed. Thirdly, the reach of the Regulations could be broadened by reliance on the HRA.

The following matters should be considered:

- impact of the HRA and recent European Court of Human Rights (ECtHR) cases;
- unfair dismissal provisions of the Employment Rights Act 1996;
- the Employment Equality (Sexual Orientation) Regulations 2003 implementing European Council Directive 2000/78/EC;
- s 28 of the Local Government Act 1988;
- the *Fitzpatrick* and *Mendoza* cases in the field of housing;
- directions of reform.

Answer

At present, a person who is treated detrimentally in terms of housing or educational provision, or is in a number of other respects adversely treated on the ground of sexual orientation, will find that no anti-discrimination legislation specifically covers his or her situation. However, a person who is refused promotion or dismissed from a job or suffers employment detriment in some other respect on this ground now may have a remedy under the Employment Equality (Sexual Orientation) Regulations 2003, which implement European Council Directive 2000/78/EC. Thus, some protection is available but the protection is clearly inadequate when compared with that available in respect of race or sex discrimination. Owing to the current gap in the law, leaving discrimination on this ground to go relatively unchecked in certain spheres, the HRA may be looked to as a method of providing some protection for the rights of homosexuals. Further, at the present time, certain legal provisions, discussed below, appear to imply that discrimination on this ground is still, in certain spheres of activity, approved of by the law and therefore by society. Thus, the picture, in terms of the protection available, remains very mixed although the new Regulations and the HRA represent an extremely significant step forward.

The HRA is significant in this field in three respects. First, a free-standing action could be brought under it, relying on s 7(1)(a), against a public authority allegedly discriminating on this ground. Secondly, any body, including private bodies allegedly discriminating on this ground in reliance on legislative provisions in, for example, housing could find that the use of s 3 of the HRA means that the discrimination is outlawed. Thirdly, the reach of the Regulations could be broadened by reliance on the HRA. A person discriminated against on grounds of sexual orientation could seek to rely on Art 8, either read with Art 14 or on its own. Article 14 only operates in conjunction with another Convention Article, but even where that other Article is not itself breached, a breach may be found when it is read with Art 14.

In *Lustig-Prean v UK* (2000) and *Smith and Grady v UK* (2000), the ECtHR found that the ban on homosexuals in the armed forces infringed Art 8 and Art 13. Its absolute nature meant that it could not be viewed as being in proportion to a legitimate aim. The ruling of the Court could be relied upon when seeking review of a decision or policy of a public authority which is discriminatory on grounds of sexual orientation. In *Salgueiro da Silva Mouta v Portugal* (2001), the Court relied on Art 14 in finding that a breach had occurred where a parent was denied contact with his child on the ground of sexual orientation. The use of the HRA and Convention in this context will be considered below, but this essay will first examine the scope and possible efficacy of the Employment Equality (Sexual Orientation) Regulations 2003. Clearly, the HRA need only be relied upon if the new Regulations are inapplicable to discrimination on this ground.

Prior to the coming into force of the Employment Equality (Sexual Orientation) Regulations 2003, if a lesbian or homosexual had been employed for at least one year before dismissal, the law of unfair dismissal under the Employment Rights Act 1996 offered some protection. However, a dismissal was fair if it was for a substantial reason of a kind to justify dismissal. Where the dismissal was on grounds of sexual orientation, a wide interpretation might be given to the meaning of 'reasonable'. In *Saunders v Scottish National Camps* (1981), the applicant, who was employed as a maintenance handyman at a boys' camp, was dismissed on the grounds of homosexuality, although his duties did not ordinarily bring him into contact with the boys. His dismissal was, nevertheless, held to be fair on the ground that many other employers would have responded in the same way. Now, however, a person in Saunders's position could rely either on a more restrictive meaning of 'reasonable', in keeping with changed attitudes towards homosexuality, or on the new Regulations. Under the Regulations, the dismissed employee would have to show that, on grounds of sexual orientation, the employer had treated him or her less favourably than it had treated other persons. In other words, if the employer had singled out the employee on this ground for dismissal, that would amount to unlawful discrimination.

The Regulations cover under s 6 a number of other forms of employment detriment. In relation to such detriment, such as a failure to promote, the applicant must show, under s 3, that he or she has been treated less favourably on the ground of sexual orientation than other persons. Motive appears to be irrelevant; the question at this stage appears to be merely whether the applicant has been treated in a particular way and other persons have been treated more favourably. Then, following the ruling of the House of Lords in *James v Eastleigh BC* (1990) (a sex discrimination case), the applicant must show that there is a causal relationship between his or her sexual orientation and the treatment; in other words that but for his or her sexual orientation, he or she would have been treated as favourably as other persons are or would have been treated.

The Regulations also import the concept of indirect discrimination in employment (under s 3(1)(b)), thereby outlawing practices which, while neutral on their face, have a disproportionately adverse impact on persons due to their sexual orientation. Making allowance for indirect discrimination means that the Regulations cover not only isolated acts of discrimination, but also institutionalised discrimination. This reflects the pluralist approach; it takes account, for example, of endemic practices of discriminating on this ground in, for example, certain police forces. In asking not whether a person can, in theory, comply with a condition, but whether he or she can do so in practice, it broadens the area of morally unjustifiable differentiation.

There are four stages in operating this concept. First, it must be shown that a condition has been applied to the applicant. Secondly, it must be shown that the condition is one which puts or would put persons of the same sexual orientation as the applicant 'at a particular disadvantage when compared with other persons'. The term 'particular disadvantage' will now have to be interpreted as cases arise. It may be taken to mean that considerably fewer persons of a particular sexual orientation are able to comply with the condition than other persons. Thirdly, the claimant must show that the condition puts him or her at a particular disadvantage; in other words, the claimant must be a 'victim' due to the application of the condition: test cases cannot therefore be brought by pressure groups such as Stonewall. Once the claimant has proved these three requirements, the burden of proof shifts to the employer to show, if possible, that the condition is a 'proportionate means of achieving a legitimate aim'.

The Regulations clearly represent an extremely significant step forward in providing protection for discrimination on this ground, although they only cover employment. However, they are qualified since being of a particular sexual orientation can be 'a genuine and determining occupational requirement', although it must also be 'proportionate to apply that requirement in the particular case'. In relation to religious organisations such as Church of England schools, it appears to be especially easy to fulfil this test, thereby allowing many such organisations to discriminate openly on this ground. Such organisations can discriminate if *inter alia* the employer is, on reasonable grounds, not satisfied that the applicant meets a requirement to be of a particular sexual orientation.

Discrimination against homosexuals in the field of education was enshrined in s 2A of the Local Government Act 1986, inserted by s 28 of the Local Government Act 1988 and amended by s 104 of the Local Government Act 2000; it prohibited the deliberate promotion of homosexuality by local authorities or the teaching of 'the acceptability of homosexuality as a pretended family relationship'. Thus, local authorities could still fund certain groups so long as this was aimed at benefiting the group rather than at promoting homosexuality. Robertson in *Freedom, the Individual and the Law* (1993) argued that s 28 did not have a significant effect in schools, as local authorities do not directly control the curriculum. However, s 28 served to ratify and legitimise intolerance of homosexuals in education and outside it. In opposition, the Labour Party pledged to abolish s 28 and in government brought forward a Bill in order to do so in 2000. The Scottish Parliament repealed s 28 as far as Scotland is concerned under ss 25–26 of the Ethical Standards in Public Life (Scotland) Act 2000. The Labour Party's original Bill was defeated in the House of Lords, but the intention of the government continued to be to repeal s 28. This was eventually achieved by s 122 of the Local Government Act 2003.

A person discriminated against in the field of education, such as a pupil forced – in effect – to leave a school or other institution owing to homophobic bullying, which appeared to be condoned by the authorities, could consider bringing an action in negligence against the institution in question or the education authority. However, he or she could also bring an action under s 7(1)(a) of the HRA, relying on Arts 8 and 14, so long as the institution was a public authority. Article 2 of the First Protocol might be used to argue that education in accordance with one's own philosophical convictions must include the need to allow some teaching about the homosexual way of life. If necessary, this guarantee could be used in an attempt to challenge any use of s 2A of the Local Government Act 1986.

Housing legislation tends to enshrine and rely on a limited notion of the 'family', and therefore it has led to discrimination against homosexuals living in a settled partnership. In *Fitzpatrick v Sterling Housing Association* (1998), the Court of Appeal had to consider whether the homosexual partner of a deceased tenant could take over the tenancy under the Rent Act 1977, which limited such succession to persons who had lived with the original tenant 'as wife or husband' or were a member of his 'family'. The court, by a majority, found that the term 'family' was to be construed in the conventional sense, bearing prevailing social attitudes in mind. It was found that a 'family' was an entity which consisted of 'persons of the opposite sex cohabiting as man and wife'. Ward LJ, dissenting, pointed out that a number of other European countries had begun to allow same-sex couples to enter into property agreements on the same basis as unmarried heterosexual couples and that the US Supreme Court had recently found that a family should include 'two adult lifetime partners whose relationship is long term and characterised by an emotional and financial commitment and interdependence'. He found that 'the trend is to shift the focus ... from structure and components to function and appearance'. In other words, if a group acts as society expects a family to act, it is a family. He found that the exclusion of same-sex couples from the protection of the Rent Act, which would follow from the preferred interpretation of the majority, amounted to an assertion by society that their relationships are judged to be 'less worthy of respect, concern and consideration than the relationship between members of the opposite sex'.

On appeal, a bare majority of the House of Lords, in a landmark decision (*Fitzpatrick v Sterling Housing Association* (1999)), found that the term 'family' could be taken to include a cohabiting couple of the same sex. If it could be taken to include a cohabiting heterosexual couple, it was found that the term could be taken to include a homosexual one since, in principle, it was the bond and commitment between the two persons, not their sexual orientation, which was significant. The Lords did not consider, however, that a person could live with another of the same sex as his 'husband or wife', but in *Ghaidan v Godin-Mendoza* (2003), the Court of Appeal took a step further; it found that Sched 1, para 2 of the 1977 Act infringed Art 14. That breach could be remedied by construing the words 'as his or her wife or husband' in Sched 1, para 2 as if they meant 'as if they were his or her wife or husband'. In reaching this decision, the Court found that Art 14 would be engaged even where there was 'the most tenuous link with another provision in the Convention'. It considered that the positive obligation on the part of the State to promote the values that Art 8 protected was wide enough to bring legislation that affected the home within the ambit of Art 8 (*Marckx v Belgium* (1979) was applied and *Michalak v Wandsworth LBC* (2002) was followed). The facts of the applicant's case did therefore fall within the ambit of Art 8 as that Article was understood for the purposes of Art 14.[1]

It may be concluded that under the HRA, the potential clearly exists for aspects of discrimination on the ground of sexuality to become illegal – by incremental steps – in the fields in question in UK law. Although Art 14 is limited by applying only where there is discrimination in relation to another Convention right, the *Mendoza* case demonstrates that a merely tenuous link with another Article is sufficient to allow for the application of Art 14. Nevertheless, another Article must have some application to the circumstances. The HRA is only applicable where a legislative provision creates discrimination or where a public authority discriminates. It would clearly be preferable to pass more comprehensive anti-discrimination legislation – on the lines of the Race Relations Act – especially as where neither the Regulations nor the HRA apply, there are wide gaps in the protection currently offered.

Note

1   It could be pointed out that other Convention Articles could be relevant in respect of, say, the provision of housing benefits or benefits linked to housing. *Schuler-Zgraggen v Switzerland* (1993) – a sex discrimination case – gives indications as to the kind of argument that could be used where an adverse presumption on grounds of sexual orientation was made against the applicant. In *Schuler-Zgraggen*, the applicant received a full State invalidity pension as a result of illness which incapacitated her for work. After the birth of her child and a medical examination by the invalidity insurance authorities, the applicant's pension was stopped and the applicant appealed the decision. Without an oral hearing, the appeal court ruled that because the applicant was a woman with a child, it had to be assumed that even without her disability she would not have gone out to work. The applicant complained that she had been denied the right to a fair trial in civil proceedings within the meaning of Art 6(1) of the Convention, and had suffered discrimination within the meaning of Art 14 taken together with Art 6(1). Her claim succeeded; the Court said: 'the advancement of the equality of the sexes is today a major goal in the Member States of the Council of Europe and very weighty reasons would have to be put forward before such a difference of treatment [as occurred in the instant case] could be regarded as compatible with the Convention.' It could probably now be argued that the elimination of discrimination on grounds of sexual orientation is also an important goal of the Member States of the Council of Europe.

Question 45

'The domestic anti-discrimination scheme is limited in its coverage and ineffective in practice. Even after recent improvements and the implementation of the "Framework Directive" such criticisms still have force.'

Discuss in relation to discrimination on grounds of sex, race, sexual orientation and disability. Do you consider that current inadequacies in the scheme could be addressed by reliance on the Human Rights Act 1998?

Answer plan

This is a fairly tricky essay since it is very broad: a large number of areas of law are relevant. Your answer will have to be selective and this should be made clear at the outset. The potential to use the HRA clearly renders this field complex. Discrimination on grounds of sexual orientation in employment was covered from December 2003 by the Employment Equality (Sexual Orientation) Regulations 2003 implementing European Council Directive 2000/78/EC, the 'Framework Directive'. Discrimination on this ground in employment but, importantly, also in the other spheres mentioned can also be addressed in certain circumstances by using the HRA, and relying on Arts 8 and 14. The HRA is significant in respect of discrimination generally in three respects. First, a free-standing action could be brought under it, relying on s 7(1)(a), against a public authority allegedly discriminating on one of these grounds. This possibility is, however, most likely to arise in practice in relation to discrimination on grounds of sexual orientation. Secondly, any body, including private bodies, allegedly discriminating on one of these grounds in reliance on legislative provisions in, say, housing could find that the use of s 3 of the HRA means that the discrimination is outlawed. Again, this possibility is of most relevance to sexual orientation and possibly disability since the Race Relations Act (RRA) 1976 and the Sex Discrimination Act (SDA) 1975 cover housing. The RRA, SDA and Disability Discrimination Act (DDA) 1995 could in theory be widened in reliance on the HRA, or situations that they do not cover could in some circumstances be addressed by using the HRA. However, the reach of the RRA, the SDA and, to a lesser extent, the DDA means that there are not many situations that could be addressed by the HRA which could not be more properly addressed by the specific legislation that covers them. In particular, the HRA only applies to public authorities, while the RRA, the SDA and the DDA apply to both public and private bodies. The answer needs to make these quite difficult points in relation mainly to the second half of the question.

The following matters should be considered:

- recent changes to the scheme created by the RRA 1976 and the SDA 1975: the Sex Discrimination (Indirect Discrimination and Burden of Proof) Regulations 2001 and the Race Relations Act 1976 (Amendment) Regulations 2003 – implementing EU Directives; the Race Relations (Amendment) Act 2000;
- the impact of the DDA 1995, as amended;
- the Employment Equality (Sexual Orientation) Regulations 2003 implementing European Council Directive 2000/78/EC;
- remaining procedural and practical difficulties;
- the possible impact of the HRA taking account of recent European Court of Human Rights (ECtHR) cases; the *Mendoza* case in the field of housing.

Answer

The domestic anti-discrimination scheme on grounds of sex, race, sexual orientation and disability has undergone a number of improvements recently as a result of amendments which have both broadened its coverage and improved its efficacy in practice. Discrimination on grounds of sexual orientation was not, until the Framework Directive was implemented in the Employment Equality (Sexual Orientation) Regulations 2003, covered at all by any specific legislation. Thus, it is fair to say that the domestic anti-discrimination scheme has undergone dramatic changes in the last five years. However, problems still remain as this essay will indicate. There are still gaps in the coverage – some very significant ones – and aggrieved persons still experience difficulties in using the schemes successfully. The essay will go on to consider the role of the HRA in terms of addressing inadequacies in the scheme.

The anti-discrimination scheme created by the RRA 1976 and the SDA 1975 has recently been improved as a result of the changes made by the Sex Discrimination (Indirect Discrimination and Burden of Proof) Regulations 2001 and the Race Relations Act 1976 (Amendment) Regulations 2003. The Race Relations (Amendment) Act 2000 inserted s 19B into the 1976 Act, thereby ensuring that discrimination (direct or indirect) by a public authority in carrying out its functions was brought within the ambit of the Act. These changes have, in the case of the 1976 Act, widened the reach of the scheme and, in the case of both statutes, eased the burden on applicants to an extent. However, as this essay will argue, applicants continue to face practical difficulties in bringing a case. Further, these changes have not in themselves created improvement in the remedies available in respect of anti-discrimination claims. Thus, applicants still face obstacles in bringing a claim and may not – even if they are successful – obtain an effective remedy.

The DDA 1995 is modelled to an extent on the SDA and RRA schemes; the DDA adopted the concepts of direct discrimination and victimisation used in the SDA and the RRA and a body was set up to promote and monitor the scheme, although it initially had an advisory role only. However, the DDA scheme differs in some important respects from the earlier schemes. In general, it is narrower in scope than the earlier legislation, in terms both of its application and of the forms of discrimination covered. Originally, the Act only applied to employers who employ more than 20 people. It is now applicable to those employing more than 15 (s 7(1)). By 2004, this figure is to be reduced to apply to employers who employ more than two employees. Thus, many small businesses will still fall outside its scope. Most significantly, the Act does not import the concept of indirect discrimination in its full sense, although, as indicated below, the concept of direct discrimination is broader than that used in the SDA and the RRA. Also, direct discrimination can be justified.

The DDA does not make discrimination on the ground of disability generally illegal; as with the sex and race legislation, it only outlaws it in the contexts in which it operates: employment (Pt II), disposal of premises (s 22) and the provision of goods and services (s 19). The Act was also amended and extended by the Special Education Needs and Disability Act 2001 to place duties on schools and on the providers of post-16 education and related services. The Act applies to all employers who have 15 or more employees, but it excludes a number of occupations, including the police, firefighters, barristers, prison officers, the armed forces, and those working on ships or aircraft. Unlike the provisions in respect of employment, which do not apply at present to businesses with fewer than 15 staff, the service provisions apply across the board. These provisions require traders not to refuse service to disabled people or to offer an inferior service. The Special Education Needs and Disability Act 2001, which adds s 28A to the DDA, covering schools, and s 28R, covering further and higher education, leaves the full field of application to orders made by the Secretary of State in respect of coverage of certain educational institutions under s 28R(6)(c), and in respect of the services covered within schools under s 28A(3). The provisions regarding education added to the DDA in 2001 will come into force as appointed by the Secretary of State.

Until December 2003, a person discriminated against on grounds of sexual orientation had no obvious means of redress, although the HRA could be invoked in certain circumstances, as discussed below. But the Employment Equality (Sexual Orientation) Regulations 2003, implementing the Framework Directive, cover under s 6 a number of forms of employment detriment. In relation to such detriment, such as a failure to promote, the applicant must show, under s 3, that he or she has been treated less favourably on the ground of sexual orientation than other persons. The Regulations also import the concept of indirect discrimination in employment (under s 3(1)(b)), thereby outlawing practices which, while neutral on their face, have a disproportionately adverse impact on persons due to their sexual orientation. Making allowance for indirect discrimination means that the Regulations cover not only isolated acts of discrimination, but also institutionalised discrimination.

It is clear that there are still a number of gaps in the coverage of this anti-discrimination scheme. The SDA does not cover private clubs; nor has it been amended in relation to operational police work as the RRA has. The Employment Equality (Sexual Orientation) Regulations 2003 only cover employment – as their name indicates. Discrimination in other fields on this ground is not covered. Even where protection from discrimination applies, applicants face procedural and practical difficulties in obtaining redress.

One of the main difficulties facing applicants under these schemes is to show that the adverse treatment is discriminatory – that is, it is on grounds of race, sex, sexual orientation or disability and not on neutral grounds. In *Dornan v Belfast CC* (1990), it was found that once the woman has raised a *prima facie* inference of discrimination, the burden will shift to the employer to show that the differentiation occurred on non-discriminatory grounds. In other words, although the plaintiff began the case bearing the burden of proof, it could shift to the defendant once a certain stage was reached. Thus, the formal burden of proof remained on the plaintiff, but once it appeared that a minimum threshold of proof of discrimination was established, the burden shifted to the defendant. The position was clarified under the Sex Discrimination (Indirect Discrimination and Burden of Proof) Regulations 2001: the complainant need not prove her case, merely the facts of the case, from which the court or tribunal should draw inferences of discrimination if the employer does not provide a satisfactory explanation. Regulation 41 of the Race Relations Act 1976 (Amendment) Regulations 2003 inserts s 54A into the RRA, effecting a similar change in race cases. These amendments have clearly eased the burden on applicants. Under reg 29 of the Employment Equality (Sexual Orientation) Regulations 2003, the burden of proof on applicants is similarly eased.

The concept of direct discrimination within the DDA 1995 involves showing, in relation to the fields covered, that the applicant has been less favourably treated for a reason related to his or her disability than a non-disabled person has been or would be treated. The claimant bears the burden of showing that the differential treatment is on grounds of disability and not for some neutral reason. Discharging this burden of proof may be problematic, although it may sometimes be clearly apparent that the employment detriment was on grounds of disability, and attention will shift to considering whether the disability fell within the Act and whether the detriment can be justified. The decision in *Dornan* will probably, however, apply in disability discrimination cases and will mean that once an inference has been raised that discrimination has occurred, the burden of proof will shift to the employer to prove that the decision in question was made on other grounds.

When seeking redress, the applicant tends to be in a very vulnerable position; the position of the parties is usually unequal, especially if an applicant is bringing the claim against his or her employer. The applicant will be afraid of being labelled a troublemaker, perhaps of being sacked for reasons apparently unrelated to the claim, or of losing promotion prospects. There may be continual pressure not only on the applicant, but also on any workmates who have consented to act as witnesses in the claim, and they may withdraw their consent to act.

The weakness of the remedies is unlikely to encourage claims, and the complexity and technicality of the substantive law may also act as a deterrent. It may do so in any event but, coupled with the lack of legal aid, the task facing the applicant may appear overwhelming. These two factors are exacerbated by, and also contribute to, the lack of experience tribunal members have of discrimination cases. The legal rules bearing on claims of indirect discrimination in particular are so complex that the applicant may be especially vulnerable to pressure to withdraw or settle the claim. The lack of public funding, meaning that many applicants are not legally represented, leads to a poor quality of decision making and to the charge that the employers' lawyers may manipulate the members of the tribunal, due to their lack of experience in the area.

It is argued that the HRA may have an impact in filling the gaps in this anti-discrimination scheme (indeed, it has already had some impact in respect of discrimination on grounds of sexual orientation), but it is hard to see that the HRA could be used to challenge the procedural and practical weaknesses of the schemes. The impetus for reform in those respects is likely to continue to come from the EU. In terms of gap-filling, the HRA is significant in respect of discrimination generally in a number of respects, although its impact is inherently limited. First, a free-standing action could be brought under it, relying on s 7(1)(a), against a public authority allegedly discriminating on one of these grounds. This possibility is most likely to arise, in practice, in relation to discrimination on grounds of sexual orientation since the protective scheme on that ground is limited to employment. Secondly, any body, including private bodies, allegedly discriminating on one of these grounds in reliance on legislative provisions in, say, housing could find that the use of s 3 of the HRA means that the discrimination is outlawed. Again, this possibility is of most relevance to sexual orientation and possibly disability since the RRA and the SDA cover housing. The DDA covers disposal of premises (s 22) and this provision appears to be narrower than those of the SDA and the RRA.

The RRA, SDA and DDA could in theory be widened in reliance on the HRA, or situations that they do not cover could in some circumstances be addressed by using the HRA. However, the reach of the RRA, the SDA and, to a lesser extent, the DDA means that there are not many situations that could be addressed by the HRA which could not be more properly addressed by the specific legislation that covers them. In particular, the HRA only applies to public authorities while the RRA, SDA and DDA apply to both public and private bodies.

Further, there is at present no free-standing right not to be discriminated against under the Convention. Article 14 only operates in conjunction with another Convention Article, but even where that other Article is not itself breached, a breach may be found when it is read with Art 14. A person discriminated against on grounds of sexual orientation could seek to rely on Art 8, either read with Art 14 or on its own. Discrimination on grounds of sexual orientation is linked to the rights protected under Art 8 since *inter alia* a person might be placed in a dilemma regarding his or her sexual orientation: if it is disclosed, employment or other detriment might follow. Sexuality is clearly an aspect of private life. In *Lustig-Prean v UK* (2000) and *Smith and Grady v UK* (2000), the ECtHR found that the ban on homosexuals in the armed forces infringed Art 8 and Art 13. Its absolute nature meant that it could not be viewed as being in proportion to a legitimate aim.[1] The ruling of the Court could be relied upon when seeking review of a decision or policy of a public authority, which is discriminatory on grounds of sexual orientation. In *Ghaidan v Godin-Mendoza* (2003), the Court of Appeal relied on Art 14 read with Art 8 in finding under the HRA that discrimination had occurred in respect of housing on this ground.

However, it is more difficult to bring claims of discrimination – on grounds of race, sex or disability – in employment or in the provision of services within the scope of Art 8, since such discrimination would not normally be linked to the right to respect for private life or the family. In *Botta v Italy* (1998), the ECtHR considered a claim that the lack of disabled facilities at a seaside resort violated the applicant's right to equal enjoyment of his right to respect for private life under Art 8 read together with Art 14. The claim was rejected on the basis that 'social' rights, such as the participation of disabled people in recreational facilities, fall outside Art 8. Therefore, Art 14 did not apply.

Clearly, however, there may be circumstances in which Art 8 or other Convention Articles could be invoked under the HRA in respect of the anti-discrimination scheme. In *Schuler-Zgraggen v Switzerland* (1993), the applicant received a full State invalidity pension as a result of illness which incapacitated her for work. After the birth of her child and a medical examination by the invalidity insurance authorities, the applicant's pension was stopped and she appealed the decision. Without an oral hearing, the appeal court ruled that because the applicant was a woman with a child, it had to be assumed that, even without her disability, she would not have gone out to work. The applicant complained that she had been denied the right to a fair trial in civil proceedings within the meaning of Art 6(1) of the Convention and had suffered discrimination within the meaning of Art 14 taken together with Art 6(1). Her claim succeeded; the Court said: 'the advancement of the equality of the sexes is today a major goal in the Member States of the Council of Europe and very weighty reasons would have to be put forward before such a difference of treatment [as occurred in the instant case] could be regarded as compatible with the Convention.'

It may be concluded that practical problems still bedevil the anti-discrimination scheme and that individuals have not been able to use the legislation very effectively in practice in order to bring about change. This situation may continue to improve as further EU Directives are introduced effecting further improvements to the scheme. The scope of the scheme has widened dramatically in recent years, although gaps are still apparent. The HRA is likely to have most impact as – in effect – a gap-filler in the field of discrimination on grounds of sexual orientation.

Note

1   A further example could be given: in *Salgueiro da Silva Mouta v Portugal* (2001), the court relied on Art 14 in finding that a breach had occurred where a parent was denied contact with his child on the ground of sexual orientation.

CHAPTER 9

THE HUMAN RIGHTS ACT 1998 AND THE EUROPEAN CONVENTION ON HUMAN RIGHTS

Introduction

The first edition of this book dealt in considerable detail with the so-called Bill of Rights debate – the advantages and disadvantages of introducing a written human rights guarantee. It also considered the deficiencies of the European Convention on Human Rights (ECHR) and the various possible human rights enforcement mechanisms. The reception of the Convention into UK law via the Human Rights Act (HRA) 1998 has rendered that debate largely defunct, but knowledge of the history of the Convention in the UK remains essential. Political and public support for some form of Bill of Rights grew overwhelming by the mid-1990s, but the resulting statute, the HRA, bears the marks of several compromises. In particular, it represents a compromise between the preservation of parliamentary sovereignty and protection for human rights.

The debate is now likely to centre upon the effectiveness of the HRA and the Convention as a human rights guarantee. Now that the HRA has been fully in force for over three years (it came into force in 2000), essay questions are likely to ask you to consider the improvements in domestic human rights protection which are resulting from and which are likely to result from the introduction of the HRA. Commentary on the significant early case law will be expected. Essay questions are also likely to ask you to consider gaps and inadequacies in both the Convention and the 1998 Act. Such questions will expect not only commentary on the nature of the Act and Convention, but will also expect you to rely on the early case law in your answer. The role of judges has now come under fresh scrutiny, since they hold an important new role as human rights watchdogs, yet lack the ultimate power of overriding legislation which breaches the Convention. Many different styles of essay question are possible on this large and wide-ranging topic; the following questions cover most of the debate at the time of writing. Certain relevant issues are also touched on in a number of chapters, since the HRA affects every area of civil liberties law. However, it affects some much more than others: chapters of most relevance are Chapters 1, 3, 4, 5, 6, 7 and the part of Chapter 8 that covers discrimination on grounds of sexual orientation.

Checklist

Students must be familiar with the following areas and their inter-relationships:

- the legal position before introduction of the HRA and the former difficulties of relying on the Convention in UK courts;
- the drive towards incorporation of the Convention;
- the doctrine of parliamentary sovereignty;
- the key provisions of the HRA and the Convention;
- key case law on the Convention;
- key HRA cases in the first three years.

Question 46

Critically evaluate the provisions of the Human Rights Act 1998 which are intended to ensure that legislation is compatible with the European Convention on Human Rights, and comment on their impact in practice.

Answer plan

This is a question which requires a sound knowledge of ss 3, 4, 10 and 19 of the HRA 1998, of some of the academic criticism generated by those provisions and of some of the key cases. Close analysis of those provisions of the Act, which are in some respects quite technical, is required. This is a question which is highly likely to be set at the present time. Note that the question does not require you to consider the efficacy of the Convention (ECHR) itself or the implications of receiving it into UK law. Also, it deliberately focuses on s 3 and the related provisions; it does not ask you to discuss the definition of a public authority under s 6.

The following matters should be discussed:

- the interpretative obligation under s 3: its use in practice so far;
- declarations of incompatibility under s 4: their use in practice;
- the 'fast track' procedure under s 10;
- impact of the Act on post-HRA legislation – s 19;
- evaluation.

Answer

The HRA 1998 is of immense constitutional significance. The Act provides further protection for the ECHR in UK law. Once it came fully into force in 2000, UK citizens had for the first time civil rights (in the sense of rights which may be claimed against public authorities) instead of civil liberties: instead of having residual freedoms, they have guarantees of rights. However, the likely impact of the reception of the Convention into domestic law is still unclear since the Act contains a number of complex, interesting and unusual features, which are determining and will determine its impact in practice.

The intention was not simply to incorporate the Convention into domestic law so that it became, in effect, a statute. The most significant provision, which largely determines the status of the Convention in domestic law, is s 3. Under s 3(1), primary and subordinate legislation must be given effect in a manner which makes it compatible with the Convention rights; the judiciary are under an obligation to ensure such compatibility 'so far as it is possible to do so'. This goes well beyond resolving ambiguity in statutory provisions by adopting the Convention-based interpretation which, of course, was already occurring in the pre-HRA era. Section 3 appears to place the judiciary under an obligation to render legislation compatible with the Convention if there is any loophole at all allowing them to do so.

It is now apparent that s 3(1) of the HRA may allow judges to read words into statutes (*R v A* (2001)), or adopt a broad or doubtful interpretation; in *Cachia v Faluyi* (2001), the Court of Appeal held that 'action' in s 2(3) of the Fatal Accidents Act 1976 should be construed as 'served process'. In *R v Secretary of State for the Home Department ex p Aleksejs Zenovics* (2002), the Court of Appeal added the words 'in respect of that claim' in the Immigration and Asylum Act 1999 to the end of the provision in question. Section 3(1) does not, however, allow for wholesale revision (*Re S and Re W (Care Orders)* (2002) and *Donoghue v Poplar Housing* (2001)) or, probably, the reading in of words where there is no 'gateway' to so doing. Thus, it is clear that the judges are prepared to use the powerful tool of s 3(1) to its fullest extent, even if this means twisting or ignoring the natural meaning of the statutory words or, most dramatically, reading words into statutory provisions. Thus, the judges have in some instances adopted a role which is close to a legislative one. Possibly in so doing they have pushed the interpretative obligation under s 3 too far as in *R v A*, and should instead have issued a declaration of incompatibility.

Section 3(2) provides that this interpretative obligation does not affect the validity, continuing operation or enforcement of any incompatible primary legislation. Thus, the Convention cannot be used to strike down any part of an existing statute as unconstitutional. This is clearly an important limitation. It means that parliamentary sovereignty is at least theoretically preserved, since prior and subsequent legislation which cannot be rendered compatible with the Convention cannot be struck down due to its incompatibility by the judiciary.

If a court cannot render a statutory provision compatible with the Convention, despite its best efforts, the person wishing to rely on the right (whether claimant or defendant, etc) will have to suffer a breach of their Convention rights for a period of time. This is clearly unsatisfactory; the solution chosen by the Labour government was to include s 4 in the Act. Section 4 allows certain higher courts to make a declaration of incompatibility, while s 10 allows for a 'fast track' procedure, whereby a minister may by order amend the offending primary or subordinate legislation if there are compelling reasons to do so. A number of comments may be made on this procedure. In general, executive amendment of legislation is objectionable. However, parliamentary scrutiny of the order is provided for under s 12. Further, the usual objections to such a procedure are arguably inapplicable since the order is intended to bring UK law into harmony with Convention, thereby raising human rights standards at the expense, in many instances, of the executive.

Other objections to this procedure are less easily overcome. The minister is under no obligation to make the amendment(s) and may only do so if there are compelling reasons. In other words, the fact that a declaration of incompatibility has been made is not, in itself, a compelling reason. Thus, there may be periods of uncertainty during which citizens cannot rely on aspects of their Convention rights. Further, in some instances, a declaration of incompatibility may not be obtained for some time. If, for example, a lower court (a court outside the meaning of 'court' within s 4(5)) finds in criminal proceedings that the police have bugged a person's home in accordance with the Police Act 1997, but possibly contrary to Art 8 (providing a right to respect for private life) of Sched 1 to the 1998 Act, the court may be unable to exclude the evidence derived from the bugging, since that would probably be contrary to the 1997 Act. The court cannot make a declaration of incompatibility and the defendant would have no interest in appealing to a higher court in order to obtain such a declaration, since it would provide him or her with no personal benefit. No damages could be awarded due to the provisions of s 6(2). Thus, change to particular parts of the law in order to ensure compatibility with the Convention rights may be slow in coming.

The courts may seek to address the inadequacy of the declaration of incompatibility procedure – awarding the claimant a 'booby prize' in two ways. First, the lower courts may come to be very reluctant to find that a statutory provision is incompatible with the Convention. Given the broad and open-ended wording of the Convention, it will often be easy to find that compatibility exists. In the example given above, the lower court could seek to twist the wording of the Police Act 1997 to ensure compliance with Art 8. The danger in this approach is that, instead of 'levelling up', that is, bringing UK law up to the level of the Convention standards, UK courts may level down – adopt the interpretation of the Convention which gives the lowest possible level of protection. It is suggested that this occurred in *Brown v Stott* (2001), in which Art 6(1) was watered down in order to avoid having to declare s 172 of the Road Traffic Act 1988 incompatible with it. Secondly, the defendant – often a public authority – may tend to appeal to a higher court on the issue of compatibility, arguing that, once the relevant UK law was properly interpreted, it could be found to be in compliance with the Convention. The defendant would hope that a higher court would be prepared to adopt a more creative interpretation than the lower one and that the interpretation obtained would be favourable to him or her. This occurred in the *Alconbury* case (2001). These tendencies, while avoiding making declarations of incompatibility, are tending to place aspects of Convention rights in a doubtful and precarious position. This is especially a matter of concern where criminal proceedings are in question, due to the implications for the defendant while the matter of compatibility is being resolved.

Declarations of incompatibility in civil proceedings are perhaps less likely to occur. The Convention, as a civil rights measure, consists of a series of rights guaranteed to the citizen against the power of the State. That power is usually, although by no means always, encapsulated in the criminal law. A glance through the pages of texts on the ECHR as an international instrument will show that proceedings brought against Member States often began as criminal proceedings in the Member State. Thus, many cases in which Convention rights are invoked in UK courts are criminal ones, and the question raised tends to concern an aspect of criminal procedure (see *R v A* (2001) and *R v Offen* (2001)). Articles 6 and 5 are frequently invoked since they protect *inter alia* a fair criminal trial and the right to liberty of the person.

Nevertheless, Convention issues are arising in civil proceedings, either substantively under, for example, Art 8 (*Re S and Re W (Care Orders)* (2002)) or procedurally under Art 6(1) as in *Alconbury*. If the Convention guarantees affect an area of the common law which applies between private individuals, such as breach of confidence, the common law will be interpreted or reformed to harmonise with the Convention (see *Douglas v Hello!* (2001)). If a statute affects the legal relations between private individuals (for example, employment statutes which will cover private companies and their employees), s 3 applies.

However, if a statute governing part of the civil law was found in a lower court to be incompatible with the Convention, the claimant or defendant would be denied a remedy, although their Convention rights had been breached. The claimant or defendant could in theory appeal to a higher court, arguing that no incompatibility arose. However, since public funding is likely to be unavailable, only those persons who can fund the action themselves will have any certainty that they will be able to do so. Others may be able to do so on a contingency fee basis, but Convention-based cases tend to be especially unpredictable, and therefore lawyers may not consider that the chances of success are sufficiently high.

Probably there is not much previous legislation which cannot be rendered compatible with the Convention,[1] but it is clear that any such legislation will persist for some time, even though the HRA is fully in force, since it is largely a matter of chance whether a suitable case comes to court. Subsequent legislation is in a somewhat different position due to the provisions of s 19. Under this section, when a minister introduces a Bill into either House of Parliament, he or she must make and publish a written statement to the effect either that, in his or her view, the provisions of the Bill are compatible with the Convention rights, or that, although he or she is unable to make such a statement, the government wishes, nevertheless, to proceed with the Bill. If the latter statement is made, it is possible that the judiciary will allow the provisions of the legislation to override the Convention just as they would if a clause was included in it stating 'this statute is to be given effect notwithstanding the provisions of Art X of the Human Rights Act 1998'. On the other hand, s 3 would still apply and the judges should therefore strive to achieve compatibility through interpretation even if ultimately it is impossible to do so.

The formal difference between declarations under s 19 and the more usual form of notwithstanding clause (as used in the Canadian Charter) will become apparent if the minister makes a statement to the effect that the legislation is compatible with the Convention, but subsequently it appears that it is not compatible. It would seem that, in such circumstances, the judiciary would do their utmost to ensure compatibility, even going so far as to disregard the absolutely plain meaning of statutory language in order to do so, on the basis that Parliament must have intended this to occur. Their duty to do so will arise both from the general need to construe legislation in order to ensure compatibility with the Convention if at all possible (s 3), and from the particular need flowing from s 19 to do so where subsequent legislation was thought to be compatible with the Convention when introduced into Parliament. All legislation passed post-HRA has been declared compatible with the Convention under s 19 so far except the Communications Act 2003. It was thought that a declaration could not be made due to the ban on political advertising which was continued under the Act. The lack of a declaration was due to the view taken that s 321(2) (the ban on political advertising) was incompatible with Art 10 – based on the decision of the European Court of Human Rights (ECtHR) in *VGT v Switzerland* (2002). However, it can be assumed that the rest of the Act was viewed by Parliament as compatible with Art 10. Therefore, it should be treated in the same way as any other Act of Parliament. Indeed, arguably, s 3 of the HRA should be applied to s 321(2) and the judiciary might find that the section is in fact compatible with Art 10 or that it can be rendered compatible through interpretation.

In conclusion, it may be said that, for the reasons discussed, the impact of the HRA is being realised slowly in practice. Nevertheless, it represents a radical change in the traditional means of protecting civil liberties. It has become much less likely that legislation will be introduced which will have the clear effect of limiting a liberty, since such legislation might eventually be declared incompatible with the guarantees of rights under the Act (s 4) and an application to Strasbourg might well be made, eventually forcing a change in the law. Further, when the legislation was introduced, the relevant minister would have to declare that a statement of compatibility could not be made under s 19 – something that ministers are clearly reluctant to do due to the political embarrassment which would be created – although they are prepared, exceptionally, to do so as indicated above. Even future illiberal governments would probably be deterred thereby from an obvious infringement of the Convention guarantees. Similarly, existing legislative protection for a Convention right is probably unlikely to be repealed, since a citizen might then challenge the failure to provide the right under s 7(1)(a), so long as the right was one exercisable against a public authority. Thus, the Act, despite its complexities and limitations, represents a break with previous legislative tradition; due to the operation of s 3 it is creating a much greater awareness in the judiciary of fundamental human rights issues. However, while the operation of s 3 has had this laudable effect, it may also be pointed out that the judiciary should bear in mind the mechanisms of the HRA which were supposed to preserve parliamentary sovereignty – ss 3(2) and 4 – and show a greater preparedness to use them.

Note

1   An example could be given which would illustrate the complexity of the process of reform. Section 10 of the Contempt of Court Act 1981, as currently interpreted, is arguably incompatible with Art 10 of the Convention due to the ruling to that effect of the ECtHR in *Goodwin v UK* (1996). Thus, s 10 is a clear candidate for reform under s 3 of the HRA, but it is almost certain that no declaration of incompatibility is necessary. A court could simply reinterpret s 10 in the light of the ruling of the ECtHR, overturning the ruling of the House of

Lords in *X v Morgan Grampian Publishers* (1991), which led to the ruling in *Goodwin v UK*. This would be a bold move, but it appears to be required by the provisions of s 3. At present, the House of Lords has, however, avoided a finding that *Morgan Grampian* has been overturned on the basis that there was sufficient flexibility in the *Goodwin* case to allow the two to be reconciled: see *Ashworth v MGN* (2002).

Question 47

In terms of enhanced human rights protection, do you consider that it would have been better to have introduced a tailor-made Bill of Rights for the UK rather than enacting the Human Rights Act 1998?

Answer plan

A fairly demanding question, which requires a quite detailed knowledge of the European Convention on Human Rights (ECHR), the HRA 1998, early decisions on it and key Convention decisions. It is also necessary to say something about the differences between an entrenched Bill of Rights and the HRA in terms of enhanced human rights protection, although it should be pointed out that a Bill of Rights need not be entrenched.

Issues to be discussed include:

- the possibilities available in terms of constructing a tailor-made Bill of Rights;
- exceptions to the primary rights of the ECHR;
- the effect of the margin of appreciation in certain European Court of Human Rights (ECtHR) decisions;
- general restrictions on Convention rights;
- weaknesses of some substantive Convention rights, for example, Art 14;
- deficiencies of the HRA in comparison with an entrenched Bill of Rights – early HRA cases illustrating the problems.

Answer

The HRA 1998 has given the ECHR further effect in UK law, as will be discussed, using the mechanism of an ordinary Act of Parliament. It has not sought to entrench its own provisions or the Convention, and it has not introduced any new rights apart from those of the Convention. The possibility of introducing a tailor-made Bill of Rights has been considered but rejected. Apart from the cumbersome nature of the process of deciding on the rights to be protected, a Bill of Rights might have taken too much account of the interests of the government in power at the time when it was passed. However, although producing a tailor-made Bill of Rights would certainly have been difficult, it can be argued that the UK should nevertheless have attempted it, rather than incorporating the ready-made Convention, which is arguably defective in content. This essay will argue that the attempt should have been made to introduce a Bill of Rights which would have been unique to the UK. It will also consider the possibility of entrenchment, which is associated with Bills of Rights – as in the US. The HRA is arguably a weak mechanism for the protection of human rights when compared to an entrenched Bill of Rights.

The Convention is a cautious document: it is not as open-textured as the American Bill of Rights and it contains long lists of exceptions to most of the primary rights – exceptions which suggest a strong respect for the institutions of the State. These exceptions have at times received a broad interpretation in the ECtHR, and it is likely that such interpretations will have a great influence on domestic courts as they apply the rights directly in the domestic arena under the HRA. For example, Art 10, which protects freedom of expression, contains an exception in respect of the protection of morals. This was invoked in the *Handyside* case (1976) in respect of a booklet aimed at schoolchildren, which was circulating freely in the rest of Europe. It was held that the UK government was best placed to determine what was needed in its own country in order to protect morals, and so no breach of Art 10 had occurred. The decision in *Otto-Preminger Institut v Austria* (1994) was on very similar lines: it was found that the 'rights of others' exception could be invoked to allow for the suppression of a film which might cause offence to religious people since, in allowing such suppression, the State had not overstepped its margin of appreciation. A somewhat similar course was adopted in *The Observer and The Guardian v UK* (1991) (the *Spycatcher* case), which will be considered in some detail as an example of the readiness of the ECtHR to afford a wide meaning to the exception provisions of the Convention.

The newspapers claimed that temporary injunctions granted to restrain publication of material from *Spycatcher* by Peter Wright violated the Art 10 guarantee of freedom of expression. The court found that, although the injunctions clearly constituted an interference with the newspapers' freedom of expression, those in force during the period before publication of the book in the US in July 1987 fell within the exception provided for by para 2 of Art 10 in respect of protecting national security. The injunctions had the aim of preventing publication of material which, according to evidence presented by the Attorney General, might have created a risk of detriment to MI5. The nature of the risk was uncertain, as the exact contents of *Spycatcher* were not known at that time, since it was still only in manuscript form. Further, the court ensured the preservation of the Attorney General's right to grant a permanent injunction; if *Spycatcher* material had been published before that claim could be heard, the subject matter of the action could have been damaged or destroyed. In the court's view, these factors established the existence of a pressing social need, which the injunctions answered.

The court then considered whether the actual restraints imposed were proportionate to the legitimate aims represented by the exceptions. It found that the injunctions did not prevent the papers from pursuing a campaign for an inquiry into the operation of the security services, and though preventing publication for a long time – over a year.– the material in question could not be classified as urgent news. Thus, it was held that the interference complained of was proportionate to the ends in view. It is suggested that in this ruling, the court accepted very readily the view that the authority of the judiciary could best be preserved by allowing a claim of confidentiality, set up in the face of a strong competing public interest, to found an infringement of freedom of speech for over a year.[1]

In other areas, there has been an equal willingness to allow the exceptions a wide scope in curtailing the primary rights. In *Council of Civil Service Unions v UK* (1988), the European Commission on Human Rights, in declaring the unions' application inadmissible, found that national security interests should prevail over freedom of association, even though the national security interest was weak, while the infringement of the primary right was very clear: an absolute ban on joining a trade union had been imposed. It is worth noting that the ILO Committee on Freedom of Association had earlier found that the ban breached the 1947 ILO Freedom of Association Convention.

However, these were all instances in which the doctrine of the 'margin of appreciation' had an influence on the decision in question. In other words, the view was taken that in certain particularly sensitive areas, such as the protection of morals or of national security, the domestic authorities had to be allowed a certain discretion in determining what was called for. In less sensitive areas, the ECtHR has been bolder. In the *Sunday Times* case (1979), it determined that the exception to Art 10, allowing restraint of freedom of speech in order to protect the authority of the judiciary, was inapplicable in an instance where the litigation in question, which could have been affected, was dormant. The court has also been relatively bold in the area of prisoners' rights, holding in *Golder v UK* (1975) and *Silver* (1983) that a prisoner's right to privacy of correspondence must be respected, and rejecting the UK government's arguments that an express or implied exception to Art 8 could be invoked.

It is not possible at the moment to come to conclusive general findings about the response of UK judges under the HRA to interpretations of the Convention rights at Strasbourg; however, some observations can be made. The judges are failing to take the view that they should not apply a particular decision because it has been affected by the margin of appreciation doctrine. In other words, they could be said to be importing the doctrine 'through the back door', even though it is an international law doctrine that has no application in the domestic sphere. To an extent, this was the approach adopted in the leading pre-HRA case of *R v DPP ex p Kebilene* (1999); although the doctrine itself was rejected, the outcomes of applications at Strasbourg were taken into account without adverting to the influence the doctrine had had on them. Arguably, a similar stance was taken in the post-HRA case of *Alconbury* (2001). Thus, the watering down effect at Strasbourg of this doctrine may also be occurring under the HRA. The judges are also giving full weight to the express exceptions under Arts 8–11 of the Convention, even where possibly Strasbourg might have decided on a different outcome. This may be said of *Interbrew SA v Financial Times Ltd* (2002), where the Court of Appeal found that on the facts of the case no protection for a media source need be given.

Apart from the express exceptions to Arts 8–11, there are also general restrictions to the operation of the rights. All the Articles except Arts 3, 4(1), 6(2) and 7 are subject to certain restrictions, either because certain limitations are inherent in the formulation of the right itself, or because it is expressly stated that certain cases are not covered by the right in question. Even the right to life under Art 2 is far from absolute: 'unintentional' deprivations of life are not covered, and the use of necessary force is justified even where it results in death. Derogations from certain of the rights are also possible. Now that the Convention has been incorporated and the interpretative jurisprudence of the Court is being used in domestic cases as a guide (s 2 of the HRA), such exceptions and restrictions tend to offer judges a means of avoiding a controversial conflict with the government, and possibly make it unlikely that a radical impact on UK law will exist in the long term. Woolf LCJ had made it clear that Convention rights should be argued only where they truly apply and that any sudden explosion of human rights arguments, where strictly unnecessary in UK courts, will not be supported. Indeed, the domestic courts have succeeded in finding exceptions even to rights that appear to be largely unqualified such as Art 6(1): this was evident in *Brown v Stott* (2001) and in *Alconbury* (2001). They have done so by relying on a case at Strasbourg, *Sporrong and Lonnroth v Sweden* (1983), in which it was said that the search for a balance between individual rights and societal concerns is fundamental to the whole Convention. Thus, it may be argued that the domestic judiciary have explored methods of watering down the rights which might not have been so readily available had a tailor-made Bill of Rights been introduced.

However, the judges do have an important function in giving the language of rights primacy, even if, eventually, an exception to a particular right is allowed to prevail. The Strasbourg jurisprudence and the rights themselves make it clear that the exceptions are to be narrowly construed and the starting point is always the primary right. This is in contrast to the previous position in which the judges merely applied the statute in question without affording much, or any, recognition to the freedoms it affected. This could bring about important changes in relation to such statutes, including the Public Order Act 1986 and the Official Secrets Act 1989. In considering the effect of such statutes, their human rights dimension should at least, in future, be recognised even if, as in the *Shayler* case (2001), it has not yet prevailed. A tailor-made Bill of Rights could hardly have afforded greater primacy to the primary rights, even though, in theory, it could have included exceptions that were more narrowly drawn and perhaps a greater number of absolute rights on the lines of the First Amendment in the US.

However, it can also be argued that a tailor-made Bill of Rights could have contained a more extensive list of rights including social and economic rights. In particular, it could have included a free-standing anti-discrimination guarantee. Such a guarantee is now contained in Protocol 12 of the Convention, but the UK has not ratified it and – as would therefore be expected – has not amended Sched 1 to the HRA to include it. In contrast, Art 14 of the Convention prohibits discrimination on 'any ground such as sex, race, colour, language, religion', but only in relation to any other Convention right or freedom. It has been determined in a string of cases since *X v Federal Republic of Germany* (1970) that Art 14 has no separate existence , but that, nevertheless, a measure which is in itself in conformity with the requirement of the Convention right governing its field of law may, however, infringe that Article when it is read in conjunction with Art 14, for the reason that it is discriminatory in nature. In *Abdulaziz, Cabales and Balkandali v UK* (1985), it was held that although the application of Art 14 does not pre-suppose a breach of the substantive provisions of the Convention and is, therefore, to that extent, autonomous, it cannot be applied unless the facts in question fall within the ambit of one or more of the rights and freedoms. Thus, in one sense, Art 14 may be ineffective in strengthening the existing provisions of sex discrimination and race relations legislation which tend to be invoked in the context of employment, because general employment claims fall outside the ambit of the other rights and freedoms.

Yet, conversely, Art 14 is having an immediate impact on certain forms of discrimination which are unlawful in situations where another Convention right or freedom does apply, since Art 14 prohibits discrimination on any ground, not just the UK's current grounds of sex, race and disability. Convention case law exists on discrimination on the basis of sexual orientation, transsexuality, religion, lifestyle, political opinion, residence or wealth. In *Salgueiro da Silva Mouta v Portugal* (2001), the Court relied on Art 8 and Art 14 in finding that a breach had occurred where a parent was denied contact with his child on the ground of sexual orientation. In *Ghaidan v Godin-Mendoza* (2003), the Court of Appeal found that Sched 1, para 2 of the Rent Act 1977 infringed Art 14. That breach could be remedied under s 3 of the HRA, by construing the words 'as his or her wife or husband' in Sched 1, para 2 as if they meant 'as if they were his or her wife or husband'. In reaching this decision, the Court found that Art 14 would be engaged even where there was 'the most tenuous link with another provision in the Convention' (*Petrovic v Austria* (2001)). It considered that the positive obligation on the part of the State to promote the values that Art 8 protected was wide enough to bring legislation that affected the home within the ambit of Art 8 (*Marckx v Belgium* (1979–80)). The other grounds protected under Art 14 are likely to be argued in UK courts very soon and are likely to shake up the UK's narrow discrimination law considerably, at least as far as the activities of public authorities are concerned. (It should be noted that further protection against discrimination on a number of grounds will be introduced when the Framework Directive is fully implemented, but since it only covers employment it will still be likely that claimants will seek to close the many gaps in the protection by reliance on Art 14 (with another Article) under the HRA.) Further, it should be remembered that ECtHR cases clearly state that discrimination on grounds of sex or race will be very difficult to justify (for example, *Schmidt v Germany* (1994)). Thus, Art 14 may have a greater impact than at first appears; nevertheless, the addition of Protocol 12 to Sched 1 to the HRA would clearly provide a far wider protection. A tailor-made Bill of Rights could have introduced its free-standing anti-discrimination guarantee.

The HRA itself has limitations in terms of enhanced human rights protection. The choice of the HRA as the enforcement mechanism for the Convention means that the Convention is incorporated into domestic law, but not entrenched on the US model; thus, it could be removed by the simple method of repeal of the HRA. Moreover, the judiciary cannot strike down incompatible legislation. Entrenchment was rejected in order to maintain parliamentary sovereignty and to avoid handing over too much power to the unelected judiciary. This means that Parliament can deliberately legislate in breach of the Convention. It also means that if prior or subsequent legislation is found to breach the Convention in the courts, and cannot be rescued from doing so by a creative interpretation, it must simply be applied (see *R (H) v Mental Health Tribunal, North and East London Region and Another* (2001)). Thus, citizens cannot always be certain of being able to rely on their

Convention rights domestically. An entrenched Bill of Rights on the US model would have provided them with that certainty and, at the sacrifice of parliamentary sovereignty as traditionally understood in the UK, would have therefore delivered an enhanced degree of rights protection.[2]

In conclusion, it should be pointed out that the Convention was never intended to be used as a domestic Bill of Rights. It has been argued that creation of such a new guarantee from scratch would be an incredibly difficult and complex task, and so it is understandable why the incorporation of the Convention has been chosen as a (comparatively) quick and easy 'fix'. However, it may further be argued that due to the deficiencies of the Convention as a human rights guarantee for the UK, there should be a commitment towards creating a new Bill of Rights in the future, once it can be judged to what extent the HRA has been a success. Once the impact of the HRA can be more fully evaluated, there will be room to consider whether further entrenched rights legislation is necessary and the form it should take. If such a course were taken in the UK, then it would be brought into line with the experience of most of the other European signatories. These States already possess codes of rights enshrined in their constitutions, but the majority also adhere to a general practice of incorporation of State treaties into domestic law, either automatically, as in the case of Switzerland, or upon ratification, as in the case of Luxembourg. The dual system of the Convention rights and a domestic code of rights seems to operate well in these countries. Thus, the HRA could become an interim measure to secure the further protection of the rights provided by the Convention, in the hope that a domestic Bill of Rights would later cure the gaps, defects and inadequacies of the Convention. If a domestic Bill of Rights is ever created (in spite of the current government's lack of will to do so, as evidenced in the White Paper, *Bringing Rights Home* (1997)), then the two documents could exist side by side in UK law and each could be invoked when its protection of rights on a point was stronger than the other.[3] However, while the deficiencies identified here leave room for argument that, at some stage, a supplementary and complementary Bill of Rights should be enacted in order to create a more tailor-made and comprehensive human rights guarantee for the UK, the likelihood that this will occur does not appear to be very great. The very reasons for settling on the compromise of the HRA would almost certainly preclude it.

Notes

1 Further features of this decision could be considered: the court seems to have been readily persuaded by the Attorney General's argument that a widely framed injunction was needed in July 1986, but it is arguable that it was wider than it needed to be to prevent a risk to national security. It could have required the newspapers to refrain from publishing Wright material which had not been

previously published by others until (if) the action to prevent publication of the book was lost. Such wording would have taken care of any national security interest; therefore, wording going beyond that was disproportionate to that aim.

2   It could be pointed out that there are advantages in incorporating the Convention as opposed to introducing a domestic instrument. In particular, if a right is violated here, since primary legislation mandates the violation, the possibility of recourse to Strasbourg remains.

3   An example could be inserted here. Cyprus adopted a course similar to this when it became independent in 1960. It used the Convention as a drafting prototype for certain fundamental rights and freedoms, which then became part of its new constitution. The Convention itself was incorporated into the law of Cyprus and was then invoked before the Cypriot courts as a supplementary aid to interpreting corresponding articles of the constitution. This apparently circular method is not without success and does seem to highlight weaknesses in the constitution.

Question 48

The Eastern European democratic State of Mandislavia is considering how best to guarantee the human rights of its citizens. Mandislavia is already a signatory to the European Convention on Human Rights but it has not incorporated the Convention into its law. You have been employed by the Mandislavian Law Commission to draft a consultation paper detailing the options available to the government in this matter. Drawing on the experience of the UK, compare and contrast the main relevant methods of ensuring human rights in Mandislavia.

Answer plan

This is a new take on a standard question, which requires consideration of a wide range of options in guaranteeing human rights. Essentially, the main options which must be discussed and evaluated are:

- becoming a signatory to the ECHR (the Convention) without incorporating it into domestic law;
- becoming a signatory to the Convention and incorporating it into domestic law;
- creating a free-standing declaratory Bill of Rights;
- creating a Bill of Rights enforced by a tailor-made court.

Answer

The Mandislavian government needs to decide to what extent it wishes to guarantee human rights within its jurisdiction and, hence, to what extent it needs to amend or overrule its existing law and legal system. Some of the available options are little more than window-dressing and would merely provide an additional legal remedy for a citizen who believes that his rights have been infringed; others would have a dramatic effect upon Mandislavian law and would override all existing and future contradictory provisions. There are essentially four main options available: becoming a signatory to the Convention without incorporating it into domestic law; becoming a signatory to the Convention and incorporating it into domestic law; creating a free-standing Bill of Rights to perform a declaratory function; or creating a Bill of Rights with a court to supervise and enforce it. Each of these options will be evaluated in turn.

The first option would put Mandislavia into broadly the same position as that held by the UK until the HRA 1998 came into force on 2 October 2000. Until 1998, the precarious and disorderly state of civil liberties and human rights in the UK was a strong argument in favour of the adoption of some form of Bill of Rights. In certain areas of civil liberties, the existing statutory and case law safeguards against abuse of power were less comprehensive and arguably less effective than in many other democratic countries. Citizens of the UK did enjoy a reasonable level of tolerance of individual behaviour, but there were serious gaps and the tolerance itself, because it was not bolstered by a formal guarantee of rights, was fragile, especially in times of crisis. The law sought to protect certain values such as the need to maintain public order but, in doing so, curtailed the exercise of certain freedoms because nothing prevented it from disregarding them. Thus, human rights had a precarious status, in that they only existed, by deduction, in the interstices of the law. Individual citizens who believed that their human rights had been violated either had to find an available domestic action and remedy or try to take a case to the European Court of Human Rights (ECtHR) in Strasbourg. Although the Eleventh Protocol has recently speeded up the Strasbourg system and should reduce the cost of an application, it is still a slow and expensive process with a high chance of failure; average Mandislavian citizens might find their rights a little more than illusory if this were the only guarantee given.

If the second option were to be taken, Mandislavia would find itself in a situation remarkably similar to that currently at play in the UK since the HRA came into force. In contrast to the previous situation, the HRA now represents a minimum guarantee of freedom. Certain fundamental values have been placed, theoretically and temporarily at least, out of the reach of any political majority. Citizens of the UK no longer have to rely upon the ruling party to ensure that its own legislation does not infringe freedoms. When laws are passed which conflict with some fundamental freedom, courts will now have to interpret such laws in the light of the Convention and consider to what extent the freedoms may legitimately be curtailed. This is in stark contrast to the prior situation, where the courts had no choice but to apply an Act of Parliament, no matter how much it might breach the Convention.

The HRA has therefore created a far more active judicial role in protecting basic rights and freedoms. If a court considers that either a new or existing statute which is under its consideration infringes the Convention rights or freedoms, then it may issue a Declaration of Incompatibility (s 4 of the HRA), upon which it is hoped the government will act promptly (s 10). The use of s 3(1) of the HRA is more significant, since it demands that legislation should be construed compatibly with the Convention rights if it is possible to do so. The judges have been – in certain contexts – very pro-active in using s 3 (see, for example, *R v A* (2001)). The interpretation of the US constitution indicates what could happen in this country; vast edifices of civil rights have been constructed out of innocuous and ambiguous phrases. The generality of terms of the Convention means that its interpretation is likely to evolve in accordance with the UK's changing needs and social values; this is, in any case, one of the basic principles of Strasbourg-based Convention jurisprudence, since the Convention is intended to be a living document which is not bound by time or venue, but can develop to suit both in any jurisdiction. Thus, it is likely that soon there will be two versions of the Convention relevant to the UK: the domestic version as incorporated by the HRA, and the existing opportunity to take a persistent grievance to Strasbourg. In the first three years of the operation of the HRA, it is not apparent that the senior judiciary are determined – in general – to take a dynamic approach to the Convention rights (see *AG v Punch* (2003) and the *ProLife Alliance* case (2003) – both in the House of Lords). Thus, it may be said that in the UK – which had already protected human rights within the common law – some resistance to the Convention as a 'foreign' instrument is apparent. However, depending upon its political and legal systems, the existing protection for human rights and the degree of independence enjoyed by its judiciary, this option might be an attractive one for Mandislavia, albeit perhaps as a first step towards a Bill of Rights tailored to the needs and mores of that State.

In the UK, incorporation has already had a number of advantages. Citizens may obtain redress for human rights breaches without needing, except as a last resort, to apply to the ECtHR in Strasbourg. This saves a great deal of time and money for the citizen and thus greatly improves access to justice. The range of remedies available under the HRA is the same as in any ordinary UK court case, and so includes injunctions and specific performance where appropriate, rather than simply damages. British judges are presumably already making a greater contribution to the development of Convention rights jurisprudence in Strasbourg. However, a major disadvantage, or at least a source of anxiety, is the doubt as to whether British judges can be trusted to give a vigorous interpretation to the Convention. The British judiciary are in general highly regarded, but they are an elite group, drawn mainly from a certain stratum of society and therefore, to varying degrees, out of touch with the working class. They have been trained in techniques of legal analysis which include deciding cases without the responsibility of considering their social repercussions; it is doubtful whether three days of human rights awareness training will have overturned years of this practice. The new role of the judiciary, which is more important and therefore more overtly political, might mean moves towards more political involvement in their appointments – a development which has taken place in the US. The interpretations given by judges to the Convention may greatly dilute its impact. The UK still has no privacy legislation; the HRA appears to have a good chance of providing the impetus to create a far more comprehensive right to respect for private and family life (see *Douglas v Hello!* (2001) and *Campbell v Mirror Group Newspapers* (2002)) than the patchy and piecemeal one previously protected under various other names in domestic law.

At present, the Convention has been afforded further effect in domestic law, but not entrenched; thus, it could be removed by the simple method of repeal of the HRA. It is submitted that this is a sensible situation at present, both in terms of the maintenance of parliamentary sovereignty and to avoid handing over too much power to the unelected judiciary. Whether it is similarly sensible for Mandislavia depends upon information which is not provided in the question as to independence of the judiciary, the political system and the current status of human rights in that State. In summary, the new scheme should allow the relatively fast, but incremental improvement of the UK's recognition and enforcement of domestic human rights. Certain weaknesses are identifiable within the HRA and the Convention, but the method chosen is a reasonable compromise or first step towards a rights-based culture in UK law and society, and could serve the same function in another State.

The third option would be to create a Bill of Rights specific to Mandislavian needs. The UK has repeatedly rejected this option; perhaps the Mandislavian government would have a more open approach to the question. The House of Lords Select Committee, as long ago as 1978, was unanimous on this issue: 'To attempt to incorporate *de novo* a set of fundamental rights would be a fruitless exercise.'

Starting from scratch and developing a Bill of Rights for the UK would almost inevitably have been a burdensome task, because the political parties (and the various pressure groups) would have had enormous difficulty in reaching agreement on it, while the process of hearing and considering all the representations made by interested parties would have been extremely lengthy. This is suggested by the experience of Austria, where a Commission was set up to draw up a code of fundamental rights. After 12 years, it had produced only alternative drafts of two rights. Apart from the cumbersome nature of the process, a Bill of Rights might have taken too much account of the interests of the government in power at the time when it was passed. Again, without further information, it is difficult to guess whether Mandislavia would face such problems.

Although producing a tailor-made Bill of Rights would certainly have been difficult, it can be argued that the UK should nevertheless have attempted it rather than incorporating the ready-made ECHR, which is arguably defective in content. It is a cautious compromise document: it is not as open-textured as the American Bill of Rights and it contains long lists of exceptions to most of the primary rights, exceptions which suggest a strong respect for the institutions of the State. These exceptions have, at times, received a broad interpretation in the ECtHR and it is likely that the resulting cases will have a great influence on domestic courts when they come to apply the rights directly in the domestic arena for the first time. For example, Art 10, which protects freedom of expression, contains an exception in respect of the protection of morals. This was invoked in the *Handyside* case (1976) in respect of a booklet aimed at schoolchildren, which was circulating freely in the rest of Europe. It was held that the UK government was best placed to determine what was needed in its own country in order to protect morals and so no breach of Art 10 had occurred. The Convention was never intended to be used as a domestic Bill of Rights. It has been argued that the creation of such a new guarantee from scratch would be an incredibly difficult and complex task and so it is understandable why the incorporation of the Convention has been chosen as a (comparatively) quick and easy 'fix'.

However, it may further be argued that, due to the deficiencies of the Convention as a human rights guarantee for the UK, there should be a commitment towards creating a new Bill of Rights in the future, once it can be judged to what extent the HRA has been a success. After the HRA has been fully in force for 10 years, there will be room to consider whether further entrenched rights legislation is necessary and the form it should take. If such a course were taken in the UK, then it would be brought into line with the experience of most of the other European signatories. These States already possess codes of rights enshrined in their constitutions, but the majority also adhere to a general practice of incorporation of State treaties into domestic law, either automatically, as in the case of Switzerland, or upon ratification, as in the case of Luxembourg. The dual system of the Convention rights and a domestic code of rights seems to operate well in these countries. Thus, in Mandislavia, the Mandislavian equivalent of the HRA could be viewed as an interim measure to secure the further protection of the rights provided by the Convention, in the hope that a domestic Bill of Rights would later cure the gaps, defects and inadequacies of the Convention. If a domestic Bill of Rights was ever created, then the two documents could exist side by side in Mandislavian law and each could be invoked when its protection of rights on a point was stronger than the other. Thus, the Convention and the HRA which incorporates it are positive steps towards the greater priority and recognition of rights in the UK, particularly in courts, and could be adapted to suit Mandislavian needs and culture.

The final, and by far the strongest and most radical solution for Mandislavia, would be to create a domestic Bill of Rights tailor-made to Mandislavian needs and mores, and supervised and enforced by a specific domestic court. This would follow the model of many other European States and would be particularly apt if Mandislavia either already has a written constitution and a constitutional court or, alternatively, is willing to create both. This option has the advantages, *inter alia*, of clarity, supremacy of human rights over conflicting law and ease of access by citizens to their rights. However, much depends on the method of appointment of judges to the court, since the American experience has demonstrated that political divisions can impede justice and that political neutrality may be difficult to maintain. However, the existence of such a strong declaration of rights, combined with a court empowered to strike down legislation and overrule executive actions which infringe those rights, is a high ideal for which to aim and one which might well be apt for Mandislavia in future, if not under present conditions.

Question 49

Critically evaluate the extent to which the Human Rights Act 1998 is bringing about change in the substantive law in the 'civil liberties' field and the extent to which it is likely to do so.

Answer plan

This is currently becoming an extremely common type of examination question, although it may appear in many forms. The question is confined to the 'civil liberties' field and within that field you will have to be selective – and make your selection clear at the outset. So, for example, you need not consider commercial law since, although the HRA has implications in that field, it itself cannot be termed the field of 'civil liberties' – at least for undergraduate purposes. In order to answer the question, it is essential that you should be able to explain and evaluate cases on selected rights of the ECHR (the Convention), and further to predict whether and how UK law will have to change in the coming years to reflect those Convention rights and the relevant jurisprudence. Changes that have already occurred should be identified. When a question is phrased as generally as this one, students should avoid the temptation to refer to a long list of instances where domestic law will be likely to be challenged; it is crucial to include some depth of argument and analysis of the case law. Examiners may also ask students to refer to one or more specific areas of domestic law, such as criminal law and evidence, or to refer to one or more Convention rights, such as privacy, expression, discrimination or torture. It is therefore essential that students have detailed knowledge of current issues concerning Convention rights and their status in domestic law. If the question is phrased generally, it will be necessary to be selective about the rights referred to in the answer and to make it clear that this is what you are doing in the introduction.

The following matters must be considered:

- the ways in which the HRA 1998 is able to have an impact on domestic law;

- leading European Court of Human Rights (ECtHR) cases which raise issues about the UK's enforcement of human rights in key areas – for example, privacy, police powers of covert surveillance, freedom of protest;

- examination of the current and probable impact of the HRA in the areas chosen;

- evaluation – the role of domestic courts and Parliament in interpreting and giving effect to the new rights.

Answer

Under s 3 of the HRA 1998, many statutes are being opened to rights-based scrutiny and, in exceptional instances, are vulnerable to declarations of incompatibility issued by a higher court under s 4. A tide of legislation apparently designed to ensure compliance is also underway, including, for example, the Regulation of Investigatory Powers Act 2000 and the Terrorism Act 2000. Since October 2000, public authorities within the UK have been under a duty to act in compliance with the Convention. Since the term 'public authorities' includes the courts, it is clear that very significant changes in UK law are likely to occur, if only by necessitating checks that current common law doctrines are in compliance with the Convention rights. Such changes are already underway, as discussed below. Courts are being deluged with arguments based on the Convention, and so the existing case law of the ECtHR has become a vital tool for interpretation purposes, although it is not binding (s 2 of the HRA). However, it remains to be seen to what extent new rights will be created in areas of the law where rights are, at present, weak; and whether the interpretation of Convention rights taken by the government (as evidenced in new Bills put forward to Parliament) and by the judiciary will be similar to that taken by Strasbourg. Obviously, if those interpretations rely on a watered down version of the rights, the impact of the Convention will be lessened.

It should be remembered that neither the HRA nor the ECHR on which the latter is based give human rights free rein within domestic law; each has its own exceptions and limitations. The key HRA provisions, especially ss 3(1), 3(2), 6(1) and 6(2), show that it is intended to create a delicate political balance: the rights which it contains only bind public authorities unless incompatible primary legislation means that they must act in contravention of the right (s 6(2)). Existing legislation which contravenes the rights is not automatically invalid, but remains in force under s 3(2) whether or not a declaration of its incompatibility is made under s 4. Article 13 of the Convention, the right to an effective remedy before a domestic court, has 'disappeared' from the text of the Act. It would be possible, although unlikely, for very little change to result from the whole exercise if Parliament regularly decided to take advantage of its power to legislate contrary to the rights.

The Convention was itself a compromise document which attempted to identify core values applicable in a range of very different signatory countries: it contains few economic and social rights; most of the rights it does contain have exceptions for such matters as national security and the prevention of crime. The doctrine of the 'margin of appreciation' has traditionally allowed a significant leeway to States as regards the means and the methods of upholding rights, and the rights and freedoms within the Convention sometimes have to be balanced against each other in the same case, since, for example, one person's exercise of freedom of expression may infringe another's right to respect for his or her private life. In spite of these and other limitations, it is, however, possible to predict many fields of law which will require at least re-evaluation in the light of Convention rights. Since the potential areas of change in the 'civil liberties' field are so many and varied, the current and future impact on three will be examined here: privacy; police powers of surveillance and freedom of public protest.

In the field of public protest, it is now clear, due to the HRA, that the Convention must be taken into account. Where protest is in question, there seems to be a preparedness evident from the decision in *DPP v Percy* (2001) to look to Art 10. In other words, protest is not merely treated under the HRA as a form of disorder as it often was in the past, but as an exercise of freedom of expression; the freedom of expression dimension is recognised – even afforded weight. When a new public order statute is passed, its impact on freedom of assembly and public protest will have to be considered so that it can be declared compatible with the Convention rights under s 19. Clearly, it is possible that a minimal interpretation of the Convention requirements may be relied upon, but at least the human rights dimension of such statutes will be recognised. They will not be considered in Parliament, only in terms of their ability to curb the activities of football hooligans or late night rowdies, as in the past. Thus, s 41 of the Criminal Justice and Police Act 2001 was considered to be compatible with Arts 10 and 11. Clearly, the courts may take a different view when cases arise under it; if so, they can use s 3 of the HRA to seek to bring s 41 into conformity with the rights if that has not already been achieved.

There is no substantive right to privacy in either domestic law or, strictly speaking, under the Convention. However, domestic law has long recognised a collection of disparate privacy-related rights, which fall within the scope of land law, tort, criminal law and a handful of statutes. Article 8 of the Convention requires respect for family and private life, and it is this requirement which is aiding in bringing about change in domestic law now that the HRA is in force. Whilst the relevant ECHR cases are qualified and the ECtHR has arguably tended towards caution in its interpretation of Art 8, it was clear from the inception of the HRA that both respect for private life and for family life would require more clarity than they had in domestic law. Since Art 8 is not binding upon private bodies (such as newspapers), the common law doctrine of breach of confidence is being utilised to create something very akin to a right to privacy, in the sense of protection for personal information (see *Douglas v Hello!* (2001) and *Campbell v Mirror Group Newspapers* (2002)). The case of *X and Y v The Netherlands* (1986) held that the State is under a positive obligation to ensure respect for an individual's private and family life, even where the interference comes from a non-State source, such as another private individual. Since the court itself is a public authority under s 6 of the HRA, it has a duty to develop existing common law doctrines, in particular, in this instance, breach of confidence, compatibly with Art 8. In the case of *Douglas v Hello!* (2001), it appeared that due to the influence of Art 8, s 12 and to an extent s 6, a right to respect for privacy was emerging from the doctrine of confidence. The findings in *A v B and C* (2002) curbed this development to an extent, but it is clear that those who wish to assert 'privacy rights' against private bodies will have to rely on confidence, but they can seek to rely on the courts' duty under s 6 in relation to the development of that area of law.

Rights to respect for private life, the home and the family can be enforced directly against public authorities and by this method it is possible that eventually something like a tort of invasion of privacy will emerge, as the barriers between the right under Art 8 and the right developing under the doctrine of confidence break down. The emerging right has, of necessity, limitations and exceptions to allow for the contrasting Convention rights to freedom of expression and freedom of information, for example, to be enforced. Section 12 of the HRA suggests that freedom of expression may take priority over any emerging right to privacy where there is a conflict, although there have been indications that the judiciary do not accept that this is the correct interpretation (*Douglas v Hello!* (2001)).

The legal basis for powers of covert surveillance and of interception has undergone a change, partly as a result of the inception of the HRA. In this instance, the change has been statute-based, rather than relying on judicial interpretation. There is a right to peaceful enjoyment of the home under the Convention (*Sporrong and Lonnroth v Sweden* (1983) and *Powell and Rayner v UK* (1990)). Invasions of the home or office, even when carried out under warrant by State officials, are open to special scrutiny (*Niemietz v Germany* (1993)). The interception of communications and covert surveillance must be carried out only in accordance with stringent safeguards and with an easily accessible method of appeal for an aggrieved party (*Khan v UK* (2000) and *Klass v Germany* (1979)). The Regulation of Investigatory Powers Act 2000 was introduced in order to provide a broader statutory basis for surveillance and interception in order to ensure that the 'in accordance with the law' requirement of Art 8(2) was met. The Act probably meets that objective. However, arguably, it fails to meet the standards laid down at Strasbourg in terms of proportionality and necessity under Art 8(2), since it provides such wide powers for the interception of communications and for surveillance accompanied by a low level of protection for the privacy of citizens.

It has been argued that the HRA has so far had a patchy impact on certain existing areas of civil liberties law. The interpretative obligation under s 3 and the court's duty under s 6 have affected the interpretation and application of the existing law in certain instances. Further, as indicated above, legislation has been introduced post-HRA which has been said by the government to be in compliance with the Convention and which is apparently intended to ensure that the exercise of powers by certain State bodies is human rights-compliant. Such legislation includes the Regulation of Investigatory Powers Act 2000, which has already been discussed, and the Terrorism Act 2000. However, it is arguable that the Terrorism Act, with its extremely broad definition of terrorism, and the Regulation of Investigatory

Powers Act, which places 'directed surveillance' on a statutory basis but provides very meagre human rights safeguards, are based on minimal readings of the Convention.[1] Thus, it is concluded that, while an awareness of the human rights dimension of legislation and of the common law is becoming apparent, the pace of change is likely to be very slow. This is largely due, it is suggested, to the readiness with which minimal interpretations of the Convention rights can be adopted both by the judiciary and by the government in introducing legislation into Parliament.

Note

1   The example of Part 3 of the Anti-Terrorism, Crime and Security Act 2001 could also be given. A broad statutory basis for the sharing of personal and other information by public authorities has been created, which affords minimal respect for Art 8 rights.

Question 50

Critically examine the implications of introducing the Human Rights Act 1998 as the UK's human rights guarantee.

Answer plan

This is a reasonably straightforward essay question, which is likely to be commonly set. However, it is important that the answer should not degenerate into a list of advantages and disadvantages of the Act and the Convention. The implications include: comparison with the previous situation; the changed role of judges; the impact on public authorities; and the new dimension to all domestic legal cases which raise human rights issues. One further implication, which should be touched on briefly, is the choice of the HRA mechanism as opposed to the introduction of a Bill of Rights on the US model.

The following matters should be discussed:

• comparison with the pre-HRA position, examples of statutory provisions;

• impact of the Act on post-HRA legislation – s 19;

• the interpretative obligation under s 3: examples of its use in practice;

• the change in the judicial role;

• the impact on public authorities;

• the choice of the HRA mechanism – as opposed to entrenching the Convention;

• evaluation.

Answer

Until 1998, the precarious and disorderly state of civil liberties and human rights in the UK was a strong argument in favour of the adoption of some form of Bill of Rights. In certain areas of civil liberties, the existing statutory and case law safeguards against abuse of power were less comprehensive and, arguably, less effective than in many other democratic countries. Citizens of the UK did enjoy a reasonable level of tolerance of individual behaviour, but there were serious gaps and the tolerance itself, because it was not bolstered by a formal guarantee of rights and was fragile, especially in times of crisis. The law sought to protect certain values, such as the need to maintain public order but, in doing so, curtailed the exercise of certain freedoms because nothing prevented it from disregarding them. Thus, human rights had a precarious status, in that they only existed, by deduction, in the interstices of the law.

For example, the Public Order Act 1986 contains extensive provisions in ss 12 and 14 which allow stringent conditions to be imposed on marches and assemblies. Such conditions are intended to enhance the ability of the police to maintain public order, but they are not balanced by any provision in the Act which takes account of the need to protect freedom of assembly. Equally, the Official Secrets Act 1989 arguably provides a more efficient means of preventing the disclosure of official information than did its predecessor, but it was not intended to allow the release of any information at all to the public (although later statutes have done just that).

Not all statutes suggested the same reluctance to protect the freedom which their provisions may infringe; the Contempt of Court Act 1981, while primarily concerned with protecting the administration of justice, contains provisions in s 5 for allowing 'discussions in good faith of public affairs ... if the risk of prejudice to the particular legal proceedings is merely incidental to the discussion'. However, the Contempt of Court Act 1981 was, in fact, passed in response to the ruling by the European Court of Human Rights (ECtHR) in the *Sunday Times* case (1979) that UK contempt law had infringed Art 10 of the Convention. The Contempt of Court Act may be contrasted with the Broadcasting Act passed in the same year, which allowed the Home Secretary to prohibit the broadcasting of 'any matter or class of matter'. This is typical of a number of provisions in domestic law which had the potential to undermine human rights very significantly and would have done so had not discretion been exercised in their interpretation and invocation. This essay will argue that the Convention, as afforded further effect in domestic law by the HRA, appears to provide a better safeguard than the previous reliance placed upon such forbearance. In particular, it should largely obviate the need to enforce rights at Strasbourg, as occurred in the *Sunday Times* case.

In the field of judicial review, the standard will no longer be that of *Wednesbury* unreasonableness or that of a heightened *Wednesbury* test; under the HRA, the body in question must abide by the right itself.

In contrast to the previous situation, the HRA now represents a minimum guarantee of freedom. Certain fundamental values have been placed, theoretically and temporarily at least, out of the reach of any political majority unless the government decides to seek to persuade Parliament to pass legislation which deliberately infringes the Convention rights. The HRA allows it to do so (see s 19(1)(b) and s 3(2)), but it is notable that apart from the Communications Bill 2003, no Bill has been presented to Parliament unaccompanied by a statement of its compatibility with the rights. Even the Anti-Terrorism, Crime and Security Act 2001 was accompanied by a statement of compatibility, although the government had to derogate from Art 5(1) in order to make the statement. Formally speaking, citizens of the UK no longer have to rely upon the ruling party to ensure that its own legislation does not infringe freedoms. They can at least be sure that the government has made some effort to ensure that a Bill is Convention-compliant before it becomes an Act of Parliament. If, despite the statement of compatibility, laws are passed which conflict with some fundamental Convention guarantee, courts will now have to interpret such laws in order to bring them into compliance with the Convention, if at all possible, under s 3 of the HRA (see *R v A (No 2)* (2001)). They must also do so in respect of pre-HRA statutes.

The courts have to consider, taking account of the Convention jurisprudence under s 2, to what extent, if at all, the freedoms may legitimately be curtailed. If, having striven to achieve compatibility, it is found to be impossible, a court of sufficient seniority can issue a declaration of incompatibility (s 4), although it will merely have to go on to apply the law in question (see *R (H) v Mental Health Tribunal, North and East London Region and Another* (2001)). The position under s 3 is in strong contrast to the prior situation, where the courts had no choice but to apply a provision of an Act of Parliament, no matter how much it might breach the Convention (although where there was ambiguity, a Convention-friendly interpretation was usually adopted in the years immediately preceding the inception of the HRA).

The HRA has therefore created a far more active judicial role in protecting basic rights and freedoms. If a court does issue a Declaration of Incompatibility, it is expected that the government will act promptly to take remedial action – although it does not have to do so (s 10). The interpretation of the US constitution illustrates what could happen in this country, although clearly to a lesser extent; vast edifices of civil rights have been constructed out of innocuous and ambiguous phrases. The generality of terms of the Convention means that its interpretation is likely to evolve in accordance with the UK's changing needs and social values; this is, in any case, one of the basic principles of Strasbourg-based Convention jurisprudence, since the Convention is intended to be a living document which is not bound by time or venue, but can develop to suit both in any jurisdiction. Thus, it is possible that soon there will be two versions of the Convention relevant to the UK: the domestic version as incorporated by the HRA and interpreted domestically and the Convention as interpreted at Strasbourg, providing a still-existing opportunity to take a persistent grievance to the ECtHR.

Incorporation of the Convention under the HRA has already had a number of advantages. Citizens may obtain redress for human rights breaches without needing, except as a last resort, to apply to the ECtHR in Strasbourg. This saves a great deal of time and money for the citizen and thus greatly improves access to justice. The range of remedies available under the HRA is the same as in any ordinary UK court case, and so includes injunctions and specific performance where appropriate, rather than simply damages. British judges are already making a contribution to the development of a domestic Convention rights jurisprudence (see, for example, *R v Lambert* (2001), *R v Offen* (2001) and *R v A* (2001)). However, a major disadvantage, or at least a source of anxiety, is the doubt as to whether UK judges can be trusted to give a vigorous interpretation to the Convention. The British judiciary are, in general, highly regarded, but they are an elite group, drawn mainly from a certain stratum of society and therefore, to varying degrees, out of touch with the working class. They have been trained in techniques of legal analysis which include deciding cases without the responsibility of considering their human rights repercussions, although it is fair to say that their attitude to such repercussions was changing in the years immediately prior to the inception of the HRA (see *ex p Simms* (1999)). It is doubtful whether three days of human rights awareness training will have overturned years of adoption of their traditional stance. The interpretations given by judges to the Convention may greatly dilute its impact. The watering down of Art 6 which occurred in *Brown v Stott* (2001) exemplified this problem. Further, the new role of the judiciary, which is more important and therefore more overtly political, might eventually mean moves towards more political involvement in their appointments – a development which has taken place in the US.

Conversely, it may be argued that UK judges have at times shown themselves capable of bearing in mind the public interest in, for example, freedom of speech. Apart from *ex p Simms*, a clear example comes from Scott J's ruling in *AG v Guardian (No 2)* (1988) (the *Spycatcher* case), which boldly rejected the argument that the need to maintain confidentiality outweighed the public interest in freedom of expression. The judges have shown themselves capable of activism in the area of privacy in *Douglas v Hello!* (2001) and the *Campbell* case (2001), although *A v B and C* (2002) may be viewed as sounding a clear cautionary note. The HRA appears to have a fair chance of aiding in the creation of a more comprehensive right to respect for private and family life than the patchy and piecemeal one currently protected under various other names in domestic law.

Apart from its implications for legislation, public authorities have been greatly affected by the inception of the HRA due to the requirements of s 6. Under s 6, it is unlawful for a public authority to act in a way which is incompatible with a Convention right. This is the main provision giving effect to the Convention rights: rather than incorporation of the Convention, it is made binding against public authorities. Under s 6(6), 'an act' includes an omission, but does not include a failure to introduce in or lay before Parliament a proposal for legislation, or a failure to make any primary legislation or remedial order. Section 6(6) was included in order to preserve parliamentary sovereignty and prerogative power: in this case, the power of the executive to introduce legislation. Thus, apart from its impact on legislation, the HRA also creates obligations under s 6 which bear upon 'public authorities'. Such obligations have a number of implications. Independently of litigation, public authorities must put procedures in place in order to ensure that they do not breach their duty under s 6. A number of public authorities and bodies that have a public function have already undergone HRA training and have had to modify their practices in response to the HRA. Thus, the HRA has had immense implications for all bodies in the UK that are public authorities or have a public function. In stark contrast to the previous situation, such bodies act illegally if they fail to abide by the Convention rights. Previously, unless forced impliedly to adhere to a particular right legislatively (for example, under s 58 of the Police and Criminal Evidence Act 1984, imposing on the police, in effect, a duty to abide by one of the implied rights within Art 6(1)), they could disregard the rights in their day-to-day operations with impunity.

Of course, much turns on the interpretation of the term 'public authority'. The case law stemming from *Donoghue v Poplar Housing and Regeneration Community Association Ltd* (2001), *R (on the Application of Heather) v Leonard Cheshire Foundation* (2002) and *Aston Cantler v Wallbank* (2003) indicates that the courts are moving towards a narrow interpretation of the term in relation to the notion of a 'public function' (s 6(3)(b) of the HRA). While bodies exercising public functions are public authorities, the term 'public function' is beginning to receive a narrow interpretation. In *Aston Cantler*, the House of Lords found that factors to be taken into account in determining whether a public or a private function is being exercised include: the extent to which, in carrying out the relevant function, the body is publicly funded, or is exercising statutory powers, or is taking the place of central government or local authorities, or is providing a public service. Clearly, this relatively narrow interpretation could mean that a citizen who considers that his or her Convention rights have been infringed by a particular body may be unable to show that it is a public authority and will therefore have no redress under the HRA. His or her only remedy might be to take a case to Strasbourg. In such a circumstance, it would appear that the HRA has failed to provide a sufficiently broad protection.

So far this essay has indicated that the HRA has immense implications for the interpretation of legislation and for the operations of a large but still limited number of bodies in the UK. However, there are limitations on its impact. The choice of the HRA as the enforcement mechanism for the Convention itself has implications, since at present the use of a different mechanism is precluded. At present, the Convention is incorporated into domestic law, but not entrenched on the US model; thus, it could be removed by the simple method of repeal of the HRA. It is submitted that this is an acceptable situation at present, both in terms of the maintenance of parliamentary sovereignty and to avoid handing over too much power to the unelected judiciary. Moreover, the judiciary cannot strike down incompatible legislation. However, it does mean, as indicated earlier, that Parliament can deliberately legislate in breach of the Convention. It also means that if prior or subsequent legislation is found to breach the Convention in the courts and cannot be rescued from doing so by a creative interpretation, it must simply be applied. Thus, citizens cannot always be certain of being able to rely on their Convention rights domestically.

In conclusion, the new scheme should allow for the incremental improvement of the UK's recognition and enforcement of domestic human rights. Certain weaknesses are identifiable[1] within the HRA and the Convention, but the method chosen represents a reasonable compromise between protection for human rights and parliamentary sovereignty. It represents a first step towards creating a rights-based culture in UK law and society.

Note

1   Obvious deficiencies of the HRA include: the missing Art 13 (guarantee of a legal remedy for infringement of a Convention right); the exceptions made in the definition of 'public authority'; the narrow definition of a 'victim'; the fact that most of the ECHR rights which it incorporates are heavily qualified or weak (Art 14) and the lack of a direct power by which courts could strike down offending legislation. Each of these could be discussed in greater detail.

INDEX